Language Recreated

HAROLD SKULSKY

Language Recreated

Seventeenth-Century
Metaphorists and the
Act of Metaphor

*The University of
Georgia Press*
Athens and
London

Paperback edition, 2012
© 1992 by the University of Georgia Press
Athens, Georgia 30602
www.ugapress.org
All rights reserved
Designed by Barbara E. Williams
Set in Garamond #3 by Tseng Information Systems, Inc.

Printed digitally in the United States of America

The Library of Congress has cataloged the
hardcover edition of this book as follows:
Skulsky, Harold.
    Language recreated : Seventeenth-Century metaphorists
    and the act of metaphor / Harold Skulsky.
    294 p. ; 24 cm.
    ISBN 0-8203-1361-0 (alk. paper)
    Includes bibliographical references (p. 235–285) and index.
    1. English poetry—Early modern, 1500–1700—History
    and criticism. 2. English language—Early modern,
    1500–1700—Style. 3. Aesthetics, Modern—17th century.
    4. Poetics—History—17th century. 5. Metaphor.
    I. Title.
PR545.M37S58   1992
821'.409—dc20   91-7901

Paperback ISBN-13: 978-0-8203-3858-3
    ISBN-10: 0-8203-3858-3

British Library Cataloging-in-Publication Data available

Chapter 8 first appeared in slightly different form as
"'The Fellowship of Mystery': Emergent and Exploratory
Metaphor in Vaughan," *Sel* 27 (Winter 1987): 89–107.

To my mother,
and the memory
of my father

Contents

	Introduction 1
Chapter One	The Act of Figuration 9
Chapter Two	The Paradigm Figurative Speaker: Divine Linguistics 33
Chapter Three	God's Tumbler: Pseudometaphor, Sacred and Profane 48
Chapter Four	Illusions of Strangeness and Shocks of Recognition 77
Chapter Five	Metaphor Dramatized: Deceit and Irony 94
Chapter Six	Figuration and Retort 140
Chapter Seven	Thinking in Metaphor: Windfalls and Searches 168
Chapter Eight	The Fellowship of the Mystery: Emergent Metaphor in Vaughan 199
	Afterword 223
	Appendix A 227
	Appendix B 231
	Notes 235
	Index 287

Language Recreated

Introduction

THIS IS A BOOK ABOUT how figurative language behaves in a major tradition of English poetry: seventeenth-century lyric. People used to call the six most conspicuous poets of this tradition "metaphysicals." I think a better case could be made for calling them "metaphoricals" in a broad sense that would cover a whole range of disruptive (or mock-disruptive) maneuvers in communication. Before studying these maneuvers I will introduce a way of looking at them. It's a way I think my six poets would have recognized as at least implicit in the standard lore on style and interpretation in their literary culture, and far more richly and subtly implicit in their own craft. Certain distinctions I will be drawing, such as reference, sense, and force, would take some explaining, but the poets wouldn't need much prompting to catch on; respect for these distinctions is registered in their practice if not spelled out in the theories they had at their disposal. Codified or not, craft is a kind of knowledge: you know *what* you're doing if you really know *how*.[1]

I will be recommending that readers approach poems and especially figures of speech as things done rather than made. If I'm right, figuration is a social act that manages to be as odd as it is commonplace. Naturally, I think that a rigorous understanding of what you do when you turn a phrase sharpens your enjoyment of the master turners of phrase. That is mainly what I'm up to here. But the pervasiveness of figures is interesting in itself. You can hardly get through a sentence without tripping over the remains of a metaphor, if not the living creature itself. This is why the phenomenon is an ideal entering wedge for intellectual subversion.

Imagine somebody eager to set up shop as a language skeptic or a critical anarchist, or a chic and sophisticated relativist. He or she wants to argue for one of the following theses:

Text meaning is a figment.

Texts are radically ambiguous.

The traditional notion of a text—something written to comply with a particular system of communication—is incoherent somehow or other.

The system of communication any given text is written in isn't a historical fact but varies from community to community, generation to generation, or university to university.

The novice hell-raiser couldn't do better than to play the scandalous possibilities of metaphor for all they're worth. Portray it as an imp of the perverse in the funnyhouse of language, a mass producer of irreducible ambiguities. Or argue that the funnyhouse is *full* of imps, or *made* of imps, since there's really no sensible criterion of literalness. If I'm right in what follows, the charges are mischievous; the accused is innocent on all counts.

But your choice of grist for the mischief mill will have been shrewd enough to set you up in trade—and that's the point: metaphor is central, and centrally problematic. Get clear on what it is to speak and interpret figuratively, and you can fairly expect corresponding clearness on other puzzling and global features of the act of communication. The master turners of language, the masters of trope, have secrets to tell beyond what their poems say. This is my second motive for a study of trope in the major seventeenth-century poets: in addition to showing how the notion of figurativeness can illuminate a body of great poetry, I also hope to show how the poetry can return the compliment by illuminating the notion of figurativeness—and the tragicomedy of human interaction in which figurativeness arises.

In chapters 1 and 2 I'll give a detailed account of the notion and begin showing how the account can sharpen our eye for the tricky and varied ways in which the notion gets embodied. First let me tell a cautionary tale of what happens when the wrong kind of sophistication lures readers into fudging the distinction between the literal and the figurative. The resulting bundle of confusions is what I call Hotspurism, for reasons that will be clear once we consider a revealing passage in a somewhat earlier poet than the ones I will be concerned with in this book—but like them, a compassionate but probing observer of the ways that points get missed.

Here is Worcester beginning to brief Hotspur on the risky conspiracy against Henry IV:

> And now I will vnclaspe a Secret booke
> And to your quicke conceyuing Discontents,
> Ile reade you Matter, deepe and dangerous,
> As full of perill and aduenturous Spirit,
> As to o're-walk a Current, roaring loud
> On the vnstedfast footing of a Speare.[2]

The thing is a metaphor with a simile tucked inside it, of course. Worcester is nowhere near a book, much less unclasping one, much less comparing an episode in the nonexistent narrative under the nonexistent clasp with the spectacular piece of military daring that has occurred to him. Worcester is talking about secrets, not books; about risky plots, not spearwalkers. But he has mistaken his man.

Hotspur ignores the point and latches onto the last vivid image he hears: "If he fall in, good night! Or sinke or swimme!" What follows is a sequence of metaphors in praise of risks worth taking—if they *are* metaphors; they're more like hallucinations:

> By heauen, me thinkes it were an easie leap
> To plucke bright Honor from the pale-fac'd Moone,
> Or diue into the bottome of the deepe,
> Where Fadome-line could neuer touch the ground
> And plucke vp drowned Honor by the lockes.[3]

The general idea is that Hotspur can earn new honor no matter how seemingly unattainable, and redeem lost honor no matter how seemingly hopeless the loss. But if Honor is bright enough to be worth fighting for, what is she doing in the care of the pallid goddess of mutability? If she's worth rescuing, why the contemptuous manhandling? What's the point of *this choice* of figures?

The speaker is obsessed by the literal meanings—the figures themselves. He couldn't care less to supply, much less to attend to, the form that should underlie them—the figurative sense:

> He apprehends a World of Figures here,
> But not the forme of what he should attend.[4]

He's a negligent reader of other people's metaphors, and a disastrous reader of his own. Here he is a little later, reacting to the misgivings expressed by a potential confederate in a begging-off letter that Hotspur has been reading aloud with frequent angry interruptions: "O, I could diuide my selfe, and go to buffets, for mouing such a dish of skim'd Milk with so honourable an Action!"[5] But the act of dividing oneself and going to buffets isn't the same, figuratively construed, as buffeting oneself; it's two half-selves buffeting each other—in a word, a spasm of ambivalence. Hotspur doesn't notice that he's confessing an impulse to take his friend's part, as well as an attack of self-reproach for having tried to recruit the friend.

His weakness as a reader of his own metaphors is the heading under which we're invited to think about his failure of self-knowledge. A little later we hear from his wife about his dreams of battle: "Thy spirit within thee hath beene so at warre. . . ."[6] If his own metaphor is taken seriously, one of the warriors arrayed against Hotspur's spirit—is Hotspur's spirit. But Hotspur, who needs most of all to take his metaphor seriously, can't take it at all. His lack of the linguistic versatility needed to negotiate between the literal meaning and the figurative is an analogue and perhaps a symptom of his lack of the political versatility he needs to resist his uncle's manipulations.

The classical term for the first kind of versatility is Aristotle's *eutrapelia*—the good talker's nimble sense of timing and tact, his flair for turning the conversation in one direction or another, his ingratiating impudence.[7] The classical term for the second versatility is *polytropia*—the virtue of the wily Odysseus, the man of stratagems; literally, the man of many turnings. Both the virtuoso of speech and the virtuoso of sharp practice are masters of *trope*, of turning; they're variant practitioners of the same virtue. In fact, Odysseus is the incarnation of both. So, in a smaller way, is Hotspur's adversary, the apparently feckless Prince of Wales; and that's the essence of Hotspur's tragedy. Unlike Hal or the old pols in his own party, Hotspur is no connoisseur of double meanings. But unfortunately the old Roman rhetor seems to have had a point: people are metaphorizing creatures.[8] Getting the point of a metaphor is the condition of getting along with them—and with oneself.

In literary criticism, the Hotspur syndrome takes the treacherous form of acting as if the point of a metaphor were a fantasy or fiction expressed by its literal meaning. Thus one critic describes the tropes in Herbert's "Praise (III)": "[God's] actions in heaven are represented in strangely materialistic terms. He saves Herbert's tears in a heavenly bottle (like a poor box, Herbert tells us)." These are, says the critic, "efforts toward literalness" on Herbert's part.[9] But the literalness is the critic's; to judge (as we should) by the speaker's ongoing argument, he is no naïf expecting to find a pantry in heaven. We don't have terms for expressing the storage power of memory literally; "materialistic terms," turned into metaphor, generally have to serve.

Another critic praises the vitality of Donne's lines about the lovers' "eyebeams," which "twisted, and did thread / Our eyes upon one double string": "The notion of a loop of string with four eyes on it disturbs. . . . We wince at the thought of transfixed eyes."[10] We don't wince if we don't skip over the mention of *eyebeams* in our eagerness for a hallucinatory rush. Eyebeams are beams of light propagated by the eyes themselves. By explaining "double string" straightaway, they forestall any thought of piercing or transfixing; there's nothing in the treatment of the metaphor to get in the way of the figurative point of this particular twisting and threading: the lovers were gazing fixedly into each other's eyes and seeing nothing else. The critic's Hotspurism keeps him from respecting the difference between this kind of figuration and the graphic violence of another Donne speaker's prayer to "let our eys be riveted quite through / Our teeming brains,"[11] where everything conspires to get us to read the riveting as riveting.

Elsewhere the same critic applies the same technique of systematic inattention deliberately, as if it were a method of reading:

> Sometimes [Donne] makes the poem's whole metaphoric level a study in changing states of matter. If we watch what happens in "A Valediction: of weeping," we can see this. Bearing the reflection of the girl's *face*, the tears become coins from their rounded shape, and their enclosure of a midget human being suggests that they are wombs. Then they become fruits. Then they drop and become water again. The indecision about what the tears are made of is accompanied by a continual change in what they're being imagined materially to consist of.[12]

The critic thinks he's discussing the metaphoric level, but what he says is true, if it's true at all, only of the literal level. Actually, Donne's speaker hasn't *failed* to make up his mind about what the tears are made of because he hasn't *tried;* his indecision on this score is an artifact of the critic's whim of taking the troublesome words literally. In the speaker's impromptu dialect, "coining" is imposing one's image on something; "minting" is the resulting value of the something (for the "coiner," at least); a "pregnant" tear is a tear that looks as if it contained a little person; for grief to have "fruit" is for it to have effects. The critic admits as much but prefers to read the poem in a language of his own invention—a language in which the poem wasn't written—that is, to replace Donne's text with another.

It's hard to see how this approach to reading could satisfy anybody who has ever made or got the point of a figurative remark. But perhaps this is how: adopt a language of commentary—say, critic-ese—exactly like English except that "reading" doesn't mean reading, and so on for all the crucial terms of the theory to be followed; in critic-ese these terms mean things that make the theory true by definition, and hence thoroughly convincing. Of course, the web we weave will be tangled; if we are somehow reminded that critic-ese isn't English, we are in for a rude awakening. But this wouldn't be the first theory in the history of literary criticism that had a good run in spite of similar disadvantages.

Sometimes the motive for critical Hotspurism is honest confusion brought on, ironically, by losing track of one's own critical metaphor: "'Sprinkl'd and taught' is like 'dust and sinne' in joining two orders of significance. . . . It begins to be idle to speak of the literal level and the figurative level, since they coexist so visibly on the same plane."[13] If it's "idle" to distinguish between levels of meaning, then how did the critic manage to notice two orders of "significance"? "Plane" can't mean level of *meaning* here; if it means anything it means level of *syntax:* Herbert's metaphors "coexist" in the same phrases or clauses with nonmetaphorical equivalents. But this doesn't hide the levels distinction; it calls attention to it. Puzzling metaphors are (as the ancient rhetoricians say) risky. The speaker has decided to play it safe.[14]

But you don't need an ancient rhetorician to tell you this. In the poems in question, the distinction seems pretty hard to miss: in one, what somebody gets sprinkled with and taught by are *precepts,* and in the other the speaker is *guilty* of dust and sin. But precepts aren't literally drops of liquid; and dust, not being an action at all, isn't an action you could literally be guilty of. Where did the critic get the idea that it is idle to draw the levels distinction? My guess: the false equation that results from taking "plane" and "level" literally.

My last specimen will have to stand for the countless ways in which, thanks to Hotspurism, metaphor has become the unhappy occasion for a lot of heavy pseudophilosophical weather: "[Metaphor] states that one thing is another. Metaphor (and allegory, which is metaphor) deals not with likeness but with essences. So, of course, do symbols, the extreme of metaphors. They can *reconcile* seeming contradictions because their terms can be "different from" and "same as" simultaneously; nor is this in defiance of logic; for metaphors deal with reality at the level of universals"[15] (italics mine). But as soon as you notice that the terms (say, in "flesh is grass") only *seem* to contradict each other, they stop *needing* to be reconciled. And this happens because you've stopped taking some of them—"grass," in this case—literally. This particular critic has been led by Hotspurism to imagine that metaphorical talk is somehow restricted in subject matter; it's always about "reality at the level of universals." Other critics agree about the restrictedness but think the subject matter is fantasies, not realities. But in this case, as often, extremes meet: like Hotspur, both parties apprehend a world of figures here, but not the form of what they should attend. They are victims of confusion about the difference between literal and figurative sense, and in the conceptual darkness they've taken one thing (the more accessible one) for the other.[16]

THE ACADEMIC BRAND of aphasia I'm talking about doesn't cripple people in their daily conversation, as they would be crippled if they lost the ability to make figurative sense and to make sense of figures. What drops out here is simply the ability to make sense *about* figurativeness. Craft (to repeat) is a form of knowledge, and the craft of figuration, though not the mastery, is just part of the repertoire of survival—for the conversational animal. But, as witness the strange adventures of these and a host of other experienced critics, *episteme* isn't *theoria:* you can *know how* to do something, know (in this sense) *what* you're doing, and yet not know what you know. I think that the seventeenth-century masters of turning had an educational advantage over us in this respect—in fact, that they owe their mastery partly to easy familiarity with the makings, at least, of an adequate theory of figuration: the Aristotelian and Augustinian traditions of commentary on the arts of discourse and interpretation.

In what follows I try to take advantage of their advantage. To do justice to the subtleties of figuration in the poetry I'll be discussing, I need an adequate working notion of the phenomenon. I'll argue shortly that the conversation-game notion I nominate for the job is *implicit* both in Aristotle's treatment of metaphor and in the later classical and Renaissance treatments that reflect his influence. For the *explicit* formulation, I'm solely responsible.

The blame, or credit, for that explicit formulation will have to include the fact that if my account of metaphor is sound, the following modern views (among others) are at least highly questionable: that the meanings of a subject and its metaphorical predicate interact so as to transform each other (Max Black); that really novel or creative metaphorical statements aren't really statements, just fresh ways of looking at things (Black); that metaphor gives structure to concepts, or even to reality itself (Paul Ricoeur, George Lakoff and Mark Johnson, Nelson Goodman); that feelings and mental images are part, rather than merely effects, of metaphorical sense or reference (Ricoeur); that metaphor so pervades language as to make a joke of the notion of determinate or determinable meaning (Nietzsche, Derrida); that the only sense of a metaphorical term is its ordinary sense (Donald Davidson); that the notion of vernacular or literal language is empty (Davidson).[17]

If a speech-act theory of texts allows force and meaning to vary with the intentions of the speaker or listener—giving Humpty-Dumptyism and anachronism a purchase—then my account of figuration isn't a speech-act theory.[18] And it isn't an example of reader response criticism either, at least in one popular version; my account doesn't locate meaning in responses unless they're moves allowed by the communication game being played.[19] In general, the approach I'll be presenting shouldn't be associated with any approach on the market that lets reading vary freely either with individual interpreter or with interpretative community. For better or worse, the classical view entails that there are such things as wrong moves in reading, and brilliance won't redeem them. The player up at bat may move like Nijinsky, but a foul is a foul.

Elsewhere I've tried to say just why the apocalyptic or romantic theories of metaphor I listed two paragraphs ago strike me as variously self-refuting.[20] In this book I'll content myself with making the best positive case I can for the classical view. The one exception to my rule of forbearance is Davidson's claim (vernacular as an empty notion). This might well seem to be terminally bad news for the whole enterprise being launched here. It needs to be acknowledged somewhere in this book. On examination, the news from Davidson's argument turns out to be fairly good: unexpected support from a hostile quarter. The reader will find a detailed treatment of the issue waiting in appendix A. Meanwhile, I'll be proceeding as if there are such things as languages.

Chapter One

The
Act of
Figuration

*1. The Act of Speaking Figuratively:
Oddity, Charity, Trope*

X bursts out laughing at a funeral service. As he walks past Parson Y, the clergyman says gravely, "You laughed." The sentence is obviously true on this occasion—too obviously. With X as audience, it carries coals to Newcastle. Construed as a report, it's pointless. Given X's and Y's mutual knowledge of X's misbehavior, and given Y's calling, Y has turned a sentence adopted by the vernacular for use as an *assertion* into a sentence that circumstances give the force of a *rebuke*. Maybe the relevant train of thought goes this way: assertions vouch for the propositions they express; vouching won't do here; so the force of the utterance as delivered isn't assertive. But obviously Y has *some* attitude or other toward the proposition that X laughed. Find the attitude and you find what Y did in saying "You laughed." You find the force of the utterance. Process of elimination does the rest.

This is the kind of figurative strategy that the Greek rhetoricians classify as a *schema*, a gesture or attitude struck in words. The schema, metaphorical or not, affects the *force* of an utterance—typically, the kind of act being performed in delivering a sentence: assertion or oath or threat or promise or rebuke. Unlike a schema, a trope affects the *sense* of an expression—the criterion for applying it.[1]

Consider what the murderers say when Macbeth asks if they're kindly disposed toward their oppressor: "We are men, my Liege."[2] Again, the sentence as uttered is pointlessly true; but this time what needs reinterpretation isn't the vernacular force of the sentence; asserting is a good move after a question. Here the culprit is "men," which can't be taken at face value. In context the vernacular meaning has to yield to another one related to it in some familiar way, maybe by a loose kind of implication.

When it comes to feelings about oppressors, the relevant truism or folklore assumption about being men is that they're the kind of creatures that keep track both of injuries and of chances to get even. "Men" here means creatures like that.

In one form or another, Parson Y and the murderers have brought off the communicative act of figuration. They did it by uttering sentences that meet three requirements:

A. If you take them as sentences in the vernacular, there's something confusing about them.[3] For example, they deny or affirm a talk-postulate—something already agreed on (at least tacitly) by the parties, or something there's an established practice of agreeing on in the parties' community. Logical absurdities ("My lord is not my lord"; Sundays are pillars) would be the extreme of (explicit or implicit) axiom denial; platitude and tautology ("My lord [Antony] is Antony again"; "What will be, will be") would be the extreme of axiom affirming. Or the sentences interrupt a developing line of discussion in mid-course by changing the subject. Or they're out of character for the speaker.

B. They must be uttered in a community that recognizes a familiar and manageably small array of tropes, or recipes for using one meaning to specify another (more about these later).

C. If the language being spoken isn't quite the vernacular, but another exactly like it except that the troublesome expression means something else in the new language, something you get by applying a familiar trope recipe to the vernacular meaning, then the trouble (see A) disappears.

That something else in C is the figurative sense. It's what the expression means in this "place," to use Quintilian's metaphor, even if it doesn't by "nature."[4] "Place"—context—is what "changes" the "proper" or "natural"—the vernacular—meaning and force of an expression. Of course, expressions generally have more than one "proper" sense, and the relevant sense of an expression "changes" from one "place" to another. But you don't arrive at the figurative meaning by choosing one of the "proper" ones. You do it once that choice is made and found wanting—by making it your point of departure for a semantic search. In Quintilian's faintly

American metaphor, you get the figurative point only if you dig it, or dig it out.[5] What you dig it out of is a "proper" meaning, and the digging tool is the system of tropes.[6]

Figuration is a communicative *act*. Like other acts it can be either unintentional or unconscious or both. Foot-in-mouth disease often takes the form of not noticing what the immediate occasion has done to the meaning of one's harmless remark. And bringing the act off doesn't guarantee that communication will result. We can't be kept from talking figuratively by the mere fact that either we or our audience somehow fails to notice the fulfillment of A, B, and C and so misses the figurative point. Communicativeness doesn't owe its existence to success; the readiness is all. By playing on just this fact, Donne and Herbert show interesting connections between the speech contract and the social contract in general. In their dramatic studies of people fooling themselves and others, language is the bad angel—as if the eighth deadly sin were the sin of crooked talking (or crooked listening; see chapter 5).

Still, what the fulfillment of A, B, and C makes our sentences ready *for* is our partners' understanding of what we meant to say. Like other social transactions, this one won't work unless the parties keep their sides of a particular kind of bargain. The terms of the bargain are disarmingly simple: you say what you meant to say, and I find what you meant to say by checking what you said. So far we have talk as a special case of commutative justice. The trouble is that even when figuration lives up to the spirit of the contract (by meaning what the speaker means), it still violates the letter (by not meaning it in the vernacular). The figurative speaker is running the risk of being held to the letter. He can minimize the risk by giving his audience a fair chance at recognizing that requirement C has been satisfied—a fair chance at solving the metaphor. A metaphor is a kind of riddle, says Aristotle; he adds usefully that good riddles are a source of metaphors that are *fair*.[7]

The speaker's audience has its own side of the bargain to keep: it too must play fair. Here is another—an ironic and hazardous—connection between linguistic response and moral responsibility. In the ethics of the courtroom, the classic remedy for rigid justice is attentiveness, empathy, tact, flexibility. Metaphor is an opportunity for its audience to exercise the same virtue (or cluster of virtues) in the domain of interpretation. And in both domains fairness won't come easily without a touch of the fox, a knack for Turning when the time is right.

II. The Impromptu Dialect of Conversation

The third and crucial condition of the figurativeness of a sentence as uttered went this way. There's a meaning M—say, *fallible*—that you get by applying a familiar trope recipe to a vernacular meaning of the troublesome expression—say, "human." Now suppose that the language being spoken *isn't* the vernacular but one exactly like it except that the troublesome expression can, and on this occasion does, mean M ("I'm only human; don't blame me"). On this supposition the trouble disappears. M is the figurative meaning. If this is right, we're in a position to say exactly what the figurative speaker is doing: *he's putting on a display of a new dialect. He's teaching it by speaking it.*

When you talk figuratively, you subject a piece of language to what Aristotle calls carryover[8]—reapplication to a new range of things, related to the old range in some conventionally standard way. (For the way, see the discussion of trope a bit further on.) The old range is just its range in the communal language. The metaphorist has managed to get a familiar expression evaluated according to its meaning in an impromptu dialect of that language. The familiarity is deceptive. A figurative expression is a *foreign* expression.[9]

"If someone maintains on the contrary that these [figurative senses] are multiple [vernacular] meanings," says Luther, "I reply: if you will have it so, I don't resist. But then what lexicon will it be that would teach us the words, since such figures are up to the whim of their users, or (as the phrase goes) subject to their pleasure?" "As Horace teaches: 'You will speak strikingly if your clever combining of words makes a familiar word a new one.' . . . If you want to make these striking innovations 'proper meanings,' what will be the end of it? . . . Persius speaks of the 'shirted onion'; so must we write [in our lexicon]: 'Take note: *shirt* means onion peel'?"[10] Luther doesn't deny that that's what "shirt" means in Persius's new language, only that the meaning belongs in a dictionary of the old one; and here for "new" we might just as well read "foreign." This particular semantics lesson will be worth recalling a bit later in our story (chapter 2): the father of Protestant reading theory is canny, subtle—and Aristotelian.

On the view we're looking at it's a happy coincidence that "I learn" and "I understand" are both covered by the same Greek word; catching on is a kind of learning. And the excitement of catching on is the excitement of getting through the phases of the semantic initiation, from confusion to quest to enlightenment. It's the *process* that's exciting—the passage by way of association or analogy from the old meaning to the new. The reward is an understanding of how the word is being used in context—not the achievement of some banal or inadequate paraphrase of that understanding.

Here is where Hotspurism gets another illusory purchase. By "decoding the message" of the hyperboles about lovers in "The Sunne Rising," "I risk a banality which Donne transcended—the universe *does* revolve around them; their bed *is* the center; nothing else *is*." The critic ends this enthusiastic line of argument triumphantly: "Who can quarrel with that?"[11] It depends on what "that" is. Nobody has much to gain by quarreling with the lover; pending good evidence to the contrary, let's take it for granted that he's telling the truth. The question is: what truth is he telling? And here the quarrel is with the critic, if his claims are any more than a pointless repetition of the lover's language. If they have a point, it would be that metaphors escape banality by inducing us to take them literally. But if we really did this, we would have to conclude—unfairly—that the speaker is not a witty amorist but a rather banal kind of psychotic. If the claims are literal, then they aren't hyperboles at all but mere falsehoods.

What saves "Nothing else is" from the banality of decoding is that it isn't a code to start with, but part of a creative act: the display of a new language in which (unlike English) "is" means (roughly) *has preeminent value for us*. What saves the experience of understanding it from the banality of decoding is that the appropriate response is also creative: we learn to think in the new language—not to substitute the italicized phrase for "is" by reference to a written or unwritten translation manual, but to understand "is" in the new sense.[12] To learn to think in the new language, we have to reconstruct the act of speaking it.

What gets created by these coordinated acts of creativity is at least a temporary community united by a new medium of communication, the impromptu dialect. That dialect, when metaphors die, becomes a new stage of the vernacular. But unlike the vernacular, it isn't a transparent medium. Figurativeness is an opportunity to renew the *sense* of language as an instrument of collective purpose—just because it requires a tacit social contract even if what the figurative talkers are doing with their metaphors is no more than spiteful abuse. The *perception* of language is what especially strikes Hobbes about figuration as a cooperative act: "As the sense we have of bodies consisteth in change and variety of impression, so also does the sense of language in the variety and changeable use of words. I mean not in the affectation of words newly brought home from travel, but new and withal significant translation to our purposes of those that be already received, and in far-fetch'd but withal apt, instructive, and comely similitudes." [13] The remark goes nicely with Davenant's remark, in the document Hobbes is replying to, that language is "the onely Creature of man's creation." [14] On Hobbes's showing, the act of metaphorizing is a reenactment of this creation.

Of course, the essential job of figuration is to say something, not to comment silently on the something or the saying. But figuration *does* its job by speaking and demonstrating a new language that is outwardly a twin of the old. So the act of figurative speech is doubly a demonstration. To be understood, the agent has to *point* at his act somehow as he performs it.[15] And this opens up the possibility of his tacitly or implicitly commenting on the act as he points at it. The figurative utterance is not only a use but in effect a quoted specimen, often marked as such by punctuation or speech melody. But quoting something transforms it into a name of itself (" 'cat' " names "cat"), and naming something is a natural step toward saying something more about it than that it's there. With appropriate cues, figuration can be made to talk about itself.

III. Talk-Postulates: Pragmatic Rules of Language

What tips us off that the language being spoken may not be "ours"? Construed as "ours," what's being said flouts a *truism*—"commonplace" or all-purpose thesis in classical jargon, "talk-postulate" in mine. The classical treatment of persuasion deals with such truisms elaborately, if only because they're a staple of persuasion as well as (what I'm interested in here) a ground of intelligibility. An assumption can be relied on in talking if it's a possible opinion, acceptable at least for argument's sake to the talkers or to a working consensus in the surrounding culture. (Aristotle appeals alternatively to a consensus of the "wise," so long as these are people generally *agreed* to be wise.)[16]

Talk-postulates are doubly noncommittal. You don't express belief in them when you "take them for granted" in the communicative sense. And you don't refer to what they're about when you use them figuratively. The literal reference isn't enriched by the figurative, it's replaced. Calling a gross feeder a pig takes derogatory pig lore for granted *without* endorsing the lore—and without mentioning pigs. If listeners try to resist by defending pig daintiness, they merely change the subject and show that the speaker hasn't gotten through to them. If they change the subject on purpose because they're more interested in pigs than table manners, they're simply exercising their privilege of opting out of the conversation, and launching a new and irrelevant one. But even if their behavior isn't *mis*understanding, it remains *non*understanding or unresponsiveness. This will be true, and important, even if the speaker really *does* underestimate pigs.

To take a more sensitive example, Spenser's narrator shows us the "house" of the rational soul—the human body—besieged by the appetites it should be controlling. The besiegers have been twisted into mindless destructiveness by the Fall. Taken figuratively, the siege isn't a siege. It's a metaphor for the problem of self-control—posed with emphasis on the vicious circularity that makes it worrisome: how do we ever manage to back up one side of the desire contest—the reason side—when we can't back it up unless it has won? Taken literally, the siege *is* a siege—more specifically, it's an uprising of dispossessed peasants or masterless men:

> loe! with outragious cry
> A thousand villeins rownd about them swarmd
> Out of the rockes and caves adjoyning nye:
> Vile caitive wretches, ragged, rude, deformd,
> All threatning death, all in straunge manner armd;
> Some with unweldy clubs, some with long speares,
> Some rusty knives, some staves in fier warmd. . . .[17]

Now it's a safe bet that Spenser really does believe that churls in arms are always "churlish"—that any uprising of "villeins" in the etymological sense is "villainous" in the colloquial sense. It's also a safe bet that he would say so if he were talking about such uprisings. But his act of reliance on a churl talk-postulate isn't an act of referring to churls. To find that reference in the passage is to misread Spenser's metaphor by taking it literally.

Above all, his act of reliance doesn't commit him to an antichurl *belief*. So it isn't trustworthy evidence that he believes the worst about peasants in arms, much less that he has a "virulent hatred and fear of the lower orders."[18] Citing the reliance as if it *were* trustworthy evidence is naïve. What's more to the point here, citing it as a contribution to reading the passage is just a mistake—a mistake about what's involved in conversational taking for granted. The penalty one pays for making this kind of mistake is the usual penalty of Hotspurism: one misses the point.

Some things get taken for granted by everybody competent in the communal language, and some by narrower groups within the language community. If we want the narrower version of competence, we need to know what kind of talk is going on and who's doing the talking. If these things aren't clear, then it may also be unclear just which or whose talk-postulate a metaphor is based on. To add to the confusion, the basis of the metaphor may not be a talk-postulate for anybody *yet*—not until we find out something new about the things picked out by the literal sense. This promissory, or "harsh," metaphor will just be self-defeating. But harshness, the seventeenth-century rhetoricians tell us, is a far cry from nonsense. In a dialogue of Plato, at least, it's an essential part of the underlying "character" or style.[19] The terminology is worth pausing over: a genre of conversation is a complex role, the linguistic counterpart of a behavioral type or "character." A distinctive way of presenting oneself adds a distinctive set of talk-postulates.

This complication gives the metaphorist a chance as well as a topic for reflexive comment on the act of figuration. In "The Sunne Rising," Donne's speaker claims that he and his lady are (figuratively) the only "princes"—that is, the only supremely fortunate people. Princes literally so called "do but *play* us"—only *appear* or pretend to be fulfilled. It's tempting to argue that to use "king" or "prince" even as a figurative term of praise is "to accept the conventional scale of values, with kings on top."[20] But the temptation should be resisted. It's Hotspurism again—the same kind as in the Spenser example.

Taken figuratively, these aren't terms for monarchs at all. They don't even refer to monarchs by implication. If there were such a reference—if "king" in this context meant *person as happy as a king*—then it would be pointlessly contradictory for the speaker to go on to claim that kings aren't "kings"; that is, that kings don't enjoy metaphorical kingship. A king in the required figurative sense is simply a supremely happy person. Of course, the word wouldn't have gotten to mean this if there weren't a talk-postulate ascribing supreme happiness to kings. But the change in meaning allows the talk-postulate to be repudiated without contradiction. The denial that kings are "kings" plays on the difference between literal and figurative sense, and between working with a talk-postulate and seriously committing oneself to a belief.[21] And the act of play, in turn, has the force of a skeptical comment.

IV. Talk-Postulates versus Overlapping Communities

There's a bit of unfinished business here. We still have to allow for the possibility that the speaker *isn't* flouting or pretending to flout a talk-postulate of the community he's in dialogue with. We may just have mistaken that community for ours. (The two communities may fool us by overlapping considerably in language and language mores.) In short, we may think we're part of the audience when we're really eavesdroppers. Here the fairness principle doesn't *fail*. It simply doesn't apply in an unqualified form. To take the speaker figuratively is to practice censorship by appropriation. "Is Vaughan's language 'figurative' when he depicts the mind animating every creature as a 'star,' a 'seed of the sun,' a 'grain of light'? Isn't this literally true for followers of Hermetic philosophy, who regard the whole creation as shot through with the 'vital fire' that the stars pour down on the world?"[22] The short and superficial answer here is no; being made of star stuff doesn't make something a star, and being implanted in a medium doesn't make something a seed. On the other hand, we would be practicing ventriloquism on Vaughan's text if we translated his star-stuff theory into something more appealing to our official version of common sense—that is, to *our* system of talk-postulates.

Suppose a speaker taken literally says of some future event that the rocks are groaning with eagerness for it to happen. This offends our common sense grossly. On the fairness principle, what's being called eagerness isn't eagerness but some other state that is associated with it, indicated by the context, and compatible with our notion of being a rock. One eligible candidate would be the state of *being just on the verge* of moving (or coming loose—e.g., if we're reading an account of an impending landslide). But in "And do they so?" Vaughan's speaker, taken literally, says the same thing of the Second Coming (that even rocks are watching for it) and takes back his earlier view that the only vegetable or mineral "sense" is the capacity to be influenced by the stars. In other words (he explains), he had thought such creatures "senseless" and "inanimate." Now he realizes that they're not only watchful but *good* at watching. "Th'Elect can do no more." The speaker doesn't share our views about what it is to be a rock.

In this case the sophisticated counsel of fairness is to take the text literally. In fact, it happens that we aren't eavesdropping on a transaction in some alien language community (say, of Hermetic enthusiasts). Vaughan doesn't presuppose that rocks are sentient; he asserts it, implies it (by claiming that the elect don't outdo them at watching and waiting), and frankly retracts an earlier figurative defense of the sentient rock thesis. It takes a little work to avoid being taken "fairly" and figuratively against your will when you're defying a talk-postulate of your language community. "You can't mean that" in such a case isn't orthodoxy in shock but a pragmatic rule of language.

V. *Biographical Facts versus Talk-Postulates*

I said just now that our acceptance of a talk-postulate that rocks aren't sentient doesn't rule us out of Vaughan's community. It doesn't leave us mere eavesdroppers. But culturally we're eavesdroppers all the same, in danger of making plenty of other mistakes about the business end of the language seventeenth-century poems are written in: the frame of reference. One avoidable mistake is to distort or replace the frame—the structure of talk-postulates. I think that's the real point of Ellrodt's complaint that reading poems as autobiography, or as presupposing biographical information, "runs the risk of simultaneously corrupting our pleasure and our aesthetic judgment. A poem that moves us thanks to our knowledge of the author's life is a bad poem or a poem we are discerning badly. The pleasure or emotion one gets out of it is the pleasure, the emotion, of a novel and not of a poem."[23] As it stands, this goes too far. There's nothing to keep the right facts about the poet's life from allowing us—in fact, putting us under a (communicative) *obligation*—to read his poem as we would a novel. The right facts are the ones that are also talk-postulates for the poet's intended audience—postulates the text meshes with to make a point. Ellrodt's complaint is well taken only when it comes to the ones that aren't. Only then is one *rewriting* the poem by (1) inventing a relevant talk-postulate, or (2) inventing a mesh with one the poet could have used but didn't. In 1, the poem isn't the only thing that gets rewritten. The language the poem was written in gets rewritten too. Existential psychoanalysis, the approach to texts favored by Ellrodt himself,[24] is a cautionary example of method 1.

Suppose your author has introduced a metaphor—say, "sponge" as a person-epithet. To psychoanalyze existentially, you proceed roughly as follows. Replace the work the sponge metaphor *belongs* to with an inventory of cases in which the author uses "sponge" (literally or figuratively) *elsewhere*. If the list is long enough, defend the thesis that the author had a thing about sponges. The figurative sense of the expression in the work you started with—that is, the sense yielded by conditions A, B, and C (see section 2)—can be disposed of easily. Claim that it's merely a fig leaf, an excuse for indulging guilty pleasure in public without embarrassment. If possible, think up or dig up a motive for the obsession and offer that motive as the real, humanly compelling, and hence authentic meaning of "sponge."

Here Ellrodt's objection hits dead center. Our sponge critic has insisted on manufacturing his own background assumption. But background assumptions are pragmatic rules of language. He's reading the work in a language in which it wasn't written. If the "sponge" poet were simply the hero of a psychological novel in which the poems were embedded as devices of characterization, then the existence of the obsession (hammered home by repetition) might very well develop into an ad hoc background assumption. Otherwise we have a case of taking out of context—methodized.

A recent practitioner of the method quotes part of the following passage from Donne's sermons, beginning with "take into" and ending with "drops out his moisture":

> You may have a good Embleme of such a rich man, whose riches perish in his travail, if you take into your memorie and thoughts, a Spunge that is overfilled. If you presse it down with your little finger, the water comes out of it. Nay, if you lift it up, there water comes out of it; If you remove it out of his place, though to the right hand as well as to the left, it poures out water. Nay if it lye still quiet in his place, yet it wets the place, and drops out his moisture.
>
> Such is an overfull, and spungy covetous person: he must pour out, as well as he hath suck't in; if the least weight of disgrace, or danger lye upon him, he bleeds out his money; Nay if he be raised up, if he be prefer'd, he hath no way to it, but by money, and he shall be raised, whether he will or no, for it. If he be stirr'd from one place to another, if he be suffered to settle where he is, and would be, still these two incommodities lye upon him, that he is loathest to part with his money, for anything, and yet he can do nothing without it.[25]

The existential psychoanalyst comments:

> Donne's mind, delightedly dabbling with its oozy toy, is concerned with religious instruction only in the most tenuous sense, though he does manage to hitch his sponge to the religion eventually by explaining that he intended it as an image for a rich man who soaks up money and "bleeds" it out when threatened. The connection is arbitrary: it is sponges Donne wants to talk about, and men don't have to be rich to give him an excuse for it.[26]

If you read the uncut version, the sponge analogy is the opposite of tenuous. The preacher doesn't set us up for a single surprise. He does his "hitching" to start with and not "eventually," as an afterthought. In fact, he isn't even using his own metaphor; he is explaining somebody else's. "Sponge" is already entrenched in seventeenth-century slang as a figurative description of greedy people who are ripe for extortion (see *OED*). The relevant talk-postulates create a *salient* resemblance between the two notions—and a resemblance that's salient isn't tenuous. There are other salient examples of metaphorical sponginess; weepiness is one ("her who still weepes with spungie eyes"). But this just reinforces the point. Donne may or may not have his private reasons or motives for talking about sponges, but what he manages to say about them is constrained by the system of communication he has to use to say anything at all. What he has managed to say here is that some rich men are like sponges. They give up their substance at the slightest pressure.

In version 2 of the novelistic fallacy, an autobiographical talk-postulate is taken as something the text means even though the text doesn't connect with it either by trope or by the loosest form of implication. So the poet is forced to express something we independently know about him—express it in spite of himself and in spite of what he wrote. Take an example from Sidney, a passage in which his sonnet speaker tells "Stella" (Penelope Rich) that he doesn't aspire to intellectual or military or political achievement so long as he wins her heart. Now the poet's friends and primary readers will know the author *does* aspire to those things—and the poet can hardly help *knowing* they know. His ambitions are a talk-postulate the novelizing critic has to do justice to somehow. But how? The speaker must be using his mistress's "sexual favors" as a "metaphor for his worldly aspirations."[27]

But this move has the disadvantage of yielding an absurdity. If the mistress's sexual favors are a metaphor for power, then the speaker is telling her (or his eavesdropping friends) that he doesn't aspire to power so long as he gets—*the power that he aspires to*! The trope won't march. Let's try a scheme. As they overhear the sonnet speaker lying to Stella, Sidney's friends will appreciate the "witty irony" of the lie.[28] But here the novelizer runs into another snag. No irony has been spelled out yet. Exhibiting an act of lying doesn't make an irony unless it also makes a point—or lets a point be made—about the lie being exhibited. And for a point to get made, the text itself, or still other talk-postulates, will have to flag the aspect of the lie that the alleged point is about. A pointless irony isn't an irony.

In one respect the novelizing strategy is sound. The existence of an autobiographical talk-postulate isn't enough. We need to show that the text mobilizes the postulate to make a point by means of some trope or scheme. Thus when the Donne speaker in "The Sunne Rising" or "The Canonization" tells his mistress that their affair is a more than adequate compensation for a ruined career, Donne's coterie readership will know—and Donne will know they know—that for the author career success was the supreme value; so (for the novelizer, at least) the speaker's *more* than adequate somehow has to mean *less*. But how?

Maybe the speaker's hyperboles can be taken for exaggerations—willfully whopping lies—betraying his real lack of conviction.[29] But this would misrepresent the workings of a trope again. Hyperbole isn't exaggeration unless you take it literally.

Obviously, some poems do allude topically. The key mistake in the novelistic fallacy is to go on as if poems inevitably do this, thanks to sociopsychological "encoding." But this jargon is just a confession of a priori faith, in the modern form of scientism; and even an up-to-date confession of faith won't shift the burden of proof. Talk-postulates have to mesh with something in the text. In the Donne poem we need to rule out the possibility that the speaker is being shown in a mood of genuine elation. In the case of genres with a story-telling dimension, including the genre of love lyric, the speaker can be beyond the reach of a biographical talk-postulate even if he's the author. But I'll have a bit more to say on that score further on (in chapter 5).

VI. *Meaning Transformations: Metaphoric*

Every figurative interpretation involves putting a canceled literal sense through one of the meaning transformations, or tropes. Take the metaphor-transformation, which is usefully defined by one seventeenth-century authority as a pattern of reasoning: the meaning of the expression as used *follows* from its canceled meaning once this is coupled with a relevant talk-postulate—say, "If something is a lion it's bold." Together with this proposition, the literal sense of "King Louis is a lion" yields its figurative sense.[30] On this account the act of metaphorizing is a kind of innuendo, with an important qualification. What we tease out of the vernacular sense is what the speaker is *actually saying* in his nonvernacular language. He isn't merely getting *us* to say it to ourselves while he plays safe by saying something harmless. The vernacular sense isn't what he's saying, and it isn't harmless. The incongruity is a smoking gun.

Aristotle's class-inclusion account comes to the same thing. Metaphor goes from species to genus. Being a lion implies being bold if and only if (as a matter of logic or talk-postulate) the class of lions is included in the class of bold things. In the vernacular the expression to be metaphorized ascribes membership in a class (say, rabbits). After metaphorization—that is, as a term of the impromptu dialect—the expression ascribes membership in a genus the species is included in (things easily frightened). The ex-name of *one* fearful species is now a way of describing members of *any* species as fearful.

VII. Simile as Metaphor

Donne *explains* the talk-postulate underlying his sponge metaphor by drawing a comparison. He isn't *paraphrasing* the metaphor. A metaphor isn't shorthand for some comparison or other. If "sponge" meant *like a sponge* in "A rich man is a sponge," the saying would be pointless; everything is like everything else, if only in being a thing. The lover's claim that kings aren't "kings" in "The Sunne Rising" would be logically absurd if the metaphorical occurrence of "kings" meant *like kings*. This distinction is essentially what sixteenth- and seventeenth-century writers on the subject found in Aristotle's standard discussion: metaphorical terms are a kind of mean between vernacular ones, which we already understand, and foreign ones, which we don't understand at all. Metaphor generates its own understanding. It demands an effort at learning (uptake) that comparison spares us. "Achilles is like a lion," for example, is literal, mentions lions, and leaves open the question of how Achilles is like them. "Achilles is a lion" is figurative, mentions no lions, but—once the context guides us to the new meaning of "lion"—spells out the answer to the question.[31]

But Aristotle takes a different tack in a tantalizing aside: a simile isn't a comparison after all. The notion of likeness belongs at most to its literal sense, not the one in which it's actually being used. In the actual sense of a simile, likeness plays no part.[32] To use Aristotle's illustration, "He pounced like a lion" is equivalent to "The 'lion' pounced." Given the standard lion lore, both versions of the Homeric tag specify the kind of "pouncing" Achilles did (ferocious or predatory). Neither merely generalizes. Both are figurative. And neither figurative sense refers to lions.

I think there's more to be said for this metaphor theory of simile than for the comparison theory of metaphor. When you warn somebody not to tangle with Bill because Bill is like a dragon, you're not saying that Bill and dragons share some unspecified trait. You're specifying the trait. For some behavioral trait T that will scare your listener, you're saying that Bill has T. "Being like a dragon" means (figuratively) just *having T*—say, *being fierce*. And it doesn't mean being as fierce as a dragon, either. One needn't maim or kill to be "like a dragon" in the required figurative sense. The illusion of reference to dragons or to dragon standards of fierceness is created by taking the phrase literally—by misreading. The vernacular sense of the phrase isn't its meaning here. It's a cue to check our talk-postulates about dragons for the nonvernacular sense of the expression in this context. Far from being the key to the functioning of metaphor, the simile is itself metaphorical.

I think that Aristotle's view is standard right down to the period that will mainly interest me in this book. Writers in his tradition often join the foreign-language theory of metaphor with the Ciceronian formula that metaphor is shortened simile, but there's no contradiction here. Cicero's point is just the obverse of Aristotle's: if simile is metaphor *with* "like," metaphor is simile *without*, in Cicero's terms, by "contraction" to a single word: "a word put in a place that belongs to a different word, as if it had been put in a place of its own." By the standard of vernacular meaning, the place (context) doesn't belong to it; by the standard of the impromptu dialect, it fits.[33]

VIII. *Tropes (Nonmetaphoric) and Schemes*

One last crucial thing to remember about metaphor is that it isn't the only trope. The price of forgetting this is to come up with counterexamples to the classical account of metaphor that aren't metaphors in the first place.[34] Theorists could spare themselves this gaffe if they took a long look at the nicely articulated traditional trope system. A full-dress treatment of the system would be out of place in a general study of figuration. At the same time, the study is meant to show a distinctive kind of cooperative activity halfway between a game and a rite—a trope dance of educated moves and educated responses. Moreover, besides being virtuoso tropists, the poets I'm concerned with sometimes invite their partners in the dance to *think* about their steps as well as do them. So a few remarks are in order.

The nonmetaphor tropes all add in one way or another to the effort of applying metaphor. In metonymy the literal implications of a referring term don't apply: the lawyer addressing the bench isn't addressing a bench or anything saliently like one. For a relevant relational property implied by the literal sense or by a talk-postulate—say (for benches) being *sat on* by somebody—the metonymic sense fixes reference by picking out the relational partners of the given kind of thing: metonymic "bench" is somebody who *sits on* a bench—in the context of a courtroom, a judge. To reach the metonymic relation, you invert the one you start with. Since a cup is not a beverage, what you drink when you drink a cup *full of* something (by the inverse relation) is something that *fills* a cup. Mercy in the literal sense is *exemplified by* certain people; but the metonymic "mercy" that "murders, pardoning those that kill,"[35] consists of people who *exemplify* mercy. And so on, for other standard metonymic relations: part, whole; composite, ingredient; agent, patient; source, product; user, instrument, purpose.

In schemes of thought, an expression is conventionally specialized for performing *one* speech act but actually used to perform *another*. What's figurative here is the conventional *label* we're apt to assign the act at first glance. I'm not literally asking about your time-telling abilities when I say, "Can you tell me what time it is?"; "asking" is (or was, when the scheme was alive) a metaphor for *requesting*. I'm not literally forbidding my guest to broach a topic when I say, "Don't tell me you're leaving"; "forbidding" is a metaphor for *expressing regret*. When the poet pretends to shift his object of address to his lute from the haughty lady he nevertheless keeps on talking to, "turning away" (*apostrophe*) is a metaphor for *slighting*. In the right circumstances, "threat" can mean *promise*, "promise" *threat*, "statement" *command*, and "insult" *flattery*.

In each case the form of an act of speech conventionally meets a speech-act description that can't be taken literally in the given circumstances. The act is the scheme, the description is a trope; the scheme is taken literally or figuratively according to how the trope is taken. In one of Donne's and Herbert's tragicomic scenarios, a speaker either tries and fails to get his scheme taken literally, or manages to miss the point himself. (See chapter 5, "diversionary *littera*.")

In the scheme of slantwise talking (*plagiotes*), the cues of figurativeness are subtle enough to be missed, but the speaker can't lose. His choice of ostensible speech act delivers the suggestion anyhow, in the form of what the naïve listener thinks is his own conclusion. Thus if Socrates is taken literally in Plato's *Apology*, he's pleading in his own defense. But in effect, given the kind of man he shows he is, he's really accusing his accusers. For the literal-minded, the reasonableness of the defense masks the bitterness of the indictment, and yet they still get the makings of the indictment. In the same way, the ostensible defense plea functions under the circumstances as a slantwise tribute to the speaker, but the urgent demands of self-defense throw the self-praise into "shadow."[36]

Again, Pericles' funeral oration goes straight from praise of the dead to exhortation of their survivors, skipping the traditional middle part—the lament. "The whole artifice of the scheme lies in the way things are mixed," says the classical authority on slantedness I'm paraphrasing here (Dionysius of Halicarnassus). Making one's men weep is no way to whip up their fighting spirit. The real point of the praise is to build morale in the troops—right down to the contrast Pericles draws between the Athenian dead and the enemy.[37] As usual, the best example can be found in Homer, when Achilles shows that he sees the slant in Phoenix's sentimental reminiscences of nursing and training the child Achilles—coupled with Phoenix's lip service to the plan of refusing to help Agamemnon. "Don't muddy my spirit with your moaning and groaning—all to favor mighty Agamemnon." Dionysius comments: "You see how the pupil unveils his teacher's artifice."[38] In fact, says the same critic a little further on, "there's no such thing as a simple speech, innocent of scheme."[39] *Every speech act had better be tested for slant.*

Since the trope generated by a scheme isn't a word actually used by the speaker, the hearer can't signal his understanding of the impromptu dialect by playing along with his partner's usage. Thus you can't coherently agree or disagree with "A likely story" (delivered ironically) merely by saying, "Yes, it is likely," or "No, it isn't likely." The speaker isn't giving a demonstration of a dialect in which "likely" means *unlikely*. As usual in schemes, the trope is in the label for what the speaker's sentence form is conventionally used to *do*. Here that *label* can't be taken literally. Ordinarily this behavior would count as an *assertion* of what the sentence says. Here the act is figuratively an assertion and literally a mocking recitation.

Ironic reciting is always silent comment on the lines being recited. In the classical jargon, irony is less a saying than an "indicating."[40] In the current example, what gets indicated at isn't the mock remark that the story is unlikely, but the speaker's conviction that the remark is absurdly wrong. The ironist is an actor who takes the role of his own opponent and disavows the lines in the act of saying them. We won't be meeting many ironists of this kind in Donne and Herbert, but we *will* be meeting forms of "indicating" that are even more complicated and nervously self-aware (see chapters 3 and 4 on simulated speech acts, chapter 5 on implicit quotation).

One curious way in which figurative interpretation is encouraged, if not forced, to be aware of itself, is *metalepsis:* beginning with the literal sense of an expression, each of a series of tropes is applied to the result of the one before. The result of the last trope in the series is the figurative sense. Hermogenes considers a text in which the literal sense, *flow down*, is transformed by application to flowers into *gradually fall away*, which is transformed in turn by application to hopes (described here as "flowers") into *gradually vanished*.[41] In metalepsis, says Erasmus, "we go step by step toward what we are showing. Consider 'He hid it in the inky caverns.' By inky caverns, black ones are understood; by black ones, utterly dark; and by this, at last, bottomlessly deep."[42]

Charles Butler gives some useful samples of the quick chain calculation involved here. On "with iron turn away thy grief": "'Iron' for *death* [i.e., suicide by stabbing] is a metalepsis. 'Iron' for *sword* or *iron weapon* is a metonymy of material, and 'sword' for *death administered by sword* is a metonymy of efficient cause."[43] An example from John Hoskins shows how snags in reading at widening levels of phrase structure can order the links in the chain. In the phrase "swords . . . hungrie of blood" the doubly incongruous "hungrie" is influenced first to mean *desirous* by the rest of its own phrase ("of blood"), and then to mean *fit for* by an expression ("swords") that "hungrie" is associated with only as a member of a whole modifying phrase. You track down the figurative sense by passing from narrower syntactic structures to wider ones.[44]

In theory at least, the chain of trope could go on indefinitely. Here is Emmanuele Tesauro explaining why a slave in Plautus is derisively called "Mill City": "Taking the city for the city walls, the walls for the circumference of the circle, the circumference for the act of going round the center (viz., the millstone), and the going for the goer: *you see with what speed, and by how many steps, your thought must descend in a single moment to reach the idea.*"[45] This gives a sense of the cognitive buzz that a seventeenth-century reader gets out of the rapid metaleptic drop—like Alice's trip down the rabbit hole. Like other trips figuration calls for, the end of this one is a kind of empathy. We start by thinking in our language and come out in the speaker's. (For more on metalepsis, see, for example, chapter 8 on Vaughan's "The Night.")

IX. Imagery and Re-presenting

So far I've been taking it for granted that what meaning is the meaning *of* is some piece of language or other. I think this assumption is right. Right or wrong, it was the standard working theory in my poets' century. So it's at least part of what they were trained to *think* their metaphorizing was all about. In what follows I'll continue to assume that words and phrases are the meaning bearers—public signs fit for communicating our ideas. But on the seventeenth-century account there are private signs to be considered, too. These are the immediate bearers of meaning. If public signs are the medium of communication, these others are the medium of understanding.

We understand, say, "cat" by virtue of having *an idea* of what would show that something we encounter is a cat. The public sign needs to elicit a private sign: the concept (*noema, concetto,* conceit) of what cats are like—that is, what sort of sense images (*homoiomata*) justify belief in the presence of things denoted by "cat." In the traditional psychology, the idea too is a kind of word, a private synonym of the public word.[46]

With the help of the mental sign account, a seventeenth-century critic in the tradition can say that a metaphor "expresses one idea [*concetto*] by means of another."[47] On this account, the literal sense (idea) doesn't drop out; it *is* the means of expression, "the unexpected image of the object being represented."[48] "If you say, 'The meadows are agreeable,' the only thing you represent to me is the greening of the meadows. But if you say, 'The meadows are laughing,' you will make me see the earth as a man with a soul, the meadows as his face, the agreeableness as his happy laugh."[49] Tesauro's "represent" keeps the root meaning *make immediate,* as familiarized by Quintilian:

> Vividness or (as some call it) representation goes beyond ease of understanding: if something is easy to understand, it's open to the mind: if it's represented, in a certain sense it reveals itself.[50]
>
> Any speaker receptive to the experiences the Greeks call imaginings will have exceptional power over his hearers' emotions. In imaginings the sense images of things not present are re-presented to the mind—so much so that we seem to be seeing them with our own eyes, and to have them present to us.[51]

None of this is as clear as it might be, especially the suggestion that a smiling face can be "the unexpected image of the object represented [the meadow]." "Image of a face" in this jargon means *perceptual evidence that a face is there*. Well, how can evidence of a face become evidence of a meadow? What the laugh image is generally evidence of (or would be in an actual case of perceiving) is the presence of something "agreeable." It's an ideogram with the same figurative sense as the word "laugh" itself. It doesn't represent the meadow itself but some property or other of meadows.

Still, there's a crucial difference between *drawing* the relevant implication of "laughing face" and *spotting* the relevant trait in the image. We get our notion of agreeableness in the first place by learning how to spot it in experiences of meadows and faces. So figurative uptake reenacts a basic step in language learning, or any learning. That's what Thomas Sprat likes about figures of speech. They "bring Knowledg back again to our very senses, from whence it was first derived."[52]

This account of imagery dominated thinking about figuration in the seventeenth century. When the poets refer to imaginative processes stimulated by figurative writing, this is the sort of thing they're referring to. The account has the additional advantage of being highly persuasive.[53]

X. The Game of Figuration

As a pattern of play in dialogue, figuration belongs with command, request, narration, threat, question, answer—with speech acts assigned by Aristotle to the craft of *hypocrisis*, or conversational cue response.[54] *Hypocrisis* in the sense of role-playing derives from the primary meaning: one's real dispositions to real acts of speech are part of one's character, and one's make-believe dispositions to make-believe acts of speech are part of one's *character's* character. (Social games have their dangers, of course; *hypocrisis* doesn't degenerate into "hypocrisy" for nothing—as the seventeenth-century metaphorists know well and mischievously remind us.) What kind of person takes the lead in the game of metaphorizing, or is capable of developing the knack?

Aristotle's is the standard answer. The metaphorist is simply the conversational side of Plato's *euphues*, the innately keen person who sees analogies in a flash. A *euphues* is curious and penetrating about other people, and he can translate his penetration into empathy. If he's a playwright, he acts out his characters' possible reactions and puts in the one that strikes him *from the inside* as the most plausible. He's a quick study who builds easily on what he learns—in the tricky Greek sense of "learn" that covers conversational uptake as well as education.[55] His seventeenth-century incarnation is the Wit, the writer and speaker whose powers of figuration are palpably there behind whatever he writes and speaks. In Tesauro's phrase, he has a genius for representation.[56] He's the chorus master, the master of the revels, the natural leader of the game.

The game begins with a move of apparent anarchy or impudence on the leader's part. The metaphorist *seems* to have broken the rule of truth telling or propriety in the vernacular. But of course you can't break a rule of a game you're not playing. As it turns out, he isn't speaking the vernacular but introducing a language that overlaps with the vernacular. The anarchy is a benign form of practical joke. Being let into the joke and the resulting community is the reward of getting over a moment of imbalance or cognitive dissonance. Aristotle compares this kind of setup with the comic poet's technique of resolving ambiguity by non sequitur at the end of a parody of the epic hero's obligatory arming: "And on his feet he had—corns."[57] An anxiety is being teased and put to rest in the figurative interplay: the fear of losing control of a perceptual resource as fundamental as hearing and seeing. The hearer finds himself not only in control, but in control of a new organ of perception—his mastery of the impromptu dialect.

The appropriate reply to a metaphor is another metaphor that supplies the first one with a mock confirmation. This response game works on a very familiar principle. People play it all the time.

Let's say we have a figurative way of expressing some relation.

Correcting or eliminating shortcoming S = "curing" S.

Inventing something new = "minting" it.

A setting appropriate to a kind of activity A = the "theater" of A.

A hole toward one end of something = its "eye."

Vertical supports of something = its "legs."

Taken literally, these relation metaphors classify the things they relate. If the world is a theater of human affairs, then these must consist either in putting on plays or in watching them; if chairs have legs and needles eyes, then chairs and needles are animals. In this last case, neither my discussion nor the culture has allowed "animal" to make a figurative point about chairs and needles. In the other cases, the classification sometimes makes figurative sense (roughly, for "disease" read *involuntary failing;* for "coin," *conventional sign;* for "putting on plays," *pretending*), and the relational metaphor gives the illusion of implying and hence confirming the statements that emerge on a figurative reading.

The implying is only a figment of literal reading. A shortcoming can be "cured" without being involuntary. Something new can be "coined" without involving a convention. An activity can have a "theater" without involving pretense. Yet the game of mock confirmation is as hard to avoid as figuration itself. Sin has its physician, its medicines, its hospital, its convalescence, its remissions, its relapses. Words are stored in a treasury, have a face value, prove sterling or counterfeit, are exchanged. Human affairs have their stage managers, come off according to script, occur against backdrops, have prologues, interludes, and climaxes.[58]

One reason why the game is in no danger of going out of style is that mock confirmation can promote real inquiry. If social behavior is a theatrical performance, we might look for a social type we could call a "prompter," or a social strategy we could call a system of "cues"—in some contextually appropriate sense of these words not necessarily implying make-believe. If we found them, it wouldn't matter whether or not our discoveries confirmed that social behavior is a kind of pretense. They would remain discoveries.

But beyond the heuristic value of the game, it can't go out of style any sooner than figuration, to which it's the inevitable response. Confirming the metaphor is affirming our partnership in creating the common language by speaking it.[59]

Sometimes a stroke of luck brings two supreme *euphues* face-to-face, and we get a chance to watch a supreme game of confirmation:

> OLIVIA. Give vs the place alone; we will hear this *diuinitie*. . . .
>   Now, sir, what is your *text?*

VIOLA. Most sweet Ladie—
OLIVIA. A *comfortable doctrine,* and much may bee saide of it. Where lies your *Text*?
VIOLA. In Orsinoes bosome.
OLIVIA. In his bosome? In what *chapter* of his bosome?
VIOLA. To answer by the *method* [i.e., by metaphorical confirmation], in the *first of* his hart.
OLIVIA. O, I haue read it; it is *heresie*. Haue you no more to say?
VIOLA. Good madam, let mee see your face.
OLIVIA. Haue you any Commission from your Lord to negotiate with my face? You are now out of your *Text*.[60]

And a new game begins.

XI. *Conversation, Tradition, and Reading*

A living culture always maintains a number of overlapping conversation games and communities at once—some wider, some narrower. In the running conversation carried on by the generations of a literary tradition, certain metaphors never stop getting confirmed—like most of those I've already mentioned. They acquire the status of a special kind of talk-postulate, or *topos*. Take the traditional metaphor of the mind as a "book." Suppose the impromptu dialect of some latecomer assigns mental "book" a more specialized meaning—say, *running interior autobiography*. His dead predecessors in the tradition are in no position to answer back; does this weaken the claim of the tradition to the status of a conversation? If not, does the oddity of the conversation call for a change in the notion of figurative meaning?

I don't think so. There are all sorts of conversations in which some of the partners either don't have the chance to answer back or needn't take it: sermons, political speeches, hucksters' spiels, deliberative meetings in which the members drop in and out randomly. And there are all sorts of conversations in which the place and time of sending an utterance are more or less remote from the place and time of getting it: messages delivered by courier or semaphore or telegraph or radio or television or postman. And there are kinds of conversation, including some of the ones I've mentioned and such others as SOS's and the cries of street vendors, in which the uttering party isn't addressing anybody in particular but everybody in range of his utterance.

The transaction between the maker of a text and the reader of a copy is a conversation of all these kinds. The reader needn't answer back. He's usually not in the author's presence and has to interpret expressions like "that tree over there" as equivalent to expressions like "a tree near the speaker and somehow pointed out by him." He usually isn't named or singled out as belonging to the audience, but belongs only by being within range. Speaking to a *particular* addressee means using the addressee's vernacular and talk-postulates as one's point of departure for the impromptu dialect. Speaking to *whoever is in range of one's utterance* means using one's own vernacular in the hope or expectation that nonnative speakers—posterity—will learn it.

For the seventeenth-century poems I want to look at, this means that we are readers—are in range of the text—only more or less. These poems were written in a seventeenth-century system of conversation—in *their* English, not ours, even though ours grew out of it. I've heard people argue, against this, that poets use the transhistorical language of an unfolding tradition; but you don't use stages of your language—syntax, meaning assignment, or talk-postulates—that haven't come into existence yet. You don't, that is, unless you're God.

With this reference to God, I turn from the classical account of figurative speaking and understanding to the special case of the divine metaphorist and his human audience.

Chapter Two   The Paradigm
Figurative Speaker:
Divine Linguistics

THE TRADITIONAL Christian account of God's approach to conversation was at least as familiar to seventeenth-century writers and readers as the classical account of figuration in general. It's simply the speaker's-eye view of the standard commonplaces about the Bible reader's approach to the same conversation. The word par excellence is the recorded utterance of the speaker par excellence, who gets his written message across by complying with the rules that make understanding possible for his finite partners in conversation. Without these rules there could be no Golden Rule. Without this unspoken covenant, no spoken ones. In the Reformation version of the Fourth Gospel, what was with God in the beginning wasn't *Verbum*—the word as a basic unit of talk—but *Sermo*—the word as the principle of talk itself: the divine communicativeness.[1]

We can spot the *Sermo* of Protestant theology at work in the divine dialogue in book 3 of *Paradise Lost*—if we catch the echoes of the future in God the Son's appeal to God the Father:

>   should Man
> Thy creature late so lov'd, thy youngest Son
> Fall circumvented thus by fraud, thou joynd
> With his own folly? that be from thee farr,
> That farr be from thee, Father, who art Judge
> Of all things made, and judgest only right.[2]

The appeal turns out to be a parody-in-advance of Abraham's appeal to God in Genesis 18. There, Abraham dares to bring his doubts "even to the face of God himself":[3] "Then Abraham drewe nere, & said, Wilt thou also destroie the righteous with the wicked? . . . Be it farre from thee from doing this thing, to slay the righteous with the wicked: & that the righteous shulde be euen as the wicked, be it farre from thee. shal not the iudge of all the worlde do right?"[4] The point of the parable is clear enough. Maybe it's more Miltonic-libertarian than Protestant. The Christ who dares to press God for an explanation of God's ways to man is the source of what is Abrahamic in Abraham. But *Sermo* is at work on both sides of the two momentous interviews. The same patient communicator who holds himself accountable to his son submits to close questioning by a defense attorney who is also his creature. The distinctiveness of the dialogue in heaven is also revealing on this point. In the orthodox perspective, the partners are two persons with one being. There's conversation— timeless conversation—*inside the essence* of this God.[5]

In the beginning was Conversation. This isn't a bad motto for the portrait of the divine *euphues* on display in Augustine, Irenaeus, Tertullian, Aquinas, Luther, and Calvin. At the end of chapter 1, I called God's way with trope a special case of the laws of figuration.[6] What's "special" here isn't that his way breaks or bends the laws, but that it embodies them to perfection. As the performance of the Speaker par excellence, God's dialogue with his prophets and readers is *the* model of how to turn the language of all of us, language as usual, into a language of just you and me, emerging here and now.

1. *The Literal Figurative*

This transformation is the point of Aquinas's insistence that what he calls the "literal" sense of a parable isn't the "figure," or strict sense (say, *merchant's pearl*), but what is "figured" (*kingdom of God*).[7] "The meaning of a metaphorical expression in the Scriptures is 'literal' because the words are being uttered to convey that meaning"[8]—not, in short, because that's what the words mean in the vernacular. "Literal" sense in Aquinas's parlance is sense in context. In a figurative context this won't be a strict or vernacular sense but a sense assigned by the speaker's new idiom. (In the idiom of the parable, for example, "pearl" doesn't literally denote nacreous oyster secretions at all.) To the confusion of some modern historians, this use of "literal" is standard in Reformation discussions.[9] What words "immediately suggest," their sense in the (vernacular) language God starts out by talking, is simply raw material for "literal"—actual, and especially figurative—sense.

This usage is hard to ignore. It's all over the place in seventeenth-century exegesis, and the motivation for it is interesting. But as a rival or replacement for the classical usage that survived it, it's more trouble than it's worth. In what follows I'll stick to the familiar as well as ancient usage: for "literal," please read *strict* or *vernacular*.

II. Augustinian Reading: Mastering God's Dialect

Like any figurative sense, God's is sense by default. It isn't there unless the speaker, taken literally, seems to be ignoring or undermining his repeatedly avowed aim of teaching. In God's case, it's certain to be there if the speaker seems to be misbehaving. As applied to Logos, the presumption of rationality isn't just a provisional rule of fairness or charity. It's guaranteed by faith.

Suppose that a literal reading of a Bible story is countereducational. Let's say it gives us what seems to be a crime committed by God, on God's orders, or by a person who prefigures Christ. This fact is our cue to look for the figurative sense of the crime attribution.[10] For the same reason, what's trivial if literal isn't literal. For example, God seems to be wasting his time and ours by forbidding us to muzzle the threshing ox.[11] "Doth God take care for oxen? Or saith he it altogether for our sakes?" Obviously, for ours: "threshing ox" and "muzzling" are figurative, and Saint Paul goes on to show how something in the wider biblical context—a key passage in the Psalms—fills in the morally relevant sense.[12]

In the same way, apparent oddities are only apparent; God doesn't play dice with his text. A mysterious change in a historical name ("Abimelech" for "Achimelech") can warn us that the historical reference in the psalm title is figurative. The same goes for a title reference to a historical episode (David's flight from Absalom) that has little or nothing to do with the psalm being introduced.[13] In getting at the relevant sense, you don't simply discard the literal implications, say, of "ox." On the contrary, the metaphorical sense is *among* those implications and reachable by "careful examination."[14] On this approach, the corrupted name may turn out to be a description, and not a name at all. The discovery procedure here is a matter of applying tropes, which (says Augustine) occur in the Bible in a complexity and profusion that unschooled readers hardly suspect—not (he adds) that you need schooling to know the tropes, which are so natural to speech that you can illustrate nearly all of them from the language of the marketplace.[15]

What the incongruous literal sense of a figurative expression is incongruous *with* is the context,[16] and one central lesson Augustine teaches his Reformation disciples is a notion of context fitted to the dual authorship of the Bible. When you read the Psalms, your immediate partner in conversation is David. So a hazy figurative use of "shield" in one psalm may be cleared up by the Psalmist's uniform practice elsewhere, not by a different use of "shield" in Saint Paul. The Epistles define a different conversation. On the other hand, the reader's ultimate partner in the transaction with Scripture is God. Where David's intention isn't cleared up by the Davidic context, God's may be. The context of *his* authorship includes the whole Bible.[17]

If none of the possible meanings is singled out by context, they don't dwindle into meanings the text merely *would* have had in different non-actual cases, leaving the text potentially meaningful but actually meaningless. This particular speaker is incapable of equivocating, so his meanings don't just hang in eternal suspense. The *legitimately* possible meanings of a scriptural passage—the ones generated by the laws of figuration—are all actual. The sense of that kind of passage needs to be read off as a conjunction, a complex unity.[18]

The thing to watch in all of this is that the traditional Christian theory of divine figuration is simply the classical theory of figuration applied to the case of a Speaker whose divinity is among the talk-postulates that enable us to follow him as he shapes our language into his own.

Augustine's discussion of talk-postulates has the shrewd relativism we might expect of an old rhetoric teacher. God's choice of commonplaces is like his choice of language—it depends on his choice of primary audience. Words get different meanings in the different actual and possible languages they belong to—and so in the different societies that observe the *convention* of speaking one language rather than another.[19] In the same way, resemblance isn't enough to make one thing a sign of another unless the relevant point of resemblance is singled out by a *convention*.[20] To complicate the situation further, which convention gets used varies widely with context, and so—to the point of contradiction—does the resulting figurative sense.[21]

So we need conventions—talk-postulates spelling out the salient traits of, say, snakes—to cover the variety of metaphorical points snakes can be used to make. Biblical meaning depends on lore about animals, vegetables, minerals, crafts, numbers, and history.[22] Suppose it's a highly conspicuous item of serpent lore that the cunning of serpents par excellence is a habit of *letting the body take an unavoidable blow to save the head.*

Then we have reason to think that the trope should work on this concrete description, not on *the cunning of serpents*. We need to know that, by convention at least, the two descriptions refer to the same behavior.[23]

III. The Trope of Silence

The moral enforced but not drawn by a biblical narrative is a *kind* of figurative sense—the meaning of a silence where the silence is a speech act (act of omission, that is); like the silence of Psalm 51, as read by Augustine: Nathan's rebuke has jolted the Psalmist into facing his guilt.

This particular psalm isn't the allegorical "veil for mysteries"[24] Augustine often finds. Here (if we follow Augustine) David is being nakedly autobiographical. The enabling talk-postulate identified by the title reference to Nathan is a scandal we've read about elsewhere in the Bible:[25]

> Whoever you are, if you've sinned, and hesitate to repent for your sin because you despair of salvation, listen to David sobbing. To you God hasn't sent Nathan his prophet, to you God has sent David himself. Listen to him crying out and cry with him. Listen to him sobbing and sob too. Listen to him weeping, and join your tears with his. Listen to him being corrected, and rejoice with him. If sin could not be barred from you, let not the hope of forgiveness be barred.
>
> This man before you, this David, couldn't say, "I didn't know what I was doing." He knew well enough how great an evil it was to touch another's wife, and how great an evil it was to kill the husband, who was unwitting and not even angry. So men who have sinned in ignorance achieve God's mercy—and men who sin knowingly achieve, not just *any* mercy, but "great mercy."[26]

David himself doesn't generalize his moral experience this way—not explicitly. The context prompts Augustine to read the silence. The reading doesn't proceed (as in metaphor) by replacing the words with a figurative sense. David's silence (passed through the required trope) *is* the (figurative) generalization—or an instruction to draw it. And by complying with the silence, Augustine allows himself to testify on the Psalmist's behalf.[27]

The resulting generalization goes from *did happen to me* to *can happen to at least some people*. Something like formal reasoning is going on—relevant Bible history doing duty as a premise in an argument with the conclusion left to us.[28]

IV. Prefiguration: Event as "Utterance"

God isn't the only historian who works this way. But he has another use for his narrative that *does* look like something beyond the reach of creaturely historians. He can make two events enough alike to let a literal description of the earlier one serve in the right context as a metaphorical description of the later one. Moses is simultaneously a historian of the ark's voyage and a prophet of the Church's troubles. The historical event (E) occasions this kind of history-prophecy (P), and so (by metonymy) is said to prophesy the future event (F).[29]

Augustine often talks as if this relation of signifying had only two members, not three: one event or person figuratively refers to another—$\langle E, F \rangle$ rather than $\langle E, P, F \rangle$. But a thing gets to refer—to name something—only if it's available for use in saying things *about* what it names; that is, only if it's part of a *language:* a sign system with *predicates* as well as names. It's just nonsense, and not merely odd, to say that some biblical events and persons hook onto predicates to form sentences, metaphorical or otherwise.[30] So we're entitled to an explanation of what Augustine is getting at, if anything, in remarks like the following:

> Where Paul mentioned allegory [Gal. 4:22–31], he found it not in words but in circumstances: when from Abraham's two sons, one by a handmaid, the other by a free woman—a circumstance, not a saying—Paul showed that the two Testaments were to be understood.[31]

> [The stone Moses used to remove the water's bitterness, the rock Jacob placed at his head, the animal Abraham sacrificed instead of his son] are *things* in such a way as to be signs of other things too.[32]

On Augustine's showing, the allegory isn't carried by things in themselves but by things *mentioned* or *reported* (in a metaphor-generating context). As in my schematization of a moment ago, the relation is $\langle E, P, F \rangle$, not $\langle E, F \rangle$. When Augustine gets around to writing his own life story in the *Confessions*, he interprets his undertaking as Mosaic history writ small. The sequence $\langle E, P, F \rangle$ is realized by the sequence ⟨life, story of the life, figurative message hidden in the text of the story⟩. By describing his experiences he's also following the prompting built into the experiences by his divine partner in conversation. He's taking both parts in the conversation—his own in the history of his life, and God's in what the history says when read as the metaphor God has arranged the life to make.[33]

Despite contrary appearances, Augustine isn't describing a nonverbal sign language, much less a way of communicating peculiar to God. He's simply applying to divine metaphor his account of metaphor in general, an account in which we meet the same problematic phrases: "Signs are metaphorical when the things we refer to literally are themselves used to refer to something else: as we say 'bovis' [ox] and by these two syllables understand the animal usually so called, but by that animal in turn we understand an evangelist; which is what Scripture referred to (on Paul's reading) in the text: 'Thou shalt not muzzle the threshing ox.' "[34] In Augustine, meanings too are things (compare "He said some interesting *things*"); what refers figuratively to evangelists isn't oxen but the concept we use to pick them out, brought up in a context that lets us know which piece of the ox concept is the new meaning of "ox." The allegorical meaning of Abraham's sons belongs to the story, not to the sons. In short, the divine historian gets the meaning across by condescending to follow the usual rigmarole of figuration. His meanings are the same kind as those of human speakers: contextual and conventional, not "intrinsic and natural."[35] They need to be human kinds of meaning to do any good. An event signifies by proxy—by prompting speech that signifies.

On the other hand, God doesn't *find* the event resemblances that ground his metaphors; he *makes* them—in reverse order: the earlier event is patterned on the later. To "prefigure" some experience of Christ or his disciples, "upon whom the ends of the world are come,"[36] is to be a stage in the working out of the "ends"[37] to which the "world" (i.e., history) is a means. In order of conception, if not execution, ends cause means, future shapes past. Paul's key metaphors for "prefiguring" all tell the same paradoxical story: the prefiguring event is an outline impression[38] stamped on the past by the future; it's the future's shadow[39] streaming backward; it anticipates the form of the later event without the "completeness" or "fullness" that time gives to the later one.[40]

But as an exercise in communicating by spectacle, there's less oddity in prefiguration than meets the eye. What God does with actual scenes is what the emblem artist does with pictures and the masque producer does with tableaux: the caption, or *literal* description of the spectacle, is *figuratively* true of something else.

V. The Limits of Metaphor: Gesturing toward the Ineffable

If God uses one epoch or world phase as an emblem of another, he also uses the world as a whole as an emblem: "Things were made so that they could be likenesses of God's goodness." "Because God's goodness couldn't be represented perfectly, given the distance between him and the creatures, that goodness had to be represented by a variety of things, so that they could compensate for each other."[41]

But here the likenesses grounding God's metaphors seem to break down: "Nothing can be said in the same sense of both God and creatures."[42] In this one case, Maker and made have absolutely nothing in common—the Maker is in a class by himself. Hands don't literally have any power, so "hand of God" is a bogus metaphor;[43] in general, creatures have this or that in common with God only in the Pickwickian sense that they *depend* on what has it.[44] Metaphors for God's attributes, in short, are nothing but metonymies in disguise.

But the whole pedagogical value of using the name of something observable (say, "notebook") for something unobservable (say, "memory") is lost if the metaphorical sense applies only to the unobservable thing. You're better off talking about God in literal terms: "As far as what such terms [as "good" and "wise"] mean, they apply to God strictly, more strictly than to creatures, and are said of him by prior right."[45] If we *must* use metaphors, they had better be negative: "What God isn't is made clear to us more readily than what he is."[46]

For any divine attribute A, we have a Hobson's choice. We can say God has A, or we can call him by the name of a creature that "has" A only by proxy, only by being related somehow to God. Neither option solves the riddle of what A is. Why prefer the second, which gives the illusion that we are already familiar with what it is to have A?

Calvin answers with a comparison and several metaphors of his own:

> It's easy to refute the anthropomorphites, who were led to imagine that God has a body by the mouth, ears, eyes, hands, and feet assigned him in Scripture. Who is so witless as not to understand that *God babbles with us in a way, as nurses are in the habit of doing with children*? These forms of speech don't so much clarify what God is like, as fit the knowledge of God to our inadequacy. For this to happen, one has to come down a good way from God's altitude.[47] (Italics mine)

But a knowledge of something lower than God isn't a knowledge of God; on Calvin's showing, what ends up fitting our inadequacy is inadequate. The nurse analogy is more reassuring. Baby talk is like small talk and other conversational amenities that make each partner "you" to the others. We can call the resulting sense of mutual attention or presence *rapport*. In conversation it's even more fundamental than confidence. Herbert's divine host in "Love (III)" starts off by establishing it with his recoiling guest by drawing "nearer to me, sweetly questioning." If Calvin is right, God the Father's "incarnation" in Old Testament metaphor is the same kind of gesture. It's a conversational act of drawing near.

According to Calvin's version of the theory of accommodation, God's self-descriptions are no more figurative than literal. They're schemes, not tropes. What carries figurative sense is our first-impression label for the speech act of uttering them. As applied to that act, "self-description" turns out to mean *rapport gesture*.

The same goes for his descriptions of his mind: "Though [God] is beyond any passionate disturbance, he testifies that he is angry with sinners. . . . When we hear that God is angry we mustn't imagine that something in him has been moved. Instead we should think that this manner of speaking has been taken from our experience, because whenever God passes judgment he assumes the expression of someone flashing out angrily."[48] "Being angry" in context turns out to be a metaphor for *condemning;*[49] a *would-be* metaphor, that is. Here again God's otherness repels the real thing. We draw a blank when "judging" is used to name a process in his mind. The best we can do to fill in the blank is: *(unknown) cause of God's angry expression*. If the Christian metaphorists have any determinate idea of him at all, it's that he's the speaker par excellence, and a figurative speaker at that—a speaker willing to start us off in our own language as a means of bringing us to his. The wit and tact on both sides of Herbert's dialogues between the sinner and God are homage to this assurance. Even the terrified sinner of Donne's divine sonnets pays a kind of homage to it in his panicky effort to put off doom with talk, like Scheherezade.

VI. *Adapting versus Reading*

Of course the Augustinian God doesn't describe himself for the fun of it. Even though his self-descriptions will remain a riddle until we're face-to-face with the Speaker, the urgent news that goes with them can be understood now, and the relevant notion of understanding is strictly realist: the news is something you *discover* in the text, not something you smuggled into it. That's why a theory of the figurative *speaker* is on the Christian agenda. For the figurative *listener* the theory translates easily into a "method of discovery" without which we're doomed to "discover" only the stuff we smuggled in.[50]

God is a *euphues* who makes his metaphors hard, not to punish the slower listeners but to challenge the quicker ones.[51] Nearly everything the quick ones dig out is available elsewhere in some unproblematic passage or other.[52] Still, understanding is a matter of life and death; fundamental beliefs are involved. The slow—the ungifted or untutored or superficially clever—are apt to be seduced by flashy misreading.[53] In a crisis of doctrine, unproblematic passages are the only suitable evidence, even though a misreading eventually discredits itself by jarring against things in the context.[54] Self-correction won't work if misreading gets to be a habit, or (worse yet) if it begins to tickle the misreader's vanity. That's why readers can't be allowed to put even wholesome things in Moses' mouth.[55]

Here we run into a puzzlement. By Augustine's standard, many of his *own* transactions with the Bible are, at best, wholesome misreadings. So are the notorious medieval allegorizations that break a fundamental rule of figuration by responding to no cue of incongruity in the literal sense; they refuse—with a vengeance—to leave well enough alone. This is a theme the Reformation made its own. "For in *no* writing, much less God's, is it legitimate to catch at figurative readings for the pure lust of it. We should avoid them and rely on the simple and pure and primary meaning until either the context or obvious absurdity forces us to acknowledge a figure." "The question [of what the text says] is not what the lust for trifling is *capable* of delivering, but what conscientiousness is *obliged* to deliver."[56]

All the stranger that much of what Augustine does with the Bible doesn't qualify as reading by the standards he holds himself and others to when the doctrinal stakes are high. The same contrast shows up in the practice of the Reformers. A passage isn't a proof text if the proof is an allegorization.[57] Yet Calvin tells us how much he likes Ambrose's "exceedingly elegant" allegorical conceit that Jacob impersonating his elder brother to earn his father's blessing is the faithful soul using Christ's merit to win God's approval.[58]

Calvin's applause looks flatly contradictory until you draw the crucial Augustinian distinction between reading proper and Ambrose's kind of reading-derived activity. Not every legitimate response to a passage is an act of understanding it. After understanding it, you can build a conceit on it—that is, put it into a new context in which it *is* figurative. In Augustine's phrase, you can "carve"[59] a spiritual sense out of a historical text as long as you don't throw out the history. This isn't reading, though it presupposes reading. It's a kind of pious repartee—retort without irreverence. As in the Ambrose case, it may even respond to a sign of figurativeness—the moral dubiousness of the Jacob story taken literally.

This is where the Papists go wrong, according to the Reformers: they "confuse the sense of the Bible with its adaptation or application to a use, which can be various and multiple even while the sense remains one and the same."[60] It's no accident that some of the most ingenious of Augustine's adaptations come up in the meditative parts of the *Confessions*. He isn't *reading* the relevant texts here. He's using them to think with. And the context in which they're ingeniously figurative isn't the Bible but the *Confessions*. Adaptation is figurativeness by transplantation. Augustine is a master of the art, as he is of all the arts of figurative speech. In this respect as in others, the seventeenth-century metaphorists are highly Augustinian.

VII. Antimetaphorism

It seems that God is not only metaphorical in himself but (by prompting adaptation) a cause of metaphor in others. So it's strange to find metaphor among the ways of God that need to be justified to man. Reservations about metaphor crop up at the beginning of systematic discussion. Aristotle recognizes that one incarnation of the *euphues* is the philosophical charlatan who uses word magic, like Empedocles' description of the sea as earth-sweat, to make a problem disappear. The same goes, he says, for "inanities and poetic metaphors" like describing the act-property of *being just* as an "original" that gets "copied" by individual acts of justice.[61] One revealing reason Aquinas gives for insisting that figurative meaning in Scripture is the meaning of an expression as the expression is actually used—what he confusingly calls the literal sense—is that God is innocent of the charges that figuration is open to: he doesn't equivocate, much less lie.

In fact, these are the charges that are leveled against metaphor, and refined on, by seventeenth-century writers like Hobbes, Sprat, and Locke.

People's use of language "to counsel and teach one another" is corrupted when they "use words metaphorically: that is, in other sense than they are ordained for, and thereby deceive others."[62] By deceiving, Hobbes seems to mean the familiar ploy of faking a logical conclusion by switching in mid-argument between the literal and figurative senses of a key term. Reasoning can't proceed if meanings aren't held constant. Figurative expressions, like evaluative ones, "can never be true grounds of any ratiocination," though Hobbes allows that metaphors are "less dangerous, because they profess their inconstancy."[63]

It's not clear why Hobbes thinks a metaphorical sense, once introduced, is less "constant"—or shiftier—than an "ordained" one. Most words have enough alternative *literal* meanings for a double-talker to monkey with. The real grievance here seems to be against *pseudo*metaphors that replace literal sense with no sense at all—riddles without solutions. Consider the jargon of the theologians: "If it be false to say that virtue can be poured, or blown up and down, the words *inpoured virtue, inblown virtue*, are as absurd and insignificant as a round quadrangle."[64] Sprat makes the same complaint, but more angrily: "Who can behold without indignation, how many mists and uncertainties these specious Tropes and Figures have brought on our knowledge?"[65] They are "specious" in the sense that they hold up a distractingly flashy "species," or image (the literal sense), between the reader's understanding and what they really mean in context, if anything.

The "trick of *Metaphors*" is a "beautiful deceipt." Sprat didn't need Quintilian to tell him that "the use of metaphor is a gift of nature; so that even uneducated and undiscerning people use it all the time"[66]—though he was probably familiar with Quintilian's influential discussion. But it takes sophistication to make a sophist. This, and not romantic primitivism, is probably the Royal Society's basic motive for "preferring the language of Artizans, Countrymen, and Merchants, before that of Wits and Scholars."[67]

Even seventeenth-century enthusiasts of metaphor tend to show uneasiness at unguarded moments. Take Tesauro: when you hear arguments laced with metaphorical wit, "they take the understanding by surprise. They look conclusive at first meeting. But closely studied they melt into empty deceptions, as Black Sea apples are beautiful and red to look at. But bite into them and they leave your jaws full of smoke."[68] Tesauro is no enemy of metaphors—consciously, at least. But metaphorical wit as he describes it is just applied sophistic—all the subtleties in Aristotle's catalogue of logical deceptions, used to exhilarate this time instead of to swindle. Maybe the Black Sea apple is free, but your mouth still ends up full of smoke. It's a questionable form of "entertainment." Tesauro's moral discomfort is obvious.

One item in Quintilian's tribute to metaphor finds its way into the Renaissance grievance list. Metaphor was invented as a technique for "stirring up minds." It works by setting off inflammatory *phantasiae*, or mental images. So if you get good at it, you can achieve "enormous emotional power."[69] The Elizabethan George Puttenham appreciates this possibility, but with less enthusiasm. In fact, for somebody offering lessons in figuration he's strangely off-putting about his stock in trade. Figurative expressions aren't samples of compliance with new rules of language. They're simply "trespasses in speech." Still worse, they're "wresters of upright judgment" (applied sophistic, in short—the Aristotelian theme again). Worst of all, they "inveigle and appassionate the mind." The logic twister shares this tool with the demagogue and the false prophet.[70]

The seventeenth-century antimetaphorists take up this theme, too. If a metaphor is "sharp and extraordinary," says Hobbes, it's fit "only for an accusation or Defense at the Bar."[71] Locke recapitulates all this in his attack on "the arts of deceiving wherein men find pleasure to be deceived." Figurative expressions "are for nothing else but to insinuate wrong ideas, move the passions, and thereby mislead the judgment, and so indeed are perfect cheats."[72]

Locke is describing a chain of psychological cause and effect. Ideas first get insinuated, or sneaked into, our consciousness. They're *wrong* ideas (or fantasies)—wrong because they belong with the literal sense, which doesn't quite go away when we dismiss it in favor of the sense in context. We respond to the fantasies as well as to the figurative sense. This confusion is why "rabbit" is even more insulting than "coward." From wrong idea to wrong passion to wrong judgment, metaphor on the showing of Puttenham and Hobbes and Locke turns teaching and counseling upside down.

VIII. *Metaphor Vindicated: The Augustinian Defense*

You can worry about metaphorical wit and eloquence and still admit that they have their uses. They're fit for pleading at the bar, says Hobbes. Eloquence is a weapon, says Sprat. What would happen if good people "cast it away" and only bad ones "retain it"?[73] Not only creatures use it—and here we come to the puzzle we started with—so does the God of Augustine's tradition. God could cure the soul without relying on speech and spokesmen. But he *does* rely on them.

It just isn't true, as one axe-grinding modern critic has it, that in Augustine human skills "cure" what is *really* cured by God. The important fact that God *makes* the skills effective implies that they *are* effective.[74] Eloquence without wisdom is a spreader of rot, says Augustine. But if the point of preaching is to do the most good, the wise preacher had better be armed with the force and art—with the eloquence—to make the wisdom count as much as it can.[75] Deploying those resources calls for an insight into other minds that goes beyond force or art,[76] but the whole point of Augustine's qualification here is that, rightly deployed, these things work. Metaphors redeem as well as inflame. They redeem by inflaming.[77]

For Augustine this is just a fact of historical observation. He cites his own spectacular success in talking the Mauritanians of Caesarea out of their gory annual war game, the Horde. "Many . . . experiences have taught us this: what a wise man's grandeur of style has *done* to people, people have *shown*. They've shown it by cheering, but no more by cheering than by groaning. Sometimes they've shown it even by tears. Ultimately they've shown it by changing their lives."[78] And where there's style, there's art. There are rules that make this particular art possible—the *praecepta dicendi*. Speakers don't—in fact they can't—bring them off by thinking about which to follow, but only because the only way to bring them off is not to think about them at all.[79] And they can be learned the same way, by imitation and practice—the way people learn to talk in the first place.[80]

As for the charge that metaphor is a kind of lying or equivocation, "it isn't lying when terms that mean one thing as a result of meaning another [i.e., figurative terms] are directed to the understanding of a truth."[81] In fact, the unspoken agreements that make figuration work are sensitive enough to changes in context to let you switch meaning from phrase to phrase without equivocation, as Augustine does while explaining the phenomenon of metaphor synonyms: "The things [in Psalm 91] that are 'wings,' are a 'shield,' too, because they're neither wings *nor* a shield."[82] As usual, absurdity on a literal reading rules out the literal reading.

Some of the seventeenth-century metaphorists are subject to fits of antimetaphorism. Vaughan says that truth gets "lost / In fine conceits, like streams in a sharp frost."[83] Traherne dismisses metaphors as nothing but clouds and vapors and gilding (the surrounding arguments show that these metaphors of his aren't ironies at his own or his speaker's expense—just honest stupidities).[84] Donne apologizes for his vice of seeking "poeticness," pleading the Prophets' example by way of excuse. But luckily these poets are also more or less Augustinian. For the Master, the Prophets' example can't excuse metaphor only because it recommends it, along with the rest of the supreme Speaker's performance.

Still, antimetaphorism is a little more valuable than mere confusion. It's confusion paying tribute to an important fact that we're going to meet again in various forms. Metaphor is an act—an act of speech, a social act. Like every social act, even a move in a game, it is liable to special corruptions all its own. There's an etiquette, even an ethics of metaphor. Maybe there's a ghost of an awareness of this in old apologetic formulas like "so to speak" and "as it were." The figurative speaker feels the need to go through the motions of getting permission from the people he's imposing on for the liberties he's about to take with the common understanding.[85]

Against this background, Locke's sermon on metaphor sheds some, though not all, of its obtuseness:

> Words, especially of languages already framed, being no man's private possession, but the common measure of commerce and communication, it is not for anyone, at pleasure, to change the stamp they are current in nor alter the ideas they are affixed to; or at least, when there is a necessity to do so, he is bound to give notice of it. Men's intentions in speaking are, or at least should be, to be understood, which cannot be without frequent explanations, demands, and other the like incommodious interruptions where men do not follow common use.[86]

Locke fails to appreciate that figuration itself is an act of giving notice: without cues, no metaphor. And he fails to appreciate that metaphors, like jokes, are gratuitous: reason not the need. In fact, he's under the spell of a figurative untruth: that the metaphorist revalues coins of the king's realm rather than puts coins in circulation in a realm of his own. But Locke is right about a speaker's duty to try to be understood, and about the inconvenient demands the figurative speaker lays himself open to.

We make these demands of the figurative speaker, or of the text in his absence. In return we offer figurational charity. If I were asked what this book is basically all about, I would answer: the hazards and pleasures of this exchange.

Chapter Three   God's Tumbler:
Pseudometaphor,
Sacred and Profane

I'LL BEGIN AT THE bottom, with the null case. In the poems we study here, the seventeenth-century metaphorist abuses our figurational charity by making his figurative sense frustratingly hard to get, and especially by tantalizing us with a figurative sense that isn't there. He imposes on us and gets away with it. Eventually we'll need to ask why he would take this kind of risk, and whether the result is figuration at all. But the first question—the key to all the others—is precisely how the trick is done.

1. Pseudometaphor as Speaking in Tongues

In a silly and luminous moment of the balcony scene, Romeo tells himself a story. Two of the fairest stars ask Juliet's eyes to take their place while the stars attend to "some business." If the request were taken up,

> The brightnesse of her cheeke would shame those starres,
> As day-light doth a Lampe, her eye in heaven
> Would through the ayrie region streame so bright,
> That Birds would sing, and thinke it were not night.[1]

Let's cooperate by following the standard rules, starting with figurational charity: take it as given that the speaker isn't a lunatic. He isn't talking about stand-in stars but using "stand-in star" *talk* to go on praising Juliet as he has been doing. Then what? At first glance it seems that what he's really saying about her needs to be fetched from afar, across a metaphysical distance—from possible worlds in which stars are capable of "business" trips and "entreaties" and changing places with eyes. But there are no such possible worlds (things with these properties wouldn't *be* stars or eyes). So we get nowhere asking what's literally true of stars in the relevant worlds. What's true in every absurd possible world is—anything at all. So we've drawn a blank. Metaphorical sense is something that saliently follows from literal sense. Unfortunately, nothing follows saliently from Romeo's fantasy.

Diagnosing *mixed* metaphor takes us no further. It doesn't help us to work at the fantasy piecemeal. "Business" and "entreat" had better be discounted altogether, not made respectably astral thanks to an arbitrary reading. Apparently they don't belong to a new language being improvised on the spot. Instead, they're there to motivate the role exchange that lets Juliet's cheek outshine stars and Juliet's eyes make daylight in the eighth sphere, and thus convey what seems to be the point: that Juliet's face is "brighter" (i.e., "fairer") than the stars.

Romeo's story isn't *mixed* metaphor, but *pseudo*metaphor. What's figurative here isn't the thing that's ostensibly being *said* but the thing that's ostensibly being *done* in saying it: the story *telling* can be figurative even if the story isn't. But what speech act is Romeo performing here if the "story-telling" label doesn't literally apply? And will the answer to this question, if there is one, also do for Crashaw's elaborate scherzo on the same story, with the Christ child's eyes and brow turning down the stars' and sky's requests for a similar exchange of jobs?

> Here with eye, there with star, but with equal brightness, both are gleaming: heaven's face and the heavenly face of the child. Look how well either's business would suit the other! How well a transfer of realms into one another's sway would suit them—if that eye of heaven were to stand in this brow's heaven; or if the boy's star here were to stand in heaven's brow.
>
> If the boy's star here were twinkling in heaven's brow, heaven would think this eye no less its own. Heaven's eye there, if it were standing in this brow's heaven, would think itself no less in a heaven of its own.
>
> Heaven could make so beautiful an exchange with the brow of the child, and the stars with his eyes. . . . Heaven and stars would wish it—but wish it in vain. Look here: the brow of the child, the eyes of the child, say no. . . .[2]

What Crashaw apparently liked in Romeo's performance, and exaggerated in his own, is the way a vivid illusion of figurative meaningfulness gets conjured up for a fantasy narrative by its figuratively meaningful ending (the face's "refusal to trade" = its resistance to comparison—hence its vast superiority—to the sky). In short, Crashaw liked and exploited a standard trick for bringing off pseudometaphor.

But he doesn't need any tutoring in this art from Romeo. He himself is the notorious past master of it. In fact, the subject of this chapter—pseudometaphor as figurative speech act—might just as well be described as the art of Crashaw.

I didn't write "notorious" lightly a moment ago, by the way. At its best or worst, this art is bound to strike modern readers as frigidly precious to the point of craziness. Often this is because the modern readers are quite right. (Maybe the eye-star story is an example.) But often enough it's because they don't have the training to respond fairly to the cues they're getting—or not getting. They aren't in possession of the rules of the game. This is a pity. In some Crashaw poems the game in all its extravagance is well worth playing in itself, to say nothing of what playing it can teach us about what greater poets than Crashaw are up to.

Another of Crashaw's virtuoso effects is just the reverse of this one. You start with a metaphor and draw a rapid succession of fantastic consequences from it by taking it literally. We know more or less what it is for a melody to *flow* through consciousness. Roughly, it's for notes to form a "plyant series" (*Musicks Duell* 61)—for musical sounds of varying pitch to be heard in a smooth sequence. Now for the fantastic consequences. If the nightingale's song flows, then it's a liquid—a liquid that was

> still'd out of her Breast,
> That ever'bubbling spring; the sugred Nest
> Of her delicious soule, that there does lye
> Bathing in streames of liquid Melodie. (65–68)

If her song is literally a stream and her breast is the source, then before the song emerges it must form a breast-pool in which her soul can literally bathe—a "sugred Nest."

It's easy to overlook the catch: the torrent *isn't* literal, and the figurative sense of the song-bath, if any, calls for an analysis readers don't have time for if they're busy following Crashaw, who jumps from one metaphor for origin to another—from breast as the spring of a song-river to breast as the seed plot of a song-harvest. He applies the same fantasy logic to the harvest. If it's literal, then think of rows of song-stalks:

> in ripend Aires
> A Golden-headed Harvest fairely reares
> His Honey-dropping tops, plow'd by her breath
> Which there reciprocally laboureth
> In that sweet soyle.   (69–73)

The airs-ears pun and the mention of breath invites us to think that the rest of this hallucination (read in context) supplies appropriate song meanings for "ears," "heads," "tops," and "Honey-dropping," and a singer meaning for the "plowing" of "that sweet soyle." But the profusion doesn't let us find any such meanings. Instead, it helps us give in to the illusion that we *have* found them, when all we've been offered to think about is the vaguely monstrous wheat field of the literal reading.

That pseudometaphorical golden crop "reared" up out of the "soyle" reminds the speaker of a chapel

> Founded to th' Name of great Apollo's lyre.
> Whose sylver-roofe rings with the sprightly notes
> Of sweet-lipp'd Angell-Imps, that swill their throats
> In creame of Morning Helicon, and then
> Preferre soft Anthems to the Eares of men,
> To woo them from their Beds, still murmuring
> That men can sleepe while they their Mattens sing:
> (Most divine service:) whose so early lay,
> Prevents the Eye-lidds of the blushing day.   (74–82)

The nightingale song, in its new incarnation as cathedral "quire," gives way to a song sung inside it. With the angelic demons (or cupids) gargling breakfast cream in preparation for an antiphonal concert, we've frankly given up the pretense of a metaphor for a bird-song's interior—whatever that would be. We've been impudently closed up in somebody's reverie.

The same reverie masquerades as a metaphor for how the Magdalene's tears affect the cherub who sips them for breakfast in "The Weeper":

> Euery morn from hence
> A brisk Cherub somthing sippes
> Whose sacred influence
> Addes sweetnes to his sweetest Lippes.
> Then to his musick. And his song
> Tasts of this Breakfast all day long.   (25–30)

We gather from the previous stanza that the tears are being sipped from the "bosome" of heaven. The cherub is being suckled by God. But this is no help, just another layer of mystification.

For what it's worth, learned sense can be made of angelic breakfast. In the standard theology, cherub contemplation is "daybreak knowledge," knowledge of things as they exist in God's mind.[3] So God's mind is the "bosome" that drinks the upward-streaming tears in the preceding stanza. God's *idea* or timeless vision of the weeper's repentance is what refreshes the cherub "every morn."[4] Does this help us accept Crashaw's induced reveries as metaphors? Hardly. "Bosom," "drinks," "breakfast," and the rest have been fused into the false unity of mixed metaphor. What fascinates or disgusts or distracts us here is the role reversal of a bosom that drinks—a bosom itself provided with a mouth to suckle.[5]

Academic readers like to point out that the monstrous fantasies conjured up by a literal reading of Crashaw's mixed or bogus metaphors are like the transformation stories in Ovid and his Renaissance imitators: decorative, erotic, and cruel. But there's one big difference. For our purposes, the difference is crucial. Take a pair of scenes that one recent critic uses to back up the theory that Crashaw got his poetics from Góngora.[6] In the Góngora work, Acis is compensated for being crushed to death by the jealous Polifemo. With the usual Ovidian gallows humor, the compensation is to get liquefied:

> With boundless violence he [Polifemo] tore away
> The greatest summit of the lofty rock,
> Which to the youth [Acis] on whom he hurls it is
> An urn immense, a pyramid not small.
> In tears the nymph [Galatea] implores the deities
> Of ocean, deities whom Acis calls:
> They nod agreement, and the blood crushed out
> By the relentless rock—was crystal pure.
> No sooner had the fateful precipice
> Fallen on his limbs in pitiful oppression
> Than all the thickest trees there had their feet
> Shod with the liquid seedpearl of his veins.
> At last the flowing silver, his white bones,
> Licking the flowers and silvering the sands,
> To Doris reaches, who with tears of pity
> Greets him a son-in-law, hails him a river.[7]

Now compare this with what Crashaw says about what persecuting a martyr does to the persecutors:

> What did their Weapons but sett wide the Doores
> For thee: Fair, purple Doores, of loue's deuising;
> The Ruby windowes which inrich't the EAST
> Of Thy so oft repeated Rising.
> Each wound of Theirs was Thy new Morning;
> And reinthron'd thee in thy Rosy Nest,
> With blush of thine own Blood thy day adorning,
> It was the witt of loue o'reflowd the Bounds
> Of WRATH, & made thee way through All Those WOUNDS.[8]

Almost every word in the Crashaw is figurative, and what's being figuratively *said* has nothing to do with bizarre transformation, or even with the physical appearance of anything:

> Without knowing it, the persecutors of martyrs were acting on Christ's behalf ("for thee").
>
> They were enlarging sinners' access to grace through sacrifice (setting wide the doors), sacrifice that is both bloody and majestic ("purple," or royal red).
>
> The martyrdoms were testimonies by precious blood sacrifice ("Ruby windowes") that celebrated the renewal ("inrich't the EAST") of Christ's often-reenacted triumph over death and sin ("Thy so oft repeated Rising").
>
> The martyrs' every wound was a symbol of Christ's renewal ("Thy new Morning"), and symbolically restored Christ in majesty ("reinthron'd thee") in the bloody place where his ascent, or Resurrection, had to begin ("thy Rosy Nest").
>
> With a reenactment of Christ's own sacrifice ("with blush of thine own Blood"), the martyrs celebrated Christ's glory ("thy day adorning").
>
> It was the alert persuasiveness ("witt") of God's love that prevailed over ("o'reflow'd the Bounds of") God's anger, and spread Christ's gospel ("made thee way") by means of the martyrs' testimony ("through All Those WOUNDS").

The close-knit texture of literal and figurative language mimics a surreal description. Hotspurism has a field day here—with Crashaw's blessing. We get windows that turn the sunrise red (rather than vice versa), nests functioning as thrones, wounds as sources of daylight, Christ walking through wounds. A *cue* for figurative interpretation has become an *obstacle*, an end in itself. Góngora's main show just doesn't work this way at all. His tangles of literal and figurative meaning (liquid seedpearl, flowing silver, and one other I'll get to next) are isolated grace notes in the telling of a story—not a mock story. What's grotesque and precious in Góngora is the event he's telling us about.

The most ingenious of Góngora's grace notes here is worth a closer look by way of introduction to still another kind of pseudometaphor, the pun: "all the thickest trees there had their feet / Shod with the liquid seedpearl of his veins." The *feet* of trees get *shod* with the river—and we're momentarily diverted by a semantic illusion of forest trolls. How is this brought off?

Try leaving feet out: if we'd been told that the trees were wading in the river, or even that the trees were shod with the river, the effect would have been weakened considerably. The key to the trick is that "shod" taken literally is closely associated with "foot" in its older literal meaning. We're seduced into taking "shoe the foot of" as a unit, and hence into repeating the history of the language by needlessly applying the metaphor transformation to "foot" to generate its alternative meaning, *bottom part*, or *foundation*, as if that meaning were still figurative. The cream of this kind of practical joke is the momentary embarrassment of being tricked into learning our own language.

In metaphor resurrection, an older literal sense distracts us from a newer by false verbal association. In punning, the literal sense distracts us by false relevance to what we've been talking about. Pun relevance is just a decoy. If the pun word is taken in isolation, the decoy sense fits fine. But when the listener gets around to integrating the word into the sentence it's part of, the decoy sense won't work. On the sentence level where actual *saying* happens, pun sense is nonsense. In the following outrageous wit game with Christ's wounded feet, the speaker is showing off for Mary Magdalene:

> This foot hath got a Mouth and lippes
>   To pay the sweet summe of thy kisses;

> To pay thy Teares, an Eye that weeps
> Instead of Teares, such Gems as this is.[9]

Atomistic relevance with a vengeance. Mouths, lips, and eyes taken literally and one at a time belong to the same domain as feet, and combine to give us a decorative nightmare glimpse of a sadly amorous foot-face—a glimpse we get by taking the features as literally as the foot.

It's typical of Crashaw that the grotesqueness here is more violent than earlier renditions of the same conceit. Mark Antony says that Caesar's wounds "like dumbe mouthes do ope their Ruby lips / To begge the voyce and vtterance of my Tongue."[10] In Crashaw's idiom, Caesar's wound-mouths wouldn't content themselves with begging dumbly for some tongue's "utterance" when they could beg out loud for the tongue itself. This doesn't mean that there's no respectable figurative sense in which Christ's wounds are "mouths" and "lips." (They're means of expressing what their suffering owner is going through.) But in Crashaw the sense that shamelessly absorbs all our interpretative energy and attention is the disreputable sense that isn't there: the *literal* story of a conscientious foot that acquires lips and eyes in the hope of repaying a debt of kisses and tears.[11]

Here and elsewhere in Crashaw, we might almost think that classic medical texts had been combed for nomenclature to exploit. All his favorite mannerisms are in Celsus and Galen—the heart's ears or stomach or head or wings, the stomach's mouth, the nose's backbone[12]—except that in the textbooks these aren't mannerisms but necessities. In Crashaw's devotional poem, gap-filling metaphors aren't being invented to fill gaps. They're little detonations of festive but serious punning—punning without the clown white.[13]

If figurative sense is systematically drowned out or faked this way, then it must be beside the point.[14] In particular, attempts to search for it will be mostly wrongheaded. It won't do, for example, to rearrange Crashaw's troublesome phrases into sentences of one's own concoction when the ones they're in turn out to be uncooperative.

Take the following:

> When some new bright Guest
> Takes vp among the starres a room,
> And Heaun will make a feast,
> Angels with crystall violls come

> And draw from these full eyes of thine
> Their master's Water: Their owne Wine.[15]

It does no good here to read what the speaker *should* have said into what he said.[16] The angels *aren't* using the Magdalene's tears to celebrate repentance, hers or anyone else's, but to celebrate someone's glory. The wineless Christ *doesn't* fail to take joy in someone's repentance. The waterless angels *don't* fail to recognize signs of grace. If there's a rough parallel between the water-wine at the wedding in heaven and the water Christ turned into wine for the earthly wedding feast at Cana, the parallel is too rough to bail us out: the drink served in heaven doesn't *turn into* wine; it's both water *and* wine, depending on the drinker.

If we insist on a figurative reading, then we may as well go on to ask exactly what the angels are doing when they (metaphorically) draw off tears and drink them. Why *are* tears being used to celebrate glory rather than repentance? And what's the figurative point of the obvious play on the invitation of Donne's disillusioned speaker in "Twicknam garden":

> Hither with christall vyals, lovers come,
> And take my teares, which are loves wine.

Clues have been generously crammed into the lines—too generously. The thickness of the clues obliterates the facts, if there are any.

We're left with a choice. We can keep the crazy literal sense—bibulous angels toasting bright newcomers among the stars from crystal vials filled with a fresh consignment of the Magdalene's tears—or we can escape the craziness by putting in a substitute text masquerading as a paraphrase of the (nonexistent) figurative sense. For better or worse, the crazy choice is the right one.

Mental imagery, says a pioneer in figuration study, is a continual accompaniment of thinking, *especially when thinking hits a snag.*[17] The process of interpretation has hit a snag here. As usual, the result is imagery. Again, conversational charity suggests a rule: where it isn't easy to see how the doer could avoid knowing what he or she is doing, the deed counts prima facie as intentional. What we're dealing with isn't an accident but an act, a calculated, emphatically repeated act of speech. The question is: which one?

In a worship context, at least, the act is a familiar idiom of preaching—so familiar it doesn't have a name (devotional cheering, let's say). If the speaker's solo demonstration works, he not only teaches the congregation how to do it but brings them along with him. In the tradition of Christian poetics, the supreme model of cheering—intimate and public at once—is Augustine's performance in the meditative parts of the *Confessions*. An example more or less at random:

Vocasti	Thou didst call
et clamasti	and cry
et rupisti	and split
surditatem meam	my deafness!
Coruscasti	Thou didst flash
splenduisti	and flare
et fugasti	and scare away
caecitatem meam!	my blindness!
Fragrasti, et duxi	Thou gavest forth sweetness,
spiritum,	I drew breath,
—et anhelo tibi!	—and pant for thee!
Gustavi	I tasted
—et esurio et sitio!	—and I hunger, and I thirst!
Tetigisti me	Thou didst touch me
—et exarsi in pacem tuam!	—and I flamed out unto thy peace![18]

In fact, Crashaw's taste in pun-subverted metaphor is recognizably Augustinian; consider again a few samples from the *Confessions:*

Receive Thou the sacrifice of my confessions from the hand of my tongue.

Neither could I guess nor had I felt what savourous joys the hidden mouth that was in her heart was browsing upon from Thy Bread.

I let out the tears that I was holding in that they might flow as they would, strewing them beneath my heart; and on them did my heart find rest.

I drive away those fancies with the hand of my heart from the face of my recollection.

Thou hadst pierced our heart with the arrow of Thy love, and we bore Thy words fixed in our bowels.[19]

In terms of the orthodox Christian psychology of religious experience, these derangements fail to *say* anything precisely because they succeed in *signaling* and (if the speaker is lucky) *evoking* something: the emotion of feeling or tasting or being "wise" to the fact that the beloved is right here and not simply nearby.

For Latinate Christendom, wisdom is "sapience"[20] in the root sense in which you "savor" what you enjoy immediate contact with.[21] It's the earthly blessing Jesus promises the pure in heart when he says that "they shal se God."[22] The speaker gifted with *sermo sapientiae* has the right to claim that he and his sympathetic audience have moments of knowing God's presence in a sense closer to the carnal than the intellectual sense of "know." As drawn by Campanella, the contrast intended here is between contact and detachment. Heard as something happening outside us, a tune is merely beautiful. Felt as a movement of the inner sense that it strokes and purifies, it's sweet.[23]

Augustine's own moments of devotional cheering are highly typical—sensual (even when renouncing the senses), ardent, exclamatory, and unembarrassed. Restraint is meaningless here:

> And what do I love, when I love thee?
>   not seemliness of body or fairness of season or brightness of
>   light—lo this friend to the eyes—
>   not the sweet tunes of all kinds of songs,
>   not the sweet smell of flowers and balm and incense,
>   not manna and honey,
>   not limbs welcome to the embraces of the flesh:
> not these do I love when I love my God.
>
> And yet I love a kind of light and a kind of voice and a kind of
>   smell and a kind of food and a kind of embrace, when I
>   love my God:
> the light, voice, smell, food, embrace of my inward self, where
>   there flashes to my soul what place does not confine,
>   and where there resounds what time does not snatch away,
>   and where there wafts forth sweetly what the wind does
>   not scatter,
>   and where there savors what eating does not diminish,
>   and where there is fixed what fullness does not uproot.
> This is what I love when I love my God.[24]

In Campanella's analogy, intimacy with God is a tune tickling the inner ear—the vibration of a mind tempered by God's mind. In Jean Gerson's analogy, it's a God-ward sparking or flaming of appetite that starts in rational understanding and outruns it. What registers on the mind surging with "emotional knowledge"[25] isn't an image or concept of the thing loved but the emotion itself.

But being an emotion, this is a kind of knowledge that naturally engages the imagination, too. In Crashaw, as in Augustine and Saint Teresa and many others in this tradition, the resulting imagery goes well with the wished-for loss of rational detachment: incoherent, unstable, monstrous. It's also good for undermining rational detachment in the listener.[26] You don't give anybody who has never felt it an idea of this joy, any more than you give somebody blind from birth an idea of the inner experience of color.[27] What you do, if you can, is induce the experience.

In this tradition, self-extinction and union are the leading metaphors for the experience of profound rapport in the dialogue with God. It's worth remembering that they *are* metaphors. Otherwise we miss the self-affirmation in this particular way of praying to "die"; that is, "die" to a rejected way of life. We also miss how values get revalued in the prayer for "death": intellect dethroned in favor of emotion, light in favor of heat. Taken literally, mystic "union" with God is just another version of dying— by loss of individual identity. But Christianity is precisely about the *saving* of the individual. In the talk-postulates of the mystical tradition, the soul becomes "one" with God when it wants all and only the things God wants.[28] "In his will is our peace"[29] just paraphrases the essence of mystic union in mainstream Catholic teaching. Prayer for oneness with the Christian God is either blasphemy or metaphor.

So Crashaw ends "The Flaming Heart" by asking Teresa to let him imitate her progress from intellect to love to "death":

> By thy large draughts of intellectuall day,
> And by thy thirsts of loue *more large* then they;
> By all thy brim-fill'd Bowles of feirce desire
> By thy *last Morning's* draught of liquid fire;
> By the full kingdome of that *finall kisse*
> That seiz'd thy parting Soul, & seal'd thee his;
> By all the heau'ns thou hast in him
> (Fair sister of the SERAPHIM!)

> By all of HIM we haue in THEE;
> Leaue nothing of my SELF in me.
> Let me so read thy life, that I
> Vnto all life of mine may dy.   (97–108; italics mine)

The prayer for self-extinction is a figment of Hotspurism. In the last three lines the speaker expects "me" to survive—freed from the burden of an unwanted *content* ("my SELF" = my self-will).

Crashaw's shock use of pseudometaphor is designed to inspire an ecstatic letting go—and to defeat its nightmare twin: the kind of depression or numbness or boredom that goes by the traditional names of sloth and *accidia* (uncaring): "Many are weake, and sicke among you, and many slepe." "Slouthfulness casteth into a deep slepe." "It is now time that we shulde arise from slepe: for now is our saluation nerer, then when we beleved it."[30] As Augustine recalls this experience from a safe distance, it's like serenely watching oneself drown. The attraction here is the terminal pleasure of letting go and not having to try any more: "As in sleep, I was sweetly oppressed by the load of the world. My meditations on thee were like the efforts of those who wish to awaken but are overcome and drowned again in the drowsy depth. . . . And I had no answer to thy saying 'Awake thou that sleepest and arise from the dead and Christ shall give thee light,' . . . but only sluggard and slumbrous words: 'Soon,' 'Soon, look you,' 'Let me be awhile.' "[31] Paul's rallying cry from Ephesians is one way of breaking the trance; the figurational high jinks of devotional cheering are another.

It's almost but not quite right to say that Crashaw aims to produce "ecstasy, a poetic equivalent to the trance state"—to "concentrate our attention upon some sensuous object like the crucifix, some sensuous symbol like wounds or tears, while the poet . . . creates an atmosphere which lulls the critical intellect while the poem insistently repeats the motif."[32] The stress on trance and lulling misses the point. The speech-act force or mood of mock metaphor and mock story telling isn't taps for the intellect but reveille for the will: "Awake thou that sleepest and arise from the dead." Within the fiction of a Crashaw hymn, the "thou" is the speaker of the poem. There's nobody else around. But the poem itself is a public performance. The "thou" is anybody within range.

The traditional Christian psychology of intense prayer helps us to one last essential point about the panegyric use of mock metaphor in Crashaw. Lust and anger in that psychology aren't just animal drives. There's an intellectual version of each. Intellectual lust is rational desire for a good for the sake of its goodness. Intellectual anger is rational eagerness to take on the struggle for an arduous good.³³ What Luis de León finds amazing in the contemplations of Teresa's Carmelites is how something "extremely difficult" has been carried off with "holy competition" and a kind of nonchalance: "They've transformed the exercise of heroic virtues into a delicious pastime."³⁴ A mystic is an activist, a prayer is an exploit, and the stimulant language of devotional cheering is a call to arms.

When Crashaw comes anywhere near to spelling out his motives, these are the motives. The aspiring soul will find that "the Armory of light . . . yeelds to holy hands."³⁵ She should use it, and not think of "leaving her chast abode / To gad abroad."³⁶ Otherwise

> some other heart
> Will *git the start*,
> And *stepping in before*,
> Will *take possession*. . . .³⁷   [Italics mine]

She should

> improve that precious houre:
> And every day,
> Seize her sweet prey.³⁸

To crown the hunt, she's promised the "power"—of all things—"to rifle and deflower"!³⁹ To put it mildly, it seems that "to have a God become her lover" is to take the active role.

The erotic and violent images brought on by mock metaphor are illustrations of literal meanings that won't work. But the required figurative meanings either don't exist or turn up only if the text is chopped up and computed rather than read. The devotional twins of eros and aggression aren't the *meaning* of the troublesome expressions but their exclamatory *force*—the point of the act of speaking them, and the effect they're designed for: to shock the joyless mind into wonder, and (if all goes well) out of wonder into joy.

II. *Consecrated Wit*

But force varies with context. The context of mock metaphor isn't always devotional cheering. Actually, the sad foot-face we met a few examples ago is such a case: the literary setting of the crucifixion bagatelle is epigram, not hymn. Instead of rapture, we get (burlesque) reflection. The speaker isn't sure if Christ's wounds are mouths or eyes—but he knows each wound is either one or the other. How so? The problem is how to provide a bizarre remark with a context in which the senses assigned to the incongruous terms add up to a remark that's *not* bizarre.

The context of stanza 2 is a wound description. Let's try reading "mouth" as *red-rimmed opening,* "full-bloom'd" as *puffed,* "lips" as *borders,* "roses" as *red objects,* and "blood-shot eye" as *red-suffused opening:*

> Lo! a mouth, whose full-bloom'd lips
>   At too deare a rate are roses.
> Lo! a blood-shot eye! that weepes
>   And many a cruell teare discloses.[40]

Read as neutral description, the remark sheds some of its bizarreness. It's no longer hallucinatory; in fact, it's true. But now it's pointless— and the *pointlessness* is bizarre; the speaker is addressing these important wound facts to the crucified Redeemer in his last agony. To add insult to injury, we have the complaint that the roses are too dear—as if this particular kind of "rose" ever came cheaper. The speaker is clownishly pretending to take his own metaphor literally. But pointlessness is itself a standard cue for figurative reading. Besides, the salient implication of "full-bloom'd lips" is far from neutrally descriptive. Unfortunately, it's laudatory: they're things that enhance sexual attractiveness! If this is the elusive figurative sense at last, we were better off without it.

Still another interpretative context is provided next. This time the reason the wounds are eyes or feet is that they represent the foot's or its owner's solution to the problem of repaying the Magdalene's kindness. At this point the speaker favors her with the remark we've already looked at:

> O thou that on this foot hast laid
>   Many a kisse, and many a teare,
> Now thou shalt have all repaid,
>   Whatsoe're thy charges were.
>
> This foot hath got a Mouth and lippes,
>   To pay the sweet summe of thy kisses;
> To pay thy Teares, an Eye that weeps
>   In stead of Tears such Gems as this is.[41]

This offers an explanation of predictable outrageousness for Christ's wanting eyes and mouths on his foot. What it doesn't do is offer a context that assigns a figurative meaning to the original wound description. Instead, it introduces new pseudometaphors of its own. What is it for wounds to pay back tears and kisses? We have a right to ask the last stanza to let this mean, say, *reward penitence with redemption*. Though this would be impossibly loose theology,[42] it would be theology, and not another joke.

What we get instead is another joke—a tactic for forcing us back to the literal sense. It seems that the Weeper is being repaid with interest:

> The debt is paid in *Ruby*-Teares,
> Which thou in Pearls did'st lend.[43]

A fantastic problem has been finessed by an equally fantastic solution in the punch line of an epigram.[44]

It's ironic that the wit depends on the strategies of mock metaphor, of balking a respectable figurative interpretation. Maybe this is what the genre demands: give the epigram a (figurative) point and it loses its (literalizing) *pointe*. But why a joke, elegantly turned or not, about the sacrificial heart of Christian redemption?

Why, for that matter, are we getting distracted in another of these performances from the real and cosmic mysteries of the Nativity to the paltry pseudomystery of how to find the Christ child a bed that will allow him "not to lye cold, yet sleepe in snow"?[45] Again the quandary owes its phantom existence to taking things literally ("snow" and "cold")—that is, to getting them wrong.[46] Why *this* kind of fiddling with pseudometaphor? Exclamatory pseudometaphor in Crashaw's hymns turned out to be a devotional speech act. It's harder to see how frivolous "problem" solving at the edges of the Gospel story could be one too—or which one it could be. It's more like the illuminated monkeys capering in the margins of a Book of Hours.

If wit is reason burlesqued, the speaker of the sacred epigrams is the model of wit. His two favorite impersonations are the crazy explainer and the still crazier quibbler. In both capacities, the burlesque of reason depends on getting us to play along with a mock metaphor.

The explainer specializes in saving appearances with theories that work well enough if you take them literally; that is, if you agree to misread them. How did five loaves manage to multiply at all, much less by a factor of a thousand? The hidden cause is obvious: "What would ye more? Here food it selfe is fed." What made the water at Cana turn into wine? Natural bashfulness, of course: God's presence brought on a blush. Why did Peter cut off the ear of one of Jesus' would-be captors? Elementary again: wasn't Peter soon to deny his Master? One less witness to hear him do it! Why did a miraculous healing of lameness convince the Lystrians that Saint Paul was the god of *wit*? Answer: well, who else *but* Mercury could have talked a cripple into being fast on his feet?[47] In many of the sacred epigrams, it's Jesus' miracles that the speaker is upstaging with his explanations.

What the explainer does for causes, the quibbler does for logic. His reasoning boggles—if you take it literally. Partaking of Christ's body and blood is amazing enough. But Christ is the *Shepherd*. So what's logically *implied* by the Eucharist is even *more* amazing: the flock is led to pasture—by the Pasture! Again, the Gospel account shows the prison gates yielding to Peter of their own accord. But the truth is, you *have* a key if you have the functional equivalent. Peter's key was—the fact that he didn't need any! Again, Jesus disqualifies the hypocrite from criticizing the motes in other people's eyes because he has a "beam" in his own.[48] But what could be better for focusing sharply on something flimsy or minute than an "optical beam" (i.e., microscope)? The hypocrite's is powerful enough to give him a close-up view of—nothing! Again, you might think there aren't any clothes too good for the king of heaven. But the crucifiers found some: the motive for shedding his blood was sartorial![49] The comment on the Eucharist sums up the effect of the others. If the speaker is to be believed, what has him in awe isn't the mystery of the sacrament but the pseudomystery he teases *out* of it.

He was a stock character long before he found his way into Crashaw's sacred epigrams. Here he's up to the same old tricks he polished up in Crashaw's Jesuit models, or occasionally in Donne's Holy Sonnets.

The red soul's only hope for forgiveness is that Christ's blood "dyes red souls to white." But in one outrageous parting couplet the blood

> hath this might,
> That being red, it dyes red soules to white.[50]

As if what's really mighty about it isn't redemption but the parlor magic of being one color while dying things another. At least once, the Donne counterpart of Crashaw's epigram speaker manages to achieve a unique high (or low) in sacred impudence. He's been wondering where he can find the True Church—the lady he's eager "to seek, and then make love [to]." He turns to Christ:

> Betray kind husband thy spouse to our sights,
> And let myne amorous soule court thy mild Dove,
> Who is most trew, and pleasing to thee, then
> When she'is embrac'd and open to most men.[51]

In what *seems* to be the speaker's metaphor, Christ revealing his Church is a husband egging on his wife to prostitute herself. But prostitution refuses to be tamed into a metaphor for sharing. The seedy literal sense can't help figuratively ascribing seediness to the speaker's request. Of course all of this is a false alarm; the sex scandal is a figment of mixed metaphor: *(Christ's) bride* and *(the Christian knight's) mistress*. Read the metaphors one by one, and the figment evaporates into the harmless if unfresh news that the more people join ("woo and embrace") the Church, the better the Church's head ("husband") likes it.

But the speaker aggravates the confusion by poising "trew, and pleasing" against "embrac'd and open" as if he were winding up with a mind-boggling paradox (the divine wittol)—in short, as if he were taking himself literally. So as in Crashaw we get mock misunderstanding of mock scandal. This is the sort of nonsense one talks only to people who can be counted on for twice the ordinary benefit of the doubt.

That counting on is the essence—the sacredness—of the sacred epigram as a conversational gesture. It's an act of extraordinary trust. But the sacred witticism—the joke as an idiom of prayer—doesn't merely *count* on charity. It *dares* it. It pays a festive *tribute* to it. For our entertainment, the sacred Jester puts on an act of taking his own descriptions literally and thereby getting them bizarrely and decoratively wrong. But a negative plus a negative makes an affirmation. To counterfeit *mis*understanding is to celebrate understanding, especially the silent understanding of intimates. It isn't accidental that "conversation between intimates" is precisely how prayer is defined in the tradition we're looking at.[52] The Jester's entertainment is a celebration of love.

The Old French tale of Our Lady's Tumbler[53] comes from the ancient heart of the tradition that gives us Crashaw's holy Jester.

The latest young[54] recruit to the monastery of Clairvaux is a *menestrel*.[55] (Keep in mind that this dismissive word is a vulgarization of *ministerialis*—somebody skilled in a *ministerium*, a craft or service.) The poor fellow "didn't know how to pursue any *mestier* [from *ministerium*, "craft" or "service"] of which the people there had need [also *mestier*]. For he had lived only by tumbling and springing and dancing. How to hop and leap is what this man knew, and he knew about nothing else, for he knew no other 'reading.'"[56]

In deep chagrin at not being able to worship like the others, the tumbler comes to a decision:

> "I will serve God's mother in her abbey—with my *mestier*. The others serve with chanting; I will serve with tumbling.[57] I don't know how to chant or read to you. But I want at least to choose out for you all my beautiful games. Now let me be a young goat hopping and leaping before her mother."[58] Then he tumbles and leaps and makes the turn of Metz about his head by way of celebration; bows to the image, adores it as reverently as he could, and afterward does for her the turn of France, then the turn of Champagne. And then he does the Spanish turn and the ones they do in Brittany, and then the turn of Lorraine.[59] For it pleased him wonderfully, and he did it so willingly that not a day was skipped on which he could do his best to entertain God's mother.[60]

The monk who spies on this strange ritual may be sarcastic, but he is clearly right: "*Par foi,* this man is having a good maytime, and a finer holiday revel than all of us put together."[61] Later, after witnessing the miracle the story is leading up to—the Virgin appears to fan her exhausted "minstrel"-minister with a white cloth—the same eavesdropper confesses: "The man I see here is holy."[62] For, as the storyteller explains, in revealing the tumble worship to third parties, God also revealed that he rejects no one who turns to him in love, whatever the lover's *mestier*.[63]

Insistent repetition makes the implied equation of the parable clear enough: games, entertainment, revelry, maytime, service, and divine love are fused in the sacred tumbler's *mestier*. It was the art and pastime of David, the wise fool whose dancing and leaping before the sacred ark were bound to inspire some people's contempt precisely because "worldlings are not able to comprehend the mocions that moue the children of God."[64]

Once again, that motion or emotion or gift of rapport is a kind of "wisdom": the "sapience" or savoring of the inner conversation with God.[65] With his foolish wisdom incomprehensible to worldlings, the sacred tumbler is simply doing what Wisdom herself did at the creation, when she was "daily [God's] delite rejoycing alwaie before him. And toke my solace in the compasse of his earth, and my delite with the children of men."[66] What Geneva and King James render as "rejoice" is given as "play" by the Vulgate. (Neither quite captures the nuance of a word that covers instrument playing as well as game playing, and comes from a root meaning *laugh*. But they're close enough to let the accent of Wisdom's memoir get into the old devotional tradition that survives in Crashaw.)

The commentary tradition adds a bit to this. It seems the audience for Wisdom's "play" or the tumbler's or the jester's is wider than God. In defiance of gender, Wisdom is really Christ, and "the solace and passetime whereof is here spoken" is Christ's love for humanity, "the worke of God in whome wisdom toke pleasure: in somuche as for man's sake the Diuine Wisdome toke man's nature."[67] The mock metaphor of the sacred epigram returns the compliment of this incarnational "passetime." Like the tumbler's high jinks before the Queen of Heaven, it looks like impudence to a superficial eye, and for that very reason means love.[68]

III. Pseudometaphor and Profane Wit

The speech act of figuration-mocking means one thing in a hymn, and still another in a sacred wit-poem. Expectably, we can learn a lot about what goes on in the sacred kind from the secular—say, a Donne poem like "Loves growth."

The speaker's belief that his love is "pure" has been shaken. Love turns out to "endure / Vicissitude and season, as the grasse" (3–4). "Grasse" doesn't help much with "pure," but it narrows down "vicissitude and season." The speaker's love-"grass" is in its winter phase: he loves her less than he did. But when we get what starts out to be a repetition of this idea of cyclic decline, with "infinite" doing duty for "pure," we're in for a surprise: love-"grass" is unlike grass-"grass" in being lush in winter—and luxuriant in spring:

> Me thinkes I lyed all winter, when I swore
> My love was infinite, if spring make'it more.   (5–6)

More—*not* less?[69] The principle of charity sends us back to reinterpret "vicissitude" and "season": we were mistaken to think they implied a cycle.

But we *weren't* mistaken! If the change in love the speaker had in mind is the one he's now successfully gotten across—no cyclical but a linear process of growth—then in the earlier sentence he failed to say what he meant. Our willingness to take the blame is reflex charity again, charity abused by the speaker.[70] What kind of standard trope takes us from *vicissitude* or *season* to *steady increase*? There is none. Forcing your reader to reread a phrase this way is equivalent to repeating the phrase in a new sense—in this case a Humpty-Dumpty sense rather than a figurative one. The lady has been teased a little for the sake of a pleasant surprise: a lover always shifting—for the better.

Unfortunately, even this happy kind of shiftiness is proof that love isn't "pure," "abstract," or "infinite." Objects and dispositions change, for better or worse, only if they're forced to by the changeful "stuff" they're made of or rooted in. So the "stuff" in which love grows must be "elemented" (13)—made of the four elements that underlie change, not the fifth element, or "quintessence" (8), that defies it. Love is "impure" and non-"abstract" and "finite" by metonymy—by belonging to the flesh, which is all these things because it's an unstable mixture of "all stuffes, paining soule, or sense" (9). The speaker's affirmation turns out not to be as affirmative as he thought. There may be no ups and downs in love's growth, but given its materiality there can't help being love cycles of *some* kind or other—say, shiftings of attention between soul and sex, in which "love sometimes would contemplate, sometimes do" (14).

And here the metaphor mocking brings a shift in the mood as well: the pleasant surprise about the "seasons" of love-"grass" is tempered by news of what this infinite growth is a growth *of:* the "pain" of "soul" or "sense"; "medicine" that "cures all sorrow / With more" (7–8). "Cure" turns out to mean *aggravate* in the speaker's mischievous lexicon. And the disease being cured by aggravation is love itself. This time the speech act being served by the mischief is a verbal gesture of restrained hostility, not a caress—restrained because the key phrases are nested in subordinate clauses: "But *if* this medicine, love, *which* cures all sorrow / With more. . . ."

Whether or not the speaker's love endures "vicissitude," his argument endures it with a vengeance. "But" brought on a worry. Now "and yet" brings on an attempt at reassurance:

> And yet no greater, but more eminent
> Love by the spring is grown.   (15–16)

This is more metaphor mocking—another play on "grow." It seems that "growth" in eminence, unlike growth in size, can happen even to the "quintessence" or star stuff. Stars aren't "enlarg'd" when they look large, only "showne" (18). In the evolving lexicon, "grow" has come to mean not only *grow* but *seem to grow*. Like the stars, the blossoms that seem to "bud out" in the love-"spring" aren't quite *love;* they're love *deeds,* of which love is simply the steadfast "root." As the speaker said earlier, love alternates between contemplating and doing. The deeds grow, but their contemplative source stays the same.

At last we have a respectable metaphor that does the trick—or does it? With spring, the speaker doesn't love more intensely, as he feared, and so he needn't dismiss the purity or infinity or abstractness of his love; he's only being more demonstrative. But why demonstrative now and not before? Because the blossoms are being put forth by an *"awakened* root." Before it woke up, it was asleep. The mixed metaphor subverts itself: whatever corresponds to root-"sleep" in love, it isn't intensity. To be blunt, it's boredom. So the *root* changes as well as the blossoms—and changes for the worse after all.

Mock metaphors about grass and blossoms won't be bullied into a semblance of fulfilling the speaker's driving wish for a notion of "growth" that goes well with "purity" and permanence. But maybe another kind of mock metaphor *will:*

> If, as in water stir'd, more circles bee
> Produc'd by one, love such additions take,
> Those like so many spheares, but one heaven make,
> For, they are all concentrique unto thee.   (21–24)

Whatever "circle" means as applied to love, how does this argument show that love is now "no greater, but more eminent"? It doesn't. Having a common "center" doesn't acquit the love-"circles" of being "additions" to love, and being parts of one system doesn't acquit them of being many. All of these quibble fantasies masquerading as metaphors have defeated themselves one by one. In spite of the strenuous arguing, love is still a thing of vicissitudes: still finite, fleshly, and impure.

The speaker ends by irrelevantly describing love's growth, or "new heat," as a war tax the king doesn't give back once the war is over. It's useless to ask who or what pays this confiscatory tax of "heat," or what is to prevent the wealth of the love-realm from being taxed beyond its limit. Once again this isn't metaphor. It's fantasy—hope keeping alive by escaping into nonsense.[71] But the speech act makes up in *force* for what the speech lacks in *sense:* the mock-metaphorical assertion of purity and infinity isn't an act of *asserting* at all. It's an oath or promise, like the "swearing" the lover did all winter—a private law he imposes on himself drawn up in the "shall" idiom of solemn commandment: "No winter shall abate the springs increase" (28). There's a tragicomic pathos here. The speaker will try to keep up his "heat" in spite of the fleshly limitations he acknowledges—acknowledges by an energetic show of struggling not to.

The figuration mocker imposes on his hearers doubly, because figuration is *already* a mock something. But mock vernacular, or impromptu dialect, *adds* to the senses of troublesome expressions. Mock metaphor shrinks their senses to zero. What gets enriched in this case is the *act* of semantic troublemaking. Mock praise in "Loves growth" carries out a promise. Mock *x*-ing can even loop in on itself, where the speaker turns out to have been demonstrating and tacitly *commenting* on remarks he seemed to be *making;* the figurative force of ostensibly saying something is mentioning or reciting or quoting it.

Taken literally, the Renaissance humanist on busman's holiday is writing in praise of the egg, ant, fly, flea, or louse; of mud or smoke; of blindness, deafness, or folly. But here the ostensible praise talk is really talk *about* praise, or about the particular exercise in praise under way at the moment. Showing off here becomes speech-act figuration that curves in wickedly complicated loops. The notorious ancient model is Favorinus's homage to quartan fever.[72] When Menapius's Renaissance imitation tells us that nothing could be better for helping keep track of time, or ordering our lives, or reducing anxiety by limiting pain to the foreseeable,[73] we're being invited to have second thoughts about the *intrinsic* value of the benefits even a fever can confer—and so on for the benefits of blindness and deafness and folly.

The lady in Donne's "A Feaver" may be under the weather, but she would hardly be inspiring the ornate clown dancing of her lover's get-well message if she were so ill, or so ill-read, that she couldn't appreciate the fine points of the dance. In this variation on the Favorinus scenario, fever is brought on as an accused felon; what it needs and gets isn't another encomiast à la Favorinus but an attorney.

The mock brief starts obliquely, with a mock warning to the lady:

> Oh doe not die, for I shall hate
> All women so, when thou art gone,
> That thee I shall not celebrate,
> When I remember, thou wast one. (1–4)

The speaker pretends to take his own word "all" literally when it has to mean "all other." If she's inconsiderate enough to die, she'll be among the women who will suffer by comparison with—her. Meanwhile, responsibility for her death is quietly shifted in advance from the fever to the fever patient. Whether or not she dies is up to her.

On second thought, it isn't up to either. It's impossible. Being the world herself (the speaker's world, at least), she can't conceivably leave the world behind, and so can't conceivably die (5–8). Or suppose she can. Suppose she's the *soul* of the world (she is to the *speaker*, at least): then what she leaves behind is merely her carcass—a world in which fairness and worthiness are phony or worse (9–12).

How does *this* back up the thesis that she's bound by either duty or logic not to die? It doesn't. Taken figuratively (that is, taken correctly), this particular mock argument is a caress, like the argument that a fever that burns up the world this way has to be the world-purifying fire prophesied in the Apocalypse. Like the fire in the prophecy, this one can't consume anything but the lady's few impurities; it can't last long or do any harm (13–20). But the nub of the attorney's defense is that criminal guilt requires criminal intent, and the fever is as well-meaning as it is unthreatening:

> Yet t'was of my minde, seising thee,
>   Though it in thee cannot persever.
> For I had rather owner bee
>   Of thee one houre, then all else ever.   (25–28)

According to one reader, this final stanza shows Donne egotistically admitting that he wants to own the lady, and "would want it even if it meant burning and wasting her like a disease."[74] But the point of resemblance between the speaker and the fever is explicit; it is that each would rather own the lady "one houre, than all else ever." This doesn't imply that destruction is inflicted by both sorts of lover, or desired by either. That inference comes from the question-begging assumption that the poem is a sadistic slice of life. The point is rather that the lady's beauty is alluring to everything in the world, even to a fever. We're being regaled with a mock explanation of the fever. The explanation is an outrageous compliment to the lady.

As a matter of fact, the way the final stanza has been introduced by its immediate predecessor rules out sadistic longings. It turns out that the lady can't be burnt or wasted by anything or anyone. In short, the narcissistic author theory is a distraction from the conventional cues of the game being played. Not the least important of these cues is the familiar voice of the Wit.

What is the figurative meaning of this fever exoneration? More generally, why try to amuse the fever patient by joking about her fever? To repeat: if she were obviously in a very bad way, the attempt would be crazy to start with. To be amusable, she has to be at least uncertain about whether she's in a bad way. But grant that this requirement is met: why the sick joke?

The speaker is refining Celsus's standard medical advice about bedside manner in such cases: beware of aggravating the fever by worrying the patient.[75] For example, beware of acting as if her appearance worries *you*. For the lady's benefit, at least, the speaker takes it for granted that the fever is doomed, not the patient. She's absolutely sure to recover, as far as he's (supposed to be) concerned. So he regales her with the familiar wit game of working up pseudoexplanations for truisms. The force of this playing of the game, and of the mock defense as a whole, is simply to register confidence that everything is all right. Confident or not, the speaker has been captured in an unsentimentally adroit, and therefore convincing, exercise of *tact*.

Maybe, with the right prologue or epilogue, the same words could have been the instrument of a gesture of contempt or malice or preening self-absorption. But no such gesture has been successfully carried off, thanks to the principle of charity. As applied to figurative speech acts, that principle is the semantic twin of the presumption of innocence—with this important difference: the accused is only *held* innocent until proven guilty, whereas the fever praiser just *is* reassuring his lady unless he does something to forfeit the benefit of her doubt.

Mock praise in "The Autumnall" refuses to be disposed of so easily. There's no delicacy or tact in defending the lady's wrinkles from an insult you yourself cook up—especially if you make the defense itself an elaborate insult:

> Call not these wrinkles, *graves;* If *graves* they were,
>   They were *Loves graves;* for else he is no where.
> Yet lies not Love *dead* here, but here doth sit
>   Vow'd to this trench, like an *Anachorit*.

> And here, till hers, which must be his *death,* come,
> He doth not digge a *Grave,* but build a *Tombe.*   (13–18)

It isn't fair to deny indignantly that the lady's wrinkles are graves, only to turn around and concede that they're graves after all—in the Pickwickian sense that they're just right for the kind of love that first uses them to mortify itself, then leaves them as a memorial "tomb." In other words: as long as love and she last, loving her is a good way to do a really spectacular penance.

The same cavortings of illogic turn up here and there in the rest of the speaker's elaborate case for cherishing middle age in a mistress. Since being fifty is "long sought"—people spend a long time getting there—being fifty has to be pretty desirable (33–34). Since the things we love are transitory, the tail end of life has to be one of them (36–37). Since love's natural "lation," or tendency, is to go downhill, it will save energy to "ebbe out" with withering beauties. "Panting after growing beauties" is just defying gravity, with the usual embarrassing result (47–50).

Like Falstaff's tall tales, the sophistries of the "autumn" enthusiast are "open, palpable." They have to be. You need to spot his free invention to *appreciate* it, "for it is worth the listning to"—worth hearing "what trick? what device? what starting hole" the speaker will come up with next.[76] The master of tall tales or tall arguments is a master of what the rhetoricians call "invention"—*discovery:* "The braine of this foolish compounded Clay man, is not able to inuent any thing that tends to laughter, more than I inuent, or is inuented on me."[77]

I've been calling the metier of Donne's typical speaker mock praise, or mock explanation. But now a flaw has turned up in the labeling. The object of the mocking, or the takeoff, isn't praise or explanation, but fallacy in the service of persuasion. This reptilian art has had its teeth drawn by being elegantly performed, with all its twists and turns in plain view. For the mock sophister, unlike his evil twin, the availability of a good reason does nothing to discourage the search for a reason that's brilliantly and divertingly bad.

For all we know, it might well be true that

> No *Spring* nor *Summer* Beauty hath such grace
> As I have seen in one *Autumnall* face   (1–2)

a face "where still *Evening* is; not *noone,* nor *night.* / Where no *voluptuousnesse,* yet all delight." That's precisely the delicious challenge to one's dialectical sleight of hand: pull or seem to pull your true conclusion out of your outrageously false premises. The rabbit is real enough; the trick is to get the spectators to wonder, and the alert ones to figure out, how it was produced from the empty hat.[78]

The mock sophister's empty hat is the dialectical tall tale—what one seventeenth-century critic aptly calls a quibble fiction;[79] though the critic spoils this a bit by going on to confuse fiction with lying, and hence quibble fiction with sophistry.[80] Real sophistry mocks reason by working up a cheating facsimile of it. The quibble fictions on display in Donne's poems mock the mockery by brilliantly burlesquing it. The result is the same sort of double negation we get in the antics of Crashaw's holy Jester, and the same sort of affirmation: the mutual understanding of the talk community is powerful enough to defeat, and relish defeating, clever little subversions.

The subversion that started us off looking for these particular figurative speech acts was the failure of literal falsehood or absurdity or pointlessness to yield figurative sense. Failing a figurative *sense,* we look for a literal *force* or speech-act description; failing a *literal* force, we look for a *figurative* one. But the initial cue is that something ought by rights to be a metaphor and isn't. The favorite seventeenth-century move for pumping up this false expectation is the conceit: the process of exploring the consequences of what the figurative expression would mean if it were being used literally.[81]

If as their faces touch, one of his tears is flooded by a stream of hers, and if the tear is this world, then he's wise to pray for mercy, because he's in danger of drowning:

> O more than Moone,
> Draw not up seas to drowne me in thy spheare.

Again, if lovers literally belong to each other, then they sigh one another's breath; and if they literally sigh one another's breath, "Whoe'er sighs most is cruellest, and hastes the other's death."[82]

Readers who are hot for Significance and unwilling or unable to take a joke run the risk of trivializing the conceit in the very act of trying to rescue it from triviality. Thus (in "The Expiration") "the breathing out of the fatal word 'Goe!' marks {for the lovers} the end of all that makes life worthy of the name. The last sighing kiss in which they surrender all hope of earthly joy is thus a spiritual expiration only slightly removed from death itself."[83] The maudlin reverence of this paraphrase is a dead giveaway that the critic hasn't noticed what the metaphor of being "killed by 'Go!' " is *there* for—what saves Donne's poem from being as maudlin as the paraphrase. The metaphor is a shoehorn for an ensuing *mock* metaphor, or quibble fiction. It seems that to pronounce "Go!" is to be a murderer. The pronouncer deserves to be executed by the same lethal word—except that he may have escaped justice: how could he have survived the *double* lethal effect of "going" and "bidding, goe" (9–12)?

This crime story is miniature conversational escape fiction with a standard plot—the same one that informs the involuntary sigh homicide in "A Valediction: of weeping," or the involuntary heart homicide that the Queen worries about in her valedictory game with Richard II:

> RICH. One Kisse shall stop our mouthes, and dumbely part.
>   Thus giue I mine, and thus take I thy heart.
> QUEEN. Give me mine owne againe: 'twere no good part,
>   To take on me to keepe, and kill thy heart.[84]

The dialogue version of the conceit lets us see that quibble solitaire is really a disguised form of quibble repartee.[85] By subversively pretending to miss his own figurative point,[86] Donne's speaker plays the role of his own rival in a wit combat. But the crucial point is that the "rival" is only play-acting: the "Expiration" speaker is no more trying to make a fool of himself than the Queen is trying to make a fool of Richard. This time the little society whose rapport is being affirmed by double negation is a society of one.

It seems that the holy Jester and the worldly Wit are twins—celebrating the same rapport by the same holiday misrule. In fact, they are closer than twins. They are one person before and after making his commitment to the religious life. The tricks that the tumbler brought into the abbey of Clairvaux in the old tale came from Metz and Champagne and Brittany—worldly places outside the cloister.

As performers of figurative speech acts, both the Jester and the Wit are instructively different from their absurdist modern counterpart, the put-on artist, who keeps his victim guessing about whether he's being talked with or derisively manipulated with words. The alienating tease is like one of those irregularly moving platforms at an amusement park. The victim must struggle to maintain his balance, constantly awkward, even (perhaps especially) when the floor *stops* moving for an instant; i.e., a "straight" movement, which makes the victim feel he has been paranoid. As he readjusts himself to this vision, the floor . . . starts moving again.

The purest put-ons are never altogether pure, never unmistakable. . . . A remark that *may be* a put-on casts a whole conversation into doubt.[87]

Even here a conversation is stymied at the level of sense only to be kept going at the level of speech-act force. If the typical purpose of the put-on is "to prevent dialogue, to guarantee continued estrangement," that purpose is ironically frustrated. A belief *about* the continuing stream of nonsense is getting implicitly communicated: "the belief that communication is impossible."[88]

The put-on artist's implicit communication of a refusal to communicate—his demonic charade of talking *with* a victim he's merely talking *at*—amounts to a withdrawal of commitment to the other as a partner in talk and an abdication from membership in the dialect enclave defined by the conversation. But conversation lives on commitment to the enterprise in general, and on a shifting pattern of mutually known commitments to particular beliefs or talk-postulates; you may be forced to withdraw some on being asked to justify them or to show how they can all be true at once, but they're your chips in the game.[89] In the put-on, the refusal of commitment brings on the death of conversation.

This is what the Wit never allows to happen, before or after his conversion. True, as a mock metaphorist he blithely exploits his hearers' figurational charity to rule out literal readings. He signals figurative senses that don't exist. He talks nonsense. But when he talks nonsense, he doesn't refuse commitment. He celebrates it.

Chapter Four	Illusions
of Strangeness
and Shocks of
Recognition

1. The Diversionary Littera *Introduced*

High voices are *literally* high in English. You don't have to put some English sense of "high" through a standard transformation or trope to get the talk-dialect sense being applied to voices here. The relevant (acoustic) sense of "high" is *already* part of current English. If it was a metaphor at some earlier stage, the metaphor is dead. By contrast, the assembly of faithful Christians is still only *figuratively* Christ's "body" or "bride." Even if we're as familiar with these Gospel metaphors as a seventeenth-century reader of George Herbert, part of that familiarity is experiencing the relevant (spiritual) sense of the word "body" or "bride" as the last step in a transformation of some other (physical) sense. A traditional metaphor stays figurative as long as the experience of understanding it includes a reenactment of the original process of understanding.

For Herbert, poised to celebrate the resurrection of Christ's mystical body or bride, these figures-by-reenactment were apparently not figurative enough, not festive or strange enough, to do justice to the festive strangeness of the event. But he doesn't replace them; instead, he makes them intermediate stages in the transformation of a new literal sense.

In the speaker's prayer in "Dooms-day," when "all the dust" is summoned "to rise, / Till it stirre, and rubbe the eyes" (3–4), we're invited to imagine a monstrous golem or heap of matter, undifferentiated at first except for a hand rubbing an eye, and then, with a touch of clownish horror, differentiated with a vengeance: "this member jogs the other, / Each one whispring, *Live you, brother?*" (5–6). Parceled out to a legion of active demons, the shape fuzzily suggests a victim of the notorious dancing madness, or Tarantella, that we hear about next: the monster "kneels" (in the novel sense of *rising* to its knees),

> As peculiar notes and strains
> Cure Tarantulas raging pains   (11–12)

as if the dance of death had to be taken literally and Gabriel's performance were the prescribed therapy for it.

But the diverting literal sense is simply the outer box of a Chinese-box trope, or metalepsis:[1] for dust, read body; for body, read Christ's mystical "body"; for Christ's mystical "body," read the congregation of all the faithful or its individual members. This last unpacking rules out the alternative sense of "member" that gave the dust monster its demon-infested limbs.

Later on, the speaker worries about the damage that may be done to the living by the decaying bodies of the "flock," atomized, vaporized, or otherwise dispersed (20–28). The fragmentation notions prepare us for the first clause of the final prayer: "Lord thy broken consort raise." The Lord's broken consort is the Church, or bride, of Christ, pitifully scattered. But the rest of the prayer gives "broken consort" a second literal sense:

> Lord thy broken consort raise,
> And the musick shall be praise.

Gabriel's trumpet solo is going to be accompanied by an ensemble playing on different instruments—a "broken consort."

Again, like the dust monster, this whimsy gets a figurative point from the developing argument: the resources of those risen bodies will be organs or "instruments" of praise from now on. But the semantic illusion of viols and recorders striking up in the universal graveyard isn't only a vehicle of figurative meaning. It's also a preliminary diversion—an entertainment. To an unjaded eye, the idea of the Resurrection and its aftermath wouldn't have needed this buildup. But the eyes now available call for a spot of diversion to bring home the experience of that idea, even at the cost of delaying its arrival. In a word, the diversion can make it new.

Again, the novelty here isn't in the subject. It isn't even in what's actually being said *about* the subject. To "reinvent" the Resurrection would be to lie about it—in the case of the dust monster and the recorder concert, to lie with self-defeating impudence. The only thing getting "invented" here—in the usual rhetorical sense—is a metaphor. And the metaphor "reinvents" entrenched beliefs only if you take it literally; that is, only if you get it wrong.[2] Getting it momentarily wrong is what unjades Herbert's readers, and leads them eventually to get it emotionally right.

Herbert has found a way of making his primary audience look at something familiar *as if* it were new to them, while leaving the thing itself completely untouched. He doesn't accomplish this by renewing the audience's visceral sense of the global size of the event, the way Donne manages to do with his inventory of the "numberlesse infinities" who died either by the flood, or by "warre, dearth, age, agues, tyrannies, / Despaire, law, chance."[3] And unlike Donne, he doesn't remind his audience of the ironic double jeopardy the Resurrection brings to some of the resurrected: the sinful generation "overthrown" by Noah's flood and now arising only to be overthrown eternally by hellfire.[4] What gets renewed in Herbert is the festive uncanniness of a graveside reunion of people with nothing to fear and everything to celebrate. Herbert's method of renewal is metaphorical description of a familiar scene—a scene readers can reach only by a detour through a literal sense that is as eerie as it is comic.

The literal sense isn't expendable, even though it's only what the passage *would* mean if it weren't figurative. It's not only the key to what the passage *does* mean, it also passes on to that (figurative) sense the complex feelings that renew it for us. This is why interference-by-literal-meaning is an entirely different phenomenon from the pseudometaphors in chapter 3. Here the fantasy generated by the literal sense isn't an end in itself, much less the real point of the poem. Fantasy delays figurative reading, conflicts with it, and eventually modifies our attitude toward it when we eventually get it right. In what follows I'll need to refer to many other cases in which the literal meaning of a figurative expression is rigged to divert attention from the meaning in context. I'm interested in the widely varied purposes this figurational strategy is made to serve by seventeenth-century masters of metaphor. For short, call it the diversionary *littera*.

Take Vaughan's justification for preferring a life that ends in "retreate."[5] What sort of life is "retreate" being used to name? Let's review the argument.

It seems that an infant is really a fallen angel who defects from its first "race" (course of life, *curriculum vitae*?) by walking away from its "first love" (Christ?) with only a backward look at "his bright face."[6] The state of mind that qualifies as a "glimpse" of that face (10) is "a white Celestiall thought" (6). Undifferentiated whiteness is crucial here. In spite of its guilt, the infant is still blessedly *simple*minded. Instead of sorting things out as "Clouds," "flowres," etc., the infant mind knows and values them only as "shadows" of the eternity it has left behind (11–14). Even this nostalgic limbo of glimpsing and gazing is bliss compared with the disaster of worldly "understanding" (3).

The disaster is all the infant's fault. Vaughan's speaker doesn't blame its corruption on losing the status of nonspeaker (*infans*), or on moral infection by the senses. The infant teaches *itself* to "fancy" things inferior (5). Having learnt to speak, it teaches its *own* "tongue" profanity (15) and systematically corrupts each of its senses, like a witch versed in "black art" (17–18).

It may have been latently corrupt to start with, but even that *residual* simplicity was better than none. So the speaker longs to "travel back"—presumably to reverse the process of corruption by shedding first its sophisticated "fancies" and then the speech and understanding that gave those "fancies" their opportunity (21, 30). By the time he is old and ready to crumble into the urn, his "Inlightned spirit" will be "in that state I came" (25, 32)—that borderland state "where first I left my glorious train" (24), far from Jerusalem and the spirit's first love, but at least on the plain of Jericho;[7] not as good a view of the Promised Land as Moses got from the mountain opposite Jericho, but a degree of "inlightenment" all the same.

So much for the argument. Now what *is* this Jericho plain of infant awareness that the speaker wants to retreat to? The literal sense of the speaker's figurative wish makes the wished-for state seem luminously attractive and mystically remote. But that's simply the renewing effect of a diversionary *littera* on what is, after all, a wish for second childhood.

The thing being figuratively named here is old age, with its farsighted memory blurring the middle distance to link the mind with its earliest past. The diversion is disarming a prejudice by neutralizing the fear of becoming (as we say) simpleminded, the fear that gives Herbert's speaker in "The Forerunners" a bad moment as he focuses on his white hairs:

> But must they have my brain? must they dispark
> Those sparkling notions, which therein were bred?
> Must dulnesse turn me to a clod?   (3–5)

Yes, the sparkling notions must go, says the speaker of "The Retreate." But the result isn't cloddishness. On the other hand, it isn't the contemplative's way of denial, either—the climb from sense perception to pure understanding to the transcendence of understanding in union with God. "Angell-infancy," alias the simplicity of old age, is no mystic union. It barely glimpses God's face "a mile or two" away, and it doesn't say good-bye to sensation. It rids itself step by step of "notions," of categories for labeling *parts* of sense experience, until it reaches the point of gazing without recognition at objects that register only as a featureless brightness.

The literal sense of the "white Celestiall thought" or the "Inlightned" vision of "the shady City of Palme trees" distracts us only from *the thing named* by these figurative descriptions, not from *the way they evaluate* what they name. It distracts us from the figurative *reference* (the forgetfulness of old age), not from the figurative *sense* being used to single out the reference (forgetfulness as the simplifying of awareness, in preparation for reunion with "first love"). It's as if we had been told of somebody executing a contraction of jaw muscles accompanied by tension of the lips, and had been brought up short by realizing a second too late that the facial maneuver being reported was a smile.

II. Diversionary "Pantheism"

When Herbert's speaker in "The Flower" catches us off guard with

> We say amisse
> This or that is   (19–20),

we can be forgiven for taking it literally, in one of the alternative senses the sentence allows, depending on how we stress it. Stress "this" and "that," and we're being told to stop *distinguishing* one thing from another; for example, "to stop distinguishing oneself from God."[8] As the speaker goes on to say, "Thy word is all, if we could spell." Stress the "is" ("This or that *is*"), and we're being told to stop attributing *existence* to mere creatures, things that are available for pointing out and naming with demonstratives like "this" and "that."

Neither reading will do. The fatal troubles with the first come out after a moment's thought: *the speaker himself* distinguished between God and people who "say amiss" and can't "spell"—and the speaker knew what he was doing. If it's a false distinction—if God is the only one there is—then by process of elimination we get the theological absurdity that God is the someone who's being accused of missaying and misspelling.

The second reading has at least the virtue of being a theological truth[9] of importance: existence is part of God's nature, and God's alone; for a creature to be is to be in a given place at a given time; only God, or Christ the "Word" of God, simply *is*.[10] If "all" means whatever simply *is,* then "thy word is all." But on this reading too the charge of saying amiss looks grossly and mystifyingly unfair. On the former one, the speaker was as guilty of the noncrime of drawing distinctions as we are. On this one, the evidence of a philosophical gaffe on our part has been cooked: unconditional existence just isn't what anybody means by a claim that this or that *is*. If we mean anything, it's precisely that the item is somewhere or other at the moment.

Both literal senses are aggressively diversionary. All we need to do to see this is to follow the usual rule of figurational charity and check to see if these lines really are a wild non sequitur or grow naturally out of what went before:

> These are thy wonders, Lord of power,
> Killing and quickning, bringing down to hell
>   And up to heaven in an houre;
> Making a chiming of a passing-bell. (15–18)

What we do in "saying amiss" is to act as if we needed to choose "this" or "that" member of an apparently clashing pair of options: *either* killing, hellward-bringing, passing-bell-making, on the one side, *or* quickening, heavenward-bringing, and chiming-bell-making, on the other. The "wonder" of God's "power" is that the alternatives are compatible: both, or all, are God's word, his ways of bringing the right kind of moral "growth" to the "flower" Herbert's poem is about. The speaker isn't claiming that "this" and "that"—spiritual spring and winter—are one in *number*, only in *nature*.

The model for the form of this diversionary *littera* seems to be Paul's claim that in the True Church there is "nether Grecian nor Iewe, circumcision nor vncircumcision, Barbarian, Scythian, bonde, fre: but Christ is all and in all things"[11]—where "Thy word" *is* all in a figurative sense that doesn't keep him from being *in* all as well, from being as distinct from the things he's in as they are from each other.

In the concluding stanza of Herbert's "Temper (I)," sameness of kind comes once again in a boggling pseudomystical disguise of just plain sameness:

> Whether I flie with angels, fall with dust,
> Thy hands made both, and I am there:
>   Thy power and love, my love and trust
> Make one place ev'ry where. (25–28)

And once again the illusion of violent assault on common sense dissolves as soon as one notices that it's the speaker himself who distinguishes between the angel place and the dust place—and who emphasizes the distinction by talking of "both" (that is, two, not one).[12] The place he's always in, no matter where he is, is "one" only figuratively.

He gets his diversionary effect here by switching, without announcing it, to a higher level of generality. Imagine a patriot saying: "Whether I'm in York or in London, I'm in England." Only in Herbert, the level of generality being switched to is *all*-inclusive: "Whether I'm in heaven or the grave, you created both, so I'm there in what is par excellence the Place You Created—that is, in the universe." The notion of the universe as the all-inclusive place is a familiar scrap of the older physics: "You're in heaven [that is, the universe] because you're in the air, and in the air because on the earth, and likewise on the earth because you're in this place over here—the one that contains nothing but you."[13]

But we're still caught up in the *littera;* Herbert's subject up to the last stanza is his painful ups and downs of religious mood. The "places" made by God's hands are of the spirit, and so the all-inclusive "place" is finally described as the cooperative work of God's initiating "power" and the speaker's responding "trust." However foul the mood the speaker is "in," he's confident that he's also "in" the state of grace. We've been led in two steps from the strangeness of the *littera,* with its madly Heraclitean claim that the angels' way up and the dust's way down are one and the same, to the renewed strangeness of the real claim being made here: that the ups and downs of religious emotion are one and the same—not in themselves but in the loving purpose they both serve.[14]

In both "The Flower" and "The Temper," the end of the trail of semantic clues is the discovery that the individuality of persons is being *asserted*—not discredited, not wished away. Take the words literally, and you get a mysticism of self-erasure. Figure out how meanings are constrained by the previous train of thought, and you get a familiar Protestant vision of individual fulfillment. But now the familiarity no longer breeds contempt. Calvin too expects that Christ "will grow together with the Elect into one thing, *in a sense*"—that is, in a figurative sense that leaves the plural number of the celebrants intact, and promises "to each his special repayment."[15]

The nondiversionary *littera* of another Herbert metaphor for the sense of "oneness" involved here is a clasping (unity) of hands (plurality). In the individualistic notion of mystic union that Christianity can't easily do without, the limit of fusion is a deeply intimate partnership of *two*, in which "each possesseth other by way of special interest, property, and inherent copulation":[16]

> O be mine still! still make me thine!
> Or rather make no Thine and Mine![17]

What the speaker asks God to abolish here aren't individual selves, but only their private ownership; get rid of Thine and Mine, not Thee and Me. From now on, let each of us belong equally to both.

III. Diversionary "Egoism"

One of Traherne's many and bafflingly impudent diversionary *litterae* turns Herbert's on its head. Instead of a speaker who seems to be claiming or praying to be nonexistent for God's sake, we have somebody who can't get over the fact that he exists. That fact (for the speaker, at least) is unblinkable. Better still, it's glorious. Best of all, it's a source of endless satisfaction—and not only to the speaker; to God, too. If the speaker didn't exist, he would have to be invented:

> But neither Goodness, Wisdom, Power, nor Love,
> Nor Happiness it self in things could be,
> Did they not all in *one fair Order* move,
> And joyntly by their Service End in *me*.
>   Had he not made an *Ey* to be the Sphere
>   Of all things, none of these would e're appear.[18]

Things are "ordered" by how much satisfaction they could give me. I rescue the "fairness" of that order from bare potentiality by letting the world make me happy.

Granted it's more blessed to give than to receive. But the reason for this has nothing to do with altruism. It so happens that "what we giv we *best* receive" (italics mine). That's why "the Sons of Men are our Greatest Treasures," and why we love them: "He that thinks the Sons of Men impertinent to his Joy & Happiness can scarely lov them. But he that Knows them to be Instruments, and what they are, will delight in them and is able to use them."[19] Even their woes have a use, as "foyls unto thy Bliss."

> The dismal Woes wherein they crawl, enhance
> The Peace of our Inheritance.[20]

Not only do you enjoy other people's service, but God sanctions your special right to their love: "It is a Great Obligation laid upon all Mankind, & upon every person in all ages, to lov you as Himself."

> His Laws command all Men
> That they lov Me, Under a penalty
> Severe, in case they miss.[21]

In the end, what I appreciate in them is just their multiple reflection of me: "And as in many mirrors we are so many other selvs, so we are Spiritualy Multiplied when we meet our selvs more Sweetly, and liv again in other Persons."[22] So loving them is simply a roundabout version of loving oneself: "Had we not loved our Selves at all we could never hav been obliged to lov any thing. So that self Lov is the Basis of all Lov." In fact, we can and must go further; loving God is also a roundabout version of loving oneself: "Even as we lov our selves [whom] he hath so infinitly pleased, . . . we are able to rejoyce in him & to lov him."[23]

It would be a confusion to identify all this genial self-puffery with egoism. It would be to take it all literally—to read it out of context. Traherne is taking us on a detour into diversionary *littera*.

Talking about oneself as *the* end of all things turns out to be a way of stressing one's uniqueness as *one* end of all things in a *kingdom* of ends: "Thousands Enjoy all as well as wee: & are the end of all: And God communicateth all to them as well as us."[24] The "mirrors" that "reflect" us in another mock-egoistic passage aren't chances for narcissism by self-duplication. They're "Diversities of Friends & Lovers" who "reflect" us by reflecting *about* us.[25] It's just this "diversity," this otherness of his friends and lovers, that makes their concern valuable to the speaker of the *Centuries*.

The claim that giving is the best kind of receiving turns out to be equally harmless—egoism as diversionary *littera* once again. Traherne's speaker tries to show that our deepest satisfactions are nicely designed to reinforce our duties. It seems we get a lot more enjoyment vicariously, out of our kindness to other people, than we do directly, out of their kindness to us. What pleasure is supposed to be testing here is the *instinctiveness* of generosity, not its *rightness*. When we read justification into the speaker's text, the egoism we find isn't the speaker's.

The speaker's smug callousness is also at least partly a trick of diversion. "Woe" disturbingly adds to the speaker's "bliss" in "The Vision" and "Mankind is sick," but the kind of "woe" involved isn't people's agony but their "ignorance" and "faults." The point is that it's better to look at human follies with "Democritus his Mirth" than to blunder into the same follies: "their Faults shall keep thee right."[26] Above all, the moral *content* of being kept "right"—what it *is* to be that way—doesn't include looking on placidly as they stew. Whatever "bliss" is, it isn't that:

> What would we give! that they might likewise see
>   The Glory of his Majesty!
> The joy & fulness of that high delight,
>   Whose Blessedness is infinite!
> We would even cease to live, to gain
>   Them from their misery & pain,
>   And make them with us reign!   (82–88)

In short, egoistic language is being put to altruistic use.

The same goes for the dictum that "It is a Great Obligation laid upon all Mankind, & upon every person in all ages, to lov you as Himself." "His laws command all Men / That they lov Me." The only "law" of "his" that plausibly applies here is "Love thy neighbor as thy self." In short, *your* and *my* right to be loved just follow straightforwardly from *everybody's*. But that's why this egoistic right coexists with the altruism of the stanza I quoted in the last paragraph. Everybody's *right* to be loved by everybody else is precisely equivalent to everybody's *duty* to love in return.[27]

Even the apparently barefaced egoism of the announcement that "self Lov is the Basis of all Lov" is a figment of taking "Basis" literally; that is, of taking it out of context. If self-love were really the essential ingredient of all love, then the speaker would be talking nonsense when he insists that "no man loves, but he loves another more than Himself." But the speaker isn't talking nonsense. He's taking the distinction between self-love and love of others for granted: "It is in the Nature of Lov to Despise itself, and to think only of its Beloveds Welfare. Look to it, it is not right Lov, that is otherwise."[28]

In the speaker's unfolding argument, "basis" means *beginning*. Learning to love *begins* with the object one loves *without* learning to: oneself. The first lesson in love is gratitude; without self-love, says the speaker, no gratitude. But as the speaker defines it, gratitude has to be totally disinterested; it's what happens after self-love is fulfilled: "That Pool must first be filled, that shall be made to overflow."[29]

In fact, the speaker eventually reverses his seeming priorities altogether by making self-love at its most authentic depend for its content on love of others, as it does in God, who doesn't love himself "under any other Notion then as He is the Lover of his Beloved."[30]

As in Herbert, the *littera* is diversionary with a vengeance: a hair-raisingly perverse egoism is being used to shake the banality out of the old saying that the model for even unselfish love of others is love of oneself—that even the charity that ends in sacrifice begins at home. Mischief maybe—but *benign* mischief. Why should the heretics have all the fun?

IV. Diversionary "Solipsism"

Almost anywhere you open Traherne, you're likely to come across some version of the curiously self-discrediting claim that people, places, and things are contents of the mind—in particular, contents of the *speaker's* mind. Things may start outside the mind, but childhood intuition lets us know that it's their nature to end up inside:

> An Object, if it were before
> My Ey, was by Dame Nature's Law,
>   Within my Soul.[31]

In fact, the best thing the grown-up mind can do is carry this process of engulfment as far as it can go: "Heaven & Earth, Angels & Men, God & all Things must be contained in our Souls, that we may becom Glorious Personages, & like unto Him in all our Actions."[32] If we persevere, we end up in glorious defiance of logic, containing the world that contains us. At least the speaker has:

> Of it I am th'inclusive Sphere,
>   It doth entire in me appear
> As well as I in it: it givs me Room,
>   Yet lies within my Womb.[33]

And if childhood intuition is right, the mind wins this contest of containment: "The world was more in me, then I in it."[34]

Again, we miss the point if we take this Traherne idiom literally, as an announcement of some project in metaphysics. Traherne is no forerunner of Berkeley or Tweedledum, interested in persuading himself that things are thoughts.[35] And his remark about the mind of God as the model world container is no sign of conversion to a contemporary theory (Henry More's) that "the Eternal Capacity or Space is God," or that "all Spirits are . . . extended like it."[36] Space in Traherne is an "Obedient Subject" for God to "work upon" because, *unlike* God's mind, it's a permanently *empty* "capacitie"—"the Eternal Privation of Infinite Perfections."[37] The literal reading of the Traherne speaker's "solipsism" is undermined by its context, often by what the speaker has to say in the same breath.

The *littera* is diversionary again—even though you'd think sheer force of habit would protect us from misreading one of the deadest of dead metaphors, at least in English: we aren't kept by any iron law of incommensurateness-in-English from "having" things as well as thoughts "in mind," or from "taking in" facts as comfortably as we take in statements of fact. To be "in mind" is simply, and banally, to be thought about. In Traherne we're distracted from the banality by the claim that mental containment is equal or superior to physical: the world is in me not only *as well as* I am in it—but *more*.

The "more in me" diversion revives another dead wonder. If we don't literally contain the world, we literally contain something better: the idea of it. Better because, at least in the old Schoolman's view of mental representation, abstract ideas are sharply defined standards to which bodies, including the speaker's, are only fuzzy approximations. In form, the idea of the world is more the world—or what the world struggles hopelessly to be—than the world itself. "What is known is in the knower"—metonymically but excellently "in" by mental representation (like the tree "in" the picture). By contrast, the speaker's presence in the world is no more than bodily—hence fuzzy.[38] On this account of ideas, the speaker's claim is a commonplace—the reason Schoolmen give for claiming that "things are more in God than God in things":[39]

> O what a World art Thou! a world within!
>   All things appear,
>   All objects are
> Aliue in thee! Supersubstancial, Rare,
>   Above themselves, & nigh of Kin
>   To those pure Things we find
>   In his Great Mind
> Who made the World![40]

It takes a certain set of mind to think that conceiving and perceiving are wonderful all by themselves. Thus Zwingli couldn't get Calvin to see how Christ's presence in the communicants' *thoughts* could be enough to explain the Communion wonder of the Real Presence.[41] Traherne's speaker is a kind of Zwinglian here. At least when it comes to material things, being mentally re*present*ed isn't being *present* only because it's much better:

> Nay Things are dead,
> And in themselves are severed
> From Souls; nor can they fil the Head
> Without our Thoughts. Thoughts are the Reall things
> From whence all Joy, from whence all Sorrow springs.[42]

Thoughts are excellent because they're "objective" in the old Schoolman sense of being directly "objected" or presented to consciousness—and hence enjoyable. Without consciousness, no enjoyment. But in the speaker's passionate belief, enjoyment is what things are for. They fulfill themselves precisely by being present to us "objectively"—present through the mental images we delight in: "Objective treasures are always Delightfull."[43] And by the same token, external treasures are always dead:

> An Object Seen, is in the Faculty Seeing it, and by that in the Soul of the Seer, after the Best of Maners. . . . Dead Things are in a Room containing them in a vain maner; unless they are Objectivly [= as *obiecta*, or mental images] in the Soul of a Seer. The Pleasure of an Enjoyer, is the very End, why Things placed are in any Place. The Place and the Things Placed in it, being both in the Understanding of a Spectator of them. . . . And thus all Angels and the Eternity and Infinity of God are in me for ever mine. I being the living TEMPLE & Comprehensor of them.[44]

Some people, including the speaker once upon a time, fail to realize that mental images are things that splendidly and intimately *belong* to us, not just raw material for beliefs about things that don't and can't belong to us at all. People who fail to take reflective possession of their own experience don't really own anything. Their alienation is the worst kind of poverty:

> I neither thought the Sun,
> Nor Moon, nor Stars, nor Peeple, *mine*,
> Though they did round about me shine.

> For till *His* Works *my* wealth became,
> No Lov, or Peace, did me enflame.[45]

Once we've gotten the (figurative) point of world possession[46] by negotiating the diversionary *littera*, it turns out all over again that common experience has been "defied" only to be *shown*—in a light that is anything but common. "I will utter Things that have been Kept Secret from the Foundation of the World. Things Strange yet common; Incredible, yet known."[47]

In Traherne's favorite diversionary *littera,* to think of something is to possess it. Memory of a mythically bright childhood is one form of this possession—memory remarkably free of nostalgia. Well, *why* no nostalgia? One critic takes the *littera* for the meaning and explains that Traherne has a consolingly nonlinear notion of time: "No recall, no memory; a 'revival' of the impression thanks to its persistence at a deeper level."[48] But a persisting impression isn't a *past* event; it's the stuff of *present memories* of the event. *The memories are what defeat nostalgia*. The reason thoughts are better than things is precisely that they "present to me / In better sort the things which I did see."[49]

Look hard at a metaphysical theory anywhere in Traherne and you find the same fact of ordinary experience restored to its pristine extraordinariness by the same strategy of figuration.[50] Take the Traherne speaker's Jabberwocky improvement on the ancient theory that people existed before they were conceived or born: in some poems, people were in all sorts of states of being *before* they existed! In "The Salutation" the speaker is an infant—the archetypal nonspeaker. This logical oddity should tip us off that we're about to be diverted for a while by what some expressions *would* mean or imply *if* the language being spoken were vernacular English rather than an impromptu talk dialect:

> These little limmes,
> These Eys and Hands which here I find,
> These rosie Cheeks wherewith my Life begins,
> Where have ye been? Behind
> What Curtain were ye hid from me so long!
> Where was? in what Abyss, my Speaking Tongue?   (1–6)

During the eternity in which it "was nothing," it "did little think such Joys as Ear or Tongue, / To Celebrat or See" (13–16). Its present surprise at these joys comes from this long habit of not expecting them. But how can it have had such a habit when it was nothing?

The same challenge to common sense turns up in the *Centuries*, in the form of a solution to the problem posed by the "wants" or lacks God apparently suffered before the creation: "He wanted the Communication of His Divine Essence, and Persons to Enjoy it. He wanted Worlds, He wanted Spectators, He wanted Joys, He wanted Treasures."[51] How could a totally self-sufficient being be "wanting" in anything? Yet he not only wants worlds and joys, he can't enjoy those worlds "unless the Soul of Man they pleas." How can a self-sufficient being have wants that depend on some creature's existence for their satisfaction?

The solution is simple, and heroically absurd. The speaker happily skewers himself on both horns of his dilemma: "He wanted, yet he wanted not, for he had them." "But he wanted Angels & Men, Images, Companions. And these He had from all Eternitie."[52] Later on, the speaker urges his audience to "let your Wants be present from Everlasting. Is not this a Strange life to which I call you? Wherein you are to be present with Things before the World was made?" The life may be strange, but the speaker thinks he has in fact already lived it: "Did you not from all Eternity Want som one to give you a Being? Did you not Want one to give you a Glorious Being? Did you not from all Eternity Want som one to giv you infinite Treasures?" "We also were our selves before God eternaly."[53]

As usual, we're being treated to a commonplace made new by being made "strange." In Schoolman's jargon again: "Though creatures did not exist from eternity except for their existence in God, yet by virtue of this existence . . . God knew and loved them from eternity in their individual natures. In the same way, we too know, by likenesses that exist in us, things that exist in themselves."[54] *We existed* in God only in the figurative sense that God *anticipated us*. (Put this way, the thought seems banal—but once again that's just the reason why it needs to be put differently.)

Before I got here, it was a fact that I could and would get here. But God knows all facts and possible facts. So before I got here I was known to God; in that cognitive sense, and only in that sense, I was "before God eternaly" before I existed. "Thine eyes did see my substance, yet being unperfect: and in thy book all my members were written, which in continuance were fashioned, when as yet there was none of them."[55] And in that conceptual or possible existence, I filled God's wants for my kind of being, even his want of a possible connoisseur to allow him vicarious eyes and ears to appreciate his work. Conceptual or possible or "objective" being—especially being thought about by God—is more than enough to guarantee the happiness of the thinker. I was "objectivly in the Soul of a Seer"—and "Objectiv Treasures are always Delightfull."

That seeming dependency of God's on me as something actual, something his "wants" forced him to make, was only a trick of diversionary *littera*.[56] The speaker mimics the perversity of people who like to see how the world looks when they're upside down. But the point of the mimicry is to show us that it is wonderful enough seen right side up.

The grace note in that wonder is consciousness. In the order of knowledge it's simply evidence, simply a datum or given. But in the order of faith it's a "gift." Take this metaphor literally and you have the making of Traherne's favorite diversionary *littera:* if the speaker's consciousness is something *given* to him, it is something he *has*. If being conscious of the world is having it in mind, then he has the world as well.

The speaker tries hard to see with the child's innocence. But the speaker's innocence is disciplined by experience. He doesn't take his metaphors literally, and he knows what the child doesn't—

> that there was a Serpents Sting,
> Whose Poyson shed
> On Men, did overspread
> The World.[57]

Disciplined innocence is his notion of an antidote: we wouldn't adulterate the world with our "evil habits" if only we could get rid of "the yellow Jandice" of Custom that "will not let a Man see those Objects truly that are before it."[58]

The argument is exactly equivalent to Lucretius's, and may owe something to it:

> Take, to start with, the bright pure color of the sky. Take what the sky contains, the stars wandering here and there, the moon, and the sun's radiance, bright beyond all the rest: if all these were putting in their maiden appearance to humanity, if all of a sudden they were being presented out of the blue—what could be more entitled to the name of marvellous? What would the nations dare less to believe before they saw it?[59]

Lucretius tries to make the sky new by asking the reader to carry out a mental experiment. Traherne's way is what you might expect of a seventeenth-century metaphorist: the reader is led to rediscover the world by double take.

Chapter Five

Metaphor Dramatized: Deceit and Irony

I. *The Histrionic Trope*

So far I've been looking at how the great seventeenth-century metaphorists *use* the diversionary *littera*. But they also write *about* that use. They do this by bringing on imaginary users to illustrate the reasons why a figurative speaker might resort to a subtle form of equivocation by getting himself taken literally. It would be too easy to tag the resulting poems as "monologues" of various speaker "types" and then get on with the business of studying the types. The detail work had better wait a while. We can't afford to be conceptually fuzzy where seventeenth-century writers are precise.

In the classical view they inherit, literature is a representational art, pure or applied. Being made of speech, what it represents most immediately are *acts* of speech. Thus Homer is the king of poets because he's the king of mimics. All the rhetorical schemes and tropes that are good for arousing emotions are essentially representations of some speech-act type or other.[1]

One central example is dialogism, the debater's ploy of suddenly taking on the role of his opponents or of made-up speakers to give his audience the momentary illusion of hearing independent testimony to the truth of his claims.[2] Another example is irony, or "urbane dissembling," in which a whole speech-act type is subjected to serious play or mimicry; an ironist *caricatures* the saying of a particular thing so as to question the intelligence or honesty of anybody capable of *actually* saying it. The offending phrase gets marked as mere quotation by delivery or circumstance, and the speaker gets his evaluation across by innuendo (or *endeixis*).[3] You can't counter an ironic utterance of "That's a likely story" by saying "But the story *isn't* likely"—as you could if "likely," used ironically, meant its opposite.[4]

In these cases and others, the speaker's real subject is quoted speech delivered in character or a burlesque of character. And the essence of the exercise is the telling of a story whose single episode is the speech act being represented. The seventeenth-century poems I'm about to look at are stories of this kind, and the topic-comment distinction this fact brings with it needs to be respected, on pain of missing crucial points. A poem in which a speaker prays isn't the speaker's prayer.[5] It's *about* his prayer, and the reader's task is to catch what the poem implicitly *says* about it, relying on rules of interpretation like the principle of charity: failing evidence to the contrary, only the speaker, not the author, is unmasked by gaffes in good manners, elementary logic, and common knowledge.[6]

In fact, the author can prepare a rude awakening for us by giving us no gaffes, no *initial* reason to think he isn't the speaker—no reason to start our reading by assuming implicit inverted commas. This is the entrapment effect that seems to have interested Ben Jonson in translating Horace's "praises of a countrie life." In the last four lines, after seventy-three lines of "praises," we're brought up short when the author finally breaks his silence to tell us that we've been reading the thoughts of the usurer Alphius, who got no closer to rural retirement than the thoughts. This amounts to an instruction to put quotes around what went before, and reread accordingly. In the new reading the praise of farming is the speaker's futile attempt to sell himself a bill of goods his compulsions will never let him buy.

The same surprise effect of retroactive quotation occurs more subtly in *Lycidas*. Again we're given no compelling reason to distinguish the speaker from the author. In fact, the subtitle gives us reason to *identify* them: "In this monody the Author bewails a learned Friend." And again the author finally speaks up in a conclusion that implicitly directs us to reread everything before it as an act of quoting rather than saying: "Thus sang the uncouth Swain." On this rereading the elegist is the author at an earlier stage of his career; and the poem turns out not to *be* an elegy but to be *about* one—to be an act of representing one and commenting on it.

The comment is the author-narrator's implied claim that the elegiac moment has been outgrown in the course of being endured:

> At last he rose, and twitch'd his mantle blew;
> Tomorrow to fresh woods and Pastures new.

"Tomorrow" epitomizes the whole effect by hovering between quotation and use; it's the speaker's word for the author's *today,* but equally it's the author's word for the great expectations he continues to share with an "uncouth Swain" he otherwise looks back on as virtually another person.

Suppose the writer tacitly quotes, by giving us a sign that his act of utterance is distinct from the speaker's; for example, the mere fact that the speaker is speaking and not writing. And suppose the quote isn't explicitly framed, even as a parting shot. Then the quoting itself acts as a minimal frame. It says, in effect, that once upon a time somebody or other spoke or thought the words quoted here. For introducing a report, the information is far too general to have much point. So, by communicative charity, to say just this is to imply a little more: what's being introduced *isn't* a report. It's a fiction.

That's how (by trope on "once") we get the fiction tag "once upon a time" in the first place, and why speakers in poems framed *only* with this tag are never the author.

Fictional "once" means *as things didn't turn out but might have*. But there are countless might-have-been courses of events in which I have very little in common with the actual me, and somebody else is a dead ringer. A fiction is precisely a story about events that form part of countless such might have beens. So having a dead ringer for me in my fiction just isn't enough to make the fiction a story about *me*. For the story to be *about* me, the cluster of dead-ringer traits has to *refer* to me. It has to function pretty much like a proper name. But this means that the cluster has to be conventionally identified with me in my language community. Unique reference to actual things in a fiction is a matter of proper names (like "Thames") or descriptions backed up by talk-postulates (the man who wept because he had no more worlds to conquer = Alexander).

The moral of this story is that the existence of such likenesses, especially general ones or ones not in the public domain, isn't enough to make a collection of lyrics like Herbert's or Vaughan's an essay in confession or autobiography. To make the poems mean what they would have *if* the likenesses had been common knowledge and had been flagged by the text is to rewrite the poems.

II. "I" for "We": The Figure of Induction

In the seventeenth-century Christian view, the model collection of poetic speech-act representations is the Book of Psalms. These *are* appropriately framed, by their circumstantial titles at least, as David's prayers to God at particular stages in his life. But as published writings, they're prayers only figuratively. Literally, they're prayer *representations*. The acts they represent may be addresses to God, but address representations no more presuppose the existence of addresses to match than goblin pictures presuppose the existence of goblins who sat for them.

In the jargon, the published texts "apostrophize" God and address *us*. As addressed to us, they're tacit commentaries on the impurities of form and motive that are bound to creep into even the holiest of "intimate conversations with God."[7] On the Renaissance account, David's collection is to sacred *colloquia familiaria*[8] what Erasmus's is to secular ones: a compassionately practical exercise in teaching by example and precept, where the example is a representation of something said in so many words, and the precept (to borrow Herbert's definition of prayer) is "something understood."

Augustine's commentary on the Fifty-first Psalm is an attempt to understand that something—to understand it aloud by spelling out the narrative comment that implicitly frames David's quotation from a past self. The indispensable cue is the stage setting in David's title: "When Nathan the prophet came in to him after he had gone in to Bathsheba." This is enough to let us see David's point in quoting this speech, or in making it up to fit his remembered situation:

> This David [that is, the speaker] couldn't say, "I didn't know what I was doing," for he wasn't ignorant of how evil it was to lay hands on another's wife, and how evil it was to kill the husband—a husband who had no knowledge of the matter, much less any resentment.
>
> So those attain God's mercy who acted in ignorance, and those who acted knowingly attain, not any mercy at random, but *"great mercy."*[9]

On Augustine's reading, this intuition about mercy unstrained is what the Psalmist was getting at in dramatizing his guilty past. It isn't merely an arbitrary moral we draw from spontaneous outcries we've been permitted to eavesdrop on by an obliging witness who committed them to memory at the time. Calvin's Augustinian way[10] of putting it is that David the regenerate author "plays the part of someone alienated from God"[11]— someone like David the unregenerate sinner.

But Augustine himself goes into a little more detail about what "role-playing" comes to in this context—what it means to intimate (by turning out a dramatic "part" or script) that once upon a time there was a speaker alienated from God: "See who this is—it seemed that David alone was praying for forbearance: see here an emblem of *us,* and a type of the *church.*"[12] For "someone alienated from God, and destined for reconciliation with God," read "*everyone* such." For the name of a patriarch with a salient trait of character or experience, read *everyone* with that trait: "The name 'Joseph' has been put for 'brother,' so that by the proper name of him whose renown is of the first brightness among brothers, any brother might be signified."[13]

Where an expression implying "some" or "at least one" is used to mean *all,* a sample isn't being used to *prove* a generalization but to *make* one. What's inductive here isn't an argument but a trope. Even so, to satisfy Augustine's wish for a handy school label, we can borrow the term here and speak of the *figure of induction.*

The Augustinian theory of psalm language has another interesting implication. In David's inductive use of the first-person singular, any struggling Christian can convert a psalm into a figurative statement about himself merely by saying it with full sincerity, as the liturgy requires. A psalm turns out to be a hypothetical quotation from its readers or reciters—a prayer *form* rather than a prayer. In Herbert's metaphor, the reader makes a prayer of the form by signing the deed at "I":

> He that will passe his land,
> As I have mine, may set his hand
> And heart unto this Deed, when he hath read.[14]

Making a deed for Everyman to sign and assuming the role of Everyman are alternative ways of describing the use of the histrionic "I"—the figure of induction—in a speech-act representation.[15]

On Augustine's account, Davidic role-playing has an important vertical dimension. When the crucified Christ shouts out the Psalmist's question, "My God, my God, why hast thou forsaken me?" (Ps. 22:1), David is revealed to have been prophetically playing the role of Christ. On the other hand, these words presuppose that the speaker has been abandoned by God, and this is not true of Christ. So the voice from the cross is not his, says Augustine, but ours. The result is a stratifying of roles: in his distressful cry to his God, David assumes the role of Christ assuming the role of his Church in distress—Christ assuming the *persona Ecclesiae.*[16]

Persona Ecclesiae: Parson. The etymology is revealing enough to bear down on here. In Herbert's account, the priestly leading of public worship is an act of impersonation—of speech-act representation—in which the parson-*persona* appears "not as himself alone, but as presenting with himself the whole Congregation, whose sins he then beares and brings with his own to the heavenly altar." [17] In this sense, a poet in the Davidic mold is a kind of priest or parson, a *persona Ecclesiae*, with the qualification that the fictive or potential speech acts he represents tend to be acts of thought, the imagined sound of one's own voice.

III. Figuration as Psychodrama

Or is the voice somebody else's? As Augustine says at the beginning of the *Soliloquies*, it isn't easy to pin down the owner of the voice in one's head: "I had been turning over many and various thoughts for a long time, and for many days looking for myself or my good, and for the evil I should avoid, when suddenly someone says to me—whether I myself, or another inside me or out, I know not, for this is the very thing I mightily struggle to know—someone, then, says to me. . . ." [18] In the poems I turn to now, a speaker is taken in by his own diversionary *littera*. He manages to equivocate with himself. It's as if he were saying by rote lines fed to him by somebody else. For all the understanding he shows of his own speech, he might just as well *be* somebody else.

"*In* the poems" shouldn't be taken casually here. The speaker isn't the poet. And his problematically shifty speech act isn't the poem; it's what the poem represents and comments on. This tricky process of communication relies on various fragile understandings to get us to see that the string of words before us is not being directly used, but quoted. To put quoting in the grammatical terms that reach the heart of the matter: the string of words has been converted into *a name of itself*, the subject of an elliptical sentence. The predicate of that sentence is the part that's been left for us to fill in, and the fragile understandings that help us do this correctly include our talk-postulates, as well as the way the speaker has been made to violate them. Without these data, quoting and commenting are impossible, whatever the author intended.

IV. Donne

The Diversionary Littera **Dramatized:**
Truancy of the Imagination

Here's a complicated example from Donne. At first it seems that the lovers described by the speaker of "The Extasie" are literally ecstatic, in the mystics' technical sense. To use a definition supplied by Donne himself,[19] it seems that each has experienced "a *departure* and *secession, and suspension* of the soul, which doth then communicate itself to two bodies" (italics mine).

The lovers' souls "were gone out" (16, departure or secession) and "hung 'twixt her, and mee" (16, suspension). Without bodily organs, they still manage to "negotiate" (17)—in "soules language" (22), of course. So it's a conversation you can overhear only if you too are a soul in love-ecstasy. You need to be "all minde" (23). Thinking in unison ("because both meant, both spake the same" [26]), the souls congratulate themselves on having learned from ecstasy the secret of "what we love" (30). It's this: they've mixed together, or "interinanimated," themselves thoroughly enough to form a single "new" soul that is "abler" than the unmixed ingredients, or "Atomies." The new soul has gotten rid of the old ones' "defects of lonelinesse" (41–48). So "what we love" isn't "sexe" (31)—sexual otherness or "lonelinesse." We love to share a soul that can keep itself company. The speaker sums up the main point of this passage in a side remark at the end: the conversation he's reporting was a "dialogue of *one*" (74; italics mine). *QED.*

There's a complication to be faced here: we're reading a quote within a quote. Donne is quoting the speech of a narrator who claims to be quoting the thought chorus of disembodied souls. The path of least resistance would be to take the speaker's claim literally. Literal claims like this are not unheard of—from spirit mediums, for example. We would be sparing ourselves a frustrating search, since Donne gives us no hint of what the point of the soul-talk report would be if we were to apply figurational charity to it. But if we take it literally, it seems we have to take the equivalent claim of the soul chorus literally too. So: the speaker says that (*a*) a composite soul said that (*b*) it was a composite soul.

But *b* isn't trouble free. On the narrator's account, agreeing that ecstasy is possible was only a preliminary. It wasn't what this particular ecstasy was *for.* The souls are military couriers "negotiating" to "advance" the "state" of their respective "Armies," their bodies (13–16). After their self-congratulation party the agents have to get down to the business of looking after the interests of their principals:

> But O alas so long, so farre
> Our bodies why doe wee forbeare?   (49–50)

Remember that earlier the lovers aren't identified with the souls at all, but with "her" and "mee" (16)—the bodies that the souls "hung" between. Once again, "whil'st our soules negotiate there, / Wee [the bodies] like sepulchrall statues lay" (18). If we follow this identification, the souls' use of "love" to mean the desire that gets fulfilled in soul union is a misleading innovation, to put it charitably: in ordinary parlance, "love" is what gets consummated by the union of *lovers*. If the lovers were body *owners* (souls), then soul union would fit. But, at this point at least, the lovers are supposed to be *bodies*—and the union of bodies is sex.

This is suspicious. But next comes a dilemma: either the narrator's report, including the soul chorus, isn't to be taken literally after all, or the narrator is being presented as a liar.

We've been led to expect the soul-agents to get down at some point to a parley on behalf of the body-principals. But when the moment apparently arrives, the ecstasy metaphor is both replaced and undermined. Now the lovers aren't bodies but souls—body *owners:*

> They'are [the bodies] ours, though they'are not wee, Wee are
> The' intelligences, they the spheares.   (51–52)

And now the indispensable job of bodies is to mediate between souls (not the other way around, as earlier):

> On man heavens influence workes not so,
>   But that it first imprints the ayre,
> Soe soule into the soule may flow,
>   Though it to body first repaire.   (57–60)

The ecstatic "flowing" of soul into soul has to be figurative after all. It's like the airborne influence—*influentia,* in-flowing—of birth stars on the people born under them: action at a distance, through a physical medium.[20]

A medium *separates* the things it joins. Sometimes it's needed because direct contact between the things would be an absurdity,

> As our blood labours to beget
> Spirits, as like soules as it can,
> Because such fingers need to knit
> That subtile knot, which makes us man.   (61–64)

Here the revealing and discouraging analogy for the knitting of soul and soul by body is the knitting of soul and body by spirit. Spirits are needed because the body and soul they knit *can't conceivably mix*—and, by implication, soul-knitting bodies are needed for the same reason. The souls mix only by proxy—if and only if the bodies mix by sex. Without sex, "a great Prince," the composite soul, won't come into existence. The balked possibility of its coming into existence will just be a "prison" it's condemned to "lie" in (68).[21] With this admission, the narrator's whole premise collapses. The "mixt soules" (35) have been made to confirm that "mixt soules" taken literally are an absurdity—along with their dialogues and confirmings.[22]

The natural move in response to "I'm in ecstasy"—or (Englishing the Greek) "I'm beside myself"—is to ask: "In an ecstasy of what? beside yourself with what?" and wait for the provocation to be spelled out. It takes some doing to get the colloquial metaphor—colloquial in Donne's dialect of English as in ours—to generate a diversionary *littera*. If the trick comes off in this case, it's because on a figurative reading the quote within a quote seems to be pointless. It loses its force as eyewitness support for a deep theory of love. But in fact this isn't the point at all, just a prelude or foreplay of cant and compliments. The point is sexual frustration. That's what the lovers are in an ecstasy of:

> But O alas, so long, so farre
> Our bodies why doe wee forbeare?   (49)

Sexual frustration is the shallowly submerged running theme of the speaker's first twenty lines, beginning with the incoherent riverbank he has the lovers sit on—a pregnant belly swelling up, a pillow on a bed also swelling up: just the sorts of things to "rest" somebody's "reclining head" on (1–3). The pillow and head talk applies figuratively and trivially to banks and violets, literally and pointedly to the lovers' desires. In short, the bank and violet are *emblems,* just as the sweat-balm-cement between the lovers' clasped hands (5–6) is a *symptom* of the same complaint.

The ghostly go-betweens we will meet a few lines later are preceded by go-betweens that are more to the point, even if equally unsatisfactory:

the sweat of stalled desire; the eyebeams threading (and hence mediating between) eyes staring into each other. No "entergrafting" of hands, much less of gazes, is enough to "make us one," any more than "getting" reflection babies in each other's eyes is the kind of propagation the lovers are after (9–12). In our last clear picture of them, they're no longer sitting. They're lying as inertly as "sepulchrall statues" in a swoon of love in suspense. Coitus is the "victory" that fate has been "suspending" between "two equal Armies," just as lovemaking is the "warfare" that allows the bodies to be "armies."[23]

All this would be no more than comical if the diversionary *littera* were simply another pious fraud. But something obviously desirable is being energetically faked, and for that very reason pathetically despaired of: the possibility of a love between persons, and not merely their bodies—a love that isn't "dull" or "sublunary" and can survive the absence of eyes, lips, and hands because it is "interassured of the mind." There are such things as "defects of lonelinesse," and on the view of mind and body we finally get, those defects are stamped into the nature of things. Minds can't conceivably get together *before* "we're to bodies gone," and as the souls' last line assures the speaker's hearers with bogus cheer, there will be "small change" *when* "we're to bodies gone" (76).

This time the diversionary *littera* is a reflex of despair. The speaker hasn't been misrepresenting to have his way with his mistress.[24] She's a third person, not part of the current audience (if anyone is). And he has already enjoyed whatever there was to enjoy of "all the day" (20) being described. He's misrepresenting for his own cold comfort. One measure of the distance between the ecstasy he believes in and the ecstasy he would believe in if he could is the violet that turns up in both tableaux, once as the reclining head of a tantalized lover, and later as the single violet of an impossible rapport between a whole man and woman, redoubling "all which before was poore, and scant" (39). The deceptively casual phrases unmask the "extasie" that gets uneasily covered up by the speaker's diversionary *littera:* "small change"; "poore, and scant."[25]

Donne's speaker in "A Valediction forbidding mourning" uses the same ploy to meet a very different kind of emergency. We're given no reason to doubt that he and the woman he's saying good-bye to are "inter-assured of the mind" (19), but the conclusion he pretends to draw from this doesn't follow, and he gives every indication of not believing it whether it follows or not.

The relevant talk-postulate is that the more you love (not simply lust for) each other, the *worse* it hurts to be apart. The speaker doesn't reject this truism, he simply goes on as if he'd never heard of it. It seems that if an attachment goes higher than eyes, lips, and hands, then the partners "care lesse, eyes, lips, and hands to misse" than partners whose only attachment is sex (17–20). The sexual bond is "sublunary"—below the moon, in the sphere of matter. Real lovers are attached above (13–16). But in fact the speaker hasn't just *heard* of the truism being flouted here. He started off by *vouching* for it out of his own current experience. For him parting was a kind of dying (1–5).[26] That was the emergency that launched the poem: a kind of dying calls for a kind of mourning—a call the speaker claimed to think it would be "prophane" to answer (7–8). (For "prophane" read *vulgar* and [hence] *degrading*.)[27] But the profanity argument was only his first stab at a plausible way of "forbidding mourning."

The way he settles on is to fiddle with the metaphor of emotional *attachment*. It turns out that departing doesn't mean parting after all. With the help of a well-timed diversionary *littera*, the lovers are free to imagine, if not believe, that to be "two soules . . . which are one" is to be inseparable (21–24). The departure of one such soul from another may be a "breach" to the bodies. To the souls it's simply an "expansion"—though the speaker flirts with giving the show away at this point by adding that the single soul of parted lovers is "gold to ayery *thinnesse beate*" (24; italics mine). It's hard to imagine that a soul has much to gain by being forcibly subdued to a state of tension or fragility.

Thanks to diversionary *littera* again, the show isn't given away. "Gold" and "ayery" draw attention from "beate", and "thinnesse"—and hence from the state of anxiety being *figuratively* described here—to the *literal* sense and the picture it conjures up: a goldsmith's wonderful simulation of bubble film. Fine gold leaf is a tour de force of illusionary craftsmanship. But so (by the author's implication, not the speaker's) is the speaker's performance.[28]

Still, maybe the clever speaker has taken too many risks. It's time for a mock concession: "If they be two [rather than the unitary being I've been imagining] . . ." (25). This is only a *mock* concession, because so far what he's been trying to pass off as literal isn't the lovers' oneness but their attachment. The place of that attachment is a realm of "trepidations" or heavenquakes—"greater far" than earthquakes, but bringing with them no "harms and fears" (9–12).[29]

What the mock concession has maneuvered us into is one last version of the same schematic diagram:

> If they be two, they are two so
> As stiff twin compasses are two.   (25–26)

When compasses are in use, they too are *attached above,* and the compass "trepidations" too are harmless. In fact, by the speaker's account, at least, they're benign. The descriptive language has been picked out shrewdly to apply figuratively to compass legs, but literally to the parted lovers. Take the metaphor literally and your reward is a consoling fantasy. At first she "[doth] in the center sit," as he "far doth rome." But eventually she "leanes, and hearkens," and "growes erect," as he "comes home" (32).

Of course, compasses in use *don't* spiral down to zero radius to let one foot "come home" to the other. That's no way to draw your circle "just" (34). The speaker is talking about different occasions of use, and different circles, and conveniently limiting his attention to a series of circles with shrinking radiuses. As before, the comfort is an illusion: a diversionary *littera.*

The last stanza reverses the process. Instead of "lover" talk to describe compasses, we have "compass" talk to describe these particular lovers and their predicament:

> Such wilt thou be to mee, who must
> Like th'other foot, obliquely runne.
> Thy firmnes makes my circle just,
> And makes me end, where I begunne.   (33–36)

As metaphor, the "compass" talk is about love for the lady as a moral agent, about love for her firmness of purpose, but above all about the steadying influence of that kind of love on the way the lover lives his life *apart from her.* Whatever obligations he takes on in that life, her example of firmness "makes me end where I begunne" by coming full circle—by coming "home" to the things he promises to do.

Compasses are joined for a purpose. To *serve* that purpose, they're not only joined above but separated below: the separation (the radius) is as essential to the purpose as the attachment. The same (figuratively) sometimes goes for lovers. Unfortunately, a promise to come home metaphorically isn't a promise to come home at all.

At least one scholarly reader has tried to find homecoming in the passage all the same, by reading *spiral* for "circle" and *curving in a spiral* for "obliquely."[30] But this violates the most basic rule of figurative reading: unbroken clocks are not repaired. "Circle" fits into a coherent argument (about moral interaction at a distance), and "spiral" doesn't. Instead it pointlessly undermines the lover's final tribute to the guidance of his lady. To draw a spiral, the distance between the compass points has to shrink *at a uniform speed*.[31] So the firmness of the center foot (the lady) isn't enough to draw a spiral "just."

But the skewing is what makes the spiral reading a nonstarter. The "circles" in a spiral are conspicuously "*un*just." That's exactly Chalcidius's point in the classic source for the iconography of the spiral: spiral revolution is a model of *inconstancy*, "*inconstans circumvectio*." Each "circle" a spiral is made up of has to be drawn "*ut non perveniat ad exordium*"—so the stylus point *won't* "end where [it] begunne."[32]

On a figurative reading, the literal homecoming disappears; and so does the consolation. What remain are variations on the argument that "tear-floods" and "sigh-tempests" would profane the kind of love these lovers have achieved. This danger may justify forbidding mourning, but it doesn't make complying any easier. What makes it easier is the relief offered to both partners by the diversionary *littera*.

The *nature* of the relief is hard to put one's finger on—maybe a kind of self-deception. But this is answering a question with a question. What is self-deception? Clearly not the logical absurdity of secretly disbelieving something you've got yourself to believe.

One plausible theory of self-deceiving that Donne might have known about is that

> the human mind is capable of attending or not attending to an idea. The mind's failure to attend takes two forms. Sometimes inattention comes of having a will that turns away all by itself from considering the idea; as the saying has it: "He wished not to understand so as to do right." Sometimes the mind occupies itself with other things that it has a better liking to. These things divert it from looking straight at the idea; as the saying has it: "The fire (that is, lust) fell over them, and they saw not the sun."[33]

The field of thought, like the field of vision, is made up of a focus and a periphery, and the periphery has its uses. To deceive oneself about something is to keep it out of focus—to choose not to pay attention to it.

This seems to be about right. In the "Valediction," at least, self-deception is an act of therapeutic or recreative inattention. The speaker starts by acknowledging the disagreeable facts: he's going away; he may never come back; parting is a kind of death. His discussion never really denies any of this. All it does is make possible a truancy of the imagination from what his words of acknowledgment mean in context—from their figurative meaning. Self-deception isn't quite losing sight of the truth. It's just looking at it out of the corner of your eye.[34]

The Diversionary Littera Dramatized: Semantic Bad Faith

Elsewhere in Donne, the diversionary *littera* is the lover's neurotic private joke at the expense of the women he can't bring himself to trust—a joke that rebounds by being itself a violation of trust. In a purely formal way, the hearer has only herself to blame if she misses the point: the speaker has followed the rules of figuration to the letter but cleverly betrayed the spirit. Two examples in particular capture his semantic bad faith with a kind of icy elegance.

Taken literally, "The Apparition" is a threat. The speaker is telling his woman listener that he means to get even with her for murdering him with scorn. He'll come back as a ghost and surprise her as she lies with her exhausted partner, who will mistake her terrified stirrings and pinches for still another demand on his prowess and make believe he's asleep. How the ghost will take advantage of this situation the speaker refuses to say, for a reason that abruptly knocks out the props from under a literal reading of *threatening* here: being forewarned, he says, might "preserve" her, and

> since *my love is spent*,
> I'had rather thou shouldst painfully repent,
> Then by my threatnings rest *still* innocent.
> (15–17; italics mine)

If his love is spent, then her scorn *won't* murder him, and the ghost *won't* walk. So where's the threat? And where's the future injury he's threatening to get even for? If what he doesn't want "preserved" by fear of revenge is her continuing "innocence," then where's the *current* injury he's threatening to get even for?

But it's precisely her continuing innocence—of an affair with him—that he finds so maddening. And love has nothing to do with this performance. It isn't his love that's been spent, only his patience. That's the point of the stream of insults that he smuggles in as if they were conceded points: she isn't chaste or virginal at all; she's refusing sex with him out of pure hypocrisy; she has rotten taste in men, taste that the "fain'd vestall" will indulge in "worse armes" than his as soon as she's "free" of his "solicitations." In fact, she's so insatiable that the owner of the "worse arms" will be "tyr'd" to the point of "shrinking" away from her at the prospect of "more."

What would be presuppositions and threats in the vernacular turn up with different but trope-related senses or speech-act forces in the speaker's impromptu dialect. For "obviousness to everybody," read *obviousness to the speaker*, for "threatened aggression," read *aggression*. The speaker has been denied his rightful pleasure, and he needs to believe the reason isn't the woman's morals but her malice. Her being "still innocent" is beside the point for him. He just goes on the Othello-ish axiom that nature—at least as manifested in his imagination—"would not inuest her selfe in such shadowing passion, without some Instruction."[35] Where there's smoke—his fantasies of her disguised nymphomania—there's fire.

And he turns the same shadowing passion into a whip to be flicked at his listener with sadistic finesse. Even before the ghost gets through with her, she'll be reduced to a rippling bank of poplar leaves; her sweat will be frigid globules combining, separating, and chasing each other over her body—"a poor Aspen wretch" "bath'd in a cold quicksilver sweat." If the speaker succeeds in passing off his threatenings and presupposings as literal, the listener will think that the insults are merely incidental to the delivery of the threat rather than ends in themselves. She won't quite know what hit her.

Again, in "Womans constancy," the speaker takes for granted something his listener is obviously far from granting:

> Now thou hast lov'd me one whole day,
> To morrow *when* thou leav'st, what wilt thou say?
> (1–2; italics mine)

"If" would be churlish enough; "when" is worse. It's the first day of the affair, and as we're informed in a moment, they've bound themselves to each other by an "oathe" or "lovers contract." The "when" of shared expectation in "when thou leavest" is bizarre—unless we take it figuratively: for "casual assumption," read *provocative assertion*. But even as an assertion it's wildly unresponsive to the occasion, which is a love affair in its infancy. It's unresponsive unless we subject the result of our first figurative reading to a second: for "assertion," read—what?

What follows seems unhelpful. The lady is asked if she plans to resort to some of the "scapes" or sophistic evasions on his list. But the question has to be reread as a statement as soon as he goes on to call her a vain lunatic for thinking him unequal to refuting "scapes" like these—as if they had been her suggestion rather than his. This gives us the second step we were looking for in the metalepsis or serial figuration: for "assertion," read *suggestion*.

What would ordinarily be an act of predicting is turned by context into the speaker's act of assigning his partner a role in the breakup *scheduled by the speaker*. In this scenario he tentatively assigns himself no more than a supporting role: "By to morrow, I may thinke so, too" (17). But this can't be why he "abstains" from spoiling her rendition of his lines by exploding them in advance. He *already* "thinkes so." He's already decided on her *role*, so he's already decided on the *breakup*. Unless he changes his mind, he'll let the woman's argument—his argument—win by default.[36]

On the other hand, he may change his mind. So he takes out insurance by saying that he only may, not does, think so. Meanwhile the "too" in "thinke so, too" is another piece of impudence: he's been doing the "thinking" for *both* of them so far.

Feste would know what to think of this performance: "Thy minde is a very opall. I would haue men of such constancie put to Sea, that their businesse might be euery thing and their intent everie where."[37] The speaker has been obliquely (figuratively) confessing and encouraging mental opalescence. The subject of the poem "Womans constancy" turns out to be the grotesque inconstancy of the man who speaks in it. As a phrase uttered by the speaker, "Womans constancy" could only be a bit of sarcastic misogyny, a mock quotation from a hypothetical dupe of women. So as a phrase uttered by the author, the title is a quotation of a quotation, an irony at an irony's expense—in short, a diversionary *littera* that matches and subverts the speaker's.

I promised two examples, but the subject really can't be covered without a third. The version of semantic bad faith in Donne's "Nocturnall upon S. *Lucies* day" is more elaborate, and maybe psychologically deeper, than the ones we've looked at so far.

If the speaker is to be believed, he has been reduced to the purest form ("quintessence") of "nothingnesse" (15), the "Elixer" of the "first nothing" (29). The something he once was made of has been broken down ("ruined") by love and bereavement, and he has been made over ("rebegot") out of "absence, darknesse, death; things which are not" (17–18). He doesn't belong to any category or kingdom of material things—animal, vegetable, or mineral. Unlike him, all of these are "invested" by at least some properties, such as that of preferring "some ends, some means." To be at all is to be this or that kind of thing. Even an "ordinary nothing" has properties, such as the shadow's property of being produced by "a light and body." But the speaker is absolutely nonexistent—an extraordinary nothing (31–36).

We could be forgiven (but just barely) for taking all this literally: being distraught might have worn down the speaker's resistance to bizarre ideas. But the richly self-satisfied quibbler before us doesn't sound especially distraught. And figurational charity reserves the benefit of the doubt for cases in which, taken literally, the speaker is wildly contradicting one of the talk-postulates of common sense—especially when the rest of what he says at the time backs up that very postulate. This is that kind of case: taken straight, the claims aren't just bizarre. The speaker virtually rejects them in the same breath.[38]

It's not only absurd that the speaker should have no properties, not even that of being a speaker. It's false on his own showing, since his property of being a bereaved lover is the obsessive theme of everything he has to say. By the same token, in spite of his denial, he *does* have preferences for "some ends, some means"—at least *three* preferences, again on his own showing: one for being with her; one for "preparing towards" her; one for calling this hour her vigil and her eve.

Again, the speaker knows better than to claim that absence, darkness, and death are "things which are not." If they didn't exist, neither would the sad example of absence, darkness, and death that's troubling *him*.

And shadows aren't nothings. On his own showing, they exist whenever and wherever lights and bodies are lined up the right way. He's right that they aren't physical objects. But then, far from proving them nothings, he's just giving the physical conditions that one class of nonphysical objects depend on for their existence. In fact, all he could actually establish by convincing us that he's made of nothing at all—that he's a nothing-"elixer" or nothing-"quintessence"—is that *he* isn't really a physical object either, *not* that he doesn't exist.

In the same way, something that isn't animal, vegetable, or mineral is immaterial, not nonexistent.

At this point, the game with "nothing" is similar to the game with "nobody" in Hutten's notorious poem of that name: "I am that Nobody the monuments talk about. Nobody gave himself the gift of life. Nobody always existed. Nobody lived in the age when the gods sorted out ill-sorted Chaos. Nobody existed before his birth and after his death. Nobody suffers or acts against God's will. Nobody is all-powerful—etc., etc."[39] Parse the word as a proper noun, as "I am that Nobody" suggests, and you have cosmic bragging. Recognize in "nobody" a term meaning "it's not the case that anybody [always existed, etc.]," and you have a series of truisms. Parse Donne's "nothing" in "elixir of nothing" as a mass term like "butter" or "gold," and you have extravagant self-contempt. Recognize that being made out of nothing is simply not being made out of anything—that is, being immaterial—and you have the familiar if controversial view that persons aren't bodies but merely their owners: "They are ours, though they are not wee."

For self-abnegation, most of this is suspiciously boastful as well as suspicious in the ways we've just looked at. The speaker wants us to know his extraordinary nothingness in the worst way, as if he were campaigning for first prize in a vacuum contest. Studied under fine adjustment, this isn't self-abnegation, it's self-assertion. And Donne's readers, like Hutten's, are probably expected to recall the parallel of Odysseus turning his famous alias "No one" into a tactic of self-preservation. In short, an *extraordinary* nothing is a *figurative* nothing. What's out of the ordinary is the use of the word. We're being hoodwinked by a diversionary *littera*. Love and grief have *figuratively* nullified the speaker. To use the speaker's fancy metaphysical word, they've figuratively stripped him of his "properties."

By the trope rule for metaphor, the (relevant) literal implication becomes the figurative sense. To lack "properties" in the speaker's abstract sense is to lack qualities. But (in Donne's vernacular, at least) for a man to lack a "quality" is for him to lack *social standing* and a *walk of life*. Her death has left him isolated, aimless, *unqualified* for doing the business of the world. This is what it is (figuratively) to be nothing. The same implication comes out in Donne's sermon remark on the vice of *making* oneself nothing: "He that qualifies himself for nothing, does so [viz., makes himself nothing]; He whom we can call nothing, . . . is no limb of this intire body, no part of Gods universal creature, the world."[40] The speaker's nothingness, or general disqualification, isn't "ordinary" but *extraordinary*. It's just the right nothingness for somebody *extra ordinem*, outside the order of things; in short, for a total outsider.

From *nothing* to *unpropertied* to *unqualified:* we're tracing the steps of a metalepsis, or Chinese-box figuration. But we aren't done. The context forces another step. The speaker started by carefully noting the time, and like the speech itself, the time notation is superficially all about despair: the midnight of Saint Lucy's Day is the midnight of the year, when

> The worlds whole sap is sunke:
> The generall balme th'hydroptique earth hath drunk,
> Whither, as to the beds-feet, life is shrunke,
> Dead and enterr'd.   (5–8)

But this particular seasonal end implies a preparation and a beginning, and so does the end of the speech itself:

> Let mee prepare towards her, and let mee call
> This houre her Vigill, and her Eve.

If this hour is her eve, then the next is her day.

We don't quite do justice to the speaker's figurative "nothing" until we notice its pointedly theological nickname: "the first nothing," the pregnant void out of which the universe was created. What we're hearing about isn't a tomb but a womb. The first-glance appearance of self-abnegation and hopelessness is merely diversionary. These were misleading intermediate steps on the way to a figurative meaning that eventually defies them. By telling a story about the deviousness of the speaker's use of words, the "Nocturnall" manages to tell a story about the deviousness of grieving.[41]

Diversionary Littera *as the Rhetoric of Fear*

I want to wind up my survey of the diversionary *littera* in Donne by looking at how it works in the Holy Sonnets, where the speaker uses it in a hysterical effort to deceive the Undeceivable. He's obviously smart enough to know that he can't possibly get away with this, but in the face of the ultimate terror, his wit combat reflexes get the better of him. It's as if he were trying to put off the pronouncement of sentence with a nonstop filibuster, knowing that at any moment a rap of the gavel will silence him for good. His only hope is to *divert* his judge in both senses of the word.

In Sonnet 1, the speaker's religious panic takes the form of a nightmare chase in which the fugitive's escape is blocked at both ends of a corridor:

> I runne to death, and death meets me as fast,
> And all my pleasures are like yesterday;

> I dare not move my dimme eyes any way,
> Despaire behind, and death before doth cast
> Such terrour, and my febled flesh doth waste
> By sinne in it, which it t'wards hell doth weigh.   (3–8)

If "runne," "behind," and "before" are taken literally, it's easy to imagine that rushing toward death is the speaker's attempt to get away from despair. But trying to die more quickly is an *expression* of despair. That's the point of the metaphor. Far from getting away from despair, the speaker is *in* it: it's his own *despair* that's driving him toward death.[42]

His call for help at the start has the same kind of deceptiveness:

> Thou hast made me, And shall thy worke decay?
> Repaire me now, for now mine end doth haste.   (1–2)

If the work's "decay" is taken literally, we have a case of poor workmanship. The least that the Maker can do is repair what he was responsible for botching. But the results of the "decay" the speaker goes on to describe are the results of his own sin, which "weighs" the speaker's "feeble flesh" down to hell. "Decay" is a deceptive metaphor for the *work's* responsibility, not the *workman's*.

The sinner tries to have it both ways—to tell the truth in language that will carry a falsehood to a superficial reader. But the God he believes in is no such reader. The whole effort is doomed. The sinner knows this, but he looks at the truth out of the corner of his eye.[43]

Even his last desperate appeal has a futile dodge in it of the same kind:

> Thy Grace may wing me to prevent his [the devil's] art,
> And thou like Adamant draw mine iron heart.

Take "iron" literally, and it seems that the substance of the speaker's heart is naturally attracted to God, who draws hearts the way adamant draws iron.[44] If "adamant" were bound by the grammar into the same metaphor as "iron," this hopeful suggestion *would* be the meaning: "And thou, O adamant, draw [by mutual affinity] mine iron heart." But we don't need a relation of mutual affinity to plug in between figurative "iron" and figurative "adamant." "Draw *like* adamant" makes good literal sense. It isn't figurative at all. Understood literally, God doesn't need the help of the things he draws to "draw like adamant." He can draw them willy-nilly, but (like adamant) by action at a distance. "Iron" confronts figurative interpretation all by itself: we need to search our talk-postulates for a salient property associated with the *single* figurative term, and unfortunately the salient property is not reassuring.

With "iron" we have another metalepsis: things made of iron are *hard;* hard things are *unyielding*. Even at the middle stage, the relevant association with "hearts" is grim. There is nothing promising in the hardness of a "hard heart," not in the biblically charged dialect of Donne's language community. To be hardhearted is to be naturally resistant to the love of God.

The speaker's diversionary *littera* is a pathetic attempt to distract attention from the utter helplessness figuratively expressed by "iron," as well as by the argument it clinches: that "our old subtle foe so tempteth me, / That not one houre myself I can sustaine" (11–12). Tempting is the only magnetism in evidence here. The adamant that draws this iron is the devil, and "mine iron heart" doesn't really *say* otherwise. What it does is let an inattentive reader *imagine* that it says otherwise. The speaker tries to equivocate to heaven, even though in the back of his mind he knows as well as Macbeth's Porter that this ploy is doomed.[45]

"As long as you do not confess your sins, you are in a certain sense quarreling with God. . . . You are disputing with God."[46] Augustine's notion of dispute here is *litigatio,* lawyerly nit-picking; this is his metaphor for the mixture of aggression and intellectual corruption that underlies a sinner's refusal to confess. In Holy Sonnet 9, Donne seems to refine on Augustine's metaphor. The speaker puts himself forward as an attorney for people in general and himself in particular. A mass verdict of guilty has been handed down, along with a sentence of capital punishment. Both are tainted by species favoritism:

> If poysonous mineralls, and if that tree,
> Whose fruit threw death on else immortall us,
> If lecherous goats, if serpents envious
> Cannot be damn'd; Alas; why should I bee?
> Why should intent or reason, borne in me,
> Make sinnes, else equall, in mee more heinous?

Sins are all hateful, so exempting some kinds of sinners from punishment can't be fair unless their sins are *less* hateful. But the only visible difference is that the sins of the exempted are committed without intent or reason. Why should this feather turn the scale?

The argument is designed to shift the burden of proof onto God—*if* God falls for the semantic illusion of the "sins" of minerals, vegetables, and dumb animals. If he falls for the diversion, he'll hunt for evidence that intent and reason make sins *worse*. But they don't, of course; they just make sins *sins*. They're part of what sinning *is*. Unless goats and serpents disobey the moral law deliberately, their lechery and envy are not excusable but metaphorical. You don't need to be God to see through this.

In short, the lawyer's brief to the court is so desperate it's a joke: if equity is to be saved, forgive everybody—or issue summonses to rocks, vegetables, and livestock. The speaker refines on Augustine's version of spiritual "litigation"—refusal to confess—by simultaneously confessing guilt and ruling out punishment. But the refinement is self-defeating. It boils down to an attack by the lawyer on the judicial temperament of the judge, and even this glibly desperate lawyer sees the stupidity of antagonizing the judge: "But who am I, that dare dispute with thee / O God?" (9–10). Even here the lawyer is still at it. But this judge can be relied on to spot the weaseling in "who am I": speaking out of turn isn't speaking false.[47]

We're given no reason to doubt that the speaker is sincere when he ends with a powerful outburst of loathing for his sins. But he's never denied that they're loathsome, just that they're *more* loathsome than the ones he claims are forgiven. This sophism is an unacknowledged piece of sleaziness the speaker still isn't ready to give up. The heart of it is a diversionary *littera*.

Donne could easily have strengthened his speaker's unfairness argument by replacing the arbitrary exemption of nonhuman "sinners" with the arbitrary predestination of the elect; that is, replacing a bogus difficulty with a genuine and notorious one. But bogus difficulties are part of his subject in this sonnet and the others that interest me here: the unholy alliance of wit and terror.

One fruit of this alliance is the sonnet speaker's technique of dodging responsibility while admitting it. Here he is in Holy Sonnet 2:

> Why doth the devill then usurpe in mee?
> Why doth he steale, nay ravish that's thy right?   (9–10)

If "pen" can mean *authorship* or "bench" can mean *judge*, the same kind of meaning tranformation can let "accomplice to crime *C*" mean *C perpetrator*. When it comes to the theft of the speaker's soul, the devil is at most a *receiver* of stolen goods. But a literal fence can squeak by as a metonymic thief.

Actually, even "fence" is too hard on the devil, who has violated no divine rights here; giving up something you own is one way of exercising your "right" of ownership, and a damned soul is property God has given up. The *literal* usurper of God's right to the sinner's soul is the sinner, who chose to take over and empty the "temple of Thy Spirit" when "I betrayed myself" (7–8). Taken literally, the metonymies soothingly cast both him and God as fellow victims, and put God on his honor to "rise and for Thine own work fight" (11) rather than sit back and be humiliatingly burglarized by Satan.

Taken literally, the speaker's allegory in Holy Sonnet 14 gives the same impression; sin is something that *happens* to the sinner rather than something he *does:*

> I, like an usurpt town, to'another due,
> Labour to'admit you, but Oh, to no end,
> Reason your viceroy in mee, mee should defend,
> But is captiv'd, and proves weake or untrue.
> Yet dearely'I love you,'and would be loved faine,
> But am betroth'd unto your enemie. (5–10)

Even though he loves God dearly and wants to be loved back, he somehow finds himself merely "labouring" to "admit" God, and laboring in vain. As long as we think of somebody struggling to get massive city gates to swing open, this sounds plausible enough. But vainly "labouring" to "admit" God is finding it hard or impossible to accept him; it's a metaphor for inability or reluctance to love, not for loving, much less for loving "dearly."

There's a second suspicious contradiction: to be "betroth'd" to somebody is to be morally "due" or obliged to marry that person: if the speaker is betrothed to the devil, then how can he also be "due" to God and be simply *usurped* by the devil? The speaker's reasoning is either weak or faithless.

But *he* is doing the reasoning! The phantom agent called Reason who conveniently takes the blame for "untruth" is just another diversionary *littera;* you exorcise the phantom person by refusing to misread the personification. The only moral agent in "town" is the speaker. From the Protestant point of view, he's weakly and untruly reasoning away an embarrassing fact: he wouldn't be guilty of sin at all if he weren't *willing* his acts of weakness and untruth, including his acts of rationalization.

And he's the agent conveniently suppressed after passive "betroth'd."

Betrothed by whom? Betrothing is a reflexive action; you do it by "plighting" your "troth"—pledging your *own* truth or loyalty, not by having it pledged by somebody else. There's only one moral agent—weak and untrue; in fact, the town he's supposed to be locked up in is another diversionary *littera*. The closed-up thing under siege by God and praying to be "o'erthrown" is just the speaker, the same speaker who begins and ends by praying to be broken, blown, burnt, enthralled, and ravished by God—in short, to be taken *against his will*. He has been talking all along about his own resisting will and nobody else's.[48]

In Holy Sonnet 14 the speaker uses the diversionary *littera* to conjure up a convenient double—in this case a whipping-boy. The double in Holy Sonnet 6 is his own soul, which is packed off to face the ultimate terror while the speaker is safely unconscious:

> gluttonous death, will instantly unjoynt
> My body,' and soule, and I shall sleepe a space,
> But my'ever-waking part shall see that face,
> Whose feare already shakes my every joynt. (5–8)

Unfortunately, if his soul sees that face, he will, too. The "I" that does the sleeping here is an "I" merely by metonymy of owner for body. The sleep of the body-"I" will spare him nothing: what's meant by "ever-waking part" is the body's owner. That's why fear is *already* shaking his every joint. What he really anticipates after death, for his waking self, not his joints, is that his new fear will just keep on mounting until it confronts its terrible object.

The diversionary *littera* can't persuade him that the terrifying belief he's figuratively expressing is false; all it can do to relieve him is let him imagine he's denying that belief—or defying it, as in "Death be not proud" (Holy Sonnet 10). The cocky challenge to a demon Goliath vanishes as soon as you ask what it is for an event or state to be "proud," and what it is for somebody to *tell* an event or state to stop being something.

Only a person can act proud—can lord it over people. But the subject isn't a person, it's a thing. Lording it over people tends (like the thought of death?) to humiliate or cow them, so metaphor transforms the ordinary person meaning of "be proud" into an implication of the meaning, an implication that relevantly applies to this particular nonperson: *tend to humiliate or cow*.

The same patterns of figurational charity apply to the speech act being mimed here: only something that interprets signals can be coherently *told to do* something. But urging a certain result R usually expresses a wish for R to happen, so when the object of "command" isn't a signal interpreter, metaphor assigns the second-person speech-act *form* a third-person speech-act *implication:* telling death not to be proud toward *me* is saying that I wish I could stop being humiliated or cowed by *it*. Once again, taking personification literally is getting it wrong; taken figuratively, a cocky challenge is unmasked as a confession of dread.

The champion wants his listeners to imagine that he thinks death isn't "mighty and dreadfull," and that he's advancing arguments to prove his point. Why should death "swell" when it's a mere "slave to Fate, Chance, kings, and desperate men"? Why indeed—unless you refuse to be taken in by the diversionary *littera* in "slave" and spot an admission that the world is chock-full of death's *masters*—of killers that make premature and painful dying not merely possible but likely. But this is an admission that death *is* "mighty and dreadfull" after all.

In the serial drama of the Holy Sonnets, Donne's Christian soldier is another Renaissance incarnation of Thraso, the braggart soldier of Roman comedy. He's a Christian Thraso who wants his audience to imagine that his faith leaves no room for fears of death or of what comes afterward.[49]

"Audience" needs to be pressed a little here. You use conversational ploys to get around an *audience;* but here lies a puzzle: what *is* the audience of a soliloquist? How can anybody pass on thoughts to somebody who already has them? This in essence is Augustine's question once again, in the book of one-man dialogues that launches the term "soliloquy"; this is "the very thing I struggle mightily to know." The puzzle of how it's possible to lie to oneself leads to the even darker puzzle of how it is possible to *talk* to oneself. Both suggest a deep fissure in the self doing the talking. And both are part of the story Donne tells in the Holy Sonnets about a terrified corrupter of words.

But this suggests one last puzzle. Why would a Christian poet purposely inflict a terrified word corrupter on his Christian readers? Granted, this is realism of sorts: they'll all have to go through something more or less like this. But why rub their noses in it? The question could just as well be put to the Psalmist as to Donne: why *ever* stoop to showing David wondering in agony if God has given him up?

Maybe the answer is this: for an incurably fissured creature, self-preservation lies in exploiting the fissure. We need to look on at our own twistings and dodges with the same compassionate irony as we've been taught to look on at the speaker's—the same charity that forbids us to see a damned soul in the word corrupter at his ludicrous worst.[50]

V. Herbert

The Diversionary Littera *Dramatized: Semantic Bad Faith*

Herbert is just as interested as Donne in the dramatic possibilities of the diversionary *littera,* and some of his plots are strikingly parallel to those of the Holy Sonnets, although Herbert's are usually much more subtly worked out.

If you take the speaker in "Deniall" literally, *he* wasn't to blame for the mutiny that went on inside him at some earlier date; the mutineers (plural) were his *thoughts*!—disavowal by personification again:

> My breast was full of fears
> And disorder;
>
> My bent thoughts, like a brittle bow,
> Did flie asunder:
> Each took his way; some would to pleasures go,
> Some to the warres and thunder
> Of alarms.   (4–10)

The old metaphor of the soul war gets an exploitative twist here: to hear him tell it, the speaker was merely an innocent bystander at a mob scene. It takes an effort to remind oneself that in this context "some of *my thoughts* would [that is, wanted to] do such and such" is equivalent to "sometimes *I thought* of doing such and such."

The disavowal effect is reinforced by the implications of the speaker's grammatical framework:

> When my devotions could not pierce
> Thy silent eares;
> Then was my heart broken, as was my verse.   (1–3)

Maybe grammatical *camouflage* would be nearer the mark. We naturally read "when . . . then . . ." here as implying that God's refusal to listen is a thing of the past, along with the speaker's heartbreak and the gappiness of his verse. Granted, "when" doesn't *logically* imply this; the speaker wouldn't be contradicting himself if he went on to say that his devotions are still not getting through to God. But *conversationally,* "when" *does* imply that the speaker's trouble is over. His singling out of a mere stage of the trouble would be pointless. By conversational charity we presume that a speaker is innocent of pointlessness until we catch him in the act—as we do next: "As good go any where, they *say*"—present tense. So the "thoughts" are still at it.

Like the buck-passing personification, the past-tense implication (smug reminiscence) is a ploy for keeping down panic, as well as for hiding it. When the pressure gets too high, the whole charade falls apart in a single outburst:

> O that thou shouldst give dust a tongue
>   To crie to thee,
> And then not heare it crying!   (16–18)

The dust is using its tongue to raise a mutinous outcry against the cruel joke of its useless talent for raising outcries. It's not clear whether the speaker is commenting on his past sufferings or just quoting what the thoughts were saying "then." It doesn't matter. Whatever else it does, the exclamation simply points the moral of the story he has been telling—points it *now:* for as long as "then" lasted, an arbitrary God was content to be the giver of a useless gift. And clearly the scandal is still going on: "O cheer and tune my heartlesse breast, / Deferre no time" (26–27). The diversionary *littera* of third-person plural drops away, and the diversionary past tense with it.[51]

The sham of the personified thought gets more elaborate in "Assurance," where the speaker proves his good faith by shouting down a faithless thought:

> Thou said'st but even now,
> That all was not so fair, as I conceiv'd,
> Betwixt my God and me.   (7–9)

If the thought can be trusted, the speaker's league with God is "broke, or neare it." But the speaker disagrees passionately. That league is guaranteed to survive because he signed it by proxy and will keep his side of it by proxy—thanks to Christ, who can't possibly "shrink, or quail." So the "bone" that the thought intruder threw rebounds to choke the thrower, who might as well

> go on,
> Spin out thy thread, and make thereof a coat
> To hide thy shame. (37–39)

The basic sham works as usual. If the personification is taken literally, somebody is saying something the speaker totally rejects. But the literal sense won't march; the somebody is the speaker's thought, and thoughts don't literally talk. On a figurative reading, "My thought says I may be damned" means precisely that I myself think I may be.

Familiar lore suggests a way out here, one the speaker himself plays with when he asks, "Wouldst thou raise devils?" Can the speaker be merely thinking *about* the possibility of his damnation, maliciously suggested by the devil? (Recall Augustine's struggle to identify the owner of the voice in his head.) Unhappily, mere "thinking about" is ruled out here by the speaker's very first words:

> O spitefull bitter thought!
> Bitterly spitefull thought! Couldst thou invent
> So high a torture? Is such poyson bought?
> Doubtlesse, but in the way of punishment.
> When wit contrives to meet with thee,
> No such rank poyson can there be. (1–6)

The speaker isn't being tortured, poisoned, or punished by the mere idea of his own damnation, not if he vehemently believes it to be a mere idea. The poison is so "rank" because his "wit" has contrived to "meet" with it: he has assimilated the idea as a suspicion. He is agonized by it because he suspects it may be true. The resulting "thought" is a slyly personified act of *thinking that*, not just an act of *thinking about*.

It would be much easier to avoid being lulled into accepting the personification as a person if the speaker weren't arguing with it just as if it *were* a person, and with such apparent sincerity. By conversational charity we presume sincerity as long as the evidence allows. But the evidence *does* allow us to accept the emerging picture of a speaker tormented by beliefs that conflict but don't quite contradict each other. He believes that "all *is* fair" between God and him, but it's "gnawing" at him that he may be wrong. Both beliefs belong to him, even though he disowns one of them.

But the concluding flurry of metaphors in which he tries to dispose of that one for good once again tells a different story as soon as you resist a literal reading:

> Now foolish thought go on,
> Spin out thy thread, and make thereof a coat
> To hide thy shame: for thou hast cast a bone
> Which bounds on thee and will not down thy throat.   (37–40)

How does a bone of doubt or scruple choke the thought that threw it? A doubt or scruple *is* a thought. How does a thought stick in a thought's throat? How, if not by continuing to cause anguish—*angor*, "choking"—to the thinker? And again, if a thought is sensibly expected to weave a coat to hide its shame, it will be a figurative thought-coat, or *praetextus*, to hide the shame of the thinker, who calls the thought foolish but lets it "go on." Stripped of the pretext of the diversionary *littera*, this permission is no way for the speaker to disown his thought. On the contrary, it's a way of saying: this thing of darkness I acknowledge mine.[52]

If the speaker of "Church-monuments" manages to take in his listener with his essay in disavowal-by-diversionary-*littera*, it will be partly by making it unexpectedly hard to tell just what is being disavowed. He says he's picked the church crypt to pray in so that his body can benefit while he's busy praying:

> Therefore I gladly trust
> My bodie to this school, that it may learn
> To spell his elements, and finde his birth
> Written in dustie heraldrie and lines;
> Which dissolution sure doth best discern,
> Comparing dust with dust and earth with earth.   (6–11)

In the literal context of "school" and "spell," "elements" are the ABC's. The schoolboy needs to master his ABC's before he can read his pedigree. But the monuments aren't literally a school, much less a body-school. So the relevant sense of *body's elements* takes over: the body has to learn what it's made of if it's going to recognize in the dust on the tombs a symbol of what bodies come from.[53] The dust is "heraldrie and lines" because, like the signs literally so called, it tells about origins. The body will read the lines by "comparing" the dust on the tombs with the dust it's gradually dissolving into: surely a victim of that "dissolution" should find it easy to "discern" the dust pedigree.

The speaker wants the body to learn its origin because its origin is also its destination. Genealogy will help it make itself fit for the final stage of its dissolution—to "fit thyself against thy fall." Rather than give in to "wanton cravings," it can try to be as "tame" and "free from lust" as "these ashes" (17–24).

What part of this lesson is the speaker ashamed of needing to learn? For obviously the schoolboy body can't be taken literally. In the only figurative sense of *lesson* that plausibly applies to the body, the body has notoriously mastered the mortality lesson—by instinct: "The flesh abhorreth naturally his owne sorrowfull dissolution."[54] The alternative is to take the lesson talk literally and "flesh" figuratively. Who *is* in a position to listen to the lesson being taught?

The speaker says the monuments will teach his body while he's occupied elsewhere, but he stays behind: he himself is both the teacher and the pupil. The hidden trope here isn't a personification of the speaker's body. To improvise the missing jargon, it's a corporification of the speaker. In short, *he's* the "flesh," or fleshly *person*, who has yet to learn whatever is being taught.[55]

And what is *that*? One familiar aim of elaborating on the theme that "dust thou art and unto dust thou shalt return" is to put the hearers in their place: "Why art thou proud, O earth and ashes?"[56] That seems to be the point of the scornful "but" in the speaker's final clinching definition: "flesh is but the glasse, which holds the dust / That measures all our time." The glass "also shall / Be crumbl'd into dust" (20–22), though it isn't dust yet. And though the circulating "dust" inside it isn't yet literally dust either, its nickname describes its future. Flesh and blood are a contrivance for reminding us of the time, but in a short time we'll need something to remind us of *them*. The crowning joke on human reminders—"monuments" in the etymological sense—is told earlier, when the speaker is talking about the "Jeat and Marble put for signes," to point out the dead inside: "What shall point out *them*" (italics mine) when they join their contents (12–16)?

So the body is being schooled in humility. It's also making the "acquaintance" (3) of models for imitation: the tame unlustful dead (23). The speaker's decision to "intombe my flesh" is an attempt to "acquire a virtue if you have it not."

These explanations discredit themselves as soon as you try to take them seriously. The genealogy lesson is a sham. Being made out of a cheap material doesn't mean something is cheap. If the speaker accepts this nonsense version of reductionism, why is he so tender toward his "dear flesh"?

Besides, why should the imminence of *being* dust inspire the flesh to *play* dust? It's at least as likely that knowing that "tomorrow we shall die" will make it seem sensible to "eat and drink" like mad; the churchgoing speaker talks as if he never read Isaiah. And how does playing dust replace "wantonness," and so on, with the corresponding virtues? The suggestion that corpses are models of self-control is a joke, and a bad one at that.

These explanations are pretexts again. By process of elimination, the lesson of the dead that the speaker is forcing himself (alias "dear flesh") to learn—is the fact of death. Like "Death be not proud," "Church-monuments" is the story of a speaker trying to stare down his fear. It's also the story of a linguistic perversion: an attempt to own up to the fear—in language that sidesteps the admission if taken literally.

The Diversionary Littera *Dramatized:*
Truancy of the Imagination

In Herbert's dramas of hidden figuration, the intent of the trickster isn't always to carry the trick off. Sometimes being caught out is precisely the point, as if the speaker were saying: I know this would mean just the opposite if taken literally, and I know I'm courting that misunderstanding; but why not imagine the agreeable while submitting to the true? In this kind of case the speech-act force of resorting to the ploy is euphemism or irony or both.

The signal for a figurative reading of the speech act in "Miserie"—self-condemnation—is that, taken literally, the act of condemning doesn't serve the speaker's purpose. If we trust him, he's asking God to let the angels take over man's duty of praise because "man is a foolish thing" (2)—so foolish and corruptly self-indulgent that he "cannot praise thy name" (31) and "cannot serve thee" (43). God doesn't get his just "portion" when "we speak of thee," or even when "we crouch / To sing thy praises" (39–42). So the best thing for God to do is to "let him go" (43). But "we" implies "I," just as man in general implies the speaker in particular, and at the end, after a summary volley of condemnations, the speaker makes the implicit explicit: "My God, I mean myself."[57] So he among the others is "a lump of flesh, without a foot or wing / To raise him to a glimpse of blisse" (74–75). He has been a victim of his own harangue, with its crude vehemence: "a foolish thing, a foolish thing" (2) and cruder sarcasm:

> He doth not like this vertue, no;
> Give him his dirt to wallow in all night:

> These Preachers make
> His head to shoot and ake. (45–48)

Taken literally, as a reason why God should let him go, the disability plea won't survive a close look. We've already been told that man knows well enough "the spring, whence all things flow" (60). He *has* had a "glimpse of blisse," in short. If he talks "as though he knew it not," it's only that "his knowledge winks, and lets his humours reigne" (61–62). The speech itself is proof that one man at least *can* praise God when he wants to: "all brightnesse, perfect puritie, . . . perfection" (32, 36). On the speaker's showing, and especially by his example, man isn't *unable* to serve, simply *unwilling*: "He knows where he can better be . . . then to serve thee in fear" (10–12)—and fond of covering his unwillingness with talk about his incapacity:

> he still doth sing,
> *Man is but grasse,*
> *He knows it, fill the glasse.* (4–6)

The speaker of "Miserie" is condemning himself only if you take his incapacity talk literally, and not as (say) figurative malingering. But a literal reading is ruled out from the beginning. The speaker's request to "let man go," to *re*assign his job to the angels (1), would be pointless if it weren't a reaction to a standing *assignment*. Praise is an *obligation* man has incurred— one that even "the best of men" can't resist trying to get out of:

> They quarrell thee, and would give over
> The bargain made to serve thee: but thy love
> Holds them unto it. (25–27)

Impossibilities can't *oblige*. Even God can't "hold" somebody to one without absurdity. If the quarrelers have yet to give the bargain over, then they're still keeping it—a strange feat if the bargain can't be kept.

The speaker himself not only can but (inadvertently) does keep his side of the bargain by praising the other party. He simply wants to be dispensed from that headache. The safety of numbers made it prudent for him to petition on behalf of "us," but his ruse is transparent even before he drops it. He's petitioning on his own behalf, and this time what would otherwise be an act of self-condemnation is a plea for release from service—an act of begging off.

The self-condemnation is a diversionary *littera*. Here as in the next example, diversion is no expression of love, no exercise in tact. It's just self-protective diplomacy—the speech-act equivalent of a euphemism.

In "Longing" the speech act being dressed in ironic euphemism is much more terrible and desperate than begging off, although its face value is innocent enough. The speaker is urgently praying for the mercy of an essentially merciful God, a God who is not only merciful in himself but the cause of mercy in others:

> From thee all pitie flows.
> Mothers are kinde, because thou art,
>   And dost dispense
>   To them a part:
> Their infants, them; and they suck thee
>   More free. (13–18)

In the speaker's biblical metaphor, the milk of human kindness is drawn from a breast of consolations like Jerusalem's in Isaiah. The motherly God is also Isaiah's: "As one whom his mother comforteth, so will I comfort you."[58] In another metaphor,

> the world's thy book,
> Where all things have their leafe assign'd:
>   Yet a meek look
>   Hath interlin'd. (49–52)

God's care reaches to infinitesimals; no matter how closely packed the names in the list of the saved, the miraculous penman can always fit in one more line.

These sentences of the speaker's are just right for praising God. But praise isn't the act of speech they're serving here. The meaning stays the same, but not the force. As the motherly God looks on silently,

> My throat, my soul is hoarse;
> My heart is wither'd like a ground
>   Which thou dost curse. (7–9)

The speaker is being mercilessly stalled:

> Thou tarriest, while I die,
> And fall to nothing: thou dost reigne,
>   And rule on high,
>   While I remain

> In bitter grief: yet am I stil'd
> Thy childe. (55–60)

Given this strange version of motherliness, "childe" is a bitter mockery. The speaker isn't praising God. The "praise" is one spasm of bitter mockery after another. Similarly, the final "prayer" simply clinches the resulting indictment. The exquisite cruelty of this God comes out in the way he makes people wait while their wounds fester:

> Pluck out thy dart,
> And heal my troubled breast which cryes,
> Which dyes. (82–84)

The prayer, like the praise, is a diversionary *littera*. And so is the self-abasement:

> Behold, thy dust doth stirre,
> It moves, it creeps, it aims at thee:
> Wilt thou deferre
> To succour me,
> Thy pile of dust, wherein each crumme
> Sayes, "Come"? (37–42)

> Lord Jesu, heare my heart
> Which hath been broken now so long,
> That ev'ry part
> Hath got a tongue!
> Thy beggars grow; rid them away
> To day. (73–78)

This dust talk makes sense only if the sense is figurative—only if "pile" means *person with a body made of dust* and "crumme" means *expressive resource (of such a person)*. But the absurd literal sense can be relied on to appease a prince who likes to imagine his subjects as mere heaps of what their bodies are made of. What passes for mercy in that kind of prince is the urge to get rid of an annoying crowd of "beggars" before it gets any bigger.

Again we have an expression with the force of a wildly inappropriate speech act—unless (by figurational charity) we construe it as part of an improvised code. In that new code, it signals a very different act: *self-abasement* is a diversionary *littera*, a deferential cloak for *protest*. Like Lucky's sarcastic theology in *Waiting for Godot*, it's a protest against a "personal God" who "loves us dearly with some exceptions for reasons unknown."

As a serious case against the traditional account of divine Providence, the speaker's protest is a nonstarter; it's simplistic. So the point of creating him by fictive quotation is not to show what a credible challenge to faith looks like. It's to show a faith disturbed by frustration—by "longing"—and at the same time to show a figurative act of speech warped by that disturbance.

In "Love unknown," figuration is warped by the speaker's urge to impose a literal reading, or rather misreading, on *himself*. This time the literal sense is a complaint about God's prankish cruelty, and the figurative sense is a tribute to his ingenious kindness—almost exactly reversing the values of "Longing."

According to the speaker, the heart he offered his lord was thrown by a servant into a

> font, wherein did fall
> A stream of bloud, which issu'd from the side
> Of a great rock.   (13–15)

By figurational charity, we provisionally discount hallucinations on the speaker's part and look for a trope. And the trope couldn't be more familiar to Herbert's audience. "Water flowing from the cliff in the desert was a token and sign to the Patriarchs of the same thing as is figured by wine in the Sacrament."[59] What Calvin means by the "same thing" is the blood of Christ's Atonement. So far, the speaker's "sad" story is simply that he has received the sacrament and has been spiritually "washed" by it. So the first item on his "long and sad" list of mishaps is a rescue by Christ.

The second makes him the butt of a practical joke. To warm his lord's love, "which I did fear grew cold," he sent his heart to "tender" him a sacrificial lamb. At the last instant, the "offering" was abruptly passed up and his heart taken instead (29–37). Again the literal meaning is tentatively put aside. We discount hallucination, if we can.

And we can very easily. We've been helped to another commonplace of religious discourse: "[God] desired mercy and not sacrifice; and the knowledge of God more than burnt offerings" (Hos. 6:6). The speaker thought he could get away with "sacrifice," with going through the motions of worship; but God demanded and got "mercy," a real amendment of life, with all the rigorous testing it involves. So his heart was unceremoniously popped into his lord's "scalding pan" to be softened by "affliction" and even more by a cup of "holy blood" from the "board" of the Communion table (40–45). Sacrament has washed him, and now suffering and sacrament allow him to overcome his spiritual "callousness" (38).

The pun on "tender heart" in "my heart did tender it" (33)[60] works like all puns, by teasing the audience with word or phrase meanings that would obviously be relevant if they could only survive the grammatical building up of the sentence meaning as a whole. In punning, relevance is aborted by grammar.[61] Here the semantic abortion itself acquires a meaning because it's paralleled by the moral failure being described: by an easy show of *tendering*, the heart avoids the work of becoming *tender*.

Now comes the third and meanest piece of mischief: no sooner had he gotten into bed to recover his "strength" by sleeping out "all these faults," than he found the bed full of thorns. Sadly, the malicious prankster must have been the one person he had trusted with his key (47–56). But, of course, the thorns that keep one from sleeping out one's faults are a blessing; that kind of "sleep" is moral truancy. "Let a man examine himself. . . . Many are weak and sickly among you, and many sleep; for if we would judge ourselves we should not be judged."[62] A "thorn in the flesh" keeps one from being "exalted above measure."[63] In short, conscience thorns are another old friend from folklore and Christian homiletics. Everybody knows who plants those thorns:

> Leaue her to *heauen*,
> And to those Thornes that in her bosome lodge,
> To pricke and sting her.[64]

The speaker tries hard to keep his metaphors as accessible as he can. He even supplies a summary explanation at one point

> I did and do commit
> Many a fault more then my lease will bear;
> Yet still askt pardon, and was not deni'd.
> But you shall heare.   (19–22)

And he sneaks in another explanation later on by way of a convenient slip of the tongue: "I found that some had stuff'd the bed with thoughts, / I would say *thorns*" (51–52). He knows perfectly well that the "heart" that was thrown *into* the cauldron is a metonymy for the owner who escapes *from* it; again he conscientiously slips in an explanation of his own trope here (46). Above all, he knows that the essence of his "tale" is the happiness of repeatedly asking pardon and never being denied (21). He should be expecting congratulations on three signs of his master's favor. Instead he despairs of "help," expects his "faintings" to be pitied (2–3), and gets his own metaphors superfluously explained to him on the ground that *"your Master shows to you / More favour than you wot of"* (62–63).

The speaker casually remarks earlier on that the servant who took his heart knew the lord's will "Better then you know me, or *(which is one)* / Then I myself" (9–11; italics mine). Well, by the standard theology the speaker's other "friend," Christ, knows everything perfectly. So the listener isn't Christ but somebody whose knowledge of the speaker is "one" with the speaker's own. For all practical purposes, the listener is *the speaker*![65] Clearly it has to be a bizarre sense of "wot" in which the last-minute explanation he gets from his other self is more than he "wot" of. After all, he's the one who has already broken the good news that "all my scores were by another paid / Who took the debt upon him" (60–61). And he's the deviser and not very surreptitious explainer of the metaphors that give him so much trouble.[66]

Herbert has dramatized the tangles of self-deception abundantly elsewhere, but this particular tangle is unique. As usual, the speaker is busy distracting his own attention from a reality that refuses to be pushed out of the field of vision altogether. Only this time the fuzzy horror at the field's edge isn't God's hatred but his love—unknown only because nervously unacknowledged. The speaker has yet to work himself up to the act of knowing it, of consenting to be happy beyond imagination. So far, it seems, the prospect is too much for him. He needs to be told to quit his clowning. Or rather he needs to tell *himself* this—as he finally does, after sitting through his own performance in silent amusement, punctuated with a few heckling interruptions. In this eerily comic poem, the diversionary *littera* becomes a counter in a game of the self with the self, a game of gaiety and fear.

VI. Dramatic Irony

There's a good deal more to be said about the scenario types in which Donne and Herbert dramatize this form of linguistic sabotage. I hope what I've said so far gives some idea of the range of types, and shows that the main action and topic of this kind of drama is *speech* action.

On the view I've been defending, dramatizing is just narrating with the connective tissue left to be inferred. The full narrative form obscured by ellipsis is: *Once upon a time, someone said Q,* where *Q* is the text of the poem, set off in quotes. Now this expanded form brings out something important about a critical idiom I've been leaning on without comment: "the speaker of *Q*." This casual usage was harmless up to this point. But for what comes next a comment on the expanded form is in order.

Consider two ways of egging on the storyteller: (*a*) Why did the speaker you're talking about say *Q*? (*b*) You relate that someone said *Q*—said it to accomplish what? Question *b* simply attributes the story to its teller ("you") with sequel blanks for the teller to fill in; it doesn't presuppose the existence of a speaker of *Q*. Question *a* does—at least in the vernacular, where it officiously takes the storyteller at his word.

In critic talk, *a* is simply a convenient paraphrase of *b*, but given vernacular habits, the critical use of "the speaker of *Q*" is always in danger of fooling us into forgetting that our only partner in conversation is a storyteller engaged in making up a quotation. He alone is the source of the poem of which *Q* is merely the explicit part. And he is the source of everything about the quotation that establishes the point of making it up. So we always need to allow for the possibility that he's not only quoting *Q* but using it—that *Q* carries a figurative sense even when the common knowledge to base it on isn't in "the speaker's" repertoire.

When a quotation doubles this way as the author's own remark, the figurative sense of the remark is called a dramatic irony. But "irony" is potentially misleading. The speaker *in* the story isn't covering up that particular sense with a diversionary *littera*. The speech act the story is *about,* in other words, needn't be expressing that sense at all. In short, the irony is in the speech of the dramatist, not in that of the speaker. The two speeches are apt to get confused because the same words embody both. But the speeches aren't the same; one is uttered in the actual world, the other in the story world. As usual, difference in context generates difference in meaning, enabling the author to say one thing by quoting another.

Sometimes we have a borderline case: the common knowledge grounding a figurative sense isn't in the speaker's repertoire—and it's his own fault; the missing knowledge is *self*-knowledge. Here the sense *does* get expressed in the story world and would be understood by any competent listener in that world. But for moral reasons the speaker falls short of competence. He misses his own point.

VII. Donne

Speaking Better Than He Knows:
Ironic Figurativeness

In "Twicknam garden," the self-proclaimed lover has come to "this place" (a phrase he repeats compulsively) to "seeke the spring." It doesn't occur to him that finding things isn't easy for somebody who can't make them out because he's "surrounded"—that is (by etymology) *super-undatus*, overwhelmed—"with teares." This consequence of his opening phrase won't fit his immediate argument, in which being drowned in tears is simply being made miserable (by the usual belle dame sans merci). Still, the metaphor narrowed down by the argument to expressing lovesickness comes out in the logic of the emerging situation—in the author's figurative discourse—as the first in a parade of metaphors for *reality distorted in transmission*. The emotion to blame isn't very much like love:

> Blasted with sighs, and surrounded with teares,
>   Hither I come to seeke the spring.
>   And at mine eyes, and at mine eares,
> Receive such balmes, as else cure every thing;
>   But O, selfe traytor, I do bring
> The spider love, which transubstantiates all
> And can convert Manna to gall. (1–7)

What gets ingested as manna gets digested as gall, like the gruesome process that gives spiders the stuff their webs are made of.[67] But ingesting through eyes and ears is perceiving, and so the matching process of digestion is the process of interpreting what one sees and hears. Truth, not food, is being fouled here: the author has used the speaker's words to tell us that this particular spider is a spinner of lies.[68]

One lie is the speaker's fantasy that "this place" or its presiding genius is somehow insulting him, that what the spring needs is the weather equivalent of a stern disciplinarian—a "grave" frost to "forbid / These trees to laugh and mocke mee to my face" (12–13). Another more fundamental lie is the speaker's diagnosis of his distress:

> But that I may not this disgrace
>   Indure, nor yet leave loving, Love let mee
>   Some senslesse peece of this place bee. (14–16)

If we go by the speaker's dictionary, you can be actively in love and brain dead, too; in fact, that's the lover's ideal state.

By the third stanza, his self-absorption has cut him off completely; no more references to "this place." Earlier his emotion was an upside-down transubstantiation, and hence a perversion of what some believers think goes on in the sacrament of Communion, the "feast of love" par excellence. Now his tears are love's "wine,"[69] as if he were reenacting Christ's wedding miracle at Cana:

> Hither with christall vyals, lovers come,
>   And take my teares, which are loves wine
>   And try your mistresse Teares at home,
> For all are false, that tast not just like mine.   (19–22)

The tears of true love are like the speaker's—salty; but so, surely, are the tears of *false* love? The truth we're being teased with is a cheat.

But a cheat is apparently as much truth as we're entitled to expect on this subject:

> O perverse sexe, where none is true but shee,
> Who's therefore true, because her truth kills mee.   (26–27)

The exception to feminine fickleness proves the rule: a woman who's faithful to somebody else merely to spite *me*! Of course; just like those trees he told us about—"laughing" only to "mock me to my face." Every maudlin or petulant note in the speaker's love complaint is at the same time a comment, from a vantage point outside the fiction, on what it's like to be "sicke of selfe-love" and to "taste with a distemper'd appetite."[70]

Herbert

Comic Irony as the Idiom of Divine Love

When people in tragedy speak better than they know, they also speak worse. Given the talk-postulates we share with the author but not with the speaker, the speaker's own words damn him. The comic version of this tragic semantics is words that bless unawares, or that embody a chance for blessing if only they're noticed; and the master comedian in this vein isn't Donne but Herbert.

In Herbert's "Peace" the speaker's story of his spiritual career takes the form of a mythlike string of metaphors. If we take the string literally, the search for Peace is an enhanced folktale with the same basic shape as Psyche's search for Cupid. It even conjures up the same kind of uncannily featureless landscape we get in Apuleius's romance, complete with magical encounters in the same tone of mock-naive matter-of-factness.

Taking the advice of the wind in the "secret cave" to "seek elsewhere," the searcher notices a rainbow farther on:

> Surely, thought I,
> This is the lace of Peaces coat:
> I will search out the matter. (8–10)

It's a riddle, but the riddler plays fair. If a rainbow is the lace of X's coat, then X's coat is the sky; if X's coat is the sky, then X is God. If Peace is X, then God is peace (i.e., the source of peace). But the rainbow breaks up, and the speaker is disappointed again by the worm he finds at the root of the crown imperial. In short, he learns by sad experience that reflective solitude (cave), natural beauty (rainbow), and political power (crown imperial) don't bring peace.

So much for the speaker's own narration. It's metaphorical, but these are *his* metaphors, and we've been given no reason to suspect that he doesn't know what he's saying.

At this critical point in the story, the teller quotes the metaphors of the informant he meets next, the "rev'rend good old man" who tells him about a murdered Prince of Salem (Hebrew for "peace"): "after death out of his grave / There sprang twelve stalks of wheat" (27–28). The wheat of the Apostles' sacramental message has spread since; it has "a secret vertue bringing peace and mirth / By flight of sinne," and it grows in the old man's garden (22–42). Like Melchisedek, the old prince of Salem and type of Christ, the speaker's informant is a priest. "In Christ we are all priests, but unto praise and thanksgiving, and unto the offering of ourselves and ours to God."[71] The metaphorical recipe for peace is the sacrament of the Eucharist (Greek for "thanksgiving"). So *if* the speaker still knows what he's saying, his story has a happy ending, along with his search.

But actually the speech activity he's engaged in isn't *saying* at all; it's *quoting*. Until he pays attention to his own story, the search is doomed to continue. The speaker inadvertently lets us know this just before he begins the story:

> Sweet Peace, where dost thou dwell? I humbly crave,
> Let me once know. (1–2)

As of the speaker's most recent report, the search is still on. It's as if the reverend old man had never spoken.

In the act of figuration, a new language is taught and spoken at the same time, or taught by being spoken. The listeners cooperate as well as show their uptake by answering back in the new language, or developing it. "OK, have it your own way: he's the cream in her coffee. But given the way she treats him, she's allergic to coffee." There's a danger in this. Uncomprehending listeners might pretend or even think they're *using* the proposed language when they're simply *reciting* it. They're likely to produce nonsense; but with luck, they just might succeed in saying something, without knowing what.

In "Peace" Herbert gives us a case of an urgent figurative message ignorantly relayed in this way. The speaker repeats it as if he knew what he was saying. Only at the end do we realize that he doesn't. Here the effect is tragicomic: a truth he has been looking for all his life is under his nose but out of his reach—a truth he manages to give but still fails to get.

Inadvertent figurativeness interests Vaughan, too—probably because it interested Herbert first. But the effect is instructively different. The speaker of "Man" has been envying the regular habits of "mean things" like birds, bees, flowers, and magnets, all of which keep the "divine appointments" of natural law as if they were not only clocks but "watchful" clocks guided home by "some hid sense their Maker gave"—all this in contrast with man, who "knows he hath a home" but "hath quite forgot how to go there."[72] The contrast ends with a resonant definition:

> Man is the shuttle, to whose winding quest
>   And passage through these looms
> God order'd motion, but ordain'd no rest.   (26–28)

Acting on the usual presumption of innocence means trying to make this metaphor sum up the speaker's argument. But the most that figurational charity can do here is see why the speaker made the mistake of thinking the metaphor sums up his argument.

He wants to show that man is "ever restless and Irregular," and a shuttle might just qualify as restless—though as the speaker uses it, "restless" means habitually breaking one's appointments with one's master, and the restlessness of a shuttle is as punctual to its master's rendezvous as clockwork. By the same token it's as *regular* as clockwork, not only in its motion but in its function of distinguishing and coordinating the warp and woof of the fabric it turns out.[73] By ancient association, a shuttle is a *canon* or *radius,* an instrument for measuring—in this case, measuring an order it helps create. Being a shuttle just *is* being regular; so it would take some doing to get it to be a metaphor for irregularity. And the doing hasn't been tried.

In short, the speaker is wrong about what his metaphor means in the system of communication he's trying to use. The resulting mistake is the figurational equivalent of a malapropism. But a speaker's malapropism tends to be his author's point.

Here, in fact, it's *more* than one point, since the metaphor itself is transformed into still another by metalepsis: this particular shuttle is engaged in a "winding quest / And passage through these looms." It's playing Theseus to the loom's labyrinth, and it owes its safe passage to being guided just as steadily as birds and magnets—and guided by a lover. The divine weaver is a divine Ariadne, and his benign thread does double duty in the *littera* of both metaphors. For the speaker, the restless motion God "order'd" is motion *commanded.* For the author, it's motion *shaped into an order*—an order known to the weaver but not to the shuttle.

As in Herbert, a malaprop attempt at griping comes out as a celebration, letting the structure of meaning show us in one last subtle way what weavers know and shuttles don't. There's none of Herbert's comic energy in Vaughan's treatment of the figurational malapropism. What makes up for its lack is a powerful effect of gradual disclosure of meaning that we'll have to look at more carefully in chapter 7.

My last example of Herbert's drama of skewed figuration is a suitable place to call a halt; figurative speech is precisely what the speaker of "Jordan (II)" is talking about. If he's to be believed, he's a reformed metaphorist who has taken the pledge:

> When first my lines of heav'nly joyes made mention,
> Such was their lustre, they did so excell,
> That I sought out quaint words, and trim invention;
> My thoughts began to burnish, sprout, and swell,
> Curling with metaphors a plain intention,
> Decking the sense, as if it were to sell.   (1–6)

The speaker hasn't quite made up his mind here about his old motive. Was it a well-meant effort to find words "quaint" and "trim" enough to do justice to the joys of heaven?[74] Or was it a mean if unconscious longing to get paid in applause for his description?

On this second theory, metaphor doesn't *express* meaning; it *decorates* it by substituting a deviously "curly" description of heavenly joys for a "plain" nonfigurative one. But *is* there a plain description—of things that "eye hath not seen, nor ear heard" (1 Cor. 2:9)? Saint Paul doesn't think so, and it's strange that the speaker does. If there isn't, then an apt metaphor for a heavenly joy no more decorates it than "needle's eye" decorates the notion of a needle's eye. What the metaphor does is christen the joy. If heavenly joys really transcend ordinary experience, if they really "trample on [the sun's] head" (12), then the language you improvise to talk about them is an attempt to reveal, not "clothe" them (11).

But the speaker turns out to favor the fancy clothes theory, combined with a charge of narcissism:

> As flames do work and winde, when they ascend,
> So did I weave my self into the sense. (13–14)

The act of metaphorizing is an act of self-advertisement. Fortunately a "friend" saw through all this "bustle" just in time:

> There is in love a sweetnesse readie penn'd:
> Copie out only that, and save expense. (17–18)

The trouble is that the whole speech-act type on display here is misleading. The speaker is giving us a gently self-mocking memoir of how his literary vanity was brought up short by a "friend's" timely advice. The implication is that the advice took; but obviously it hasn't. The use of "decking the senses" and "curling with metaphors" is itself an act of semantic "decking" and "curling." So is the notion of thoughts that "burnish, sprout, and swell" like explosively growing vegetation; or the notion of egoism and meaning as flames, or flames as interwoven strands. If verbal artifice is a corrupt game, then he's still playing. It seems that artifice is addictive.

In fact, the parallel failure of his fellow antimetaphorist in "Jordan (I)" shows that renouncing artifice is itself an artifice: In a virtuoso display of one-upmanship the "Jordan (I)" speaker danced through some shrewdly knowing parodies of the conventions of secular love poetry, parodies that transcend themselves by taking on a crazy life of their own:

> Is it no verse, except enchanted groves
>   And sudden arbours shadow coarse-spunne lines?
> Must purling streams refresh a lovers loves? (6–8)

where the diversionary *littera* of "shadow" and "refresh" momentarily suggests a scenic description hexed into the scene it describes. The "Jordan (I)" speaker wound up with a display of rugged simplicity, all short declarative sentences almost completely unspoiled by connectives or dependent clauses: "Shepherds are honest people"—stop—"let them sing"—stop—"Riddle who list, for me, and pull for Prime"—stop—"I envie no man's nightingale or spring."

We know from his earlier performance that this spokesman for simple shepherds is no simple shepherd. The new country style is another piece of one-upmanship: he could match the city poets if he wanted to, but he scorns to do it for reasons he has just gone into. He claims to be asking for no more than fair play. He doesn't begrudge the sophisticates their nightingales and riddles, and they should return the compliment by letting honest Christian shepherds alone to sing "My God, my King."

But he has just finished a long exercise in begrudging, and his final show of artlessness is a last shot—a last artful shot, all the more artful for being borrowed from the city poets' arsenal. The whole strategy of the gruff anti-Petrarchist love poet is an oblique attack on the verbal affectations his foppish rivals go in for. Compare Sidney in the same vein:

> Some do I hear of poets' fury tell,
> But God wot, wot not what they mean by it.

We know Sidney's speaker is just putting on all that hearty cacophony ("God wot, wot not what"). Astrophil can outflorid the best of them. The point is: he disdains to do it. Like him, and like the hero of "Jordan (II)," the "Jordan (I)" speaker campaigned against figuration—a style in which "he that reades, divines, / Catching the sense at two removes" (9–10). But one style has merely been replaced by another. When it comes to speech, there's no such thing as going naked.

The "friend's" advice in "Jordan (II)" is to copy out the "sweetnesse readie penn'd" in your own experience, penned presumably by somebody else (17); that way you save the expense of penning something for yourself. But to copy out the handiwork of one penman takes another. The original may be ready penned, but the copy is a specimen of one's own handwriting. For one's own love to be "ready" for copying is for one's inner experience to be (uniquely) available for representation—representation in some medium or other. Metaphor is such a medium, and the friend's "pen" and "copy" talk shows that it's a medium he himself isn't above using.

In fact, the net effect of his advice is to do for the speaker's phobia about self-affirmation what the speaker himself has done for his phobia about metaphors: expose it as a clown version of Puritanism. The speaker hasn't been recoiling from vanity but from self-affirmation in general—as if the Gospel promises themselves weren't precisely an appeal to a higher self-interest. Heavenly joys aren't meant for an undifferentiated mass; they're meant for individuals: "The Scriptures not only promise life eternal to the faithful but a specific reward for each."[75] In Herbert's religious tradition, the Augustinian tradition, individualism is a rock-bottom axiom. It's the home charity begins at: "When it was said: 'Love thy neighbor as thyself,' at the same time the love-of-thyself-by-thee was not passed over."[76]

In one way, the speaker hasn't been individualistic or self-centered *enough:* he's been trying to write about heavenly joys[77]—things necessarily beyond his experience. The "friend" advises him to write about his own love of God, and hence to write about himself. Self-promotion is the wrong way to weave oneself into the sense. The antidote is to do it right, by bearing witness.

In the "Jordan" poems the author manages to write a defense of his art of obliqueness by letting some adversaries have their say. For this to happen, the sense of the poem has to be counterpointed against the sense of the quotation it coincides with—"while he that reades, divines, / Catching the sense at two removes."

Chapter Six

Figuration and Retort

1. *Retort as Scheme and Trope: Kinds of Retort*

As I've been insisting up to this point, figurativeness happens only in conversation, and only if the cooperative talk custom of the partners *makes* it happen. This doesn't mean that it can't happen unless the partners go along with the custom; it's not the talkers but the talk that needs to conform. When the talk does and the talkers don't—when they fail to get the point or say something they didn't mean to say—we simply have unnoticed or unintended figurativeness. What gets killed by failure to cooperate isn't meaning, it's success in getting the meaning across—in a word: communication.

But communication is a hardy organism. There is at least one kind of obstructionist behavior that doesn't kill it but signals, on the contrary, that it's still alive. I'm talking about the large family of countermoves in talk that go by the traditional name of retorts. In retort—Cicero calls it "the answerer's barb"[1]—failure to go along with one's partner's improvised meanings is itself an act of improvising meaning. Literally described, what the act communicates is a refusal to communicate. But taking the retort literally is only the first step in getting it right.

Retort in general is frankly bogus misunderstanding behavior of one sort or another, with the intended effect of letting the target know that he hasn't really been misunderstood.[2] By way of handicapping in the competitive game of repartee, the target has had the benefit of figurational charity—but that's all the charity he's going to get. The specific force of the misunderstanding behavior varies. In Cicero's convenient list, the back-talker is defeating his opponent, or frustrating his attack, or belittling him, or scaring him off, or proving him wrong, or spreading himself, or dancing away from objections.

The simplest formula is to use one's opponent's phrase to mean some-

Figuration and Retort | 141

thing subversively different from what he's just used it to mean. Cicero tells about the foot-in-mouth defense attorney who "thought that in summing up his client's plea, he had inspired pity in the judges; so on taking his seat he asked if his opposite number thought so too. 'Yes indeed, profound pity,' the other replied; 'I think there's no human being so heartless he wouldn't find your speech pitiful.' "³ In the normal conversation game, uptake is signaled by adopting one's partner's metaphor and extending it. In the retort version, only the target's literal sense is adopted and extended; the figurative sense—the sense of his phrase as actually used—is conveniently replaced.

One seventeenth-century theorist of retort illustrates the effect with the story of what happened when the triumphant Mark Antony had

> approached Athens with a great army, and had put a story in circulation that he was [the incarnation of] the god Bacchus conqueror of the East: the Athenians came out humbly to surrender up to him themselves and their city, the namesake of Athena—a thing that had never happened before. They said to him: "We pledge our [virgin patroness] Athena to you in marriage, O father Bacchus." Antony replied to them: "I accept her: but I command one thousand talents by way of dowry." The Athenians: "O master—but Jupiter accepted your mother [Semele] *without* a dowry."⁴

Up until the Athenians' winning move we have the normal game: myth language being used *figuratively* to negotiate the terms of surrender. But Jupiter's affair with Semele is a precedent for "dowry" withholding only if you take the myth talk *literally;* the Athenians have suddenly started refusing to get the point—for obvious reasons.

In a variant of retort illustrated by the same anecdote, the opponent's metaphor is replaced with a twin: the same literal sense (ostensibly) applied to the same subject matter, but with a figurative sense that's mischievously different. The unblinkable fact about the Jupiter-Semele affair is that he came to her in the shape of lightning: her marriage bed was her pyre. In short, the Athenians have found a graphic metaphor for the kind of "marriage" with Roman occupation that their city can look forward to.

The poets whose way with metaphor is the subject of this book ring a variety of interesting changes on retort. For them it becomes virtually a mode, a basis for shaping kinds of writing. Next a close look at some of their inventions.

II. Crashaw's Gospel: Coopting as Retort

When Crashaw took up the assignment of writing a series of "sacred epigrams," his models may have given him a hint for the form of retort that his enterprise eventually took on. But the hint is fuzzy at best; we don't find anything quite like the special kind of comic-allusive literary dialogue he pioneers. Jakob Biedermann comments on a picture of the boy Jesus as an apprentice carpenter sweeping up wood shavings: Jesus shouldn't waste his energy; he'll have much bigger pieces of wood to carry—and be carried by. Bernaard Baauwhuys comments on a picture of the child Jesus carrying a cross: Please stop, you're not old enough. The child's reply: I'm practising on this beginner's size just so I'll be equal to the bigger size when it comes along—and you should do the same![5]

These limp whimsies are more emblem poems than retorts. They realize the figurative implications of the pictures instead of turning those implications upside down. There are retorts *in* the poems, but the wit is the Christ child's, not the speaker's—with a donnish nod to the classics in the Baauwhuys.[6] The metaphorical notion of Christ as a master of the sharp comeback[7] can have a remarkable emotional and moral complexity in the hands of a master, and I'll come back to it when I talk about retort in Herbert. But the dialogue dimension of Jesuit epigram, though it's there, didn't have much to teach Crashaw in his special line of territory. The partners in conversation Crashaw retorts on in *Sacred Epigrams* are none other than the authors of the Gospels.

One striking way of getting directly acquainted with his approach is to confront his treatment of a particular Gospel text with something more standard by an earlier writer of sacred epigrams. In Acts 12, the chains slip all by themselves from the arms of the sleeping Peter as an angel wakes him to free him from Herod's prison. Peter "knewe not that it was true, which was done by the Angel, but thoght he had sene a vision." François Remond's speaker guesses that Peter would rather not believe his eyes: "[Not yet awake,] he fears the false shapes—shapes that bear a true image [of his release]. He looks, and thinks that what he's seeing is a figment. No wonder: maybe if he were awake he would never allow himself to be released from the prison [and hence from the martyr's glory] that he has been longing for."[8] There's no retort here at all. The speaker isn't reacting snappily to something he's just witnessed (there's no suggestion here that he's a mind reader).

But snappy reaction—by somebody on the scene—is the main ingredient in Crashaw's treatment of the same episode. The instant witticisms are an old friend from chapter 3. We're already pretty well satisfied that Crashaw's speaker can't resist a bon mot, here or elsewhere. What's of interest here is that his heckling is part of the action in the Gospel scene itself. The speaker is an eyewitness.[9] He's just been watching Peter's chains slipping off and the jail doors opening of their own accord. He can't get over it—though as usual he can't resist trying to make a good thing even better: "Iron is forgetting what iron is like! For Peter's good, the chains are donning a disguise! How thoroughly set free he'll be, set free by his own jail! How thoroughly safe, unchained by the chains themselves!"[10]

Like Lucio in *Measure for Measure*, the holy Jester is a compulsive mood breaker. He refuses to play dumb on the fringes of a great event; he would much rather upstage it by playing off it, like a vaudeville top banana with his straight man, or (more to the point) a Renaissance fool with his zany. He uses the events he thrusts himself into as cues for a retort. And since he's (fantastically) on the scene of a book he's read, he can even cheat a little here and there, by using hindsight as foresight. So Jesus warning his disciples about how the word of God falls among thorns is seconded with a prophetic retort: "I well believe it! For you too, Christ, are God, the Word, and—ah, only too obviously—you fall among thorns!"[11] As usual, the retort achieves its point only by a burlesque of missing the previous speaker's point. And as usual, the holy Jester is undaunted by the fact that the previous speaker is Jesus. A friend is somebody you're not afraid to take liberties with.

Jesus is perfectly equal to snapping out sharp replies of his own, of course: "Ye are of your father the devil, and the lustes of your father ye wil do." His persecutors retaliate by returning the compliment: "Say we not wel that thou . . . hast a deuil?" Jesus' next effort is to the point—but unfortunately, not pointed: "I haue not a deuil, but I honour my Father, and ye haue dishonored me."[12] This is just too plain, too downright, for one of the bystanders, at least. The holy Jester steps in with something more to his taste—something that plays on the central absurdity of mistaking Christ for the devil: "Being blind, you did not know God—that could happen. But I ask you: could it happen that you're so bad at spotting your own father?"[13] Again in Luke we have Christ's correction of some well-intentioned but shallow praise:

> WOMAN. Blessed is the wombe that bare thee, and the pappes which thou hast sucked.
> CHRIST. Yea, rather blessed are they that heare the worde of God, and kepe it.[14]

This is gentle, but not nearly witty enough to suit the Jester; the way to handle the woman's remark is to replace it with a straw man:

> THE JESTER [to the woman]. Suppose he had been Tabled at *thy* Teates,
> *Thy* hunger feeles not what *he* eates:
> Hee'l have his Teat e're long (a bloody one).
> The Mother *then* must suck the Son.
> (Italics mine)[15]

"[What makes you think Mary's hunger was miraculously satisfied by satisfying Jesus'?] *Yours* wouldn't have been! [On the other hand, maybe you have a point.] Her nourishment [and perhaps yours] will come later— by blood, not milk." But the woman's point about the paps' blessedness was obviously *not* that suckling Jesus was the literal equivalent of being suckled oneself. This time, with blithe high-handedness, the speaker is retorting on words he's put into his victim's mouth, and he adds insult to injury by going on to follow this up by finding metaphorical sense in the fantasy paradox of the suckler suckled, a notion he himself has just foisted on the woman and then dismissed on a literal reading. It's a tour de force of conversational mischief.

The speaker isn't shy about giving lessons in repartee to Christ. So it isn't surprising to find him elsewhere happily forcing his services on the Apostles.

The Holy Spirit has descended in fire on the heads of the disciples at Pentecost, bringing them the gift of speaking in tongues. There are the usual hecklers to deal with: the disciples aren't inspired, merely "ful of newe wine." Unfortunately, Saint Peter's retort technique is no more likely to satisfy Crashaw's speaker than Jesus': "These are not dronken, as ye suppose, since it is but the thirde hour of the day."[16] As if midmorning would stop a drunkard! This is poor stuff; surely a mock calls for a mock. The speaker comes to Peter's rescue with a virtuoso demonstration of how to mix sarcasm and rapture:

THE JESTER [to Peter's mockers]. Spread your robes wide, spread
them: the vintage of heaven is coming down; a holy vintage is
rolling from the hills of heaven. More than happy are those who
drink so good a new wine; into their laps comes the bright
winter [harvest]! Look at their heads! Look how they gleam and
gleam with heaven's wine! Gods above, who would refuse to be
drunk like *this*? The torch that lights *these* revellers home, to
keep them from stumbling, is their own wine! [17]

The retort pleads guilty to the accusation—only after reading the accusation as metaphorical applause.

The Jester thinks nothing of putting in a retort where his betters have chosen not to answer at all. Thus the High Priest accuses Jesus of blasphemy, and the charge gets put down, and trivialized, with a standard burlesque of misunderstanding—as if the priest's sin weren't (by a talk-postulate of Crashaw's religious culture) an inexcusable failure of recognition; just a crazy mistake in logic: "You attack Christ for not denying he's Christ. The charge against him is that he's—himself! Am I supposed to think you're a priest? A new brand of priest: by whom God is forbidden on pain of retribution—to be God!" [18]

Not that the rest of the speakers in the Gospel world the Jester intrudes into don't somehow catch the knack of retort from his contagious presence. Even the blasted fig tree seizes an opportunity to show off something like the Jester's mastery of the quick paradoxical comeback: dry up? delighted to; to obey *this* master's direct order to bear no more fruit—is to bear better fruit than ever.[19] Saint John, the Virgin Mary, and Christ himself talk in the same combative-whimsical idiom. Christ to Doubting Thomas: "Savage faith! Is this the way to wish to 'touch' my griefs? Cruel fingers! Is this the way to 'learn' divinity? To stop your doubting, you want to touch my wounds: the deeper wounds are the ones *you make* by doubting!" [20]

The Jester himself eventually sees the silence Jesus answers his accusers with as the retort to end all retorts—the supremely communicative refusal to communicate: "He says nothing: . . . how weighty that nothing was! He once said a word and made the world. Now he makes the world over by saying no word at all." [21]

In short, Crashaw's collection is a dialogue with gaps to be filled in from the text it assimilates to itself—a witty dialogue punctuated with retorts. But this doesn't quite capture the essence of his conversational sleight of hand here. The book as a *whole* is a single grand retort on the Gospels, which it frames, and hence includes in an expanded version. In addition to the dialogue of Crashaw's anachronistic speaker with the figures *in* the story, we have his dialogue *about* the story, with the storytellers. This comes out explicitly in the epigrams in which the storytellers are the people he interrupts.

> JOHN. Christ was walking in Solomon's porch, and it was winter.
> THE JESTER. Winter? No, no it wasn't—not in the presence of
>   that face. Or if it was winter, it wasn't the winter that comes
>   back every year, not a winter true to its own nature.[22]

In fact, Crashaw's retort on the Gospel is as lovingly elaborate as it is loving. The Jester turns up in the cast of characters at three levels of narrative: Jesus' parables, the story the Gospel tells about Jesus, and the overarching story of the Jester's challenges to the Evangelists themselves—the story of the irrepressible heckler in the margin.

III. Parody and Retort in Herbert

In what remains of this chapter I'd like to look in detail at some of Herbert's many experiments with retort.

The competitive extreme of retort is to *parody* the speech being retorted on—to match your opponent's language phrase for phrase and cadence for cadence while twisting or contradicting the sense. There's some serious parody going on in the sacred epigrams we've looked at. But Herbert's own "Parodie"—on a poem by the earl of Pembroke—is more elaborate and, in its way, more cunningly subversive than anything in Crashaw. In Pembroke's poem a departing lover is using his valediction, à la Donne, to forbid mourning:

> Soules joy, now I am gone,
>   And you alone,
>   (Which cannot be,
> Since I must leave my selfe with thee,
>   And carry thee with me)
>
>   Yet when unto our eyes
>   Absence denies
>   Each others sight,

> And makes to us a constant night,
> When others change to light,
>
> O give no way to griefe,
> But let beliefe
> Of mutuall love
> This wonder to the vulgar prove:
> Our Bodyes, not wee move. . . .[23]

This is Donne material, but obviously the heart has gone out of it. The old gestures are being executed rigidly, with a stifled yawn. But maybe something can be made of them—and here *made of* needs emphasis: Herbert finds a way of turning Pembroke's lines retroactively, with a crucial twist in meaning, into a dramatically functional part of his own poem.

The Pembroke lover has been assuring the lady that because his absence is just an illusion there's nothing for the lady to mourn. In language that mischievously echoes the lover's cadences, Herbert's speaker refuses to buy this: what prompts—and deserves—mourning is precisely the illusion. Illusions too can hurt, even when you aren't taken in by them:

> Souls joy, when thou art gone,
> And I alone,
> Which cannot be,
> Because thou dost abide with me,
> And I depend on thee;
>
> Yet when thou dost suppresse
> The cheerfulnesse
> Of thy abode,
> And in my powers not stirre abroad,
> But leave me to my load:
>
> O what a damp and shade
> Doth me invade!
> No stormie night
> Can so afflict or so affright,
> As thy eclipsed light.
>
> Ah Lord! do not withdraw,
> Lest want of aw
> Make Sinne appeare. . . .

"Withdrawal" is just as agonizing as absence. Having no sense of your lover's presence is enough to make you "half beleeve" in his absence—as the sin of despair is always tempting the speaker to do:

> O what a deadly cold
> Doth me infold!
> I half beleeve,
> That Sinne sayes true....

I think I've said enough to bring out the strategy of Herbert's retort. The lover being addressed in his poem is Christ. The reassurance we're not supposed to need but need anyway isn't the sight of the loved one but the "cheerfulness" and perceptual glow ("powers") that tell us Christ is "here." In short, the debate between the two speakers won't hold together—unless you pretend to miss Pembroke's unmissable point and take the Pembroke lover figuratively, as a metaphor for Christ, like the lover in the Song of Songs. Herbert retorts on Pembroke by replying to the poem Pembroke should have written but didn't. That revised version fills the gap in the elliptical dialogue of "Parodie"—the reassurance by Christ that launches the soul on its paradoxical agony: it's been told something it knows is true and yet doesn't quite believe.[24]

In "The Quip," retort is a crucial part of another sort of meaning entanglement. The quipsters in the story aren't literally quipsters. The quip that puts them down isn't literally a quip. And even if we take the story literally, the retort we hear about is distinctly unorthodox: it's wit by proxy. Like his counterpart in the psalm being echoed in the refrain,[25] the speaker is "as one that is dumb, who doth not open his mouth"—but his mockers won't go unanswered: "Thou shalt answer, Lord, for me."

But there's a problem about what it is to "answer" mockers called Beauty, Money, Glory, and Wit-and-Conversation—four temptations, or (in the speaker's metaphor) four troopers in the "train-band" (the citizen militia) of "the merrie world." The mockery troubling the speaker is frustration, and the self-reproach that goes with it. Here, for example, is Beauty:

> First, Beautie crept into a rose,
> Which when I pluckt not, Sir, said she,
> Tell me, I pray, Whose hands are those? (5–7)

The speaker is kicking himself for passing up pleasures, especially the aesthetically refined pleasures he likes best: after all, who owns his will—

or his resources for acting on his will (his "hands")—if *he* doesn't? On the other hand, maybe there *is* something paltry about the life of, say, a music lover, in comparison with a life spent wielding power of one kind or another; the power of the purse, for example:

> Then Money came, and chinking still,
> What tune is this, poore man? said he:
> I heard in Musick you had skill.   (9–11)

An ear for where the profit is coming from is the only ear worth developing. There's a price to be paid for *not* doing what's necessary to make it. You get snubbed by people who *do,* like Glory the fop, who "scarce allow'd me half an eie" (15). Or you meet people with a reputation for talents you have and they don't—like the allegedly "quick" Wit-and-Conversation, whose idea of being "short" is to "make an Oration" (19).

What is it to answer *for* the speaker when the person to be answered *is* the speaker? What is it to answer emotions rather than remarks? The sense of "answer for" that works when you take the story literally cancels itself as soon as you stop. But that's all right; there's an alternative sense that's just as idiomatic: Christ will *make himself answerable* for the speaker. He will *take responsibility for* him—and do it by springing the "quip" of the title:

> Yet when the houre of thy designe
> To answer these fine things [i.e., bons mots] shall come;
> Speak not at large; say, I am thine:
> And then they have their answer home.   (21–24)

But back to the story (the literal sense) again: the speaker has been insisting that Christ will answer for him—will spring a quip; where is it?

Joseph Summers suggests that "Say, I am thine" has a double meaning,[26] but I don't think this works. The speaker is making the following request of Christ: "Say, I am thine." The proposed double meaning would be: "(*a*) say *that* I am thine; (*b*) say [the sentence] "I am thine." If Jesus complies with *a,* he'll affirm that the speaker belongs to Jesus. If Jesus complies with *b,* he'll affirm that Jesus belongs to the speaker.

I have two qualms about *b,* the quotation half of this reading. The first is merely formal—though if it's well taken it has a cautionary point to make about one kind of "reading-in" (that is, misreading)—the kind that amounts to repairing unbroken clocks. The second qualm is substantive and leads us to the center of Herbert's retort design in the poem.

Now it's true that *b* tells us enough to let us know what Jesus *would* be saying *if* he used the quoted words. But the fact remains that in *b* itself, the quoted words refer only to themselves. The "I," for example, doesn't refer to the speaker—*as it would if the speaker were using it in the ordinary way*. And it doesn't refer to Jesus. It just refers to the word "I" that Jesus is being asked to say. In short, quotation is like figurativeness in *replacing the ordinary use of words*.

But that's precisely why the quotation reading seems to fail in this context. At least it fails if the argument of chapter 1 is right: if ordinary sense or reference somehow doesn't pass muster, you've been given a cue to replace or augment it, and a clue to how. If it does pass muster, you've been given neither. In that case, replacing or augmenting is a fancy way of not listening. But in Herbert's line, the nonquotation reading, *a*, passes muster very well—admittedly; otherwise it couldn't be kept as half of the alleged double meaning. I conclude that if the speaker says to Jesus, "Say, I am thine," the only way Jesus can comply (if he decides to) is by adopting reading *a* all by itself, and confirming that the speaker belongs to Jesus.

I think something more basic is wrong with the proposed double meaning: it's hard to see how the statement that Christ and the speaker belong to *each other* responds at all, much less responds sharply, to anything the mockers have been saying. Coming where it does, this half of the double meaning is pointless; so it can't do duty for Christ's retort. It can't be the quip that the title and refrain lead us to expect. (I think we're better off without the superstition that double meaning is a literary end in itself. It makes us accident-prone.)

The quip we're after is the uncontroversial half of the proposal: the speaker would like to be told truthfully that he belongs to Christ—that *all* of him belongs to Christ, including the "hands" Beauty was asking about: "Whose hands are those?" That was a rhetorical question, of course, confidently expecting either no answer or the corrupt answer that would mark the speaker out as a fellow recruit in the world's train-band. Beauty is using a question figuratively, to make a statement. And the speaker turns the tables on her by using the classic strategy of retort: he takes her literally and answers her subversively. And he answers her while going through the motions of addressing somebody else—assigning her the (figurative) status of eavesdropper on a conversation she's barred from entering. Herbert has managed to tell the story of a magnificent quip—and to make the act of quipping itself a metaphor for a defiant statement of faith.[27]

Figuration and Retort | 151

In "The Quip" the speaker's explicit refusal to answer is a covert answer: if his prayer is granted, Christ himself will do the retorting on the speaker's persecutors—though the speech he'll do this in won't be addressed to them, at least not in explicit form. For them, he too will have only silence—if his figurative speech act (of apostrophe) is taken literally. Crashaw too gave us this curious version of Christ as *Mot* incarnate, past master of retort, with his outright silence figuring in one of the sacred epigrams as the supreme retort: the "weighty nothing" that recreates the world.

The witty silence expands into a virtuoso recital in "The Sacrifice." This is Herbert's version of the old liturgical theme of Christ reproaching his crucifiers. The Gospel doesn't record any such speech from the cross, so our traditional point of departure is a traditional metaphor: for "act of reproaching," read *act of forbearing (with the FORCE of a reproach)*. "I answer nothing, but . . ." (89). What follows the "but" is the point of this particular nothing—one in the series of bitterly pointed nothings the crucifiers are too witless or pitiless to get.

Herbert's way of *adapting* the metaphor is precisely Crashaw's: instead of reproaches, we get retorts. And the retort story taken literally avoids violating the Gospel fact of Christ's silence. The retorts are hypothetical: Christ on the cross is imagining what he *could* say to each of his murderers' slanders. In the imaginary debate, with Christ acting out both parts, we get replies to the crucifiers' actual taunts and to the challenges implied by their actions.

> CHALLENGE. "It was not sound / What I taught."
> RETORT [on "sound"]. "Comments will the text confound" [i.e., for the orthodox to question Christ's orthodoxy is for a Bible gloss to attack the Bible] (54–55).
>
> CHALLENGE. "Then they condemne me all with that same breath, / Which I do give them daily, unto death."
> RETORT. "Thus *Adam* my first breathing rendereth [i.e., returns the breath of life that I breathed into him at the creation" (69–71).
>
> CHALLENGE. "It is not fit he live a day."
> RETORT (continuing the taunters' sentence). ". . . who cannot live lesse then eternally" (98–99).

CHALLENGE. "Putting my life [if they spare it] among their sins [of omission]," they're perfectly willing to accept the lesser guilt of killing me—they "wish *my blood on them and theirs*."
RETORT (reinterpreting "wish" and "blood on"). "These words aright / Used, and wished, are the whole worlds light" (106–10).[28]

CHALLENGE. "they spit on me in scornfull wise."
RETORT. "Who by my spittle gave the blinde man eyes" (133–34).

CHALLENGE. "They are wittie: / *Now prophesie who strikes thee*, is their dittie."
RETORT. "So they in me denie themselves all pitie" (141–42).

CHALLENGE. "with a scarlet robe they me aray."
RETORT. "Which shews my bloud to be the onely way / And cordiall left to repair mans decay" (157–59).

CHALLENGE. "Now heal thy self, Physician; now come down [from the cross]."
RETORT. "Alas, I did so [from heaven—to heal *you*]" (221–22).

In "The Quip" the divine wit is called on to answer for the speaker. "The Sacrifice" is an attempt to show how decisively he could answer for himself—if he thought it was worthwhile. Traditional theology makes Christ the Word Incarnate; in a typically seventeenth-century twist on the old philosophical metaphor, the Word Incarnate turns out, even in silence, to be a witticism.

The crucified Christ's single retort at the end of "Redemption" is subtler and far more laconic. It's also free from bitterness; Christ talks to a friend, or a would-be friend, who is telling the story on himself. The speaker has picked out rent-law talk as the impromptu dialect in which to describe his conversion. It seems that he wanted his "rich [land]lord" (God) to "cancell" his old "lease," or salvation contract—the impossibly hard terms of Old Testament law—and let him have a "new small-rented lease"—the easy terms of New Testament faith.

But the oddity here goes beyond figuration signaling. The speaker's choice of language is perfectly standard—but laid on so thick it's a caricature: a desire to be released from the rigidities of law is getting translated into pedantic legalese.

Figuration and Retort | 153

The speaker goes on this way:

> In heaven at his manour I him sought:
>   They told me there, that he was lately gone
>   About some land, which he had dearly bought
> Long since on earth, to take possession.
> I straight return'd, and knowing his great birth,
>   Sought him accordingly in great resorts;
>   In cities, theatres, gardens, parks, and courts. (5-11)

The speaker's first notion of how to pray for the new "lease" is a little unhappy again: the God he "sought" is a lord "at his manour." But this is precisely the Old Testament God whose edicts he's trying to get released from. The God he needs is the Redeemer, who "bought [back]" (Latin root sense of "redeem") some "land" on earth "long since" (Hebrew "Adam" is cognate with a word meaning *{red} earth*)—"long since" because in the usual theology his decision to sacrifice himself for humanity was made from eternity.[29] But in spite of the speaker's new insight, his second notion of praying for redemption is as uncomprehending as his first. He "seeks" him again as the God of the unmeek; the God who prefers "great resorts," or the resorts of the great.

Part of his failure to appreciate what redeeming entails is his choice of metaphors for prayer, and the metaphors for Christ they imply. The "fact" of the matter—Christian talk-postulate—is that in this case to redeem was to volunteer to be a victim of thieves and murderers. The speaker can't understand properly what he's praying for unless he faces this fact—without benefit of rent-law talk or great resort talk. So he faces it:

> At length I heard a ragged noise and mirth
>   Of theeves and murderers: there I him espied,
>   Who straight, *Your suit is granted,* said, & died. (12-14)

Except for "heard" (to mean *thought of* or *recalled*), we're getting a literal expression of the end of the speaker's search for terms in which to think of the person he's praying to: that person is the suffering God.

But at this point something curious happens. To describe the feeling of having his prayer answered, the speaker relapses into legalese again. Or rather, he has *Christ* relapse *for* him. The situation is absurd. In the middle of his death pangs, the landlord nonchalantly pauses to dispose of some unfinished business: he's been waiting to grant not a prayer but the "suit" we've been told about—the "tenant" will be getting his "small-rented lease" after all. Then, as if he's been postponing death to clear one last item on his agenda, he promptly dies. What's going on here?

What's going on is a retort. Christ is giving the speaker back what looks like the speaker's own metaphor—but with a critical difference in sense: redemptive "suit granting" is an act of sacrifice, not power. The retort is a very different kind of reproach from the reproaches in "The Sacrifice": it's a gentle criticism of a failure in style. But the style of what? Of the poem before us! Christ's last words, his "it is finished," are being treated metaphorically as an answer to things that haven't yet been said— an answer that manages to balance wit with compassion.[30]

IV. Retort in Herbert: Winning at No One's Expense

In the usual retort game the player burlesques failure to understand in order to imply refusal to act on his understanding. Instead of talking his opponent's language, he talks a booby-trapped facsimile of it. The booby-trapping is either an act of figuration or a figurative act; that's why it calls for attention in this study. It's also a step toward winning the game: if all goes as planned in repartee, somebody will win on points. It's tempting to go on to add: and somebody else will lose. But this would be unfair to the complexity and humor that Herbert's speaker and his God bring to their wit combats. In Herbert, repartee is never a zero-sum game. The loser always comes out a winner. A bit further on I'll have a detailed look at how this is managed. But first I want to consider two interesting pieces of external evidence that Herbert appreciates this distinction and takes it seriously: his own reflections on the paradox (or sham paradox) of uninvidious winning.

The speaker of "The Thanksgiving" has been done a transcendently good turn and talks as if he resented it. He's determined—if we take him literally, at least—to stop his benefactor from getting the better of him:

>   Surely I will revenge me on thy love,
>   And trie who shall victorious prove.   (17–18)

>   Nay, I will reade thy book, and never move
>   Till I have found therein thy love,
>   Thy art of love, which I'le turn back on thee:
>   O my deare Saviour, Victorie!   (45–48)

Love retaliation seems to hold out a more realistic hope of winning than grief retaliation. There doesn't seem to be much chance of repaying the suffering of the acknowledged "King" of grief, who is in the lead so far not only in magnitude but also in a kind of originality. Any sacrifice the speaker thinks of will be an old story:

> Shall I be scourged, flouted, boxed, sold?
>   'Tis but to tell a tale is told
>   [i.e., a tale that is (already) told].   (7–8)

I said "if we take him literally," but his way of taking "revenge" for Christ's love doesn't make this easy. For somebody who seriously expects to show Christ up, the speaker's threats make no sense. He makes no attempt to hide the embarrassing fact that the credit for his talents, if any, belongs to his opponent—that they're part of the good turn he's trying to repay:

> If thou shalt give me wit, it shall appeare,
>   If thou hast giv'n it me, 'tis here [i.e., in the
>   words I'm saying right now!].   (43–44)

And he admits quite openly, again with no competitive gnashing of teeth, that even if he wins the love contest, he won't be the only winner. His trainer is none other than his opponent, whose "book" is a divine version of Ovid's love manual—"thy art of love." In an aside he goes even further: one of the good turns he aims to match (and hence cancel) is the "predestination" that lets him do good at all (31)!

Stranger yet, the whole design of the argument is ostentatiously self-defeating. The speaker starts by admitting that he hasn't a prayer of winning the grief contest (1–4). Then he interrupts his plans for a win in the love contest by promising to follow up with plans for the grief contest he's already conceded:

> As for thy passion—But of that anon,
>   When with the other I have done.   (29–30)

And at the end he keeps his promise by discovering, as if he hadn't known it from the beginning, that he hasn't a clue to how he can repay the Passion:

> Then for thy passion—I will do for that—
> Alas, my God, I know not what.   (49–50)

I said his lust for outdoing Christ is *hard* to take literally. Actually, short of dismissing him from the start as stupid or deranged—short of violating figurational charity—it's *impossible*.

It seems fairly clear that we're dealing with a cunning and high-spirited example of the self-directed irony I looked at in detail in chapter 5. In the guise of trying to get an exclusive victory, the speaker has been systematically showing us why no victory he could win is exclusive.[31]

Not that victory of some sort is *impossible;* the things he's enabled to do, he'll do, and the wit he's been given, he has. In Herbert, shedding a corrupt fantasy of winning brings the speaker a step closer to the winning he never stops trying for. The next poem in *The Temple*, "The Reprisall," tells another version of the same story, with the same kind of festive irony:

> Couldst thou not griefs sad conquests me allow,
>   But in all vict'ries overthrow me?
>
>   Yet by confession will I come
> Into thy conquest: though I can do nought
> Against thee, in thee I will overcome
>   The man, who once against thee fought.   (11–16)

Again the speaker hasn't given up wanting victory. His rival keeps on winning—but if the speaker joins him, he too can win. The only one who'll wind up "overcome" will be "the man, who once against thee fought." But the *speaker* is that man! If he denies it, then he isn't confessing, he's indulging in a whitewash.

This is all mischief, of course; being "overcome" isn't losing. Being the man who *once* against thee fought (and so doesn't any more) is precisely the victory announced by that joyfully self-assertive *yet:* all right (the speaker argues), Christ has frustrated my aim in one direction; *yet* I still have a chance for a "reprisall" in another—I can foil his project of balking me!

The game being played in both poems is a humorous simulation of a zero-sum game—and that's the point. In some kinds of game, even if they look competitive, there are no winners unless everybody wins—and (even when God is one of the participants) no losers unless everybody loses. The wily Creator in "The Pulley," who decides to leave natural contentment out of the human makeup, freely admits that if Man lost God, God too would wind up a loser:

> For if I should (said he)
> Bestow this jewell [namely, Rest] also on my creature,
> He would adore my gifts in stead of me,
> And rest in Nature, not the God of Nature:
> So both should losers be.   (11–15)

The friendly retort match between Herbert's speaker and God is that kind of game.

"Hope" tells about a repartee between the two carried on by exchanging emblems:

> I gave to Hope [i.e., Christ] a watch of mine: but he
>   An anchor gave to me.
> Then an old prayer-book I did present:
>   And he an optick [i.e., telescope] sent.
> With that I gave a viall full of tears:
>   But he a few green eares.
> Ah Loyterer! I'le no more, no more I'le bring:
>   I did expect a ring.

In literal terms, the dialogue goes roughly like this:

> SPEAKER [giving watch]. You're taking a very long time.
> CHRIST [giving anchor]. Have patience.
> SPEAKER [presenting old prayer book]. But I've been pleading with you to come for years!
> CHRIST [sending telescope]. Try to take the long view.
> SPEAKER [giving tear bottle]. My grief doesn't make that easy.
> CHRIST [giving unripe ears]. It isn't time yet—but it will be.
> SPEAKER [abandoning the emblem dialogue]. You're dawdling. Well, I won't offer any more signs of love. I expected them to be repaid by a permanent commitment.

The speaker thinks he's gotten the last word by refusing to carry on the emblem exchange. If he's right, he's come up with a brilliant variation on the retort-by-silence; he too retorts by breaking off a conversation—but does it by *breaking* silence! But he's wrong. The order of turns has already been set, with Christ always coming second; it's Christ's turn, and Christ passes it up. *He's* the one who has the last word, and the last word is silence.

Christ's retort on the speaker's threat to stop communicating is an emblem of what stopping would be like. But it's *only* an emblem, as the green ears have already made clear; the fact that Christ isn't ready to harvest his crop doesn't mean that he's given up growing it. The speaker is glaringly unready for harvesting; he takes it for granted that gifts can buy the "ring" (Christ's gift to the soul he marries, in the old metaphor). Besides, up to the point when the speaker gets petulant and resorts to words, the partners have been communicating *in* silence; a communication *by* silence simply resumes the pattern.

We need to go a bit further. Like other Herbert speakers we've met, this one fails to notice a key fact supplied by his own narrative—a fact that nicely justifies Christ's nickname of "Hope" (that is, the person hoped for): at least one of the speaker's gifts wasn't merely given but *presented* to Christ. But then it seems clear that even if "Hope" was sometimes far enough away to "send" a gift (by messenger, presumably), at least part of the time he was close enough to be handed gifts in person!

And not only that; "Hope" was close enough to talk with the speaker— not in the routinely cooperative mode of ordinary talk, but with the special rapport of an emblem conversation. But that kind of conversation isn't nearly as impersonal as it seems. In fact, it calls for a kind of intimacy that has no parallel in ordinary conversation. The meaning-bearers in emblem talk aren't the emblems but the figurative sentences they prompt; by consenting to *be* prompted the receiver becomes the sender's organ of expression. So far the speaker has managed not to notice either Christ's presence or the intimacy with which he's manifesting it.

The best reason for hoping is that you find your hope is already partly fulfilled and you hadn't noticed it. But the speaker *hasn't* noticed this— yet. In short, the one who stands convicted of "loytering" (at least in awareness) turns out to be the speaker. It seems that if he's succeeded in retorting on anybody, it's himself.

But we still haven't gone far enough. It would be a particularly foolish example of Hotspurism to think of the listener and Jesus as literally mailing off bric-a-brac to each other. The metaphors elicited by the emblems in the dialogue are framed by the larger metaphor of the emblem dialogue itself. If the religious consciousness exchanges images with Christ at all, they will be *mental* images. The intimacy of emblem dialogue is being used to describe a dialogue that is still more intimate. The setting of *this* comic repartee is a mind. And the cream of the joke is that the mind gets one-upped by somebody else's thought without quite noticing that somebody else is there.

Figuration and Retort | 159

In "The Holdfast" the speaker is thwarted by his opponent again—but this time only to be rescued by another party to the conversation:

> I threatned to observe the strict decree
>   Of my deare God with all my power & might.
>   But I was told by one, it could not be;
> Yet I might trust in God to be my light.
> Then will I trust, said I, in him alone.
>   Nay, ev'n to trust in him, was also his:
>   We must confesse that nothing is our own.
> Then I confesse that he my succour is:
> But to have nought is ours, not to confesse
>   That we have nought. I stood amaz'd at this,
>   Much troubled, till I heard a friend expresse,
> That all things were more ours by being his.
>   What Adam had, and forfeited for all,
>   Christ keepeth now, who cannot fail or fall.

The initially overconfident speaker doesn't wind up being simply humbled by his opponent; he's devastated.

The opponent's recipe is: give the victim something to make up for a disappointment, then pretend to take it away as soon as it's accepted. Thus: to make up for the denial of the ability to obey God, give an assurance that "I might trust in God"—then pretend to take it away by announcing that trust, like obedience, is "also his [God's]." Once again: to make up for (apparent) denial of the ability to trust, give not only the ability but the obligation to confess ("we must confesse")—then pretend to take away the ability ("to have nought is ours") while leaving the obligation. This last maneuver is guaranteed to leave the poor speaker paralyzed in what *he* calls "amazement" and *we* nowadays call a classic double bind.

I was careful to say that the speaker's opponent *pretends* to take away what he gives. The curious thing is that on closer examination, in spite of the ominous "nay" and "but," his second thoughts don't really cancel out his first ones. The troublesome formulas here are "to trust (obey, confess) is his" and "to have nought is ours." What is it for trust, obedience, and confession of faith to be God's but not the speaker's? Is "to have nought" supposed to be "ours" in the same sense of the possessive?

Well, obviously obedience doesn't belong to God in the sense that *he* obeys or ought to obey God.[32] If anybody obeys, trusts, or confesses to God, *we* do. The opponent's point seems to be that God decides whether we do or can do these things; our obeying or ability to obey are God's to decide. On this reading, the sense in which we "have nought" is simply that we aren't the cause and can't take the credit for anything good we do or *can* do—not that we don't or can't do anything good.[33] In short, the speaker's "nay" and "but" are pure intimidation, distracting from the real implications of what he says. He's talking in the usual Protestant vein about human dependency on God. But he makes dependency look like paralysis.

Now it's true that the speaker is asking for it when he starts out by cockily promising ("threatening") to obey—as if he could even *begin* to do this without help (grace). But the lesson is a little harsh. In fact, so far it's not a lesson: instead of showing him where he's gone wrong, the opponent plays cat and mouse with him, then immobilizes him in a trap of "amazement." The match is very unequal; the speaker has been ambushed. He puts up no resistance at all to these maneuvers. If he's the only person available to deliver a retort to his opponent, then obviously the bout is over. Yet the opponent's key terms—"his" and "ours"—are just waiting to be given the twist that the speaker's "friend" and rescuer now gives them.

The friend does this by simply restoring the positive side of the same truth (talk-postulate) that the opponent has been using to put the speaker down:

> That all things were more ours by being his.
> What Adam had, and forfeited for all,
> Christ keepeth now, who cannot fail or fall.

In the words of the Anglican article *Of Free-Will:* "We have no power to do good works pleasant and acceptable to God." But at this point the article doesn't say *no power, period,* but no power "without the grace of God by Christ preventing [= anticipating and moving] us, that we may have a good will, and working with us, when we have that good will." This restoration is the point of the speaker's metaphorical play on the opponent's fuzzy possessives. Our free will is "his" (Christ's) by trusteeship, not ownership. He's the holdfast of things we failed to hold onto, things like the ability to trust him. He's "keeping" our free will *for* us. You keep something *for* somebody to give it back to him or her when the time comes. Meanwhile, since we're bound to lose them without the help of a trustee, they're in fact *more* "ours" by being "his." Retorts have all sorts of uses; here's another: curing despair in third parties.[34]

But who *are* the speaker's two partners in conversation? It's natural to assume that there *are* two; otherwise "*a* friend" should read "*the* friend," that is, the person just mentioned. Still, in the perspective of Protestant religious ideas the seeming rivals collaborate by performing two halves of a single function. Together they lead the speaker through the familiar stages of "rebirth": smugness crushed by a message that seems to rule out hope; hope restored by a second look at the same message. In effect, when the speaker finds himself unable to retort on God, God finds a way to retort—in fact, to double back—on himself.

The speaker manages to put up a fight in the last poem I want to consider. Thanks to his unhappy efforts, "Love (III)" is a sustained repartee—though all but two of the retorts belong to Christ.

The speaker describes Christ's efforts to get him to overcome the pain and misunderstanding that keep him from sitting down to the Lord's Supper. In the display of divine wit we're being entertained with, retort—figurative refusal to communicate—is going to be used to undo a refusal to communicate.

The metaphorical language in which the speaker gives us his memoir of religious crisis is familiar from the Book of Common Prayer: hanging back from Communion is as if "a man hath prepared a rich feast, decked his table with all kind of provision, so that there lacketh nothing but the guests to sit down; and yet they who are called (without any cause) most unthankfully refuse to come." Only in this particular case there *is* a "cause"; and the cause is precisely that the guest *knows* he's "unthankful"—more than unthankful: totally unfit to be there. In short, he's in the first stage of approach to the Communion table: in the usual jargon, he needs to be "prepared."

In particular he has to be made to understand that Paul's warning doesn't apply to him: "Wherefore, whosoeuer shal eat this bread, and drinke the cup of the Lord vnworthely, shalbe giltie of the bodie & blood of the Lord. Let a man therefore examine him self, and so let him eat of this bread, and drinke of this cup. For he that eateth and drinketh vnworthely, eateth and drinketh his owne damnation, because he discerneth not the Lords bodie."[35] On the usual Protestant reading, Paul's "worthy" can't mean *free of ingratitude,* much less *untainted altogether;* otherwise *nobody* is qualified to take Communion. The kind of love God expects and welcomes, in fact, is Luther's and Calvin's *caritas imperfecta:* love that can and will be tainted in various ways, and is acceptable all the same—just so long as it "discerns" the love that's being offered to it.[36]

Imperfect love sometimes takes the form of a misguided desire to spare the host, a desire mixed with shame and self-disgust. So the comforter needs to be careful and "bear with all the wants of the distressed; as with their frowardnesse, peevishnesse, rashnesse, and with their distempered and disordered affections." In this context, imperfect love is still love; in fact, it's evidence that communion has already started: "For it is not nature, that makes us to grieve for hardnes of heart, but grace."[37]

These are the background assumptions that make sense of the way Christ bears with the speaker in "Love (III)," to the point of consenting to play the wit game the speaker falls back on. Immediately after the speaker challenges him, Christ takes command and dominates the game to the finish. The unspoken stakes don't need to be spelled out for Herbert's audience. If the speaker isn't outwitted, he's in danger of outwitting himself.

The duel starts when the guest shies away from being welcomed rather than get his "dust" (guilt) on his welcomer. "Dust" gets its figurative point in the usual way: by how it fits into the (literal) story that apparently is being told here. The guilt that the dust is identified with isn't the guilt (if any) the guest brings on himself by drawing back; the dust has been collected *on the way* to the feast. What's being referred to is the *sense* of guilt—the sense that makes him shy away from what he thinks is an act of pollution. The love this fumbling etiquette stands in for is tainted, of course, but in Herbert's religious ethos tainted love is the best anybody can do. It's enough for Love (Christ) to work with—as he proceeds to do by drawing nearer to the guest and thereby drawing the guest nearer to him. What follows is a volley of (sometimes crisscrossing) challenges and retorts (individual challenge-retort pairings are marked below by italics and matching letters):

> Love bade me welcome: yet my soul drew back,
>   Guiltie of dust and sinne.
> But quick-ey'd Love, observing me grow slack
>   From my first entrance in,
> Drew nearer to me, sweetly questioning,
>   If I *lack'd*$_a$ anything.
>
> A *guest*$_{ab}$, I answer'd, worthy to be here:
>   Love said, *You shall be he*$_b$.
> I the unkinde, ungratefull? Ah my deare,
>   I cannot *look*$_c$ on thee.

> Love took my hand, and smiling did reply,
>   Who *made*$_d$ the *eyes*$_c$ but I?
>
> Truth Lord, but I have *marr'd*$_d$ them: let my shame
>   Go where it doth *deserve*$_e$.
> And know you not, sayes Love, who *bore the blame*$_e$?
>   My deare, then I will *serve*$_f$.
> You must *sit down*, sayes Love, and *taste my meat*$_f$:
>   So I did sit and eat.

The "sweet question" Love draws near with is "What do you lack?"—colloquial-cordial for "What would you like?" The guest finds it necessary to dodge the question with a standard retort tactic: pretending to misread a key word by taking it out of context. He responds to "lack" as if it were being used literally, to mean *don't have,* and turns this sense into a metaphor of self-disgust: what he doesn't have—what he isn't—is a guest fit for the occasion. Retort is only a witty pretense of misunderstanding. But in falling back on it the guest shows that he really *doesn't* understand the relevant standard of fitness. The shell of wit has to be cracked.

In his reply, the host chooses the gentlest possible way of doing the cracking: he bears with the wit—redeems it—by playing along with it. The speaker gets back some of his own medicine by being taken literally in turn: So you haven't brought along a worthy guest? Quite all right: You shall be he. (The "shall" of decree: I'll *make* you deserving!)[38] At this point the pressure is too great for concentration on chess; the unhappy love spills out in a kind of shorthand. The guest isn't fit to be there; even looking at Christ would compound the wrong he's already done him by being "unkind" and "ungrateful." "Ah my deare / I cannot look on thee." The sequence of ideas is absolutely crucial here; this isn't mere shame. It's because you're "*deare*" that I can't look at you. As the title promises, we're listening to a story of love. In the speaker's case, it's the imperfect love that comes out in the superstitious delicacy of his qualm about looking.

Again wit is enlisted in the service of compassion; the speaker gets a gentle but pointed retort on the key word "look": how can the *use* of vision desecrate the *maker* of vision? (Unless, of course, vision were being *mis*used; the clear implication is that in this case it wouldn't be.)

But in his use of "make" Christ has left a handle for a retort. The proverbial doublet "make and mar" makes it easy enough for the speaker to parry this time: "Truth Lord, but I have marr'd them: let my shame [that is, this self of mine that I'm ashamed of] go where it doth deserve."

The request is presumptuous, of course; the convict is giving his own judge advice on the right sentence. But in his reply Christ ignores this and focuses instead—as by implication *we* should—on the saving grace here: the passion for justice.[39]

Herbert's audience will know that this is the kind of presumption God sometimes overlooks: "Shal not the iudge of all the worlde do right?" Earlier the speaker's word for the notion he has been misapplying was "worthy." Now it's "deserve." The point of the therapeutic retort that follows is that the speaker is calling for a justice that has already been done: the score *was* settled when Christ "bore the blame."

There's an economy of effort that goes with the wit here. Christ is coming back at the speaker unanswerably—simply by reminding him of a belief he's already committed to. Remembering that act of love prompted the guest's impulsive "My deare" a moment ago and prompts it again now: "My deare, then I will serve." The speaker has capitulated, but one more retort is called for. It isn't hard to spot the key word here—provided we remember that the meal-serving story is figurative through and through: a meal is what the story would be about if it *weren't* figurative. In the impromptu dialect of the speaker's memoir, "meal" means *grace*.

Taken literally, the guest's offer to serve the meal is at least intelligible, especially given the "lordship" of the host. Taken in a figurative sense based on meal serving, the guest's offer is nonsense: there's only one person who could conceivably "serve" grace, and it isn't the speaker. So that route to a figurative sense is tentatively ruled out by figurational charity; the speaker hasn't been represented as an idiot or a lunatic. Read with the attention he's entitled to, he isn't expressing a nonsensical desire; he doesn't want to serve Christ grace any more than he wants to serve him a meal. All he's asked for in so many words is a chance to serve, period.

Like all retorts, Christ's answer, "You must sit down . . . and taste my meat," sneaks up on us; it yields only to a second hearing. It starts by sounding dismissive. But it stops sounding that way as soon as we stop taking it literally. To sit and taste this particular "meat" *is* to serve love in the only relevant sense—by participating in it. Christ is inviting the speaker to perform the central act of *worship*—or equivalently, in a perfectly standard sense of the word, of religious "service."

The "must" in "You must sit down" might well suggest that the poor speaker is being robbed of his freedom and dignity by being bullied into salvation whether he likes it or not; that is, it might well suggest this *if* the context and background assumptions were different.

Stanley Fish is put off by Christ's "dismissal as so much [*sic*] ephemera of everything that is beside [Christ's] point."[40] "'You shall be he,' for example, "does not at all touch on the matter of whether or not he *should* be he.... In terms of what the speaker desires—an earned place—it is hard and unyielding because it denies him any part in the disposition of his own case."[41] But on the usual Christian assumptions, the speaker's "earned place" is hell, his desire to go there is foolish, and Christ's unyielding effort to save him from his folly isn't hardness but love. Fish's libertarian objection to that effort isn't a reading of Herbert's poem. It's a quarrel with Herbert, and with Christian ethics in general. He's entitled to his quarrels, but not to offer them as readings.

As for Christ's alleged tyranny of denying the speaker a chance to decide for himself (if that's what the "disposition-of-case" talk means), strenuously arguing people out of their misconceptions isn't the same as fooling or forcing them into agreement.

Fish concocts a pseudo-Christian talk-postulate of his own a bit further on: "'Who made the eyes but I'... means 'you cannot escape me because you are of my substance,' and it has the effect of leaving the speaker with nothing to call his own."[42] God didn't create things out of his own substance; how pantheism has crept in here is a mystery. But suppose the Protestant's God *had* made some of his creatures out of allotments of his own substance. Fish's conclusion would still be question begging: why *can't* the speaker call his allotment his own (whatever "his own" means in this context)? Fish takes it for granted that the speaker is trying to escape Christ, period. But this doesn't follow from the claim that the speaker is trying to escape a union with Christ that he (the speaker) doesn't deserve. And it doesn't follow that the motive of the escape attempt is a desire to live free or die.

Here is Fish again, on "let my shame / Go where it doth deserve": "Behind the shame one hears the plea, let me at least have this."[43] "Behind the X one hears the Y" is a recipe for disguising claims as arguments. Who's the anonymous plea hearer? What kind of hearing is this supposed to be, an inference? a naked intuition? If an inference, where are the grounds? If an intuition, why should we accept it? Why should the hearer, for that matter? Above all, why not just take the passage at face value instead of taking it for granted that its face has to be a mask?

One way of refusing to play the receiving end of the game of figuration is literalism; for example, taking a metaphor for a fantasy (the sort of thing I've called Hotspurism). Another is the way of the ventriloquist:

replacing the unflagged and uncanceled face value of the text with what "one hears" or prefers to hear. The face value of these lines in particular is neither flagged nor canceled by the context. The speaker's apparent urge to hide what he's ashamed of fits in snugly enough with what we've already seen him do: try to keep his "dust" and "sinne" away from the Communion table.

According to Fish, the "must" in "You must sit down . . . and taste my meat" is the tyranny of a hostess pressing "cheese puffs" on an unwilling guest.[44] This reading is ruled out by both the argument's progress to this point and the identity of the cheese puffs available at this particular party. The guest has already agreed to partake of Communion—but *if* he does, he can't possibly supply the grace that is the essential course in the meal. If he partakes at all, he *must* (logical "must," not tyrannical "must") partake by receiving, not by giving.

According to Fish, "So I did sit and eat" means "What else could I do but *what I had been told*? So I did sit and eat."[45] This ignores the metaphor that "told to" would have to be if it really occurred in the poem: the speaker is doing what *Love* "tells him to do"—he is acting out of love. And the "must" he's submitting to isn't a boss's order. It simply spells out what's implied by the choice he has just made.[46]

In short, "sitting" is a metaphor for an *act of choice*—the speaker's choice—that Love has been energetically arguing for. This persuasive effort makes no sense at all if what the speaker wants to do doesn't matter.

Now at last the effort has paid off. The speaker admits that his conscientious objection to making the choice was based on a mistake. That's the point of the "then" in "My deare, then I will serve." Since I owe Love my vindication, and can stay, I want to stay to "serve" that Love. But (once again) to sit and eat *is* to serve. The speaker has been gradually brought to the happy condition of learning that he "must" do something he wants to do. This eating is a response to a hunger he is finally free to satisfy. And if serving is the speaker's idea of dignity, then his dignity has been as carefully provided for as his freedom. "So I did sit and eat."

In "Love (III)," wit play—repartee—is Herbert's metaphor for the experience of working through a crisis in faith.[47] The shape of the experience is comic, with the ping-pong rhythm of comic debate. The dramatic metaphor of active compassion as wit gets its last refinement here, allowing a compression that gives simple-looking strings of monosyllables—"So I did sit and eat" most of all—enormous emotional force in proportion to their look of simplicity. It seems that the soul in crisis is an impatient patient—subtle to plague itself and fiercely resisting its own happiness. So the would-be helper has to be fiercely cunning in response, always on the lookout for a chance to turn the resister's own words against him, since to turn them against him in this case is to turn them in his favor. And for this paradoxical coup de grâce, Herbert's metaphor is the retort.

Chapter Seven

Thinking in Metaphor: Windfalls and Searches

I. Para Prosdokian

In chapter 3, when we were considering the mock metaphors in "Loves growth," I remarked that the habit of figurational charity tends to make us take the blame when the speaker turns out to have been using a word to mean something totally unexpected—if it makes sense to speak of "using a word to mean" something it doesn't mean in any language one could conceivably be speaking. "Vicissitude" doesn't mean *increase* in the vernacular, and it doesn't mean it in the speaker's impromptu conversation dialect—not when what this particular "vicissitude" was supposed to be proving was *the impurity of his love:*

> I scarce beleeve my love to be so pure
>   As I had thought it was,
>   Because it doth endure
> Vicissitude, and season, as the grasse.

It's not that you can't get "vicissitude" to mean *increase,* or anything else you please, by working it into a suitable trope. It's just that the speaker hasn't. As he uses the word, it means *fluctuation* as usual, and we're justified by what he's been saying so far in thinking that this particular phase of the fluctuation cycle is downhill.

But now he goes on to spell out his bizarre reason for suspecting impurity: he had thought his love already infinite but now finds that it's grown. The result of this maneuver is that the speaker gets his earlier phrase repeated by forcing us to reread it, this time interpreting "vicissitude" as *increase* rather than as *fluctuation.* The unexpected meaning goes with the repetition but not with the original use. In short, what we thought he was saying the first time was precisely what he said—and what he meant to say. Otherwise his tease wouldn't have come off.

Yet *we* tend to take the blame. "The fault, *as it were,* is ours," says one critic, "for having misread the implications of 'endure,' 'vicissitude,' or 'grasse' by relying on the false pointers cunningly planted within the text" (italics mine).[1] But you can't "misread" implications that don't exist; they were canceled by the "pointers," which are *part* of the text and partly responsible for what it means. The critic's "as it were" is revealing in this connection. It evades the issue of precisely *how* we're "at fault"; and, on the other hand, it also acknowledges that we aren't literally at fault at all. The critic has managed to look past his awareness that somehow we've been had—almost as if he were his deceiver's accomplice. Why?

There's a hint of an explanation for this perfectly natural overextension of charity in Cicero's theory of the appeal of comic non sequitur in general: "You know the most familiar kind of laugh-getter, when we're waiting for one phrase and we get another. This blunder of ours makes us laugh at ourselves." "We take a natural delight in our own mistakes."[2] As it stands, this won't work, of course: being prone to mistakes is being exposed to their consequences, which aren't always delightful. But maybe the theory of mistake-"delight" can be rescued by specifying the *kind* of mistake at play here.

In the simple case, familiar to lovers of Aristophanes as the trope "against expectation" (*para prosdokian*), the speaker mischievously ties a knot in the tail of a cliché. Hermogenes gives a rudimentary example: "I wouldn't have wanted this stinking thing to happen to me, but since it has—[here the listener expects to hear "I'll live with it"]—since it has, I *still* wouldn't have wanted it to happen to me!"[3] The modern master of *para prosdokian* is Oscar Wilde:

> I believe marriage *is* a very pleasant state, sir. I have had very little experience of it myself up to the present. I have only been married once.
>
> I was obliged to call on dear Lady Harbury. I hadn't been there since her poor husband's death. I never saw a woman so altered; she looks quite twenty years younger.
>
> It is always painful to part from people whom one has known for a brief space of time.

The raw material for the trick is the commonplace, or talk-postulate—the kind of thought or train of thought that routinely gets by "for the sake of argument," or gets "taken for granted" unless explicitly challenged. If the postulate isn't up for evaluation, it just doesn't make sense to challenge it, just as it doesn't make sense to challenge "John is as greedy as a wolf" by challenging the underlying zoology. The trickster catches us off balance by abruptly and irrelevantly challenging a talk-postulate he appears to be getting ready to use. And he creates that appearance precisely by planting false pointers—by sending a signal that will throw us off *if we get it right*.

Comic zeugma is an example that comes still closer to the communicative misbehavior—licensed misbehavior—that we looked at in "Love's growth." The notorious example is Pope's remark about Hampton Court, where the Queen "[doth] sometimes counsel take, and sometimes tea." Here the rules of intelligibility being twisted are grammatical. The speaker gives us a sequence like this: $\langle \text{object}_a, \text{verb}_a; \text{object}_b, [\text{verb}_b] \rangle$, (where the deleted verb_b breaks the deletion rule by being only a twin of verb_a). Object_a ("counsel") lets us know which vernacular sense "take" is being used in; the things one "takes_a" are things one is given. Object_b ("tea") forces us to reread and hence repeat "take" in still another—incompatible—vernacular sense; the things one "takes_b" are things one helps *oneself* to (e.g., naps, steps, positions, actions, pity [on somebody]): in Pope great Anna "takes_b" tea—by drinking, not by accepting the cup. Unfortunately, "take_b" doesn't apply to object_a—unless the Queen doesn't so much hear advice as dictate what she hears.[4] We see with "delight" that we got "take" wrong the first time round; it had a bite we somehow missed.

But once again the seeing is only reflex charity. The a-sense of "take" was picked out, and the b-sense ruled out, by the presence of "counsel." Charity in this case is a presumption of consistency that we go on to salvage come what may: our second step clashes with our first—so we go back and correct our "misunderstanding" of the first.

"Counsel" wasn't a false pointer because it was ambiguous but because it was clear. The clarity was the bait. Far from getting anything wrong, we've been misled again by something we got right. As usual, the trickster relies on our *competence* to trip us up, and on our amusement to let him get away with it. Presumably, what delights us here, and in the other cases, is that we too get away with something: the trip-up—the temporary snag in communication—is a make-believe punishment for a make-believe mistake. We laugh at our pratfalls when they turn out not to have cost us anything—*because* they turn out that way. Maybe with this qualification, Cicero's theory can be allowed to stand.

Clearly the trickster has no choice but to rely on his listeners' competence. You can't lie efficiently to people who don't catch your drift, or are just guessing. So baffled expectations based on incompetence and guessing can't be raw material for *para prosdokian* (the scheme "against expectation")—or for reading in general, for that matter.

11. *Reader Entrapment versus* Para Prosdokian

There's a temptation to mistake the random mental static that inescapably crackles underneath reading and listening for part of the activity it's interfering with. One fancy way of defending the mistake would be to say that "[the reader's] temporary adoption of . . . inappropriate strategies is itself a strategy of the author."[5] But the inappropriate strategies are precisely the ones that vary unpredictably from one reader to another. So only a magician can bank on his readers' inappropriate strategies—especially arbitrary ones like jumping the gun by "positing, on the basis of incomplete evidence, deep structures that fail to materialize."[6]

A reader who goes by the "posit," or guess, method of reading is destined to see a lot of compelling examples of *para prosdokian* that aren't there. He'll find one in any seventeenth-century periodic sentence whose syntax keeps him guessing—say, this sentence of Sir Thomas Browne: "That *Judas* perished by hanging himself, there is no certainty in Scripture: though in one place it seemes to affirme it, and by a doubtfull word hath given occasion so to translate it; yet in another place, in a more punctuall description, it makes it improbable, and seemes to overthrow it."[7] Imagine a supersubtle critic arguing as follows: "*Simply by taking in* [italics mine] the first clause of the sentence, *the reader commits himself* to its assertion 'that Judas perished by hanging himself' (in constructions of this type 'that' is understood to be shorthand for 'the fact that')." But (the critic goes on) the reader is being purposely set up for a fall. When he gets to "there is no certainty," "the status of the 'fact' that had served as his point of reference becomes uncertain," and "going forward only intensifies the reader's sense of disorientation." In short, the sentence carries out a "strategy" or "action . . . upon a reader" that amounts to "progressive decertainizing."[8]

A reader who gets "decertainized" by reacting this way isn't a victim of the strategy of *para prosdokian,* or of any other strategy adopted by Browne. Browne can't be held to account for reactions to things he never did. In his seventeenth-century prose idiom, at least, initial "that" seldom if ever means *the fact that*. If it means anything, it means *the proposition (or claim) that:*

> That miracles are ceased, I can neither prove, nor absolutely deny.
>
> That Archimedes burnt the ships of Marcellus . . . sounds hard unto reason . . . and therefore justly questioned.
>
> That Snails have two eyes, and at the end of their Horns, beside the assertion of the people, is the opinion of some Learned men.
>
> That onely Man hath an erect figure, and for to behold and look up toward heaven, is a double assertion, whose first part may be true.
>
> That the sex is discernible from the figure of the eggs, . . . experiment will easily frustrate [i.e., refute].[9]

Not only would a reader who bought the "fact that" theory of "that" have to ignore Browne's uniform practice in a swarm of "that" clauses, he would also have to ignore what leads up to the "Judas" passage itself: a promise to supply a list of "*assertions* . . . drawn from Scripture . . . whereunto I would never betray the libertie of my reason" (italics mine).

Still worse, we're asked to believe that to be a reader is to "commit" oneself to an author's say-so "simply by taking it in." Worst of all, "readers" in this Pickwickian sense "read" by stopping every so often to guess at random about how the sentence will turn out. It isn't surprising that "readers" don't notice that the uncertain sentences Browne is referring to are Bible sentences, not Browne's, much less the one he does the referring in. And it isn't surprising that "readers" get just backward the *certainty* Browne is expressing at this point (about the inconclusiveness of the Bible evidence on Judas's death). But here as elsewhere it's the result that's predictable, not "readers'" misdemeanors; short of magic, Browne's sentence isn't to blame for this or any other hash that can be made of it.

But suppose the "fact that" theory of initial "that" clauses *were* correct after all. Then reading Browne's example accordingly would *also* be correct—not a "posit" on "incomplete evidence" about a "deep structure" that failed to materialize. Browne would have generated a surprise for the reader by sending a false signal of his intention. We would have (roughly): "The fact of Judas's hanging himself—may not be a fact." Once again the reader would take the blame and see with "delight" that the initial "that" meant *the proposition that*. And once again the seeing would be an illusion—

conversational charity gone awry. All we would have is the familiar pattern of *para prosdokian:* getting the reader to trip on his own competence.

We need a way of talking informatively about disorienting effects like the one I'm concerned with in this chapter. I plan to explore the advantages of one way. There are undoubtedly others. But I don't think the posit theory of reading is in the running.

III. Para Prosdokian *in Herbert*

In the subtlest version of *para prosdokian*—the version carried out in the Herbert poems I'll be looking at in a moment—a speaker seems to be continuing with the same metaphor he started with. But it *isn't* the same; the old literal sense ("vehicle" in the jargon) is getting applied to the old subject matter ("tenor"), but applied in a new figurative sense that releases the speaker to think in a new direction. It's as if this is what his words meant all the time; as if the old sense were simply his and our misreading. In short, we're being invited to regard this kind of hindsight figuration as the fulfillment of a potentiality: language that has caught up with the meaning it was straining toward. The study of hindsight figuration will lead us straight to exploratory and emergent metaphors—two kinds of thinking-in-metaphor that are powerful and inclusive enough to create the structure of whole poems.

The speaker of "Employment (II)" starts out smugly enough with some oblique self-congratulation:

> He that is weary, let him sit.
>   My soul would stirre
> And trade in courtesies and wit,
>   Quitting the furre
> To cold complexions needing it.
>
> Man is no starre, but a quick coal
>   Of mortall fire:
> Who blows it not, nor doth controll
>   A faint desire,
> Lets his own ashes choke his soul.   (1–10)

The speaker has only contempt for the depressive personality that needs "furre" and retirement to keep it warm. His complexion (balance of humors) is naturally hot—it leans toward blood and bile, not melancholy and phlegm. But he has no illusions. He knows his fire is a coal, not a star; mortal, not self-sustaining. Only activity will keep it up, the kind of activity that's favored by blood and bile, desire and anger, lust and aggression.

But though he's no star, his ambition is starlike enough—"ordain'd," in fact, by the divine will: the universe owes its order to a grand upheaval of the same ambition—to *eris,* strife, the war of each against all:

> When th' elements did for place contest
>   With him, whose will
> Ordain'd the highest to be best;
>   The earth sat still,
> And by the others is opprest.   (11–15)

The speaker too is after "place" in all the relevant senses—political appointment, power, status. He hopes to get it by his social grace and his intellect, cashed out in the form of "courtesies" and "wit," the familiar coin of the status-"trade." And the "trade" involved here is no different in principle from the one that formed the world. It's a piratical "contest" against rivals for place "with" (in the circle of) a patron. Favorite-creating and world-creating are unexpectedly close kin. The rival elements that were most aggressive rose highest in God's court. The one with the cold complexion (earth) just sat there, neglecting its own advantage, and got the oppression it deserved.

What's true of the elements is true of the vying for attention between sun and stars. Where your rival is too bright to outshine, make the most of his absence:

> The sunne still shineth there or here,
>   Whereas the starres
> Watch an advantage to appeare.   (18–20)

In short, life is no party, it's a scramble for "advantage"—

> Life is a businesse, not good cheer;
> Ever in warres.   (16–17)

And the speaker is all on fire to "live."

So far it would be hard to find a wittier exploitation of the strife or check-and-balance theory of natural order that seventeenth-century university readers would recall from tags of the Presocratics.[10] The speaker out-heretics the similarly indebted arguments in the Sophists by equating "highest" in the social rat race with "best" in God's eyes, and by going on with hardly a pause to a materialist version, or subversion, of Job's complaint that "warfare is the life of man upon the earth."[11]

The materialism seems pretty confident. For the speaker there's evidently no hole in an argument from (humor- and element-induced) *preference* to moral *rightness*. His favorite metaphor captures the reductive flavor: maybe the reason why it makes sense to describe soul-fires as choking on body-ashes, and to identify "stirring" souls with hot "complexions," is precisely that souls *are* just the business end of complexions—just human "coal" in combustion. But if that's the way things are, why not just surrender to the joyful necessity of being a coal? Rarely has an egoistic Ought been weaseled so handily out of a predatory Is.

The only misstep in the performance is the suspicious placement of "with him" (after "contest" rather than "place") in "th' elements did for place *contest / With* him [i.e., God]. . . ." At first glance it looks as if the elements were challenging God, and not each other, for "place" in a contest umpired by some third party. But in that case, what becomes of the speaker's glorification of elemental conflict? The rest of the sentence saves the argument by sending us back to reparse the phrase. If "with" meant *against*, God would be just another contestant, not someone presiding over the contest and "ordaining" its terms.

So we've been put right—or have we? Clearly we haven't. In the only available sense of "right," we were right to start with: we complied with the relevant rule (for "with" after "to contest"). If the shock reading (God as Contestant) had come after rather than before the respectable reading (God as Umpire), then we would have hindsight figuration of the kind we're interested in. What we have instead is instant retrieval of a telltale slip of the tongue.

This is where we get the surprise that undermines the speaker's whole argument beyond repair, metaphor and all. The speaker starts by shifting metaphors, at least for the moment; the quick coal is replaced by the orange tree, which brings with it a new notion of "businesse," and hence "life":

> Oh that I were an Orenge-tree,
> > That busie plant!
> Then should I ever laden be,
> > And never want
> Some fruit for him that dressed me.   (21–25)

So now we have a choice of alivenesses—live coal against live orange tree.

The meaning of the choice is clear enough. Coals lack fruit even for themselves, not to mention anybody else; egoism is morally sterile to the point of being self-defeating. If steadily bearing fruit is being alive, then being a coal, even a live coal, is being dead with a vengeance. But the surprise here is that this is a choice the speaker has somehow already made; in fact, it's apparently not so much a choice as an urge. The urge refuses to be repressed any longer and forces its way out now as a wish.

On the other hand, the speaker has contradicted himself without skipping a beat. Nothing comes up just before the wish to motivate the sudden change of direction. Maybe there has been no change of direction, no repression, and no bursting out. Maybe we were overhasty in reading "warre" and "businesse" as militant egoism, or the temperature talk as materialism. If so, it seems we heard wrong when we understood the speaker to be boasting of his superiority to fur-loving "cold complexions."

At least that's not how he's using the metaphor now:

> But we are still too young or old;
>   The Man is gone,
> Before we do our wares unfold:
>   So we freeze on,
> Untill the grave increase our cold.   (26–30)

No arrogance *here*. The speaker is as cold as the rest—too slow to bear fruit in time to catch "him that dressed me" (Christ, the archetypal "Man" and gardener of men). So evidently the temperature the speaker has been worrying about all this time has been devotion, not virility or power lust. And the war he's been aching to go to isn't the profit war but the one in Saint Paul: "No man that warreth entangleth himself with the affairs of this life; that he may please him who hath chosen him to be a soldier." [12] We'll just have to go back and reread the earlier uses of these metaphors to bring them into line with our new understanding.

Only we *weren't* mistaken, of course. And the temperature metaphor *isn't* the same. The speaker has retorted on himself, and in the process won his language back from the impulses that were fouling it up. In this kind of poem, part of repenting is rejecting one's own metaphors, and metaphors are rejected by being redeemed.

One of the crucial religious-ethical metaphors of "Employment (II)" stays undeveloped: the one in the title. It's particularly crucial in Herbert, who has a horror of *un*employment. People who are no use to others, especially God, are likely to be people God has no use for. But private horror aside, vocational activism goes with Herbert's Protestant ideal of piety: "Even in Paradise man had a calling, and how much more out of Paradise, when the evills which he is now subject unto may be prevented, or diverted, by reasonable imployment. . . . Every gift or ability is a talent to be accounted for and to be improved to our Master's Advantage."[13] The core of the metaphorical ambition being expressed here is the desire to join the company of God's household, in Paul's charged phrase; to be one of the *domestici Dei*.[14] If God has liveried servants, then he must be "the great householder of the world."[15] The arguer-from-design "sees not how a house could be either built without a builder, or kept in repair without a house-keeper";[16] on this metaphorical version of the design argument, it's because houses imply the existence of both builders and keepers, and God is both, that God has to exist.

In "Affliction (I)" the cosmic householder puts in a sinister reappearance. One of the domestics of a king confronts his employer with a long-standing grievance,[17] and we watch the metaphor march on bitterly toward an astonishing reversal.

If the servant's complaint is well taken, his employer hired him under false pretenses. The bad faith involved was the worst kind: breach of promise and malicious entrapment. First the entrapment:

> When first thou didst entice to thee my heart
>   I thought the service brave:
> So many joyes I writ down for my part,
>   Besides what I might have
> Out of my stock of naturall delights,   5
> Augmented with thy gracious benefits.
>
> I looked on thy furniture so fine,
>   And made it fine to me:
> Thy glorious houshold-stuffe did me entwine,
>   And 'tice me unto thee.   10
> Such starres I counted mine: both heav'n and earth
> Payd me my wages in a world of mirth.
>
> What pleasures could I want, whose King I served,
>   Where joyes my fellows were?

> Thus argu'd into hopes, my thoughts reserved   15
> No place for grief or fear.
> Therefore my sudden soul caught at the place,
> And made her youth and fierceness seek thy face.

No wonder the servant's soul caught at the offered "place" (17). His fellows in the "service" (2) were supposed to be "joyes" (14), with no "place" reserved for servants with names like "Grief" and "Fear" (16). The expected salary was double: pleasure [18] and ambition,[19] earth and heaven (11), the "delights" of nature (5), and the "benefits" of grace (6). Above all, this service was "brave" (2)—full of pomp and circumstance. The servant was especially "entwined" and "enticed" by the glory of wearing, and being surrounded by, his lord's "houshold stuff" (9–10).[20]

All this suits his frank ambition and aggressiveness. For him the status of a priest—a servant in God's house—isn't a privilege. It's a contractual claim on the divine employer that the speaker "writ down for my part" (3) at the bargaining stage.[21] These were things, the stars included, that he "counted mine" (11). In passing we get a nice touch of self-importance. Fine as the furniture might be in itself, the servant managed to add something special: "[I] *made* it fine to *me*" (8). As he describes it, priesthood wasn't a favor granted but a trophy seized—and here the witness's self-ignorance jumps out at us. In his unhappy and revealing metaphor, his soul was something greedy that "caught" at the place; a kind of hunter that *made* youth, and especially fierceness, seek the employer's face (17–18)—as if they were dogs being egged on, and the face the quarry.

The speaker blames his illusions about the status of priests on his employer. And illusions are all they've turned out to be. He expected to be a figure of reverence and finds himself a figure of fun. "The Countrey Parson knows well," says Herbert elsewhere, "that . . . for the generall ignominy which is cast upon the profession, . . . he must be despised."[22] There was no fair warning of this in the speaker's high marks and preferments at university. Now he discovers that "Academick praise" (45) was only bait in the church's trap of social marginality, isolated from the real action.[23]

Scholastic debate, "sweetened" with praise, was just a "world" of inconsequential "strife" his divine employer and recruiter "entangled" him in "before I had the power to change my life" (41–42). The ways of pedants aren't the ways that the "town" is taken with—and the town is the world of consequential strife that the speaker knows he was meant for:

> Whereas my birth and spirit rather took
>   The way that takes the town;
> Thou didst betray me to a lingring book,
>   And wrap me in a gown. (37–40)

In short, he never got the chance to find out how he really wanted to live. Instead, he was "entic'd" (1, 10), "argu'd into hopes" (15), "entangl'd" (41), and above all "betrayed" (39)—"before I had the power to change my life." The heart of the betrayal was this theft of personal autonomy.

Presumably the servant might have lived with his supposedly ill-informed decision to serve—if the employer had eventually *let* him serve. But with demonic spite, even this consolation was taken away:

> Thus doth thy power crosse-bias me, not making
> Thine own gift good, yet me from my ways taking. (53–54)

The employer made sure the gift of employment was no good—in fact, a mockery—by incapacitating the employee:

> My flesh began unto my soul in pain,
>   Sicknesses cleave my bones;
> Consuming agues dwell in ev'ry vein,
>   And tune my breath to grones.
> Sorrow was all my soul; I scarce beleeved,
> Till grief did tell me roundly, that I lived.
>
> When I got health, thou took'st away my life,
>   And more; for my friends die. (25–32)

Even though the speaker doesn't seem to notice what he's doing, Herbert's readers will recognize the familiar accents of Job and the penitential psalms:

> For my daies are consumed like smoke, and my bones are burnt like an herth. . . . For the voice of my groning my bones do cleaue to my skin.
>
> There is nothing sounde in my flesh, because of thine angre: nether is there rest in my bones because of my sinne.
>
> My bone cleaueth to my skin and to my flesh, and I haue escaped with the skinne of my teeth.[24]

The difference is that, unlike David and Job,[25] the speaker neatly puts the blame for his predicament on somebody else. In the figurative dialogue he puts in at this point (25–28), the soul has nothing to say. The noisy partner is the flesh, guileless and obviously more sinned against than sinning. In the whole narrative there's no hint of misgiving, only bitterness over the employer's bad faith. There's certainly no hint of love for the employer (with one exception I'll get to in a moment). The recruit was won over to start with by the promise of glory, or rather by what he *interpreted* as a promise of glory; or rather by what he *says* he interpreted that way. Throughout this testimony the witness is industriously cooking the evidence.

What gives him his chance to cook the evidence is his choice of metaphor: priesthood as liveried service in the household of a great lord. Manor-house talk is precisely the language of the life to be given up; it's the way of talking that "takes the town." We recognize the evidence cooking because we aren't confined to the metaphor for relevant information. In fact, the metaphor would make no sense at all to us if we were. We know—by talk-postulate, at least—that the priesthood isn't offered to its aspirants as a posh job. We also know that, since the speaker trained carefully for his ministry with a "lingring book" (39), he knows it, too.

I said that his testimony shows no hint of love for the employer, with one exception. The ultimate frustration, the one he mentions in passing but comes back to at the end of his catalogue of frustrations, is that, no thanks to God, "a blunted knife" is "of more use then I" (33–34): he's a servant his master has no use for. He wants there to be something that could be *done* with him, but unfortunately, "now I am here, what thou wilt do with me"—if anything—"none of my books will show" (55–56). But *why* doesn't his master have a use for him? The speaker's suspicion of why comes out in his daydream:

> I reade, and sigh, and wish I were a tree;
>   For sure then I should grow
> To fruit and shade: at least some bird would trust
> Her houshold to me, and I should be just.   (57–60)

If he were a tree he would not only be used but *trusted*. As things stand, he isn't used—because not trusted? And if not trusted, how *loved*? This sounds like the familiar petulance of the slighted lover.

Petulance, at least, is the note the speaker seems to be determined to end on. He also seems to be determined to carry his embittered-servant metaphor out to the bitter end. He starts by pouring a little sarcasm on the standard wisdom about how to handle affliction:

> Yet, though thou troublest me, I must be meek;
>   In weakness must be stout. (61–62)

Apparently we're supposed to see flat contradictions in the notion of meekness toward a troubler and stoutness in weakness—contradictions that will show the absurdity of the moral ideal they grow out of. Then comes the outbreak of petulance:

> Well, I will change the service, and go seek
>   Some other master out. (63–64)

The only other relevant "master," of course, is Satan. The threat is ugly and desperate enough, even though it's mostly infantile tantrum. We seem to be headed straight toward an ending made up of equal parts of abject and nasty. But at this point something astonishing happens. The speaker begins another petulant "though" clause in the voice of the disgruntled servant: "Ah my deare God! though I am clean forgot. . . ."

Now the rule for "though A is true, B is true just the same" is straightforward and utterly familiar—just right for trapping us with our automatic response: B has to deny some obviously relevant thing that A would justify one in expecting. In this case, being forgotten by a master with a reputation for being fair is good evidence that the forgetting was warranted. So given the rule for "though" and the speaker's crescendo of reproaches, we can be drearily sure of what sort of A-B sequence is called for here. It will have to be something that says, more or less: Though you don't love me, I'm worthy of love just the same. Something like this:

> Ah my deare God! though I am clean forgot,
> Thy servant hath deserv'd a better lot.

The B we get instead totally undermines our understanding of A—and not through any fault of ours: "Let me not love thee, if I love thee not" (66). The speaker has broken the "though" rule, and at the same time broken with the self that would have gone on to obey it. Viewed from the vantage point of the way he *does* go on, the A-B sequence goes roughly this way:

A. "THOUGH" CLAUSE: You don't love me—as you would if I were fit to be loved.

B. "JUST THE SAME" CLAUSE: But if what makes me unfit is that *I* don't love *you*, then punish me still further by *keeping* me unfit. In short, don't forgive me if I don't love you; because then I don't forgive myself.

The speaker has been listening to his own performance long enough to be revolted by it. And at the last moment he chucks it, metaphor and all, by turning all his reproaches on himself. This time the *para prosdokian* doesn't redeem the metaphor; it simply, and abruptly, renounces it, with an apparently sudden effort of will. Now we see our earlier hunch confirmed. Behind the figuration mask of the badly treated domestic there was the rejected lover all along, daydreaming about a transformation into something—tree or knife—worth using, if not loving. In the comic tangle that is suddenly untied here, a lover condemns himself for being unloving, and thereby proves his love to everybody but himself. With the final identification of "my *deare* God," the mask of disgruntlement has already started to come apart:

> Ah my deare God! though I am clean forgot,
> Let me not love thee, if I love thee not.   (65–66)[26]

"The Pearl" is worth a look in this connection. In "Affliction (I)" the speaker manages to corrupt the Bible metaphor of "service" by missing or ignoring the point. God's domestics aren't paid in luxuries and glory, and domestics also serve who only stand and wait. In short, God has broken promises about "service" only on a corrupt reading of the metaphor. The speaker has substituted a twin—same literal meaning, same subject matter, new and demeaning figurative sense. Something similar happens in "The Pearl," but here the comic untying is truer to the *para prosdokian* form that I'm interested in here. Instead of being renounced, the corrupted metaphor is reread, as if the new reading were what the metaphor really meant the first time around.

The victim of the speaker's manipulation is the Gospel notion that choosing to live as a Christian is striking a supremely good bargain: "The kingdome of heaven is like to a marchant man, that seketh good perles, who hauing founde a perle of great price, went and solde all that he had, and boght it."[27] Good bargains imply various things, profit and shrewdness among others. Which implications are turned by metaphor into a new sense of *bargain* depends on the context—and here is where the speaker makes his mistake. He takes the metaphor out of context. All that's meant by spiritual "merchandise" in the Bible is infinite profit:

> Blessed is the man that findeth wisdome, and the man that getteth vnderstanding. For the marchandise thereof is better then the marchandise of siluer, and the gaine thereof is better then golde. It is more precious then pearls: and all things that thou canst desire, are not to be compared vnto her. Length of daies is in her right hand, and in her left hand riches and glorie. Her waies are waies of pleasure [see "The Pearl," st. 3], and all her paths prosperitie.[28]

But for the speaker of "The Pearl," the choice to "love thee" is not only infinitely profitable, it's a tribute to the chooser's own shrewdness. So this particular "marchant man" settles down to a good brag about the "wisdom" and "understanding" that won him a treasure more precious than pearls.

The speaker knows "the wayes of Learning"; he knows both its sources and how it is transmitted—the "head" (water power) and "pipes" that "feed the [printing] presse, and make it runne." He knows political philosophy—what conscience and prudence separately put into the design of a civil order.[29] He knows natural philosophy—how to study nature by observing it either hands-off or hands-on. He knows ancient and modern geography.

He knows "the wayes of Honour"—knows the "quick returns [repartee, rewards]" of deftness in the social arts. He knows which rival is winning the contest for worldly "favours" and adoration, and what his loyalty is worth to employers, friendly or otherwise.

And he knows "the wayes of Pleasure," both its intensities ("relishes," "hot bloud," "mirth," "love") and its refinements ("lullings," "brains," "musick," "wit").[30] He is as exquisitely vulnerable to pleasure as Job was to pain; his "stuffe" too is "flesh, not brasse,"[31] and often makes him think it's unfair for reason to "curb" a nature that's really more sensual than rational.

Up until the last stanza, the response to each list of "wayes" of the world has been: "*Yet* I love thee" (italics mine). In other words, in choosing Christ the speaker has had to *overcome* his knowledge of the world. That knowledge is an *obstacle* to making the right choice. It would have excused his failure, and it glorifies his success. Part of the challenge is a credit to the world's maker: the value of what he made. And part comes out in details of the speaker's account that I've put off looking at because they need a paragraph to themselves: the sordid urges that the world panders to, and that the speaker hints at glancingly here and there.

Not satisfied with what "*willing* nature speaks," the experimental scientist pushes on to find out what nature will say when "forced by fire" (6). He starts inquisitive and ends up inquisitorial. Scientific curiosity and sadism are secret cousins. The "honour" seeker is at least as unsavory seen close up: a mercenary flunky, willing to "bear the [world's] bundle wheresoe're [the world] goes," and to "sell" his life—measured in "drammes of spirit"— to "friends or foes" indiscriminately (17–19). His beloved "glorie" is a glassblower who "swells the heart and moldeth it" to "all expressions of the hand or eye" that will win the world's vote (14–16). As for the robust hedonism surveyed under "pleasure," the speaker doesn't try to hide the parasitic hoarding that makes it possible: lives of end-to-end pleasure are "projects of unbridled *store*" (26; italics mine).

Presumably a (fallen) human nature will find all these things strongly tempting just *because* they're spiced with corruption. And the speaker doesn't claim to be superhuman. So the "yet" in "Yet I love thee" is a fairly obvious puff of the bargainer's sales resistance.

But in the last stanza, "yet" is replaced with "therefore":

> I know all these, and have them in my hand:
> *Therefore* not sealed, but with open eyes
> I flie to thee, and fully understand
> Both the main sale, and the commodities;
> And at what rate and price I have thy love;
> With all the circumstances that may move.
>
> (31–36; italics mine)

Instead of hindering, knowledge *enables* the chooser to choose right. It removes rather than adds an excuse. If by knowledge you mean acquaintance, then it might make some sort of sense to say you know a thing, even know it intimately, and "yet" manage to avoid wildly overestimating it; but only because you're using a different sense of "know": knowing by acquaintance ("I've known X intimately for years") rather than knowing facts *about* ("I've got X's number"). To know the ways of the world in the relevant sense, the speaker needs to see their real value well enough to see that the pearl in Christ's parable is the better bargain.

The change in emphasis marked by the shift from "yet" to "therefore" is self-serving, of course. We've heard all about the speaker's sales resistance; now it's time for his shrewdness. You need open eyes to strike a shrewd bargain. And you need to *claim* open eyes to *brag* of having struck one. Everything has gone predictably so far—until we're brought up short with the return of "yet."

Again the reversal is astonishing—a supreme *para prosdokian*. Without skipping a beat, the speaker in effect forces us to go back and check his argument. Both it and his metaphor have been abruptly refigured by hindsight:

> Yet through these labyrinths, not my groveling wit,
> But thy silk twist let down from heav'n to me,
> Did both conduct and teach me, how by it
>   To climb to thee.   (37–40)

Surely the speaker wasn't bragging that his *wisdom* won him the pearl. Wisdom is what the pearl *brought* him: "Blessed is the man that findeth wisdome, and the man that getteth vnderstanding. For the marchandise thereof is better then the marchandise of siluer, and the gaine thereof is better then golde. It is more precious then pearls: and all things that thou canst desire, are not to be compared vnto her." But of course he *was* bragging of wisdom—and now he's retorting on himself.

At the same time, there *was* a bargain, and one of infinite shrewdness at that. It took a divine accountant to tote up "the main sale, and the commodities" (34). But for that very reason both the bargain and the shrewdness are gifts.[32] For the gift to be genuine it has to be usable. The shrewdness is really being exercised. The merchant really chooses. But he chooses by instruction—like Theseus moving out of the maze by himself, but under guidance. The merchant is a falcon flying to his trainer's lure. Unlike ordinary trainees reduced by temporary blinding to abject dependence, he doesn't fly with seeled eyes.

In the last stanza the speaker redeems his metaphor. But since it gave him trouble, he takes the trouble to combine it with two others that cover the same meaning: the unseeled eyes and the silk twist. The redundancy can't guarantee "full understanding," but it makes it more likely. And it makes some amends.[33]

I've left my most puzzling example of *para prosdokian* in Herbert for last:

> Prayer the Churches banquet, Angels age,
>   Gods breath in man returning to his birth,

> The soul in paraphrase, heart in pilgrimage,
> The Christian plummet sounding heav'n and earth;
> Engine against th' Almightie, sinners towre,
>> Reversed thunder, Christ-side-piercing spear,
> The six-daies world transposing in an houre,
> A kinde of tune, which all things heare and fear;
> Softnesse, and peace, and joy, and love and blisse,
>> Exalted Manna, gladnesse of the best,
>> Heaven in ordinarie, man well drest,
> The milkie way, the bird of Paradise,
>> Church-bels beyond the starres heard, the souls bloud,
>> The land of spices; something understood.

In "Prayer (I)" the meaning that is reversed by the last two words doesn't belong to any particular phrase used by the speaker. Instead, it belongs to the standard label for the speech act he's performing. What the speaker *seems* to be doing, at least at the start, is a familiar kind of virtuoso figuration: the mock dictionary entry.

As usual in this kind of entertainment, none of the "definitions" in the "entry" actually spells out a sense of the word "prayer." They're all figurative descriptions of praying itself, and the challenge is to solve the implication riddle posed by the literal sense of one description after another, and to do this without breaking stride. What makes the challenge a riddle is that many, if not all, the descriptions have literal implications that are (by talk-postulate, at least) distractingly wrong. So the trick of reading is to refuse to be distracted from finding the literal implications that qualify as figurative senses—the implications that are cleverly right. We have a combination treasure hunt and obstacle course. And the course is strewn with gaudily unpredictable obstacles.

For example, there's a somewhat misleading technical sense of "breath" and "return" in which prayer *is* "Gods breath in man returning to his [the breath's and man's] birth [origin]": human prayer is supposed to be made possible by the indwelling of the Holy *Spirit*—etymologically, "breath." So in hearing prayer God is regaining (catching?) his "breath"! The quibble is a chance to capture the special intimacy of conversation with God. It's also a reminder that the act of sanctifying life is the end of a historical process that begins with the act of giving it; creating "prefigures" redeeming.

Or, to solve a much more bizarre riddle: it's precisely because God is our ally and egger-on against *himself* that it isn't an insult to call prayer an "engine against th' Almightie" or "reversed thunder," that is, thunder boomeranging against the thunderer. God's mercy *overcomes* God's justice when he enables and licenses a sinner to talk to him with utter bluntness (*licentia,* in the jargon of theological rhetoric). In one of his sermons Donne reaches for roughly the same metaphor: "God charges and discharges the Cannon [of prayer] upon him selfe."[34]

In the same context (figurative aggressions "against th' Almightie"), the notion of being allied with God against God also saves "sinners tower" (of Babel?). The tower won't do if what's meant is "resentment . . . raised against a seemingly unjust God";[35] raging at God isn't praying. But figurational charity rules out absurdities if an obvious alternative is available: "He is my goodness & my fortres, my *tower* & my deliverer."[36] If prayer is a new and good kind of Babel tower, this time the architect is God.

The witty metaphor-riddles speed after each other one or two to a line, with a rush of decorative sensuousness toward the end:

> The milkie way,[37] the bird of Paradise,
> Church-bels beyond the starres heard, the souls bloud,
> The land of spices

—only to come to a thudding stop in a phrase that couldn't be less decorative or sensuous, or less obviously witty: "something understood."

It's as if the speaker were resorting to a tactic of Saint Cyprian's, described this way by his admirer Augustine:

> These things [a purple patch in Cyprian] are said with nothing short of the most miraculously exuberant fertility of wit. But seriousness is offended by their lush profusion. On the other hand, those who love this kind of thing imagine that people who don't talk this way, but with more discipline, don't because they can't, not because good judgment tells them to avoid it. So this holy man shows both that he *can* talk this way, since he did it somewhere, and that he doesn't *wish* to, since afterward he does it nowhere.[38]

If the speaker's tactic is anything like Cyprian's, then what we've been hearing isn't a mock definition after all, but a fictive *quotation* of one. The speaker has been setting up a specimen of false wit to point at: here's the kind of thing I can do if I please, so don't put my contempt for it down to sour grapes. But if this is the implication of the speaker's ostentatiously plain ending, then we're blaming ourselves for a nonexistent mistake again. The force of quotation belongs to the foregoing words as *reread*— to a *repetition* of the words, not to the original utterance. The speaker is turning and pointing back at his own false wit. We follow the pointing finger and look again.

But there's unfinished business. What is it for prayer to be "something understood"? Taken at face value, this is utterly pointless. God (if he exists) knows everything. So given his existence, any meaningful utterance at all is guaranteed to be something understood. Figurational charity comes into play here: we'd better not take the phrase at face value if we can help it.

The obvious solution is to limit our attention to the kind of understanding that matters to us: getting across *to the person we're addressing*, whether it's God or another human being. But the obvious solution has a less obvious catch: if things people say to each other, unlike prayers, are never "things understood" by their intended audience—at least in the deep way that God understands them—then neither is the phrase "something understood" itself!

That phrase turns out to be a *para prosdokian* to the second power. First, its plainness forces us back to reread and "recognize"—as butts of ridicule—the witty riddles that went before it. But then, as its generality dawns on us, it forces us to reread *itself;* and what we "recognize" now, in vindication of the butts, is the wittiest riddle of the lot. In perhaps a shallower sense than the one it disclaims, but a sense that's far from negligible, "something understood" is something "understood" after all.

IV. *The Exploratory Metaphor*

I said earlier that studying this effect of hindsight figuration would lead us straight to kinds of thinking-in-metaphor that are powerful and inclusive enough to create the structure of whole poems. It's time to try to make good that claim.

Here's one way ex post facto meaning might create a structure: the "correction" in the reading might itself need to be "corrected" in turn, then this second "correction" is modified by a third, and so on to the end of the poem. Imagine the following scenario. The speaker starts by using a given literal sense (vehicle) to describe or name a given subject (tenor). The literal sense somehow doesn't apply. As usual, the speaker gets the benefit of the doubt. He's innocent until proved guilty of gross mistakes of both speaking and conceiving. Again as usual, a figurative sense is supplied by the way the argument fits together. But this time the story doesn't end there. The figurative sense refuses to stay put.

We start with a pairing of vehicle and tenor—something that will be a metaphor if the argument shows how the vehicle *applies* to the tenor; that is, if the argument calls for a particular figurative sense. But the sense keeps on being changed by jumps in the argument. What we're really getting is a *series* of metaphors, together with the thoughts they're part of. But the continuity of vehicle and tenor gives the impression of a single metaphor and a single thought gradually revealing themselves to meditative trial and error.

One variant of this pattern is especially interesting. Suppose the only way we can learn how the vehicle (say, *corpuscle-stream*) applies to the tenor (say, *ray of light*) is by learning something new about the tenor first. We're offered an apparently metaphorical statement as a truth—but exactly *how* it's true is something we'll have to go through a search, and successive re-understandings, to find out. Here the vehicle-tenor pairing is like the core of an evolving theory. In fact, maybe it *is* an evolving theory. This isn't the place to look further into the parallel between theory building and using tenor-vehicle pairings heuristically. But it suggests a handy name for the general phenomenon I'll be looking at in the next group of poems to be studied: the exploratory metaphor.

V. *Exploratory Metaphors in Donne*

I think the most elaborate and powerful of Donne's studies in exploratory metaphor is "Hymne to God my God, in my sicknesse." The crucial vehicle-tenor pairings are introduced in the first two sentences. Mortal fever is either the door to a church or the narrow passage (strait; *fretum*) to a wide western sea. The dying speaker is a map:

> Since I am comming to that Holy roome,
>   Where, with thy Quire of Saints for evermore,
> I shall be made thy Musique; As I come,
>   I tune the Instrument here at the dore,
>   And what I must doe then, thinke here before.
>
> Whilst my Physitians by their lore are growne
>   Cosmographers, and I their Mapp, who lie

> Flat on this bed, that by them may be showne
> That this is my South-west discoverie
> *Per fretum febris*, by these streights to die,
>
> I joy, that in these straits, I see my West. (1–11)

Here the reader gets some tentative help from metaphors already entrenched in one of the wider conversations the poem is jointly part of: its cultural tradition, in the shape of the classical atlas. It happens that the atlas conveniently associates the two vehicle-notions. "[Front] gate" and "door" are both metaphors for geographical *strait* (the Strait of Gibraltar is the "ocean door" and the "Cadiz gates").[39] As for the cosmographical man-"map," the famous Renaissance talk-postulate has it that both the human body and the human mind are "microcosms," little worlds that map the great one—though the speaker has the grace or grit to resist being lured here into a show of self-importance. What we get instead is a show of insouciance—a sardonic joke at his own expense. Thanks to his learned doctors' "lore," *his* stretched-out, fever-ridden microcosm is making itself useful. He's being a demonstration chart for a "geography" lesson ("my South-west discoverie"). So far, the only course he charts is that of his own fever.

At this point the metaphors of dying-as-"strait" and speaker-as-"map" go through a modulation together. The voyage being plotted on this chart isn't the body's but the mind's, and it's a voyage of exploration:

> I joy, that in these straits, I see my West;
>   For, though theire currants yeeld returne to none,
> What shall my West hurt me? As West and East
>   In all flatt Maps (and I am one) are one,
>   So death doth touch the Resurrection.
>
> Is the Pacifique Sea my home? Or are
>   The Easterne riches? Is *Ierusalem*?
> *Anyan*, and *Magellan*, and *Gibraltare*,
>   All streights, and none but streights are wayes to them,
>   Whether where *Iaphet* dwelt, or *Cham*, or *Sem*. (11–20)

Again we get some help from traditional metaphors. People undergoing hardship are sailing through narrows—choppy stretches with nasty currents. *Anguish* and *anxiety* are also "narrows" (*angustiae*)—the kind of hard going that brings on a panicky narrowing of the throat (*angor*). These are the emotional straits that the speaker manages to defy by making wry jokes, and now by finding a reason for "joy." In effect, stanza 3 gives "*by these streights*" in stanza 2 a new context and a new reading. A nautical strait is something restrictive that you have to go *through* to get to the free expanse at the other end.

In this context, the crack about a "South-west *discoverie*" stops being just a display of panache under stress. Hamlet is only half right about death being an undiscovered country from whose bourn no traveler returns. The speaker will soon be *joining* the unreturning travelers, and he's looking forward precisely to a "discoverie" (an uncovering; a revelation)—and at the same time to the Odyssean joy of coming home (in the old theological jargon, heaven is *patria*).[40] The opening metaphor also is enriched by hindsight. The arduous Christian life is precisely a narrow entry to that "Holy roome" ("the gate is *streighte,* and the way *narowe* that leadeth vnto life").[41]

The dying speaker's maphood also turns out to mean more than we thought. Like the flat parchment map, the flat human one's leftmost edge (death) somehow "touches" its rightmost edge (resurrection). Not literally, of course; the two outermost meridians on the parchment aren't literally "one" either. In the relevant Bible commonplace, a thousand years are a mere day from God's point of view—which is the point of view that the soul will share with God just after death. The parchment map edges "touch" by association (*metonymy*): they *stand for* the same longitude. And the human "map" edges "touch" by minimization (*meiosis*): as experienced by a consciousness outside time (reunited with God), the gap between death and resurrection is (practically) no time at all.[42]

If "death" and "resurrection" are themselves taken figuratively (as names of *sin* and *redemption,* respectively), *practically end to end* doesn't exhaust what their "touching" can be maneuvered into meaning. Sin also "touches"—calls forth, implies—redemption:

> We thinke that *Paradise* and *Calvarie,*
>   *Christs* Crosse, and *Adams* tree, stood in one place;
> Looke Lord, and finde both *Adams* met in me;
>   As the first *Adams* sweat surrounds my face,
> May the last *Adams* blood my soule embrace.
>
> So, in his purple wrapp'd receive mee Lord,
>   By these his thornes give me his other Crowne;
> And as to others soules I preach'd thy word,

>   Be this my Text, my Sermon to mine owne,
>   Therefore that he may raise the Lord throws down.   (21–30)

The speaker has been thinking in images, the images reassuringly held constant as their values shift gradually from one metaphor-homonym to another—from "map$_1$," to "map$_2$," "strait$_1$," to "strait$_2$," and so on. By contrast, "door" and "strait" have been metaphor-synonyms at each stage. As we approach the end of the poem the synonyms are joined by still other metaphorically equivalent "touchings" or coincidings: west and east in maps = tree and cross = Adam$_1$ and Adam$_2$ = sin-sweat and redemption-blood = sin-thorns and redemption-crown = (punitive) throwing down and (redemptive) raising up. The speaker has finally worked through to a confrontation with his main worry, and to a last defiant hindsight valuation of the image he started with: "I [Christ] am the dore. By me if any man enter in, he shalbe saued."[43] The deaths that are "doors" to the "Holy roome" coincide with acts of faith—with imitations of Christ.

VI. *Exploratory Metaphors in Herbert*

Herbert's exploratory metaphor in "The Temper (I)" does its exploring a bit differently. The vehicle is allowed to change, too, but not simply to be replaced like the figurative sense. Instead we get variations on a single theme, as if an experimenter were trying out different versions of a single basic explanatory hunch.

The thing to be explained is the point of the speaker's painful swings in religious emotion between the extremes of "hope and fear":

>   Although there were some fourtie heav'ns, or more,
>   Sometimes I peere above them all;
>   Sometimes I hardly reach a score,
>   Sometimes to hell I fall.   (5–8)

The width of the swing is painful in itself, so that it would bring some measure of relief if, whichever the extreme, "what my soul doth feel sometimes, / My soul might ever feel" (3–4). It seems that the swings follow each other rapidly enough to seem to merge. The swing becomes a *stretch*—giving the speaker the dominant image on which he'll play figurative variations in the form of alternative theories of why he's being put through this ordeal in the first place.

Maybe (theory 1) the point of the stretching is to torture him, by way of punishment ("racking"). If so, the punishment is surely too great, not for the victim's endurance—after all, he *is* enduring it so far—but for his modest place in the scheme of things:

> O rack me not to such a vast extent;
>   Those distances belong to thee:
>   The world's too little for thy tent,
>   A grave too big for me.   (9–12)

On the other hand (theory 2), maybe the point isn't so much punishment as continuous hostility. The "stretching" is a move in combat, like Jacob's wrestling match with the angel. If so, the speaker is a poor choice for a sparring partner. The trouble, of course, isn't that being matched with God is unfair to *him,* but that being matched with him is unfair to *God:*

> Wilt thou meet arms with man, that thou dost stretch
>   A crumme of dust from heav'n to hell?
>   Will great God measure with a wretch?
>   Shall he thy stature spell?

The irony just underscores the bitterness. This poor David is up against a Goliath no sling could equalize.

But the author has managed to introduce a second irony, this time at his speaker's expense. The speaker asks rhetorically: "Shall [I] thy stature spell?" Given the Jacob analogy, "stretch" forces a yes answer in spite of the asker. Herbert's readers will know the glosses on the Jacob episode in the Geneva Bible: "For God assaileth his [children] with the one hand, and vpholdeth them with the other." "God gaue Iaakob bothe power to ouercome and also the praise of the victorie."[44] And they'll also know that the wrestling angel is Christ. In Calvin's phrase, the match is a "curtain raiser" (*praeludium*) to Christ's main performance as mediator between the sinner and his judge.[45] By stretching the stature of his chosen antagonist, God is *making* the match equal. And in "measuring" with a wretch, God isn't simply vying with him: the nonslang sense of the word is read back into it by "spell." The speaker is becoming an instrument of measurement—of stature spelling (stature in this case being the scope of God's power to rehabilitate "wretches"). If all goes well, this particular wretch will be the "measure of all things" in a sense that turns the tables on the subversive skepticism that inspired that ancient slogan. Once again the speaker's vehicle—or vehicle-core—has changed just enough to change the sense. This time "stretching" somebody isn't racking him but making him grow. It isn't vengeance but grace.

But as usual in Herbert, the speaker is too distracted (by resentment and self-pity this time) to catch these happy ironies. Besides, he isn't interested in *stature;* what he prays for is a comfortable *littleness*, as one more chick in the divine dovecote. This fey performance is topped off with an afterthought of jocular coyness. It seems that God also stands to gain by fulfilling this hope. He'll get a nuisance off his hands:

> O let me, when thy roof my soul hath hid,
>   O let me roost and nestle there:
>   Then of a sinner thou art rid,
>   And I of hope and fear.   (17–20)

The whimsical self-prescribing and wheedling aren't just precious; they're presumptuous. They need to be taken back, and are. The move leads to the speaker's last and apparently most satisfactory theory (3):

> Yet take thy way; for sure thy way is best:
>   Stretch or contract me, thy poore debter:
>   This is but tuning of my breast,
>   To make the musick better.   (21–24)

So stretching is neither racking nor wrestling. It's tuning—the tempering that Herbert's title has kept us waiting for.

This final theory nicely clinches Herbert's ironies at the speaker's expense. The speaker has just asked rhetorically if God plans to use him to span the distance between heaven and hell—to measure the cosmos. Now, thanks to another variation on stretching, the rhetoric is taken out of the question. In at least one famously compelling vision of cosmic harmony, things hold together precisely by straining apart—like the string of a lyre or a drawn bow. Without tension, no equilibrium.[46] The speaker adds a grace note to that compelling old theme. A string of the cosmic lyre is being adjusted to the harmony of the whole instrument, "to make the musick better."

The poem might well have ended here. But from Herbert's religious point of view, at least, the extra stanza has a clinching irony of its own. The speaker has gotten all the way from querulousness to a serene confession of faith. We're being given a pragmatic proof of sorts that the tempering has finally started to "make the musick better":

> Whether I flie with angels, fall with dust,
>   Thy hands made both, and I am there:
> Thy power and love, my love and trust
>   Make one place ev'ry where.   (25–28)

In "The Temper (I)" Herbert's speaker takes the classic conservative approach to inquiry: hang onto the core of a reasonable theory in the face of setbacks—as long as there's a workable way of extending the core. The speaker tinkers slightly this way and that with his vehicle, or literal sense (mood shifting as "stretching"), until it generates the figurative sense that satisfies him. In "The Forerunners" his exploratory metaphor is more straightforwardly heuristic. The vehicle is fine—in fact, much finer than he realizes at the start. The heuristic effect is precisely that realization. The speaker turns a corner in his argument to find out suddenly that he's been misunderstanding himself. His figurative sense—the application of his vehicle to his tenor—turns out to be richer and more revealing than the application he has been working with.

Here's the speaker introducing his metaphor:

> The harbingers are come. See, see their mark;
> White is their colour, and behold my head.
> But must they have my brain? Must they dispark
> Those sparkling notions, which therein were bred?
>   Must dulnesse turn me to a clod?
> Yet have they left me, *Thou art still my God.*
>
> Good men ye be, to leave me my best room,
> Ev'n all my heart, and what is lodged there:
> I passe not, I, what of the rest become,
> So *Thou art still my God,* be out of fear.   (1–10)

Just how are white hairs "harbingers" of the loss of mental vigor? The prima facie point of this hardly seems to be worth the trouble of a metaphor. Harbingers run up ahead of a great lord on a progress to chalk the door of the night's lodging they've commandeered for him. And the commandeering may involve herding out ("dis-parking") some of the residents. So in this context being a harbinger of the loss of one's "sparkling notions" is being an advance warning, and maybe a partial cause, of the loss.

Oddly enough, the speaker's main point has nothing to do with harbingers or advance warnings. So far he's been allowed to keep his faith: "Yet have they left me, *Thou art still my God*." Provided he's assured of keeping that, he can put up with the loss of his wit:

> I passe not, I, what of the rest become,
> So *Thou art still my God,* be out of fear.

The brain can die before the heart, and that's all right with him.

The distinction between the brain and the heart is obviously crucial for the speaker. He's fooling himself when he says that he doesn't care "what of the rest become." A death sentence to the "brain" is too terrible not to appeal: "But *must* they have my brain?" "*Must* dulnesse turn me to a clod?" (italics mine). But for him faith is a moral attitude, not a state of the intellect, and it's the faithful who amount to something in the end, not the clever. So if it comes to a choice of which to give up, "brain" or "heart," he'll give up the brain.

The speaker goes on to find a clever way of being resigned without choking on his terror and bitterness. He follows the time-tested recipe for having your cake while eating it: draw a superfine distinction. On the one hand, he *is* willing to say good-bye to his verbal talents—his "lovely metaphors" (13). On the other hand, he can't stand the *way* they're leaving him: "But will you [the metaphors] leave me thus?" (14). The "thus" is spelled out in what follows. He's the one who rescued those metaphors from "stews and brothels" and "brought you to Church well drest and clad." Now what will become of his "lovely enchanting language"? "Wilt thou [the language] leave the Church, and love a stie?" (15–22).

The only decent use of *creatures'* beauty in metaphors is to apply it figuratively to their *creator's* beauty; applying it to anything else is a prostitution:

> True beautie dwells on high: ours [earthly beauty] is a flame
> But borrow'd thence to light us thither.
> Beautie [God's] and beauteous words [metaphors] should go
>   together.   (28–30)[47]

The speaker worries that once he's too senile to *see* to it that they go together, the "beauteous words" will be used by "foolish lovers" to "clothe their shame" (25–26). He found those words in profane love poetry. He made them fit for expressing sacred love. Now he's afraid that without his protection they'll backslide:

> Fie, thou [enchanting language] wilt soil thy
> broider'd coat,
> And hurt thy self, and him that sings thy note. (23–24)

Or so he claims.

But obviously devotional adaptations of profane love poetry have been around for centuries. Equally obviously, neither the speaker nor any other devotional adapter can keep his profane rivals from returning the compliment by adapting the devotions. Besides, all this pious concern is immediately deflated by the sour-grapes argument that comes next. Now it seems that "beauteous words" don't light anybody anywhere. They just embellish—*perhaps:*

> Yet if you go, I passe not; take your way;
> For, *Thou art still my God,* is all that ye
> Perhaps with more embellishment can say. (31–33)

Sour grapes are as eloquent a testimonial as a grape could hope for. And clearly the statesmanlike reason for the speaker's reluctance to let go of his knack for "lovely metaphors" won't survive a close look. It's the thinnest of disguises for the real reason, which is simply that it hurts fiercely to let go—never more fiercely than when it isn't *time* to let go.

And clearly it's not nearly time. For somebody with weakening powers of metaphor, this metaphorist is suspiciously active—suspiciously full of "sparkling notions." He may have talked himself into thinking that white hair is the beginning of the end. But his talk shows otherwise. In short, we have to do with another Herbertian comic irony. The speaker's whole performance has been so vivid that it's easy to forget he's only rehearsing. And even his rehearsal goes too far. Accepting the eventual loss of one's gifts doesn't call for surrendering them in advance, much less dismissing them as trivial.

If we need a demonstration of how untrivial metaphors can be—of how they can *make* thought rather than embellish it ready-made—we get one at the last moment from the speaker himself:

> Let a bleak palenesse chalk the doore,
> So all within be livelier than before. (35–36)

The speaker has realized that he's done his own metaphor an injustice. Only the *door* gets chalked by the harbingers. The inner state harbingers prepare for isn't bleakness but festivity: the presence of a king. The presence of some kings, of course, may not be very festive. But for a Christian the royal guest in prospect isn't one of those. When *he* makes use of harbingers, they're sent on to locate a "large upper room furnished"—a room he has already chosen—for the archetypal feast of love (Luke 22:7–15).[48] By the same token, the state of mind being described by this metaphor can't belong to a "clod." The speaker is going to have to discard his heart-brain dichotomy or else discard the metaphor. If the white hairs are really "harbingers," then they aren't simply emptying the brain. The point of intellectual "disparking" is precisely to make room for a special tenant—the one tenant who can make "*all*" within (brain *and* heart) livelier than before.

The discovery an exploratory metaphor promotes is a discovery (hindsight creation) of meaning, not a proof of anything. And here the "so" in the last sentence is important out of proportion to its size. The speaker accepts bleakness on the outside *provided* there's liveliness within, not *because* there is. As we leave him he's as serene as he can be—without guarantees.

In spite of my warning earlier on, I've made a little free here and there with the notion of meaning discovery. The truth is that the speaker can't cause his words to have meant something they didn't mean at the time. And he can't find to his surprise what they "really" meant by treating them as if they had been said in different (later) circumstances—right now, for example. Meaningfulness ex post facto is as fictitious as crime status ex post facto.

What the speaker can do is use his words again by having us reread them in a new context. The exploratory metaphor is really a series of distinct metaphors. The last is marked as *the* metaphor by coming last, and by satisfying the speaker that the thought he's after has finally been captured by the way he's got his vehicle to apply to his tenor. The thought was no more in the vehicle to start with than the statue was in the virgin marble. But the marble has its distinctive shape, and the literal sense has its distinctive implications—potential figurative senses. These are the material conditions that metaphoric invention thrives on, and they give the hidden statue a psychological reality that may excuse critical talk about "retroactive" meaning.

Chapter Eight

The Fellowship of the Mystery: Emergent Metaphor in Vaughan

WHEN METAPHORICAL SENSE is carried by grammatical *parts* of phrases or sentences, the grammar of the impromptu talk dialect is just the old familiar grammar of the vernacular. So syntax can function as a clue to sense. You solve for the unknown by relying, among other things, on how the troublesome part links up syntactically with the rest to let the whole say something relevant. If all we know about metaphorical "cats and dogs" is that it links up with "raining" as an adverb,[1] then at least we know that in the new usage the phrase describes the way it's raining. The challenge is a bit more strenuous where the grammar of the impromptu dialect differs from the vernacular; for example, where the metaphorical sense is carried by phrases or sentences taken as seamless wholes. "Cats and dogs" can't be broken down. The old grammar is no invitation to track down a distinction between "cat" rain and "dog" rain.

The job of reading is still more challenging when the metaphorical sense isn't being carried by any well-defined syntactical unit at all. Sometimes, in fact, as in the hindsight figuration I studied in chapter 7, the sense carrier has only a conceptual existence. The reader "repeats" it in a new context on the author's behalf. And sometimes the metaphorical sense just *emerges*—emerges gradually, as the hovering implication of a *series* of metaphors that begin to cluster in the mind, helped along by the unfolding argument. That's what happens in the strange maneuver I turn to now.

The emergent metaphor is to the poem what anxiety is to an anxious face: it's a quality of the whole that depends on the qualities and relations of the parts—without *being* any such quality or relation. Straightforward analyzing and summing aren't much help in finding it. Vaughan is especially good at emergent metaphor. In fact, there's a particular example that occurs tellingly in four of his best poems. I'll be tracing it through them in what follows.

The metaphor I have in mind is revealing in more ways than one. It gives a vivid picture of the tortured yearnings for secret insight that come out in many of Vaughan's religious poems. As a literary strategy, metaphoric emergence in general is just what we might expect of a poet who cherishes his privacy and yet wants to confide in his reader somehow. Before I'm through I'll have something more to say about these matters of personality. But my main interest here is the kind of contextual prompting that's needed to get a metaphor to emerge.

1. Spying and Vanity

As a religious poet, Vaughan is less obviously dramatic or conversational than, say, Donne or Herbert. But even in *his* work metaphor turns out to be best understood as a move in the game of dialogue—actually, as a move in a double game. With Herbert, Vaughan engages in affectionate repartee, volleying back the master's terms with a twist in the sense. With the reader, Vaughan plays a semantic version of hide-and-seek, the game of metaphoric emergence itself. Neither game is the zero-sum kind in which one player wins only if the other loses; both are plus-sum games of coordination, or (as a Christian poet like Vaughan might very well prefer to put it) games of charity, in which somebody winds up ahead only if everybody does. Vaughan's typical speaker is starkly solitary. Yet the enterprise he and his creator are engaged in is deeply and intricately social. It seems to be essential to acts of figurative speaking and construing that this should be so.

Of the two games Vaughan's metaphor challenges us to, the first is a spectator sport. It's precisely *allusion*, in the classical sense: utterance that *plays* on and off what precedes it. The second is a refinement of conversational uptake: by moving intently from cue to cue, the listener wins as much rapport as the reticent speaker invites or allows. In what follows, my main business is playing the second game. But to do that, we need to begin by watching Vaughan play the first. Here's "Vanitie (I)," the Herbert poem Vaughan retorts or plays on:[2]

> The fleet Astronomer can bore,
>   And thred the spheres with his quick-piercing minde:
> He views their stations, walks from doore to doore,
>   Surveys, as if he had design'd

> To make a purchase there: he sees their dances,   5
>   And knoweth long before
> Both their full-ey'd aspects, and secret glances.
>
>   The nimble Diver with his side
> Cuts through the working waves, that he may fetch
> His dearely-earned pearl, which God did hide   10
>   On purpose from the ventrous wretch:
> That he might save his life, and also hers,
>   Who with excessive pride
> Her own destruction and his danger wears.
>
>   The subtil Chymick can devest   15
> And strip the creature naked, till he finde
> The callow principles within their nest:
>   There he imparts to them his minde,
> Admitted to their bed-chamber, before
>   They appear trim and drest   20
> To ordinarie suitours at the doore.
>
>   What hath not man sought out and found,
> But his deare God? who yet his glorious law
> Embosomes in us, mellowing the ground
>   With showres and frosts, with love and aw,   25
> So that we need not say, Where's this command?
>   Poore man, thou searchest round
> To finde out *death,* but missest *life* at hand.

The fleet Astronomer "threads" the spheres in his quick-piercing mind (2). So far, clear enough: meridians and parallels are being drawn rapidly through the spheres on a mental star chart. But what is it to walk from door to door, looking the dancers over as if one "design'd to make a purchase" (3–5)? What is it to do this with a familiarity that lets one tell just when to expect a "full-ey'd" look, and when a "secret glance" (5–7)? Take all this literally, in a cluster, and you have a connoisseur of the stews on a shopping visit, even though each detail taken separately is a metaphor for something chastely astronomical—or rather, lewdly astronomical. The point of the emergent metaphor is that stargazing is really star *ogling*— and (in retrospect) that the gratifications of a "quick-piercing" mind don't bear looking at too closely.

The Diver of Herbert's next example is also looking for something it would be better to hide, and in fact something "God *did* hide / On purpose from the ventrous wretch" (10–11; italics mine). But the notion of prurient looking and searching comes back in the portrayal of the subtle Chymick who can "devest / And strip the creature naked" (15–16). On a literal reading of the whole phrase, "the creature" is a contemptuous way of referring to the person being stripped. But in the relevant Latinism, the "creature" is the material creation, whose clothes are appearances—the effects of hidden realities ("principles"). The Chymick's art is precisely the art of stripping off the effects and exposing the causes.

In the next metaphor these are unfledged nestlings—potentialities that will take wing when the predatory Chymick gets around to exploiting them. But still another metaphor brings a correction: the principles are great lords and he's their favorite suitor. He's the one with the privilege of "imparting" his "minde" in the grandee's bedchamber. Meanwhile, ordinary suitors have to cool their heels at the door until the ceremony of dressing for the levee is over. The elements won't change their nature for the asking, but they favor the projects of somebody privy to that nature; laymen (ordinary suitors) know them only by their dress (their observable effects). In this metaphorical development the rapist has vanished, to be replaced by an ironic picture of a successful parasite.

Here the images don't cluster into a single coherent image, like the visit to the stews. We're not being invited to hallucinate about a woman-bird-grandee in a nest-bedchamber being both stripped and petitioned by a nest-robbing client. Still, the notions of stripping and of watching people get dressed do manage to tie the metaphors crucially together: the unifying suggestion is a vaguely unsavory intrusion on privacy. The Chymick's grand intellectual passion is as tainted as the learned Astronomer's.

Herbert's poem turns out to be a tiny sermon on Paul's exhortation not to "walk" in the vanity of the mind.[3] The idea of including scientists prominently among these vain walkers goes back beyond the church fathers to the writers of the biblical Wisdom books. Herbert's astronomer is simply Jerome's "tenacious inquirer into nature who sends his eyes across heaven."[4] This "sending" is where the sexual metaphors come in: the eyes have their own kind of lust—the lust "to see with thine eyes the things that are secret."[5] And the lust of the eyes simply reappears in a sophisticated form in the astronomer's intellectual curiosity. In this context, Saint Paul's metaphor of meddlingly "walking about"[6] describes a perverse response to the promise "Seek and ye shall find":[7] "What hath not man sought out and found, / But his deare God?" (22–23). The ironic moral, of course, is that God can't possibly be found by walking about; he's already with us unnoticed, in the "glorious law" that he "embosomes in us."

For once in Herbert, the plot sags. In spite of the wit and formal elegance, nothing much happens in *his* "vanity"; Vaughan's may not be as neat, but it's more eventful. And the main event is an unfolding act of figurative speaking.

The speaker's story in "Vanity of Spirit"[8] is a retort on Herbert's emergent metaphors of rape and voyeurism—retort, once again, in the classic sense: the difference from the originals in literal sense is slight, the difference in figurative sense is radical. Vaughan's emergent metaphor works like Herbert's: a sequence of distinct metaphors generates still another, this time by being grammatically coordinated or "mixed" to resist being broken down:

> I summon'd nature: peirc'd through all her store,
> Broke up some seales, which none had touch'd before,
>> Her wombe, her bosome, and her head
>> Where all her secrets lay a bed
> I rifled quite. . . .   (9–13)

Taking the metaphors *separately*, we have a speaker calling nature to mind ("summoning" her), going through an inventory of natural things ("peircing" her "store"), forcing access to some secrets of nature, and inquiring intrusively into ("rifling") others hidden in parts of the organic system of the world. Taking the terms *together*, as if they jointly supplied the literal sense of a single metaphor, we have a self-confessed rapist and voyeur.

A passage in one of Vaughan's brother Thomas's philosophical potboilers has Vaughan's notion of seal breaking and Herbert's of stripping. It's close enough to serve as a gloss—on Herbert at least, if not quite on Vaughan: "Me thinks Nature complaines of a Prostitution, that I goe about to diminish her Majesty, having allmost broken her Seale and exposed her naked to the world, and now I must recall my selfe: For there is a necessity of reserving as well as publishing some things."[9] There's some confusion here. If Thomas is reserving (i.e., keeping) nature's secret, then he already knows it. But then he's *already* broken her seal. Otherwise, at most he's letting her keep her own secret. If not prostitution, there's at least a suspicious *ménage à deux*.

But unlike Thomas, or the intellectual sinners in Herbert, Vaughan's speaker isn't after the scientific discoveries that are the by-products of his search. He's after the "name" of the Creator (7). He wants to "descry"—to glimpse from a distance—"some part" of the Creator's "great light." And given the tantalizing fact that the quarry that's dodging him is everywhere at once, the speaker isn't especially committed to "walking about" like the busybody cosmographers in the Herbert poem. One of the creatures he'll need to ransack is himself. When he gets round to this, this rifler-voyeur isn't reversing course, as those other busybodies would be. He's just following through systematically with his original plan of "peircing" through *all* of nature, himself included. And if we follow the assurance of Herbert's preacher—or Jeremiah—that God's law is inscribed in the searcher's bosom or "inward parts,"[10] this stage in the search ought to turn out well.

So we're entitled to be surprised when it turns out merely frustrating. Self-examination brings him teasingly close:

> Weake beames, and fires flash'd to my sight,
>   Like a young East, or Moone-shine night,
>   Which shew'd me in a nook cast by
>   A peece of much antiquity,
>   With Hyeroglyphicks quite dismembred,
>   And broken letters scarce remembred.
> I tooke them up, and (much Joy'd,) went about
> T' unite those peeces, hoping to find out
>   The mystery; but this neer done,
>   That little light I had was gone:
>   It griev'd me much.   (19–29)

But unhappily, self-examination is no *more* than a tease. The puny candle in the mind winks out before the speaker manages to piece together the broken letters he finds there. Unlike the speaker of Herbert's "Jesu," who manages to reconstruct the divine name engraved on pieces of his broken heart, Vaughan's spiritual prowler fails to get a peek at the "mystery." So far, he's the Grendel lurking around this mead-hall. People who belong there, regular initiates, get more than a peek at their mysteries, of course. But he isn't one of them—not yet, at least. To be let into the tantalizing secret, he'll need to strip the creature one more time:[11]

> At last, said I,
> *Since in these veyls my Ecclips'd Eye*
> *May not approach thee, (for at night*
> *Who can have commerce with the light?)*
> *I'le disapparell, and to buy*
> *But one half glaunce, most gladly dye.*   (29–34)

The speaker's effort to know God, or know of him, is no surprise. The surprise is that his effort fails even when it turns in what we're told is the right direction; this is half of the retort on Herbert's preacher in "Vanitie (I)." And maybe a bigger surprise is the metaphor (of sexual violation and spying) that emerges as the effort is described—just the kind of metaphor that the preacher reserved for describing a *misdirected* search; this is the other half of the retort. It seems that it's possible to escape from vanity of mind only to be trapped in vanity of spirit: the futile attempt to spy out God's secrets in this life. These include God's "name" because, true to the spirit of retort, Vaughan is giving back Herbert's metaphors with a difference. In Herbert, the faithful heart is inscribed with its own assurance—with the name of God in his role of *Savior* ("Jesus").[12] Vaughan's spy, by contrast, hasn't been rummaging in the inner darkness for a sign that he's an adopted son of God. The spy too has been trying to decipher a name of God from traces (hieroglyphics) in his own creaturehood. But this name spells out the Creator's *secret* nature, the nature of the God that *hides* himself.[13] Same vehicle, new tenor: introspection makes way for espionage.

II. Spying and Grief

We gradually make out the same basic metaphor as we follow the story in "I walkt the other day."[14] Actually, part of the poem's challenge and interest is that we need to follow *two* stories: the speaker's story of his figurative quest and Vaughan's of the speaker's act of story telling. Vaughan's goes the usual good yarn one better by keeping us in suspense till nearly the end, not about what *will* happen, but about what *has* been happening all along. And what eventually emerges, along with a story of voyeurism, is a voyeur metaphor. The narrative art on display here is a kind of Salome's dance—one teasing equivocation dropping away to reveal another.

The quest begins. Because of winter, says the speaker, he missed finding a "gallant flowre" where he had last seen it among others as "curious" (rare? arousing curiosity? the second possibility will be confirmed later). He consoled himself with the argument that

>   there might be other springs
>   Besides this here
> Which, like cold friends, sees us but once a year,
>   And so the flowre
>   Might have some other bowre.   (10–14)

So far there's no pressing reason to suspect anything more aggressively figurative than a little stretching of "springs" and "flowres." The point is that the Bermudan equivalent (say) of the spring season is no "cold friend" to Bermudans, as the spring "here" is to the English. That generic "spring" stays with ("sees") the Bermudans all year round. Maybe the flower the speaker is after (flower *species*, that is) is in bloom there right now.

The argument seems to be a justification for looking elsewhere, or giving up, especially since the narrator introduces it by insisting that his search "lov'd not to peep and peer / I'th'face of things" (8–9). On the other hand, why this disclaimer, out of the blue? Who would have *thought* him a peeper (busybody? voyeur?) just because he wanted to have a second look at a species of flower he found magnificent (which is what "gallant" ought to mean on a literal reading of "flowre")? Besides, the disclaimer has a catch in it. It's hard to see how an addict of peeping and peering could get a thrill out of looking at the *face* of things. Surfaces are as available to a "full-ey'd" look as to a "secret glance." Maybe this is a peeper who dislikes surfaces because they refuse him a peep at what's hiding behind them.

In short, we have a right to be suspicious about the generic, or even the floral, status of this particular flower—and about the innocence of the searcher's motives.

The suspicions are encouraged by what the speaker says he did next. Rather than give up his search for a specimen of the "gallant" flower, or decide to carry on in a "bowre" that enjoys a friendlier spring, the speaker took up the nearest thing he could "spie" and "digg'd about / That place where I had seen him to grow out" (17). Given his recent disclaimer of a love for "peeping," the unintended irony of "spie" is hard to ignore. Another danger signal in the language: the plant is now a "him," in fact a "warm Recluse"—still alive, though "of us unseen" (18–21).

Where does this leave us? It's still just possible to take "flowre" literally. But if this particular *specimen* is what really matters, we still need to explain the earlier talk of other climates that might support the flower *species*. And we need to come up with the point of the sudden personification. On the other hand, hacking around blindly with an improvised spade is a strange way of showing concern for a plant; whereas (construed figuratively) it might imaginably be *a desperate effort to locate a coffin*. If we choose this second option, then values get reversed. "Flowre" comes out figurative, and "him" and "recluse" are literal. The victim of the speaker's prying is a person. But then in what figurative sense is a living person lying there buried, or a buried person lying there alive?

There's a metaphor here somewhere. The task remains to say just where.

So far in *Vaughan's* story, as opposed to his *storyteller's*, the branching possibilities that build suspense aren't narrated events but textual meanings. As in "Vanity of Spirit," the one given is the emerging shape of the forlorn busybody, compulsively digging for sights he's not allowed to see. We don't yet have the help we need to figure out what it *is* to dig that way.

After invading the "Recluse's" privacy, the speaker tried—better: *tells* us he tried—to "extort" answers to "many a question intricate and rare" (22–24). And again the figuration fends us off. What *is* it to coerce a flower into answering questions? Maybe (by the etymology of "extort") to "twist" or skew the facts about it into a phony confirmation of what one believes. This saves the literal reading of "flowre," but just barely. The "he" is as arbitrary and conspicuous as ever. Still, the literal reading can be made to fit in with the only answer the speaker managed to extort from the flower:

> he now
> Did there repair
> Such losses as befel him in this air
> And would e'r long
> Come forth most fair and young. (24–28)

"Repairing" the flower is a strange way to describe replacing last year's flower (lost in "this air") with a new one. But if what's talking about itself here is a personified *root*, then with a little straining we can make out a description of the winter dormancy of the plant.

In the alternative reading, once again, an answer is literally being extorted from a person—the occupant of a grave. "He" has somehow been forced to give an assurance of his own resurrection. The losses being "repaired" were sustained by his body and soul, which will rise again free of the nastiness they picked up in "this air." (The climate in which spring is a "cold friend" will be the fallen world's, not England's.) This glosses more details, but at a price: the unpleasant suggestion that the speaker's taste for violating privacy extends to grave raiding. And on this reading the spy is distraught to the point of not recognizing an important secret when it's spelled out to him in so many words. Firsthand testimony to a basic Christian hope gets dismissed as "all I could extort" (24).

What follows seems to confirm that we'll have to tolerate the unpleasant suggestion. "Flowre" was a euphemism. At least in the speaker's wish-fantasy, a grave *was* violated:

> This past, I threw the Clothes quite o'r his head,
>   And stung with fear
> Of my own frailty dropt down many a tear
>   Upon his bed,
> Then sighing whisper'd, *Happy are the dead!*
>   *What peace doth now*
>   *Rock him asleep below?* (29–35)

Throwing the grave clothes over the uncovered head: as the speaker looks back on it, this clumsy effort to undo the violation of his victim's privacy was full of guilty panic. He was terrified of his own (act of) frailty. So the tears that followed weren't grief alone. They were also remorse.

Somehow he still hasn't managed to get the point of what he's been told. All he's learned from the ordeal is the sentimental pessimism that it's happier to be dead and insensible than alive and awake. And on his dismissive interpretation of what went on, the paltriness of this news is easy enough to explain. His informant was a "poor root" without "wings / To raise it to the truth and light of things." He does manage to appreciate that even though its "winglessness" will let few believe this, the "root" was a source of "doctrine." But the doctrine itself escapes him:

> And yet, how few believe such doctrine springs
>   From a poor root
> Which all the Winter sleeps here under foot
>   And hath no wings
> To raise it to the truth and light of things,
>   But is stil trod
>   By ev'ry wandring clod. (36–42)

At the same time, these same lines upset the reading again. "Few" won't pass as an estimate of the seventeenth-century public for news about occult traffic with the dead; and if the loved one really has to endure being continually "trod / By ev'ry wandring clod," then we're being asked to imagine a totally unmarked grave in an open road. These absurdities disappear if the subject is really a root. Moreover, the speaker's concluding prayer fits the literal reading of "root." What he's caught sight of is one of the "masques and shadows" of an omnipresent Creator—an instance of what Vaughan elsewhere calls "*prolusions* and strong *proofs* of our *restoration* laid out in *nature*."[15] In short, the speaker has been dabbling in natural theology. The only privacy up for invasion here is botanical. So "flowre" and "root" are being used literally after all, and the person-predicates are being used figuratively.

But the natural theology was the premise of an act of self-dramatization. To use the speaker's term, the performance he's been describing was a religious *masque*—a masque he made up and starred in, for the benefit of an audience of one. This goes some way toward explaining our trouble in locating the figurative terms. The semantic rule of the masque is that expressions that apply literally but routinely to performers and props (a root exposed) apply figuratively and interestingly to objects in the fiction being acted out (a body exhumed). The buried root's greenness rates a testimonial only for the sake of what's being said in the same breath: even in decay, the loved person's body is somehow being prepared for its resurrection.[16] It's in the masque fiction about digging up the body that we get some reversal of values; in particular, a *figurative* "root"—a person—being stripped of his *literal* clothes.

But here we meet another complication. Masque fictions are figurative in their turn. Disturbing the dead to harass them with questions is an emergent metaphor for the penetration of the grave's secrets by less obnoxious and hopeless means. You can't quiz the dead, but you can quiz your memory of them and your sense of the meaning of their lives. Something like this—inquest by meditation—seems to lie behind the charade of the imaginary graveside dialogue that ends with a guiltily hurried replacement of the loved one's shroud.

In the concluding prayer the cemetery spy is replaced by a hunter who "tracks" the steps of God (49) in pursuit of his "hid ascents" (52).[17] The hunter, like the spy, wants to be shown things hidden. Above all,

> hid in thee, shew me his life again
>   At whose dumbe urne
> Thus all the year I mourn.　(61–63)

Evidently the root's emblematic survival wasn't enough to show "his life"; and neither was the elegiac masque fiction that the speaker had woven around the act of digging for the root. Whether one plays with emblems or masques, a "prolusion" can't supply the lack of a "proof."

If his concluding prayer is granted, things hidden will be gradually revealed to a speaker who loves to peep and peer more than he lets himself admit. The story telling itself mimics this pattern by only gradually resolving its ambiguities, forcing the reader into the role of semantic spy or hunter. In the process the image of an invader of graves, carried by no single word or phrase, gradually emerges and owns up to being a metaphor. The process is a lot more complex than its counterpart in "Vanity of Spirit," but in both poems an emergent metaphor that literally describes sneaky and illicit looking is used as a figurative description of the struggle for illumination.

III. Spying and Envy

"They are all gone into the world of light" is as caught up in a present moment as "I walkt the other day" is in a past one:

> They are all gone into the world of light!
>   And I alone sit lingring here;
> Their very memory is fair and bright,
>   And my sad thoughts doth clear.
>
> It glows and glitters in my cloudy brest
>   Like stars upon some gloomy grove,
> Or those faint beams in which this hill is drest,
>   After the Sun's remove.

This time the speaker is a soliloquist, sitting (2) on or near a hill (7), apparently at dusk (8).[18] To judge by his use of demonstratives here and later, his thinking is partly resonating to the sensations of the moment. But this is no random moping session. There's an urgent agenda. Like the good if eccentric Christian he turns out to be, the speaker is convinced that his dead friends are in heaven, and he's struggling desperately for a way of living decently with the conviction. The struggle takes the experimental form of trying out attitudes.

The first attitude is a nonstarter: envy, resentment, petulance. They've gone on ahead and left him in the lurch. He, in the meantime, has no choice but to spend his time "lingring" (2). Survival is a kind of hanging around stranded while one's friends are all happy elsewhere.

But the speaker checks himself immediately: even the act of remembering his friends (not to mention being with them) brightens his "cloudy brest" as starlight does a gloomy grove or "faint beams" a hill after sunset. This, of course, is a very feeble retraction; it would take more than starlight to relieve the gloom of a grove. And the sequence of ideas is revealing: the memory of his friends

> glows and glitters in my cloudy brest
> Like stars upon some gloomy grove,
> Or those faint beams in which this hill is drest,
> After the Sun's remove.   (5–8)

The conviction pumped up by "glows and glitters" subsides along with the candlepower of the speaker's analogies, and with the alliterative diminuendo of "glows," "glitters," and "gloom." Not that it really matters; what triggered the envy was a vision, not a memory: his friends' present and future sight of God, not their past friendship with the speaker. A momentary change of subject is serving as a change of attitude.

When the vision comes back, so does the attitude, in amplified form. He's thinking again of the world of light—now an "Air of glory" in which his friends are "walking" (9). As they *walk,* the light of glory (as if to join them in triumphing)

> doth *trample* on my days:
> My days, which are at best but dull and hoary,
> Meer glimering and decays.
>   (10–12; italics mine)

We get the initial impression that the friends and the air of glory are in a conspiracy to walk all over him. But the impression is only a semantic illusion created by the fact that "trampling" describes a kind of walking if you take it literally. The speaker chooses an expression of bitter envy that he can always disown. He was merely inept; he had an accidental run-in with a mixed metaphor. But if the bitterness can be disowned, the envy can't. The figurative sense is: "The light outshines my days—if you can *call* them 'days' [here repetition signals second thoughts]. You don't need anything dazzling to outshine *this* kind of daylight!" The point once again is the light that surrounds the others and excludes him, and (equivalently) the gloom he has been left to endure.

What follows is another attempt to get beyond envy, this time by a reinterpretation of the notion of walking:

> O holy hope! and high humility,
> High as the Heavens above!
> These are your walks, and you have shew'd them me
> To kindle my cold love. (13–16)

Envy, or "cold love," gets no admission to "walks" frequented not only by the speaker's friends but by his own hope and humility. This is a satisfying notion, especially if we succumb to the diversionary *littera*. By shouting triumphantly as if his personifications could be taken at face value, the speaker helps himself to a fanciful reason for not envying his friends. Two of them have taken him along after all. But again the fantasy is only the literal sense of an expression that isn't being used literally. As it happens, the sense as used—the figurative sense—is only a little less satisfying. Heaven is par excellence what hopeful and humble thoughts "walk" in. It's what they've "shew'd" the speaker by letting him see it.

Unfortunately, the speaker's soaring enthusiasm hurries him into exposing his failure to see any such thing. Death is

> the Jewel of the Just,
> Shining nowhere, but in the dark;
> What mysteries do lie beyond thy dust;
> Could man outlook that mark! (17–20)

If "the dark" meant something like *benighted worldly existence,* then the speaker would be pointing out that death shines only or mainly for benighted worldlings. But the afterlife is invisible even to *un*worldly people while they're stranded, like the speaker, on this side. They'll be able to see their jewel shine only when they're with it—in the realm that we, not they, know only as "the dark." The brilliance of death is one of the "mysteries" that "lie beyond thy dust." Seen from the hither side, where we and the speaker are, death is admittedly no jewel. It's a "mark" man can't "outlook."

The speaker's next remarks only underline the difference between the dark where the speaker is and the dark he's referring to, which is dark only because he can't see into it—can't see death "shining," or get initiated into its other "mysteries:"

> He that hath found some fledg'd birds nest, may know
>   At first sight, if the bird be flown;
> But what fair Well, or Grove he sings in now,
>   That is to him unknown. (21–24)

It's not hard to know if somebody's dead. A glance at the body-nest is enough to show that the soul-bird has flown.[19] But we don't know "what fair Well, or Grove he sings in now" (23). The speaker thinks he knows that there's a "grove" for the "bird" somewhere—fair, not gloomy like the speaker's breast-grove (6). But the rest is ignorance. So much for the claim that humility and hope have "shew'd" him what he's aching to see.

In spite of that claim, the metaphor emerging here is the familiar one of agonized voyeurism. The speaker is still on the outside trying and failing to get a peek at enjoyments they won't *let* him peek at, much less share. He can think of hope as a kind of knowing if he likes, but he can't add to his knowledge by taking thought.

Still, maybe they'll change their minds:

> And yet, as Angels in some brighter dreams
>   Call to the soul, when man doth sleep:
> So some strange thoughts transcend our wonted theams,
>   And into glory peep. (25–28)

Maybe what can't be taken will yet be given—provided that "some strange thoughts transcend our wonted theams, / And into glory peep." This phrase is a miniature tragicomedy of rhetoric all by itself. As the promised victory puffed up by all the fanfare of suspensive grammar, the anticlimax of "peep" is almost as funny as it is sad. The forlorn peeping of the speaker's predecessors in "Vanity of Spirit" and "I walkt the other day" has been licensed by wishful thinking. But it remains an outsider's stolen look.[20] Or rather, it remains that *when taken literally*. Taken together with the whole complex of details that have led up to it, it's an emergent metaphor for what corresponds to voyeurism—to the lust of the eyes—in religious experience.

Earlier the speaker compared his soul to a "gloomy grove" under a starry sky. The "stars" were friends—friends he loves but, in his painful confusion, can't help envying, too. At last something helpful has occurred to him. Why should one star envy another? He too is a star, a "captive" star "lockt up" in a tomb:

> If a star were confin'd into a Tomb
>   Her captive flames must needs burn there;
> But when the hand that lockt her up, gives room,
>   She'l shine through all the sphaere.
>
> O Father of eternal life, and all
>   Created glories under thee!
> Resume thy spirit from this world of thrall
>   Into true liberty.   (29–36)

The "star" is shut out of a glory (9) she can't do any more than peep into. But she herself is one of God's "created glories." When her jailer sets her free,[21] she won't go into the world of light so much as light up the world, or at least the part of the world she's in charge of.

Sense can be made of this vague philosophical boasting in Platonic and Hermetic terms,[22] but this doesn't keep it from being vague philosophical boasting, or from earning its keep by treating, if not curing, the strain of eye-lust the speaker is infected with—his chronic envy.[23]

As I began by pointing out, the speaker is doing his meditating on a hill, apparently just after sunset. What is he doing there? If he's like the speaker of "I walkt the other day," he's acting out a solitary masque, and by masque semantics his description of what he's doing will be literally as well as figuratively true. This will go for the description implied in his final prayer:

> Either disperse these mists, which blot and fill
>   My perspective (still) as they pass,
> Or else remove me hence unto that hill,
>   Where I shall need no glass.   (37–40)

Passing mists are blocking the speaker's telescope ("perspective"). He prays for God to scatter them. Either remove *them*, or remove *him*—"unto that hill, / Where I shall need no glass." When somebody tries to see beyond death, the faculty that gets blocked in the relevant sense is the speculative intellect. That's the situation being emblematically mimed here. As a masque prop, the "glass" is a last telling detail in the emergent metaphor of the outsider looking in, this time as an ineffectual spy on the hidden joys that Paul describes as "the fellowship of the mystery."[24]

IV. Spying and Thwarted Desire

In "The Night," that fellowship is represented by the "wise Nicodemus" of the Fourth Gospel. The "wisdom" he shows there is the simple man's wisdom, not Solomon's, but this is precisely what qualifies it to serve the speaker's purposes. Nicodemus is naïvely moved by Christ's miracles to pay a night visit to the "teacher come from God" and, true to his naïveté, winds up nonplussed by the instruction he gets.[25] Yet he apparently comes away from that visit committed, and he finds the courage to defy the jeers and threats of his fellow Pharisees when he speaks up for his master later on.[26] The last we see of him is his reappearance at the end of the Fourth Gospel, as one of the two disciples who take down and care for the crucified body.[27] So one conspicuous theme of this redemption myth is the importance of the redeemer's body, or of his having had one. God's human presence in the world gives natural man his chance. The chance is what gives the poem its point of departure: for the speaker, it's a chance he never got.

The speaker begins his reflections on Nicodemus's night visit by introducing the first of a series of parallel metaphors. Eventually these will cluster together to form the emergent metaphor I'm interested in. As usual, the emotion up for metaphorical expression, and exorcism, is envy. Lucky Nicodemus got to meet divinity ("light," 4) in the flesh, and the flesh (of Christ) is what let him survive. It sheltered him from the full force (the "noon," 2) of God's presence. It was the veil covering the hidden splendors of the tabernacle (2). More truly than Moses' tabernacle, Christ's body is the tent or dwelling of God.[28] More than the Mosaic equivalent, the flesh of Christ is the "veil" over the Holy of Holies.[29]

In short, the tabernacle-tent metaphor is highly recognizable, straight out of the letters of Saint Paul and grounded in the usual talk-postulate about history as a series of divine speech acts: God uses some events to refer to later ones that "fulfill" them (see chapter 2 on prefiguration). But all this is just the basis of the metaphor, not the point of it—the small contribution to the larger metaphor that will be emerging as the poem goes along. The point is the speaker's growing discomfort in having to think of things like veils as means of seeing instead of hindering sight.

The discomfort comes out partly in the way things get scrambled in his version of the tabernacle metaphor. Consider the order of ideas. First we get the *limitations* of the "blest believer's" privilege of seeing God—only then do we get the privilege. Even Nicodemus had to be satisfied with no more than a peep into glory:

> Through that pure *Virgin-shrine,*
> That sacred vail drawn o'r thy glorious noon
> That men might look and live as Glo-worms shine,
>   And face the Moon:
> Wise Nicodemus saw such light
> As made him know his God by night.   (1-6)

The veil lets one *look at God* and *live,* in spite of the warning,[30] just as the moon lets the glowworms *face the moon* and *shine* (hence survive) even though the light they're facing would snuff them out if it were coming straight from the source.

Can we let it go at that? The reading is a little *too* charitable. It doesn't register the fact that the speaker temporarily fudges his own analogy—look : live = face the moon : shine—by putting "shine" before "face the moon." When the listener arrives at "shine," he hasn't found a counterpart of "look." So he's been kept from seeing that "shine" is part of an analogy at all, much less that it's the counterpart of "live." Instead he gets the illusion of very different syntax with sense to match. Men are apparently being permitted two actions by the veil: (a) look and live as glowworms shine; (b) face the moon. This is almost nonsensical, but not quite. It gives the impression that instead of saving lives while illuminating them, the veil is really for damping lives down to glimmers in the moonlight. The impression won't outlast the reader's second thought, but he isn't to blame for the first. He's been given false cues. Has the speaker blundered? Or has he manufactured a bit of rhetorical immunity for feelings that will come out less discreetly later on?

We haven't quite done justice to the figurational busyness of this first sentence. The speaker is launching more than one development here. While another metaphorical voyeur of contemplation is emerging, we're also being given the beginnings of a series of metaphor synonyms. One of them is just barely observable in the speaker's puzzling admiration for "*such* light / As made him know his God *by night*" (5-6; italics mine). Why "such"—that is, *(bright) enough to* (identify God by night)? Of course, it was literally night at the time, and in the Gospel Christ's divinity sometimes literally shines. But neither fact justifies this use of "such." Added brightness is called for to stand out against the *daylight,* not the *dark.*

In what kind of night does God need more brightness to be recognizable than he would by day? A *metaphorical* "night," of course; the kind that can overlap with metaphorical "noon" without absurdity. In a later version of the same pseudoparadox, the contradiction in "did at midnight speak with the Sun" once again depends on momentarily misreading "Sun" by taking it literally. The metaphorical "Sun" Nicodemus spoke with needs no miracle to be seen at midnight (10). In the "such" case, "night" describes a state of mind. It's a metaphor synonym of "darkness and blinde eyes."

In fact, the contemplative dialect we're being forced to learn as we listen, and learn by listening, is rich in *equivalences*—charms for fixing on a particular thought and staying there. This, after all, is what contemplation is for.

Take the three metaphorical notions we've started with: veil, tent, and light-darkness (or day-night). The speaker brings back two of them immediately in his rendition of the prophetic notion of the winged sun (9)[31]—wings doubling for "veil" and "Sun" for "noon." A little later all three notions come back, in the flower "within whose sacred leafs did lie / The fulness of the Deity" (17–18): the leaves (petals) are the incarnational wings or veil once again; "fulness" is the "noon" of God's presence; and the flower is the place par excellence where the fullness of the Godhead "lies" or dwells.[32] Night-darkness-blindness; noon-sun-fullness; veil-wings-petals; tabernacle-flower. Each sequence of coreferential metaphors circles its own object of passionate concentration. The metaphorical descriptions of night that get strung together later on (25–36) are only the most explicit and passionate sequence of all.[33]

But like contemplation itself, the language of contemplation has its expansions as well as its contractions. In the expansion, terms keep on shifting their sense or reference. We get a sequence of metaphor twins, or homonyms, masquerading as a single dynamic idea (see chapter 7 on exploratory metaphor). In "The Night" the speaker explores the meanings or possible meanings of key terms this way, and in the process gradually changes his idea of the sight that's eluding him. The process ends by filling out the emergent metaphor we've already met.

"O who will tell me, where / He found thee?" (13–14). The speaker can supply part of the answer himself. It's accompanied by a shift in the tabernacle metaphor. One kind of tent Nicodemus *didn't* find his master in was the Old Testament kind—much less a temple like Solomon's (19–

20). Christ was enshrined among his own "living works" (21). The "*trees and herbs*" were his "lodge" (that is, tent [22]). The "living works" were also parties to the mystery—timid spectators who "did watch and *peep / And wonder*" (23–24; italics mine). "Peep" has its usual force in Vaughan here. Like Nicodemus, the things of nature weren't—couldn't be—quite insiders. So their way of looking had a bit of the furtiveness of the outsider who is imagining and envying them.

But the sore point is still that envy, carried this time by an exploratory metaphor. The Incarnation-"tent" we started with has been silently replaced with a Nature-"tent"—a tent it would be pointless for the speaker to think of peeping into. He's already in it, and the God-Man is no longer in it at all. The speaker has arrived too late.

Another shift in the meaning of *tent* or *dwelling* comes in as an allusion. Night is the time

> When my Lords head is fill'd with dew, and all
> His locks are wet with the clear drops of night;
> His still, soft call;
> His knocking time; The souls dumb watch,
> When Spirits their fair kinred catch.   (32–36)

With this play on the Song of Songs, values get exactly reversed: "I slepe, but mine heart waketh, it is the voyce of my welbeloued that knocketh, saying, Open vnto me, my sister, my loue, my dooue, my vndefiled: for mine head is ful of dewe, and my lockes with the droppes of the night. . . . I opened to my welbeloued: but my welbeloued was gone, and past: mine heart was gone when he did speake: I soght him, but I colde not finde him: I called him, but he answered me not."[34] Now the dwelling is the soul, and the outsider calling and knocking to be let in is Christ.[35] But she opens too late, and the quandary her lateness puts her in is the speaker's: "I soght him, but I colde not finde him."[36] Christ's retort on "seeking," "finding," and "knocking" is inescapably familiar to Vaughan's audience: "Seek and ye shall find; knock, and it shall be opened unto you."[37]

In short, the story in the Song of Songs leads (by way of the Gospel) from the soul's tent back to God's—and unfortunately back to the speaker's earlier frustration: "O who will tell me, where / He found thee . . . ? (13–14). To a frustrated *seeker*, "Seek and ye shall find" sounds more like a taunt than a consolation.

The exploratory "tent" metaphor hasn't come to rest. Night was the soul's time to watch for her chance to "catch" her "fair kinred," Christ. Now it's a benignly dark "tent" equal to heaven (38). And the metamorphoses of "tent" have brought along with them changes in the notions of *night, darkness, sun,* and *light.* "Night" has become another name for contemplation:

> Dear night! this world's defeat;
> The stop to busie fools; cares check and curb;
> The day of Spirits; my souls calm retreat
>   Which none disturb! (25–28)

And to be in the "dark" is to be ready for contemplation—"calm" and "unhaunted," that is, solitary (38).

"Sun" and "light" have been redefined to match. The sun that keeps all things awake to "mix and tyre / Themselves and others" (44–45) clearly isn't Malachi's sun of righteousness. What it *is,* is less clear. A sinner's "mixing and tyring" don't respect curfews, any more than a saint's "defeat" of the world ends at daybreak. So this corrupt "Sun" can't be taken literally, either. It's another metaphor—in fact more than one.

The rhetoricians recognize a trope in which "out of one improper term issues by signification another, then out of that improper term perhaps another, and so on, until one comes to the proper term."[38] Vaughan's morally corrupt "Sun" leads the mind on this kind of search, as if we too were groping our way toward a hidden interior:

> But living where the Sun
> Doth all things wake, and where all mix and tyre
> Themselves and others, I consent and run
>   To ev'ry myre,
> And by this worlds ill-guiding light,
> Erre more then I can do by night. (43–48)

The search goes roughly this way:

1. The light that leads people astray into mires is foolish fire, the will-o'-the-wisp.
2. But there *is* no cosmic will-o'-the-wisp—unless this notion is being used figuratively, as a contemptuous reference to the sun ("this world's light").
3. But the sun literally so called doesn't light anybody's way to moral error or confusion.

4. So (by metonymy) the notion of *sun* has a figurative meaning in its turn: the worldliness that dominates people's waking lives, night or day.

The emergent figure of the outsider longing for a peep into the Holy of Holies is coming a little closer. We can now make out a blurred suggestion of his tragicomic encounters with puddles outside the tent; in the moral darkness he envies Nicodemus for having escaped.

The "tent" metaphor undergoes one last metamorphosis. Again the stimulus is the outsider's lust for secrets—even for *hearsay* about secrets: "O who will tell me where?" Hearsay—about the supreme secret—is what he turns to one last time:

> There is in God (some say)
> A deep, but dazling darkness; As men here
> Say it is late and dusky, because they
> See not all clear;
> O for that night; where I in him
> Might live invisible and dim. (49–54)

Like people who say it's dusk here when it isn't, people who speak of a darkness in God are faint-sighted. Both kinds of people say that something is a certain way because the something looks that way to *them*. But there's a difference. The myopic time-tellers blame the darkness on the time of day; the theologians blame it on their eyes.

The speaker doesn't say this; he only implies it. But the implication is clear, and important. The implication is carried by the pointed contrast between the theologians' "dazling darkness" and the very different "late and dusky" of the time-tellers. By hedging "darkness" with "dazling," the theologians warn us not to take "darkness" literally. Deep darkness can work as a metaphor for dazzling brightness because they have something in common. They both make it impossible to see things clearly—to see them with definition and thus to see *what* you're looking at. The divine nature is deeply "dark" in this metaphorical sense, but only because it dazzles. Herbert stretches "dark" in roughly the same way, but more explicitly:

> If that bee dark we can not see,
> The sunn is darker then a Tree,
> And thou {that is, God} more dark then either.[39]

When the time-tellers say it's late "because" it looks late, they're arguing literally (and simplemindedly) from appearances to facts. *They* don't talk about a dazzling dusk. Not so the theologians. When the theologians say God is dark "because" he looks dark, "because" means *in the sense that*, not *in consequence of the fact that*.[40] The theologians aren't justifying a conclusion. They're explaining a trope.

Here again we've reached a figurative notion: God's effect on the *eye*. The subject is minds, of course. We need another step to reach the figurative sense of *eye*, the semantic interior. Minds can grasp only what they can analyze. But perfect unity can't be analyzed. No wonder God's fullness of being registers on minds only as a blank. In the impromptu dialect of theology, for "dark" read *bright*. The speaker of the last stanza hasn't taken back the first. Inside the tent, it's still noon.[41]

But now the exploratory metaphor has taken its last turn. The "tent" isn't Christ's body or the natural world or the soul. It's God, who has an interior (49) that the speaker is longing to enter and live in (54). *God is now the coveted dwelling place.* If the speaker asks here only for the right to be "invisible and dim," this isn't because his desires have suddenly become modest. In effect, "dim" is a qualifying gloss on "invisible." The speaker is praying for a degree of the divine splendor we've already been taught to call darkness. Dimness is a step toward darkness, and in the semantic revaluation of the last stanza this implies that the speaker is praying for as much "brightness" (fullness of being) as is possible to a thing that isn't God. But prayers don't grant themselves. The speaker is still outside the tent stumbling in mire, still recognizably the thwarted voyeur of the poems we've already considered.

The thwarted voyeur doesn't play a major role in other devotional poems of Vaughan, but the religious attitude described by that metaphor does—the thwarted desire for a glimpse of secret truth. It's what makes the difference in accent between Vaughan's Protestantism and Herbert's. The issue in Vaughan is what the already justified speaker can hope for before he dies. In particular, can he hope to be regenerated fully enough to enjoy a visiting "Ray" of the Johannine light? Equivalently, can he hope for a breath of the Pentecostal wind that blows where it pleases?[42] Will he be allowed to join the society of "Inlightned spirit"?[43] Unfortunately, it seems more likely that he's in for a long delay of his "invisible estate" and "glorious liberty, still late!"[44] In short, the central issue for this poet isn't love but light.

In its strategy of metaphoric emergence, concentration, and exploration, "The Night" gives us Vaughan's highly contrapuntal version of the seventeenth-century metaphorist approach to the transaction between writer and reader. These devices are just right for putting intense pressure on the etiquette of cooperation—or benefit of the doubt or patience or "humanity" or "sophisticated charity"—the etiquette we can't very well do without even in ordinary conversation. We don't rush officiously to take the figurative speaker at his word—or rather to take him at ours. We let him build up his own idiom, and we do the best we can to learn it as he and we go along. If we know what's good for us, we cultivate a hermeneutic patience.

Not all conversations are two-way; sometimes listeners have to make do with conventions of interpreting that they can apply on their own. Reading is a special case of one-way conversation. The repertoire of uptake that one falls back on in such emergencies is made to work overtime in one's negotiations with a *text,* and especially with a figurative text. Reading, in this perspective, is a steady state of conversational emergency—steadiest and most demanding when what is emerging is a metaphor.

A BRIEF AFTERWORD seems to be in order. I've tried to show how the particular metaphor that emerges in these poems captures a deep religious anxiety that Vaughan also expresses in other ways. I think it's possible, if not necessary, to push the inquiry a little further and ask if the *kind* of metaphor Vaughan has chosen also has something to tell us about what Vaughan is like as a poet, if not as a religious poet. I think it does. There's an analogy between the general effect of the emergent metaphor and the subject matter of the particular one we've been tracing.

Vaughan warns the readers of *Silex* that "you will (peradventure) observe some passages, whose history or reason may seem something remote; but were they brought *nearer,* and plainly exposed to your view, (though that [perhaps] might quiet your curiosity) yet would it not conduce much to your greater advantage."[45] The emergent metaphor suits this poetic of privacy very well. It leaves the reader in a position like that of Vaughan's metaphorical figure, peering at a meaning close enough to be just made out, far enough away to exclude him from the fellowship of the mystery.

Afterword

SOME PROFESSIONAL "close" readers specialize in finding exciting new things for other people's poems to be saying. They put the poems in an exciting "context"—an ad-lib selection from the circumstances the poems were written in,[1] or some theory that applies to that selection. Then they "closely" read the "context" as if it were the poem. Or they read the poem according to a newly devised closeness recipe designed to mesh conveniently with their choice of "context."[2] I've been trying for an exciting kind of closeness, too, but not that kind. If the account in chapter 1 is right, the approach to reading being tried out on the poems studied in this book is just the conversational model of figurative speech the poems were written to comply with. And if things have gone well, then the closeness goes no further than the reader's side of the conversation calls for—no closer than the cues in the poems allow.

About figuration the seventeenth-century metaphorists have the advantage of self-awareness, and the cunning that self-awareness makes possible. They work inside highly articulate overlapping traditions of thinking about conversation: the dialogue tradition from Plato through Cicero to Landino and beyond; the analysis of the tactics of sophistic gamesmanship in Aristotle; the treatment of wit and repartee in the rhetorical traditions of Aristotle, Hermogenes, Demetrius, Cicero, or Dionysius of Halicarnassus; manners books in the pattern of Castiglione's *Courtier* or Guazzo's *Civil Conversation*—not only the explicit treatments of repartee strategy but the practical demonstrations;[3] the practical demonstrations and instructional arrangement of Erasmus's *Colloquies*; above all, the hermeneutic schools of Augustine or Jerome or Irenaeus—accounts of the linguistic folkways of the supreme conversationalist (see chapter 2).

From the point of view of these traditions, poems too are moves in a conversation. They're *acts* of speech. The Greeks might have done as well or better to call them *pragmata* instead of *poiemata*—not so much things made as things done. It doesn't matter whether the deed is done with the tongue or the pen. A poet "makes" a poem the way somebody addressing an audience "makes" a speech—by uttering it. On this kind of view, a poem is a miniconversation inside the wider conversation of the culture it grows in. And as talkers put entrenched meanings through tropes, the languages of miniconversations become dialects of the language of the wider conversation. So in addition to knowing the grammar and vocabulary of the wider language, talkers have to know how to coach their listeners silently in the emerging grammar and vocabulary. And the listeners have to know how to be coached. Know-how can't be poetics. It will have to be pragmatics: agreed-on ways of carrying *pragmata* off.

Maybe pragmatics can even shed some light on poetics. True, the figuration of the metaphorists is extraordinary, whereas figuration itself is as ordinary as can be. It's something nonpoets do, and just possibly can't *help* doing if they're going to communicate. All by itself, a *feature* of ordinary language use can't set anything *apart* from ordinary language use. But suppose the difference between figurative subtlety in poems and figurative subtlety in nonpoems isn't a matter of kind or degree at all. Suppose the difference lies outside the figuration itself—in the fact that the poems are the (self-announced) *performances;* that they or their settings are conventionally marked out to be rated by listeners on the subtlety scale (possibly among other scales). If so, it's a waste of time to test a speech act for poemhood by checking for the presence of some exotic feature of the way it communicates. Besides, the more exotic in principle, the less communicative; the less communicative, the less a *pragma;* the less a *pragma*, the less a poem.

What the speaker is after or up against varies widely from one metaphorist poem to another, but the action of his story is always speech action, and the crisis is always a language crisis. The rhythm of his downs and ups is the rhythm of figuration, a cycle of *exapatesis* and *mathesis:* deception and learning, confusion and uptake, contact broken and contact mended, alienation and rapport. The rhythm is often abortive. Speakers fail or refuse to make themselves understood—or being understood wouldn't help.

Once upon a time it would have been tempting to say that the appeal of the metaphorist scenario is bound to last—that it's a powerful rendition of everybody's story. But at this moment in the culture of the ultrasophisticated it's a sentimental confusion to talk about human nature, much less the human predicament. And so much the worse for the ultrasophisticated. The tragicomic struggles of a language-using animal to avoid being used by its language seem to be guaranteed a reasonably steady audience among, let's say, a certain talkative brood of featherless bipeds.

Appendix A

AFTER SO MUCH harping on the difference between figurative and literal meaning, I think I should admit that there are those who argue that there is none. If they're right, this whole book rests on a mammoth error. I've considered this possibility and find no cause for alarm. Surprisingly enough, what I've found instead is confirmation from a hostile quarter—the best kind of confirmation. I'll wind up by considering Donald Davidson's version of the argument. It's both more provocative and (unintentionally) more revealing than most.

Davidson's target is the notion of a public or shared language like English or French. He isn't taking aim at the notion of a personal language, or idiolect. It's only of language in the public sense that he claims "there is no such thing as a language, not if a language is anything like what many philosophers and linguists have supposed."[1] According to Davidson, what these people think a language is like is a collection of "words and sentences as [1] uttered by a particular speaker on a particular occasion. But [2] if the occasion, the speaker, and the audience are 'normal' or 'standard' (in a sense not to be further explained here), then the first [i.e., literal] meaning of an utterance will be what should be found by consulting a dictionary based on actual usage."[2] It's easy to see why "standard" doesn't deserve Davidson's further attention. He's added just enough to the associated notion of public language (2) to fudge both it and "standard." According to that notion, a language assigns every word it contains a choice of senses suitable for different occasions—like the senses listed in a dictionary entry. If one of the choices in the set fits a given occasion, then the occasion is "standard" for using the word. In the Trojan Horse clause added by Davidson (1), the meaning of a word in a language is made up of *nothing but* the senses it has in personal languages used on particular occasions. Dismissing any of these as nonstandard or incorrect usage isn't *high-handed*. Since utterances in personal languages are all there is, it's just *absurd*.

We might wonder about how (1) can work. How can the listener understand somebody else's personal language unless it's *the listener's* language too? How can the listener understand it if it isn't a language shared by at least a pair of users—in short, the kind of *public* language Davidson rules out? Davidson's answer is: "through the intentions of the speaker." We keep on building up and revising a "prior theory" of what kind of personal language the speaker *intends* to use. We do it by finding out as much as we can about him—including the beliefs and intentions he typically gets across to us in the nonexistent public language!

But Davidson seems to have no more success than we have at doing without that kind of language. In fact, he drops the derivative notion of standard *situations* only to call on its source—the supposedly empty notion of standard *meanings*, or "lines of interpretation":

> The less we know about the speaker, assuming that we know he belongs to *our language community*, the more nearly our prior theory [our long-range theory about his use of words] will simply be the theory we expect someone who hears our unguarded speech to use. If we ask for a cup of coffee, direct a taxi driver, or order a crate of lemons, we may know so little about our intended interpreter that we can do no better than to assume that he will interpret our speech along what we take to be *the standard lines*. (Italics mine)[3]

It turns out that we can depend on strangers to interpret us along "standard" lines automatically—*just so long as they belong to our language community*. And what kind of community would that be? Clearly they don't belong to it by sharing the community diet or dress. They belong—by knowing the community *language*! If standard meaning is anything, it's meaning in that language. It isn't easy to see what's left of Davidson's provocative thesis besides the provocation.

But there *is* something left. That's why I began by saying that his thesis is revealing as well as provocative. As he describes the listener's developing theory of what the speaker is *literally* saying, the result is nearly a twin of the account I give in chapter 1 of how the listener gradually catches on to what the speaker is *figuratively* saying:

> Every *deviation from ordinary usage*, as long as it is *agreed on* for the moment (knowingly deviant or not, on one or both sides), is in the

passing theory [the listener's guesses about the speaker's deviant usages] as a feature of what the words mean on that occasion. Such meanings, transient though they may be, are *literal*. (Italics mine)

Knowing a passing theory is only knowing how to interpret a particular utterance on a particular occasion. Nor could such a language, if we want to call it that, be said to have been learned, or to be governed by conventions.

The expected field of application [of the passing theory] is vanishingly small.[4]

Some of this is likely to seem just arbitrary. For example, deviant usages are supposed to be literal. But if ordinary or standard usage is anything, it's *usage in a language*—a language in which deviant usage is anything *but* literal. Still, I don't think "arbitrary" is quite right. "Obedient" is more like it—obedient to the requirements of a theory. It's Davidson's theory that is arbitrary. It makes no room for the existence of such things as languages in the public sense. So in the theory, what we call figurative comes out literal—literal in a language too microscopically "passing" or "transient" to be called a language.

Until we check what Davidson's theory wants him to say, "transient" here looks as arbitrary as "literal." What's to keep a speaker from bringing one of his deviant meanings in again and again—as long as the talk they come up in lasts? Don't speakers do this all the time? Once new meanings are introduced, they belong to some entry or other in the dictionary of the going conversation. In fact, if they're literal in any language at all, they're literal in the impromptu dialect of *that conversation*. But again Davidson's *theory* has drafted the conversation dialect to do the work of nonexistent English or French. So the lifetime of deviant meanings and the nonlanguage that assigns them had better be "vanishingly small"—so small it's pointless to talk about "learning" them.

I said this was revealing as well as provocative. The revealing part is that Davidson's *deviations* are precisely the *figurative meanings* of chapter 1. His "passing" language is precisely the conversation dialect. True, he doesn't think that people who catch on to figurative meanings rely on convention—even though this makes a needless mystery of how any catching on short of clairvoyance is ever carried off. But we saw language surviving his theoretical death sentence. Convention does the same. In the first Davidson passage I just quoted, deviant meanings belong to expressions *when the parties agree that they do*—that is, *by convention*. And it seems that the agreement itself calls for understandings (or conventions) already in place: "[Alfred] Mackay says you cannot change what words mean . . . merely by intending to; the answer is that this is true, but you can change the meaning provided you believe (and perhaps are justified in believing) that the interpreter has adequate clues for the new interpretation."⁵ So we need conventions after all—clue conventions to make the new meaning conventions possible. For example, we need rules for transforming irrelevant old meanings into relevant new ones. None of these "trope" rules takes us (let's say) from any sense of Mrs. Malaprop's word to what she seems to think it means in English. *That's* why she's committed a malapropism and not a metaphor. But we mustn't expect too much. Davidson would have to see the implications of his "clues" more clearly to appreciate the need for tropes. It's enough that he gives us *the main contours of the account laid out in chapter 1*—in spite of his official position.

This is an old story. In quantum physics and elsewhere, powerful theories strip us of our commonsense convictions, and it seems we just have to resign ourselves to going naked. But not everything that does us this favor is a powerful theory. And when it isn't, common sense takes its revenge. After a bit, if we insist on talking theory talk, we wind up not making any kind of sense at all. Then, little by little, common sense quietly takes up its old position as the minimum requirement for being intelligible—intelligible to ourselves, not to mention anybody else. The old Roman poet says: "You can drive Nature outside with a pitchfork if you like. She'll just keep running back in."

Appendix B

RECENTLY, BAD NEWS about the classic literal-figurative distinction has come in from cognitive science; a second appendix is in order.

On the classic view, figurative uptake is made up of literal uptake *plus* something else (trope testing). Grasping, for example, what it is for mutual acquaintance X to be a "broiled haddock" should take longer than grasping (more or less equivalently) what it is for X to be an ordinary guy. Unfortunately, the laboratory assures us that as a rule figurative uptake is no slower than literal—provided the conversation has alerted the listener to the relevant talk-postulates.[1] Given the introductory priming, "Among the caviare and filet mignon, X is the broiled haddock" will get the point across as fast as "X is an ordinary guy." But if the time difference between literal and figurative *uptake* has to go, then the distinction between literal and figurative *sense* goes with it. Or, at least, so runs the argument.

It's notably awkward for the cognitive scientists that they can't get their comparison test of responses off the ground without breaking down specimens intuitively according to the distinction they're challenging—and still more awkward that their intuitions play them false. Take the following list of sentences supplied by one writer in this vein:

5. A tree is a plant.
6. A tree is a landmark.
7. A tree is an investment.
8. A tree is a rarity.
9. A tree is a factory.

The scientist argues that "all but Sentence 9 are literal statements," yet only sentence 5 "poses no recognition problem." This is because in sentence 5 "all the properties of the concept 'plant' must be true of the concept 'tree.' " By contrast, sentences 6, 7, and 8, "although literal, cannot be sensibly interpreted in this way, and so they must pose the same recognition problem posed by Sentence 9."[2]

No wonder these "literal" sentences take as long to grasp as the metaphorical one; on the scientist's showing, what's getting applied to the subject of each is only a *part* of the literal meaning of the predicate. To avoid being just false of their subjects, these *allegedly literal* predicates get a new meaning that bears a particular trope relation (part-whole or implicate-implicans) to the old meaning, or to the old meaning plus talk-postulate information. In short, all the sentences but sentence 5 are *figurative in the classic sense*—and by the scientist's own admission the literal one poses no recognition problem! With enemies like this, the classic view needs no friends.

Still another scientist comes up with a dramatic example of *allegedly figurative* sense that beats literal to the punch: "If a house painter literally kicks the bucket, then processing is slower for this phrase than if the context directs 'kick the bucket' to be interpreted as [meaning] *die*. . . . Once added to the phrasal lexicon, 'kick the bucket' becomes a dead metaphor and will not cause its literal interpretation to be accessed. The literal interpretation will require more work, because 'kick,' 'the,' and 'bucket' must be separately accessed." "Once the metaphor or figurative phrase is dead, nonliteral interpretation will be rapid and automatic."[3]

But, of course, metaphors die precisely when their meanings *stop* being "nonliteral." It's the new *literal* interpretation of "kick the bucket" that's rapid and automatic; in the lexicon this particular dead metaphor functions as a single term (like "dumbwaiter" or adverbial "cats and dogs" in "it's raining cats and dogs")—that's why the genuine word string "kick" + "the" + "bucket" is unlikely to be used and hard to spot when it is.[4] Once again, thanks to gross confusion, the classic account can thank its debunkers for a vindication.

We're told that requests that are both sarcastic *and* indirect ("Sure is nice and warm in here," reacting to a cold draft from the window) turn out to be clearer than requests that are just indirect ("Why don't you close the window?").[5] But these examples, at least, aren't very reassuring on this score; the cold draft has already added a request *expectation* to the talk-postulates underlying both requests—so in the sarcastic one the only recognition problem left is getting the point of the sarcasm ("Given the window you've neglected to close, only a fool would think it's nice and warm in here"). By contrast, without more information it's harder to rule out the possibility that the request figuratively expressed by "Why don't you, etc.?" *also* has a sarcastic point ("Only a fool would think you have a *reason* for keeping the window open in a draft like this").

Observed time equivalence doesn't establish *real* time equivalence anyhow; for all the observers have shown to the contrary, real time difference could be *unobservable*. All this would take is an obligatory process that accompanies both literal and figurative interpretation and lasts longer than either. It's hard to imagine how this possibility could be experimentally ruled out; in fact, one researcher of the debunking school thinks ruling out a masking process is "methodologically impossible."[6]

But what's decisively against the debunking is that the theory it's clearing the way for is none other than the classic theory again, in thin disguise: "Consider another of Denise's utterances to Rob: 'The sky is blue.' This utterance has a straightforward literal interpretation. None the less, . . . suppose Denise and Rob have an agreement in which . . . Rob walks the dog on sunny days. By uttering 'The sky is blue,' Denise would be . . . intending, 'It's your turn to walk the dog.' " This is supposed to show that "what is immediately evident in metaphor comprehension—the necessity for disambiguation with respect to common ground—is rampant in literal interpretation as well."[7] But clearly what's getting "disambiguated" is the figurative meaning—the meaning in the dialect of conversation—of "The sky is blue": *It's your turn to walk the dog*. And the way this is managed is by troping a "straightforward literal meaning" that happens to be pointless—just as the classic theory predicts. Again:

> Imagine a computer programmer stating "I found a bug in my program" and hearing a visiting child giggle. . . . The metaphor is still alive for the child and must be processed literally in this first-time encounter. . . . Once a phrasal entry has been created, "bug" will cease to map to *insect* in that . . . context. . . . Suppose the child can infer from the situation that the error has caused the program to malfunction. In addition, because the child knows that bugs are small, the child might add the hypothesis that program bugs are a small portion of the entire program and may be difficult to find.[8]

The metaphor-trope steps illustrated here are "discrepancy analysis [of literal sense], access to world knowledge, and analogical reasoning"—just as the classic theory predicts.

As in the Davidson case, it's the same old story; it takes more than a pitchfork, even a high-tech pitchfork, to keep Nature out of the barn.

Notes

Introduction

1. Cf. David Lewis's rehabilitation of Abelard's distinction between general knowledge *in sensu composito* and general knowledge *in sensu diviso*. See Lewis, *Convention* (Cambridge, Mass.: Harvard University Press, 1969), pp. 64, 67, 68.

2. *1 Henry IV* 1.3.190–96. I quote here and hereafter from Charleton Hinman's facsimile of the first folio (New York: W. W. Norton, 1969).

3. Ibid., 1.3.196–200.

4. Ibid., 1.3.211–12.

5. Ibid., 2.3.29–31.

6. Ibid., 2.3.55.

7. Aristotle, *Ethica Nicomachea* 1128a9–12.

8. Quintilian, *Institutio oratoria* 8.6.4: "[Metaphora] est ab ipsa nobis concessa Natura." I quote here and hereafter from the edition of Karl Halm (Leipzig: Teubner, 1869).

9. Helen Vendler, *The Poetry of George Herbert* (Cambridge, Mass.: Harvard University Press, 1975), pp. 195–96.

10. John Carey, *John Donne: Life, Mind, and Art* (London: Faber and Faber, 1981), p. 138.

11. Elegie 12.57–62. I quote here and hereafter from *The Poems of John Donne*, ed. Herbert Grierson (Oxford: Oxford University Press, 1912).

12. Carey, *John Donne*, p. 170.

13. Vendler, *Poetry of George Herbert*, p. 61.

14. Demetrius Phalerensis, *De interpretatione* 80. See *Rhetores graeci*, ed. Leonhart Spengel (Leipzig: Teubner, 1856), 3:280–81.

15. Rosemond Tuve, *A Reading of George Herbert* (Chicago: University of Chicago Press, 1952), p. 202.

16. Maureen Quilligan, *The Language of Allegory* (Ithaca: Cornell University Press, 1979), offers this confusion, in the form of a meaning swap, as "an important new distinction between . . . the literal and the metaphorical" (pp. 67–68): (a) what used to be called the self-referential use of words (now renamed "literal");

(b) what used to be called their literal meaning (now renamed "metaphorical");
(c) what used to be called their allegorical meaning (now renamed "truly literal").

17. Max Black, "Metaphor," in *Proceedings of the Aristotelean Society* 4 (1955); Black, "More about Metaphor," in *Metaphor and Thought*, ed. Andrew Ortony (Cambridge: Cambridge University Press, 1979); Paul Ricoeur, "The Metaphorical Process," *Critical Inquiry* 5 (1978): 143–59; Ricoeur, *The Rule of Metaphor* (Toronto: University of Toronto Press, 1979); George Lakoff and Mark Johnson, *Metaphors We Live By* (Chicago: University of Chicago Press, 1980); Nelson Goodman, *Languages of Art* (Indianapolis: Hackett, 1976); Friedrich Nietzsche, *Über Wahrheit und Lüge im aussermoralischen Sinn*, in *Werke* (Stuttgart: Kröner, 1921), 2: 10–11, 17; Nietzsche, *Jenseits von Gut und Böse*, *Werke* 1:20; Jacques Derrida, "La mythologie blanche," in *Rhétorique et philosophie*, *Poétique*, vol. 5 (Paris: Editions du Seuil, 1971); Donald Davidson, "What Metaphors Mean," *Critical Inquiry* 5 (1978): 31–48; "A Nice Derangement of Epitaphs," in *Truth and Interpretation*, ed. Ernest LePore (Oxford: Basil Blackwell, 1986).

18. H. Paul Grice, "Logic and Conversation," in *Syntax and Semantics*, ed. Peter Cole and Jerry Morgan (New York: Academic Press, 1975); John Searle, *Speech Acts* (Cambridge: Cambridge University Press, 1969). For relativism of both kinds in a literary speech-act theory, see Mary Louise Pratt, *Toward a Speech Act Theory of Literary Discourse* (Bloomington: Indiana University Press, 1977), pp. 81, 87–88.

19. This is more or less what Warning seems to be getting at when he rejects Vodicka's distinction between the structure of a literary work and the norms of the reader: "A particular historic norm, namely that of the author's intended public, has already entered this structure—in other words, the norm itself is already a joint determinant not only of the system of interpretation but of the code that generates the work." See *Rezeptionsästhetik: Theorie und Praxis*, ed. Rainer Warning (Munich: Wilhelm Fink, 1975), p. 18.

20. Harold Skulsky, "Metaphorese," *NOUS* 20 (1986): 350–70.

Chapter 1. The Act of Figuration

1. See Quintilian on "figures of thought," *Institutiones* 9.1.14. The speech-act dimension of the maneuver ("saying one thing and *doing* another *in one's speech*") is spelled out in (Pseudo-)Dionysius of Halicarnassus, *Ars rhetorica* 8.3. Cf. John Searle's notion of indirect speech acts, in John R. Searle and Daniel Vanderveken, *Foundations of Illocutionary Logic* (Cambridge: Cambridge University Press, 1985), p. 10. Cicero gives many examples of Gricean conversational implicature in *De oratore* 259.23–26, 269.15–19, 276.34–36, 280.3–5, 282.21–32.

2. *Macbeth* 3.1.96.

3. A number of recent writers think literal meaning is a needless theoretical

whisker ripe for Occam's razor. Not only can we do without vernacular meaning and deviation from it, we can prove in the laboratory that such things don't play any part in interpreting figurative language. Take, for example, D. A. Boswell's claim in "Speakers' Intentions: Constraints on Metaphor Comprehension," *Metaphor and Symbolic Activity* 1 (1986): 154–55: "Empirical investigations of subjects' reaction times for metaphoric and literal utterances revealed equivalent processing times when these sentences were presented in contexts appropriate to their interpretation." Cf. A. Ortony et al., "Metaphor: Theoretical and Empirical Research," *Psychological Bulletin* 85 (1978): 919–43; Roger Tourangeau, "Metaphor and Cognitive Structure," in *Metaphor: Problems and Perspectives*, ed. David S. Miall (Sussex: Harvester Press, 1982), pp. 14–35.

People who argue this way seem to be guided more by a desire for scientific progress than by a clear vision of an alternative to the old categories. Witness Boswell's promise that the view he'll be defending "does not rely on the . . . assumption of fixed lexical meanings" ("Speakers' Intentions," p. 153). The promise gets broken virtually in the same breath: "To comprehend *Billboards are warts on the landscape*, . . . listeners must make certain aesthetic judgments that are not fundamental to the *definitional properties* of the terms comprising the metaphor" (p. 153; italics mine). "Speakers' intended meaning [in using metaphor] depends on but is not a direct derivative of the *lexical constituents* used to produce utterances" (p. 153; italics mine). As used by Boswell, the italicized phrases are just stand-ins for the exorcised "lexical meanings."

Still, the question of reaction times can't be avoided simply by arguing that the distinction it discredits should be cherished because it's better than nothing. The real difficulty here is that the experimental *comparisons* demand that the distinction be somehow drawn; but (as with Boswell's performance reviewed above) the experimenters aren't rhetorically sophisticated enough to guarantee an intuitively plausible sorting out of sample. See appendix B.

4. Quintilian, *Institutiones* 1.5.7. Cf. ibid., 9.1.4.

5. Ibid., 9.2.64: "ex aliquo dicto latens aliquid eruitur."

6. Ibid., 8.6.1: "Trope is change in word or speech from their proper meaning, along with its force [*cum uirtute*], to some other."

7. *Poetics* 1458a25–28; *Rhetorica* 1405b2–5. Aristotle's word for fairness in the second passage (*epieikeia*) is also his word for judicial equity.

8. *Epiphora*. See *Poetics* 1457b7. Aristotle assigns his theory of speech acts (command, prayer, story telling, threat, question, answer) to the science of conversational response (*techne hypocritike*) (*Poetics* 1456b9–13, 1457a12).

9. A *xenikon*. See *Poetics* 1458a22–23; *Rhetorica* 1405a8–9.

10. *Rationis Latomianae confutatio*, in *Luthers Werke: Kritische Gesamtausgabe* (Weimar: Boehlau), 8:43–128; pp. 84–85 (translation mine).

11. Brian Vickers, " 'Songs and Sonnets' and the Rhetoric of Hyperbole,"

in *John Donne: Essays in Celebration*, ed. A. J. Smith (London: Methuen, 1972), p. 155.

12. Cf. Michael Dummett on Wittgenstein's distinction between a way of grasping and an interpretation, in "Comments on Davidson and Hacking," in *Truth and Interpretation: Perspectives on the Philosophy of Donald Davidson*, ed. Ernest LePore (Oxford: Basil Blackwell, 1986), p. 464.

13. "Answer to Davenant's Preface to *Gondibert*"; see *Critical Essays of the Seventeenth Century*, ed. J. E. Spingarn (Oxford: Clarendon Press, 1908), 2:65.

14. "Preface to *Gondibert*," in Spingarn 2:6.

15. One overt way of doing this is to use the mock-apologetic formula "so to speak." See Hermogenes, *De methodo vafritiae* 6, Spengel 2:430.

16. Aristotle, *Prior Analytics* 2.28; *Topics* 1.8. "Possible opinion" is *protasis* (or *erotesis*) *endoxos* (= proposition [or question] expressed in a [current] opinion) in Greek, represented in Scholastic discussion by *opinabile*. In the *Topics* passage, Aristotle supplies *paradoxon* as the contrary of *endoxon*. In *Paradoxa Stoicorum* 5, Cicero translates *paradoxon* as *inopinatum dictu*—and pointedly contrasts this with *inopinatum re*. The complementary contrast between kinds of *opinatum* is precisely a contrast between *talk*-postulates and real ones. A talk-postulate is a *dictu opinatum*.

17. *The Faerie Queene* 2.9.13.

18. Christopher Hill, *Change and Continuity in Seventeenth-Century England* (London: Weidenfeld and Nicolson, 1974), p. 182.

19. Bernaard Vos, *Commentaria rhetorica* (Marburg: J. H. Stockenius, 1681), p. 102. This use of "character" seems to be due to Demetrius (see *De interpretatione* 39).

20. Carey, *John Donne*, p. 109.

21. For this distinction, see n. 16 to this chapter, on *dictu opinatum* versus *re opinatum*.

22. Robert Ellrodt, *Les Poètes métaphysiques anglais* (Paris: Jose Corti, 1960), 2:541.

23. Ibid., 2:166.

24. Ibid., 2:149.

25. *Sermons*, ed. Potter and Simpson (Berkeley: University of California Press, 1953), 3:165.

26. Carey, *John Donne*, p. 178.

27. Arthur F. Marotti, *John Donne, Coterie Poet* (Madison: University of Wisconsin Press, 1986), p. 11.

28. Ibid.

29. Ibid., p. 156.

30. François Menestrier, *L'Art des Emblèmes* (Lyons, 1662), p. 606.

31. *Rhetorica* 1410b10–20.

32. Ibid., 1406b20–26.
33. Cicero, *De oratore* 3.156–57. Charles Butler's discussion in *Rhetorica* (1600; London: William Bentley and John Williams, 1649), pp. 1, 22, 25, is typical of its century in following both Ciceronian accounts. John Hoskins distinguishes between what a metaphorical statement says and the resemblance that grounds the metaphor; see *Directions for Speech and Style*, ed. Hoyt H. Hudson (Princeton: Princeton University Press, 1935), p. 8.
34. See the example from John Searle discussed in my "Metaphorese," p. 354. Cf. also Lakoff and Johnson's confusion of metaphor and metonymy in *Metaphors We Live By*, pp. 19, 154.
35. *Romeo and Juliet* 3.1.212.
36. Pseudo-Dionysius Halicarnassensis, *Ars rhetorica* 8.8 (in *Opera omnia*, ed. Angelus Maius [Leipzig: Tauchnitz, 1829]).
37. Ibid., 8.9.
38. Ibid., 8.11.
39. Ibid., 9.1.
40. Less *logos* than *endeixis*. See Hermogenes, *De formis* 2.8, ed. Spengel, p. 385. For the underlying verb *endeiknysthai* (= imply conversationally), see ibid., p. 388.
41. *De formis* 2.5, Spengel, p. 376.
42. *De duplici copia*, p. 46.
43. Charles Butler, *[Ars] rhetorica* (London: William Bentley for John Williams, 1649), pp. 7–8. Cf. Geraard Vos, *Rhetorice contracta* (Leyden: Jan Maire, 1640), p. 353.
44. Hoskins, *Directions*, p. 8.
45. Emmanuele Tesauro, *Il cannocchiale aristotelico* (Venice: Paolo Baglioni, 1663), p. 248; italics mine.
46. Aristotle, *De interpretatione* 1 and 4. A word doesn't link up directly with what it denotes, but rather with some class of mental experiences (*pathemata*). The members of the class in turn are likenesses (*homoiomata*) of the members of some class of things or facts (*pragmata*). The likeness class is registered as an idea (*noema; eidos noeton* in *De anima*) or definition (*logos tes ousias*). Aristotle's "idea" lives on in Scholastic psychology as the "intelligible species."
  Both Descartes and Hobbes adapt the theory of mental likeness. For Descartes see *Oeuvres*, ed. Charles Adam and Paul Tannery (Paris: Leopold Cerf, 1897), 7: 160–61; *Oeuvres philosophiques*, ed. Ferdinand Alquié (Paris: Garnier, 1967), 2: 608–9. For Hobbes see Mersenne's exposition, in the preface to *Ballistica* (1644), *Thomae Hobbes Opera philosophica quae latine scripsit*, ed. William Molesworth (London: Longman, Brown, Green, and Longman, 1845), 5:310; *De corpore* 2.5, *Opera latina* (London: John Bohn, 1839), 1:15; *Opera latina* 5:309; *Objectiones ad Cartesii Meditationes* 5; *Opera latina* 5:259; *De corpore* 7.1, *Opera latina* 1:82; *Leviathan* 4,

in *The English Works of Thomas Hobbes*, ed. William Molesworth (1839; reprint, Aalen: Scientia, 1962), 3:21; *English Works* 3:26–27; *Opera latina* 1:28. Hobbes's image theory of understanding belongs to the old *De interpretatione* tradition (*Opera latina* 5:316, Mersenne's exposition).

For modern versions of the mental term theory of images, see Wilhelm Wundt, *Völkerpsychologie* (Leipzig: Kröner, 1912), 1:594–610; Gustaf Stern, *Meaning and Change of Meaning* (Göteborg: Elander, 1931), pp. 301–2; Stephen Ullmann, *The Principles of Semantics* (Oxford: Oxford University Press, 1957).

47. Tesauro, *Cannocchiale*, p. 245.
48. Ibid.
49. Ibid., p. 246. Tesauro's laughing meadow simply rehashes the old Aristotelian advice that goes with the image theory. You make things immediate when you describe them metaphorically as acting spontaneously—as having *energeia*. The resulting image realizes or illustrates the literal sense of your metaphor.
50. Quintilian, *Institutio oratoria* 8.3.61. Cf. ibid., 8.6.19.
51. Ibid., 6.2.29–30.
52. Thomas Sprat, *The History of the Royal Society of London* (London: T.R., 1667), 2.20. On the other hand, Gustaf Stern tries to show by experiment that thinking is punctuated by imagery, *especially when the thinking is stalled* (*Meaning and Change of Meaning*, pp. 46–67).
53. Modern psychological research backs up the folklore belief or intuition that thought is not only inner talk but inner picturing. See Allan Paivio, "Psychological Processes in the Comprehension of Metaphor," in *Metaphor and Thought*, ed. Andrew Ortony (Cambridge: Cambridge University Press, 1979), pp. 166–67; Ned Block, "The Photographic Fallacy in the Debate about Mental Imagery," *NOUS* 17 (1983): 651–67. See also *Imagery*, ed. Ned Block (Cambridge, Mass.: MIT Press, 1981).
54. *Poetics* 1456a9–13.
55. Ibid., 1459a7–9, 1455a32; *Rhetorica* 1362b24, 1412a11–16. Metaphorizing is part of "urbanity" (*asteiotes*), which generates "learning" by delaying the listener's perception of the meaning (*dianoia*) of a bon mot (*Poetics* 1410b35–36). The pseudo-Platonic *Horoi* (glossary) gives "quick learning" for *euphues*, following the discussion in *Republic* 455b. Lyly's Euphues is a "sharp wit" given to "fine phrases, smooth quipping, merry taunting." Ascham glosses "he that is apt by goodness of wit, and appliable by readiness of will, to learning." See also Tesauro, *Cannocchiale*, p. 245.
56. *Cannocchiale*, p. 245: "And this begets wonder, as the listener's mind, overcome by the novelty of the speaker's phrase, contemplates the sharpness of his genius for representation [*ingegno rappresentante;* literally, 'representing intellect']."
57. *Rhetorica* 1412a19–31. Metaphorizing is not only a kind of foreign speech

but a renewing of speech—*kainologia,* or coining (ibid.). In his translation and commentary on the *Rhetorica* (Argentinae: Theodosius Rihelius, 1570), Johann Sturm elaborates Aristotle's account of metaphorical disorientation (*prosexapatesis*). It's a prank (*elusio*) that ends happily, with the discovery of unsuspected multiple meaning (fols. 370r–v, 371v). This is just about right—except that the multiplicity being discovered belongs to the talk dialect, and not to the vernacular. Cicero sums up the metaphorical prank as mock digression. Finding you're not way off the track is *maxima delectatio* (*De oratore* 3.160).

58. Weinrich's "image-fields" in "Münze und Wort" are precisely the mock theories that get mock confirmed in the game of extending metaphors. The same goes for Sister Joan Marie Lechner's "commonplaces" in *Renaissance Concepts of the Commonplaces* (1962; Westport, Conn.: Greenwood Press, 1974).

59. Demetrius (*De interpretatione,* Spengel 3:310) shrewdly points out the indirect speaker's implied compliment to the sharpness of his listener.

60. *Twelfth Night* 1.5.299–311; italics mine.

Chapter 2. The Paradigm Figurative Speaker: Divine Linguistics

1. See the Junius-Tremellius rendering of John 1:1.
2. *Paradise Lost* 3.150–55.
3. Milton, *The Doctrine and Discipline of Divorce* 2.4.
4. Gen. 18:24–25.
5. For hints in *Paradise Lost* of the Father's and Son's separate individualities ("essences"), see Hugh MacCallum, *Milton and the Sons of God* (Toronto: University of Toronto Press, 1986). For their separateness in *De doctrina* see *The Works of John Milton,* ed. F. A. Patterson (New York: Columbia University Press, 1933), 14:192; cf. Maurice Kelley, ed., *The Complete Prose Works of John Milton* (New Haven: Yale University Press, 1973), 6:66. (The evidence of Milton's heterodoxy is compelling; but see *Bright Essence,* ed. W. B. Hunter, C. A. Patrides, and J. H. Adamson [Salt Lake City: University of Utah Press, 1971].) Still, in Milton the Son wasn't created out of nothing, but out of God's (essentially communicative?) substance or nature (*Works,* ed. Patterson, 14:192).
6. Chapter one, sec. 2, A, B, and C.
7. *Summa Theologica* 1.1.10 ad 3. Cf. Henri de Lubac, *Exégèse médiévale* (Paris: Aubier, 1959), 1:180.
8. *Summa theologica* 1–2.102.2 ad 1. Cf. Bartholomaeus Keckermann, *Syntagma theologiae* (Hanau: Petrus Antonius, 1615), p. 160; also John Weemse, in *The Christian Synagogue* [ca. 1632], quoted by Barbara Lewalski, *Protestant Poetics and the Seventeenth-Century Religious Lyric* (Princeton: Princeton University Press, 1979), p. 121. For Luther's inconsistent usage, see Karlfried Fröhlich, "Fifteenth-

Century Hermeneutics," in *Literary Uses of Typology*, ed. Earl Miner (Princeton: Princeton University Press, 1977), p. 26. Aquinas redefines "literal" to clear God of the charge of equivocation (*Summa theologica* 1.1.10 *objectio*). Cf. Melanchthon, *Institutiones rhetoricae* (Wittenberg, ?1536), sig. diiiiv–eir.

9. See, e.g., William Whitaker, *A Disputation on Holy Scripture Against the Papists* [1610], trans. William Fitzgerald, Parker Society (Cambridge: Cambridge University Press, 1849), p. 405.

10. Augustine, *De doctrina Christiana* 3.10, Migne *PL* 34, col. 71; 3.12, col. 73.; 3.16, col. 74.

11. Deut. 25:4.

12. 1 Cor. 9:9–10. Cf. Augustine, *De doctrina* 2.10, Migne *PL* 34, col. 42.

13. Augustine, *Enarrationes in Psalmos*, Migne *PL* 36, cols. 605, 72. To judge from the use Augustine makes of Tychonius's treatise on rules of interpreting figures of speech, the first rule is that without a cue—anomaly of one kind or another—there's no figure. See *De doctrina* 3.33, Migne *PL* 34, cols. 84, 81.

Luther follows Augustine in making anomaly *part* of figurativeness, not just an optional warning that figurativeness is there. See *Rationis Latomianae confutatio*, in *Luthers Werke*, 8:43–128, pp. 63, 64. "We aren't trying to find out what the lust for noodling [*libido nugandi*] is *capable* of offering, but what scrupulous accuracy in interpreting [*religio interpretandi*] is *obliged* to offer" (ibid., p. 62). The tone of this is a little like that of a passage in one of the church fathers most revered by Reformers, Jerome in the *Apology* for his *Against Jovinian*, where he condemns appropriative reading as an assault on the author and asks to be condemned if he's caught doing it.

14. Augustine, *De doctrina* 3.14, col. 74.

15. Ibid., 3.29, cols. 81, 80.

16. Here and throughout, "context" includes those circumstances of utterance that are conventional talk-postulates for the kind of communication the utterance is part of.

17. *De doctrina* 3.26, col. 79. The second of Irenaeus's rules of reading in *Contra haereticos* 2.46–47 is to use literal parts of the text to clear up ostensible metaphors, never the reverse. The duty of a reader is to follow an appropriate discovery procedure (*disciplina inventionis*; Migne *PG* 5, col. 719). Cf. Augustine, *De doctrina* 3.28, col. 80. Hilary of Poitiers widens the notion of context to include the circumstances of utterance. See *De trinitate* 4, n. 14 (*PL* 10, col. 107); 2, n. 31 (col. 71).

Wherever an important issue of faith comes up, Augustine takes it for granted that reading is for finding the sense of the text, not introducing a sense of one's own. See *Contra Donatistas* 16, Migne *PL* 43, cols. 422–23, 430–31. Vital issues of doctrine should never be settled by appeal to figurative passages—not because there's no probable fact of the matter, but because disputes among experts scandalize laymen (ibid., chap. 5, cols. 397, 398).

18. *De doctrina* 3.27–28, col. 80. For Protestant redactions of Augustine's method, see William Whitaker, *A Disputation on Holy Scripture*, pp. 470, 471, and 472, respectively; George Herbert, *The Countrey Parson*, chap. 4, in *Works*, ed. F. E. Hutchinson (Oxford: Clarendon Press, 1954); Patterson, ed., *The Works of John Milton*, 16:278.
19. *De doctrina Christiana* 2.24, col. 54.
20. Ibid., 2.25, col. 54.
21. Ibid., 3.25, cols. 78–79.
22. Ibid., 2.16, col. 47; 2.30, col. 57; 2.16, col. 48; 2.28, cols. 55–56.
23. Ibid., 2.16, col. 47.
24. *Enarrationes in Psalmos*, col. 97.
25. 2 Sam. 12.
26. *Enarrationes in Psalmos*, col. 589.
27. Demetrius, *De interpretatione* 222 (Spengel 3:310).
28. See Whitaker, *A Disputation on Holy Scripture*, pp. 406–7, 408.
29. The notion of type seems to be a development of the notion of an omen, which also depends for its existence on an accompanying (figurative) utterance and its circumstances. Cf. Calchas's interpretation of the omen at Aulis (*Iliad* 2.323–29). The snake from under the altar that devours eight sparrows and their mother before Zeus turns it to stone *is* (metaphorically) the Achaean host that will consume nine years fighting in Troy before taking the city in the tenth. The omen is *opsi-teleston*. (It is to achieve its *telos* late.)
30. This implication of Erich Auerbach's account seems to have escaped his notice. See *Scenes from the Drama of European Literature* (New York: Meridian, 1959), pp. 53–54.

Lubac's discussion of another Augustinian passage (*De utilitate credendi* 3, nn. 5–6) seems to tally in principle with my account (*Exégèse médiévale*, 1:180). A less ambiguous passage than the one Lubac is commenting on is *De vera religione* 50, n. 99, *PL* 42, col. 166.

Milton's treatment clearly implies that he too sees prefiguring as a three-member relation ⟨E, P, F⟩. See *De doctrina Christiana*, Columbia Milton 16:262.

31. *De trinitate* 15.9, Migne *PL* 42, col. 1069. William G. Madsen, *From Shadowy Types to Truth* (New Haven: Yale University Press, 1968), pp. 5–6, defines a type as "a *person, thing,* or *event* that prefigures [sic] a future person, thing, or event." But "prefiguration" just means *type*. So the definition goes in a circle. "Type" has non-Pauline uses (all distinct) in the seventeenth century. Unfortunately, in Paul J. Korshin's *Typologies in England, 1650–1820* (Princeton: Princeton University Press, 1982), they all get conflated with the one we're interested in. The result is an unhistorical and hence unusable hippogryph.
32. *De doctrina* 1.2, Migne *PL* 34, cols. 19–20.
33. See Reinhart Herzog, "Augustins Gespräch mit Gott," in *Das Gespräch*,

ed. Karlheinz Stierle and Rainer Warning (Munich: Wilhelm Fink, 1984), esp. pp. 218, 222, 231.

34. *De doctrina* 2.10, col. 42. Cf. Whitaker, *A Disputation on Holy Scripture*, pp. 407–8.

35. Joseph Anthony Mazzeo, "St. Augustine's Rhetoric of Silence," *Journal of the History of Ideas* 26 (1962): 175–96, p. 179. For God's pragmatic way of making an event report both literal and figurative, see Augustine's discussion of Tychonius's rules for reading figures, in *De doctrina* 3.33, col. 84.

36. 1 Cor. 10:11.

37. *Tele* in New Testament *koine*.

38. *Typos* in the *koine*.

39. Gal. 2:17; Col. 2:16, 17. Cf. Calvin, *Institutio* 2.11.8, 2.8.31.

40. Gal. 4:4. Calvin supplies illustrations of other familiar metaphors coreferential with "type": mirror, mask (or role), "figure," "image" (*Institutio* 2.7.2, 3.20.25). In the usual account, type is to antitype as *dynamis* (potentiality) is to *energeia* (actualization) in Aristotle's biologically motivated teleology. In effect, time is an organism passing through intermediate stages on the way to realizing its essence. Thus the Patriarchs are minors under the tutelage (*paidagogia*) of the Old Law (Gal. 4:11, 3:24; Calvin, *Institutio* 2.11.2, 5, 13). Maturity in this stretched use corresponds to "time perfected" (*chronos teleios*) in Aristotle (*Metaphysics* 4.16 [1021b13–14]).

41. Aquinas, *Compendium theologiae* 101, 102. Cf. *Summa theologiae* 1.47.1, 1.45.2.

42. *Summa theologiae* 1.29.4 ad 4.

43. Lewalski, *Protestant Poetics*, p. 76, denies that Thomas allows "any real interplay" between arm and power (God's). If so, how does "arm" manage to pick out power here? God's power gets picked out by causing (rather than exemplifying) what we call "power" in arms. In short, it gets picked out by *metonymy;* Aquinas is using "metaphor" to mean tropes in general.

44. *Summa theologiae* 1.4.3.

45. Ibid., 1.13.3.

46. Ibid., 1.10.9 ad 3. At this point Aquinas is retreating to the position of so-called negative theology. See Pseudo-Dionysius the Areopagite, *The Celestial Hierarchy* 2.

47. Calvin, *Institutio* 1.13.1.

48. Ibid., 1.17.13.

49. By talk-postulate, if A is angry with B, A judges B guilty of a wrong. Richard Strier, *Love Known* (Chicago: University of Chicago Press, 1983), pp. 186, 167, claims that in celebrating an angry God Protestants repudiate "the God of the philosophers," who (according, e.g., to Cicero in *De officiis*) "never gets angry and never does damage" (p. 167). But unlike the Protestants, Cicero

is using "anger" literally, to mean (roughly) *disturbance of reason by the drive to repay a supposed wrong*. Obviously the last thing Protestant theologians want to do is accuse the Bible of calling God irrational.

50. Irenaeus's term for "[interpretative] discovery method" is *disciplina inventionis*—a heuristics of reading.

51. "Nobody doubts either that people learn things more willingly through metaphors or that things hard sought are more agreeably found" (*De doctrina* 2.6, col. 39, reading "gratius" ["agreeably"]; the Migne editor's "grauius" is an obvious slip).

52. Ibid., 2.6, col. 39; 2.8, col. 42.

53. The (scribal?) title of *De doctrina* 1.37 is typical of this line of thinking: "There is grave danger in this flawed [kind of] reading" (col. 35). In 1.36, col. 35, Augustine warns of the intellectually corrupting effect of the *habit* of straying from the meaning of the text.

54. *De doctrina* 1.37, col. 35; *De genesi ad litteram* 1.18, n. 37, Migne *PL* 34, col. 260.

55. *De doctrina* 1.36, col. 35.

56. Luther, *Rationis Latomianae confutatio*, pp. 63, 62. Cf. Melanchthon, *Institutiones rhetoricae*, sig. diiiiv–eir: "Figurative passages should be read by a fixed method [*certa ratione*], not one that varies [with the reader]."

57. Calvin, *Institutio* 2.5.19.

58. Ibid., 3.11.23 (cf. Ambrose, *De Jacobo et uita beata* 2.2).

59. *Exsculpere* (*De civitate Dei* 17.3 G).

60. Keckermann, *Syntagma theologiae*, p. 161. Cf. Melanchthon, *Institutiones rhetoricae*, sig. diiiiv–eir: "Tropology shouldn't be listed among schemes. In some contexts it's nothing but the application of Scripture to morals, where nothing of the historical sense is changed. In others we use figurative language to issue a warning about morals."

61. *Meteorologica* 357a24; *Metaphysica* 991a20.

62. Thomas Hobbes, *Leviathan* 1.4, in *The English Works of Thomas Hobbes*, ed. Molesworth, 3:20.

63. Ibid., pp. 24, 25. James Siemon makes the following strange argument: the Reformers are *icono*clasts; metaphor generates a mental *icon*; ergo the Reformers are *metaphora*clasts (*Shakespearean Iconoclasm* [Berkeley: University of California Press, 1985], pp. 1–75). But Luther and Calvin are fans of metaphor. And there's nothing in Siemon's argument to embarrass them; iconoclasm isn't about the inherent badness of images, it's about the *abuse* of images *in church* ("Homilie Against Images," *Homilies* [London: John Bill, 1632], pp. 44–45, 29). In fact, it isn't about metaphor at all (ibid., p. 41).

64. Hobbes, *Leviathan* 1.4, *English Works*, p. 27.

65. Sprat, *History* 2.20.

66. Quintilian, *Institutio oratoria* 8.6.4.
67. Ibid.
68. Tesauro, *Cannocchiale*, p. 448.
69. Quintilian, *Institutio oratoria* 8.6.19, 6.2.29–30.
70. George Puttenham, *The Arte of English Poesie (1589)* (Facsimile reproduction; Kent, Ohio: Kent State University Press, 1970), p. 166. Note that in classical theory quirky or daring metaphors require "permission." See Hermogenes' discussion of poetic license (*exousia poietike*, *De formis* 2.4; *De methodo vafritiae* 6).
71. "The Vertues of an Heroique Poem," reprinted in Spingarn, pp. 67–76, p. 70.
72. *An Essay Concerning Human Understanding* 3.10.34.
73. *History* 2.20.
74. See Stanley Fish, *Self-Consuming Artifacts* (Berkeley: University of California Press, 1972), p. 40. Fish relies on D. W. Robertson's text of the relevant passage in *De doctrina* (4.16, Migne *PL* 34, col. 104): "The benefits of teaching profit the mind . . . when such assistance is granted by God." But "adiumenta doctrinae tunc prosunt animae . . . cum *Deus operatur ut prosint*" says instead: "The helps of teaching benefit the soul . . . when *God so acts that they benefit {the soul}*" (italics mine). God's having caused something to happen implies that it happened.
75. *De doctrina* 4.5, cols. 91–92 ("ut prosit audientibus, etiam si minus quam prodesset si et eloquenter posset dicere," "profecto plus proderit, si utrumque proderit [scil., non solum sapienter verum etiam eloquenter dicendo]"). Fish, *Self-Consuming Artifacts*, p. 31, quotes the passage with ellipses replacing Augustine's comment that eloquent wisdom does more good than wisdom drably expressed. This enables Fish to claim that eloquence is "now declared superfluous, even dangerous."
76. *De doctrina* 4.5, col. 103.
77. Cf. George Herbert, *The Countrey Parson*, chap. 21: "There being two things in sermons, the one Informing, the other Inflaming; as Sermons come short of questions [i.e., catechisms] in the one, so they farre exceed them in the other. For questions cannot inflame or ravish; that must be done by a set, and laboured, and continued speech."
78. *De doctrina* 4.24, cols. 115–16.
79. Ibid., 4.15, col. 103.
80. Ibid., 4.3, col. 91.
81. *De mendacio* 10, Migne *PL* 40, col. 534.
82. *Enarrationes in Psalmos*, Migne *PL* 36, col. 1151.
83. "The World," ll. 13–14.
84. "The Author to the Critical Peruser," ll. 11–14; "The Person," ll. 17–26; "Thanksgiving for the Body," ll. 339–40.

85. See the Hermogenes reference in n. 70.

86. *An Essay Concerning Human Understanding* 3.11.11 (p. 416).

Chapter 3. God's Tumbler: Pseudometaphor, Sacred and Profane

1. *Romeo and Juliet* 2.1.58–61.

2. "MATTH. 2. In nocturnum & hyemale iter infantis Domini," pp. 37–66. The text of Crashaw I'm translating from is *The Poems of Richard Crashaw*, ed. L. C. Martin (Oxford: Clarendon Press, 1957).

3. *Cognitio matutina*. See Augustine, *Super Genesin ad litteram* 4.22, 31; *De civitate Dei* 12.7, 20; Aquinas, *Summa theologica* 1.58.6.

4. Stephen Manning, "The Meaning of 'The Weeper,'" *ELH* 22 (1955): 35–41, p. 37, explains heaven's bosom as the surface of heaven drinking in the Magdalene's tears. This is Hotspurism (see chapter 1), not an explanation. But here I think it's the response that the language is designed to elicit.

5. Having a mouth, or the functional equivalent, is straightforwardly implied by drinking. Understandably, Robert Ellrodt would rather believe against the evidence that Crashaw's phrase is designed to block rather than trigger visualization (*Poètes métaphysiques*, 2:441, 438).

6. Góngora's subject is *literally* grotesque, Crashaw's isn't. R. V. Young carries his point by forgetting this in *Richard Crashaw and the Spanish Golden Age* (New Haven: Yale University Press, 1982), p. 157.

7. Luis de Góngora y Argote, *Fabula de Polifemo y Galatea*, ll. 489–504. I'm translating from Gimenez's edition of the *Obras Completas* (Madrid: Aguilar, 1943), p. 547.

8. *To the Name above Every Name, the Name of Jesus*, ll. 216–24.

9. "On the Wounds of our crucified Lord," ll. 13–16.

10. *Julius Caesar* 3.1.267–68.

11. Critics are forever trying to rescue Crashaw over his strenuous protest. See Austin Warren, *Richard Crashaw: A Study in Baroque Sensibility* (Baton Rouge: Louisiana State University Press, 1939), p. 130; Frank J. Fabry, "Crashaw's 'On the wounds of our crucified Lord,'" *Concerning Poetry* 10 (Spring 1977): 51–58.

12. Galen, *De usu partium* 6.15, 16, Kuhn ed. 5.275 ("heart's ears," "heart's head," "stomach's mouth"); Celsus 4.1.4 and 5 (heart's or kidney's stomach); Rufus Medicus, *De nomenclatura*, ed. Daremberg and Ruelle 35 ("nose's backbone"); *The Anatomical Works of William Harvey*, ed. G. Whitteridge (Edinburgh: Edinburgh University Press, 1964), p. 252 ("heart's wings"). Cf. Hoskins, *Directions for Speech and Style*, p. 12: "the elbow of his nose."

13. Some critics acknowledge that in Crashaw's conceits "image or sensation replaces idea" (Ellrodt, *Poètes métaphysiques*, 2:434), but they write off the resulting "phantasmagoria" as "confusion" or an atrophied sense of humor. See Warren, *Crashaw*, p. 192; Ruth Coons Wallerstein, *Richard Crashaw: A Study in*

Style and Poetic Development (Madison: University of Wisconsin Press, 1935), p. 92. Ellrodt thinks that putting "images" before the "ideas" they express is the "reef" Crashaw's poetry runs aground on (2:445). But the skipper heads for the reef every chance he gets. Why not assume he knows precisely what he's doing and then see if this kind of running aground serves a legitimate devotional purpose?

14. In her pioneering study, Ruth Wallerstein amply documents the opacity of Crashaw's grotesque images—then goes on to claim that as a result, the underlying idea gets communicated independently of the image (*Richard Crashaw*, p. 85). Cf. George Walton Williams, *Image and Symbol in the Sacred Poetry of Richard Crashaw* (Columbia: University of South Carolina Press, 1963), p. 96; Marc F. Bertonasco, *Crashaw and the Baroque* (University: University of Alabama Press, 1971), pp. 104, 88. In some moods, Ellrodt sees through this line of argument (*Poètes métaphysiques*, 2:437–38). But see n. 5 to this chapter.

15. "Sainte Mary Magdalene, or The Weeper," ll. 67–72.

16. Bertonasco, *Crashaw and the Baroque*, p. 106.

17. See the reference to Gustaf Stern in chap. 1, n. 46.

18. *Confessions* 10.27. Here and hereafter I use the edition of Pius Knoell (Leipzig: G. Freytag, 1896).

19. *Confessions* 5.1, 6.3, 9.12, 10.8.

20. See Vulgate text of 1 Cor. 12:8; Isa. 11:2.

21. This idea of taste-knowledge (*sapida scientia*), or knowledge by acquaintance (*notitia experimentalis*), is endorsed by Aquinas, *Summa theologica* 1.43.5 ad 2, and Bernard of Clairvaux, *Sermones in Cantica* 85. Aquinas refers to Augustine's discussion of a form of understanding that "breaks out into an amorous passion" (*De trinitate* 4.20).

22. Matt. 5:8. This is Jean Gerson's identification. See the reference in n. 33.

23. For an interesting summary of this eroticizing tradition, see Tommaso Campanella's own commentary on Madrigale 6 of his canzone *Della bellezza, segnal del bene, oggetto d'amore*.

24. *Confessions* 10.6.

25. *Affectualis cognitio*. See Jean Gerson, *De theologia mystica*, ed. Glorieux (Paris: Desclée and Cie, 1962), pp. 261, 290.

26. See Ellrodt, *Poètes métaphysiques*, p. 438. Heather Asals believes that Crashaw's "need to confuse the picture" results from an ambition to capture the radical divisions within Being as, for example, Thomists conceive of it: to say that God "is" and that creatures "are" and that causes "are" and that qualities "are," and so on, is to say an entirely distinct thing about each item in turn ("Crashaw's Participles," in *Essays on Richard Crashaw* [Columbia: University of Missouri Press, 1984], pp. 38–39). There's some truth in the critic's appeal to the gulf between (God's and our) ways of being; but if my argument is right so far, Crashaw's project is to *bridge* the gulf, not to acknowledge or display it. Rearing back to look at things is precisely not what he's about. There's even more truth

in Coburn Freer's remarks about Crashaw's un-Protestant spiritual hedonism and lack of "self-division" ("Mirth in Funeral," in ibid., pp. 84–85).

27. Gerson, *De theologia mystica*, p. 252.

28. Ibid., p. 285.

29. Dante, *Paradiso* 3.80: "E'n la sua volontade è nostra pace." Cf. ibid., 20.138.

30. 1 Cor. 11:30; Prov. 19:15; Rom. 13:11.

31. *Confessions* 8.4. The biblical quotation is from Eph. 5:14.

32. Warren, *Crashaw*, pp. 174–75. Cf. Wallerstein, *Richard Crashaw*, p. 90. Robert M. Cooper finds nothing "odd or alien" in Crashaw's "modes of tone and image" (*An Essay on the Art of Richard Crashaw* [Salzburg: Institut für Anglistik, 1982], p. 77). This doesn't strike me as an advance on the insights of pioneers like Wallerstein and Warren.

There's an interesting moment in Hermogenes' condemnation of "frigid" or "tough" metaphors in "civic speech" (*De formis* 1.6, Spengel 292) when he remembers that these abound in the great tragedians, and in Pindar. These authors deserve a "vindication," says the enemy of "frigidity." Unfortunately, he leaves this task for some other occasion.

33. Gerson, *De theologia mystica*, p. 261.

34. "Carta de Fray Luis de Leon a las Carmelitas Descalzas del Monasterio de Madrid," in Santa Teresa de Jesu, *Libro de su Vida* (Garden City, N.Y.: Doubleday), p. xiii.

35. "On a Prayer booke sent to Mrs. M. R.," ll. 15–18.

36. Ibid., ll. 43–44.

37. Ibid., ll. 54–57.

38. Ibid., ll. 99–101.

39. Ibid., ll. 108–9.

40. "On the Wounds of our crucified Lord," ll. 5–8.

41. Ibid., ll. 9–16.

42. Redemption, for both confessions, is what makes repentance possible.

43. "On the Wounds of our crucified Lord," ll. 19–20.

44. Cf. Baltasar Gracián's discussion of the *problema conceptuoso* ("conceit-generated problem") in *Agudeza y Arte de Ingenio* 39, *Obras Completas*, ed. Arturo del Hoyo (Madrid: Aguilar, 1960), pp. 419–23.

45. "In the Holy Nativity," ll. 51–70.

46. R. V. Young explains away this performance as "the innocent banter of a humble shepherd carried away by joy" (*Richard Crashaw and the Spanish Golden Age*, p. 61). But there's nothing rustic or naïve about it.

47. "On the miracle of multiplyed loaves," L. C. Martin, *Poems of Richard Crashaw*, p. 86; "Aquae in vinum versae," p. 38; "In Petrum auricidam," p. 43; "Divum Paulum . . . Lystres adorant," p. 45.

48. Matt. 7:5. Crashaw's nonce term for *microscope* is *optica trabs*. This allows a

play on *trabs,* Jerome's translation of "beam [in the eye]."

49. "In gregem Christi Pastoris," p. 41; "In fores Divo Petro sponte apertas," p. 46; "In trabem Pharisaicam," p. 46; "On our crucified Lord Naked, and bloody," p. 100. On this last epigram and the way Crashaw adapts the mannerist Italian poet Giambattista Marino, see Wallerstein, *Richard Crashaw,* p. 97–98.

50. *Holy Sonnets* 4.13–14.

51. *Holy Sonnets* 18.11–14.

52. Calvin, *Institutio* 3.20.16; John Chrysostom, *Homily 2 De oratione,* and 12 *In Genesin.* Cf. Gregory of Nyssa's doctrine of prayer as an exercise of "freedom of speech" (*parrhesia*) (Migne *PG* 44, cols. 1124b, 497c), where the explicit model is the civil right or privilege of the same name (ibid., col. 1365). See Calvin, *Institutio* 3.20.14; Jean Daniélou, *Platonisme et théologie mystique* (Paris: Aubier, 1944), pp. 114, 119–23. Maybe the traditional "thou-ing" of God reflects the same ideal of familiarity. Cf. Christopher Hill, *The World Turned Upside Down* (Harmondsworth: Penguin, 1975), p. 247, for "thou" as a Quaker challenge to hierarchy.

53. I translate from *Del tumbeor Nostre Dame,* ed. Erhard Lommatzsch (Berlin: Weidmann, 1920).

54. Ibid., ll. 20, 652.

55. Ibid., l. 19.

56. Ibid., ll. 21–29.

57. Ibid., ll. 132–36.

58. Ibid., ll. 155–59.

59. Ibid., ll. 171–79.

60. Ibid., ll. 259–63.

61. Ibid., ll. 332–34.

62. Ibid., l. 462.

63. Ibid., ll. 289–92.

64. The Geneva gloss at 2 Sam. 6:16.

65. See n. 33 to this chapter.

66. Prov. 8:30–31.

67. The Geneva gloss on Prov. 8:30–31.

68. Joseph P. Hilyard traces Crashaw's playful use of rhyme to "something like the *jongleur de dieu* attitude that Chesterton senses in St. Francis" ("The Negative Wayfarers of Richard Crashaw's 'Hymn in the Glorious Epiphanie,'" in *Essays on Richard Crashaw,* ed. Cooper, p. 189). Unfortunately, what Hilyard means by this "attitude" is satirical contempt for the world, not the overflowing charity of a Christian *homo ludens.*

69. Murray Roston, *The Soul of Wit: A Study of John Donne* (Oxford: Clarendon Press, 1974), reads "if spring make'it more" as implying that the speaker's love "outgrows its own infinity" (p. 116). But the speaker's point is that love's growth

proves he was *wrong* to think last winter's love infinite. There's no "transcendence of natural law," no "validation of paradox" (ibid.) in the mere fact that the speaker has managed to spring a surprise on us.

70. See chapter 7 on *para prosdokian*.

71. In *John Donne* (Boston: Twayne, 1987), p. 53, Frank Warnke thinks the war tax illustrates "diminishing metaphor": it's "so inappropriate" as "to be perverse"—and "to force on the reader an emotional response that is refracted through the intellect." But the speaker's point (roughly) is that the lovers blithely set themselves above ordinary constraints—and bring off the attempt; not that, like irresponsible kings, they do this at anybody's expense. Calling love confiscatory isn't "diminishing" or "perverse" or "inappropriate" unless we insist on taking the description literally. And getting "refracted" through the intellect is just what it *is* to be a figurative sense (though in this case the intellect-prism hasn't let through much light).

72. Aulus Gellius 17.12.3 gives a sample of Favorinus's procedure. In his edition of Favorinus's surviving fragments (Florence: Le Monnier, 1966), pp. 139–41, Adelmo Barigazzi notes that the writers of the New Sophistic develop a genre devoted to witty defenses of frivolous arguments (*hypotheseis paradoxoi*). The ancient model is Isocrates' praise of Helen. Favorinus's praises of Thersites and quartan fever are more immediately indebted to Dio of Prusa's praise of hair, and Synesius's retort in praise of baldness. Favorinus's contemporary Fronto produced praises of smoke, dust, and negligence. One source of topics for this kind of exercise is the Cynic-Stoic diatribe, which pushes contempt for adversity to the point of praising its manifestations. Hence Agrippinus's praise of fever, humiliation, and exile (Stobaeus, *Florilegium* 7.17), Cicero's of filth (*Tusc.* 5.40.116). The sophists modify this genre by making it a star turn of pedantic wit rather than ataraxy.

73. *Guillelmi Menapii Encomium Febris Quartanae*, in *Admiranda rerum admirabilium encomia, sive diserta et amoena Pallas disserens seria sub ludicra specie* (Nijmegen: Reiner Smet, 1666), p. 216. The editorial introduction to this collection ("Lectori") argues that (intellectual) play is part of rationality. Compare the traditional definition of man as the laughing animal; e.g., Lucian, *Vitarum auctio* 26; Martianus Capella cap. 4, sec. 398; Thomas Granger, *Syntagma logicon* (1620), p. 55; John Carpenter, *King Solomon His Solace* (1606), p. 37.

74. Carey, *John Donne*, p. 100.

75. *De medicina* 3.5, 6.

76. *I Henry IV* 2.4.275–76.

77. *II Henry IV* 1.2.6–8.

78. Carey concedes that without external evidence "we should never have guessed that it was about [Mrs. Herbert]" (*John Donne*, p. 81). But this begs the question of whether external "evidence" can prove what the internal evidence

repudiates. Donne "bestows upon Mrs. Herbert additional years and wrinkles, so that his love for her may appear generous and selfless" (p. 83). It would be at least as plausible to argue that by adding wrinkles he rules out a reference to Mrs. Herbert altogether. Donne, after all, has "cut loose from reality" (p. 82). "The woman disappears beneath his reveries on middle age and cooling passion" (p. 82). Just so—if she ever "appeared" at all.

All of this biographical "reading" just proceeds as if genre had nothing to do with what a text can and cannot say. The wrinkles are there to launch the game of finding crazy reasons to value them, the crazier and more elaborately argumentative the better. In other words, the speaker of "The Autumnall" is the Wit who speaks in all mock encomia, and whose backstage life doesn't exist.

79. *Fingimento cauilloso*; see Tesauro, *Cannocchiale*, p. 447.
80. Tesauro, ibid., pp. 449, 450. Cf. Butler, *Rhetorica*, p. 3; Quintilian, *Institutio oratoria* 8.6.75–76.
81. De Sanctis, *Saggio sul Petrarca*; cited by S. Vento, "L'Essenza del Secentismo," *Rivista d'Italia* (1925): 314; cited in turn by Ellrodt, *Poètes métaphysiques*, p. 192, also p. 195.
82. "A Valediction: of weeping," ll. 19–20, 26–27.
83. Roston, *The Soul of Wit*, pp. 93–94.
84. *Richard II* 5.1.96–99.
85. See chapter 7.
86. Cf. J. B. Leishman, *The Monarch of Wit* (New York: Hutchinson's University Library, 1951): "Most of [Donne's] analogies [in Elegie 2] are compressed syllogisms which, as *he knows very well, for that is part of the fun*, continually commit the fallacy of the undistributed middle" (p. 80; italics mine).
87. Jacob Brackman, "The Put-On," *The New Yorker*, May 24, 1967, pp. 34–73, pp. 34, 38.
88. Ibid., p. 57.
89. See J. D. MacKenzie's formalization of rules for dialogue in "Begging the Question in Dialogue," *Australasian Journal of Philosophy* 62 (1984): 174–81. Every step in cooperative discussion depends on the partners' mutual knowledge of their respective commitments at the earlier steps. Refusing to commit oneself is refusing to take part in dialogue.

Chapter 4. Illusions of Strangeness and Shocks of Recognition

1. See chapter 1, sec. 8.
2. The reinvention thesis is Helen Vendler's, in *The Poetry of George Herbert*, p. 32. Herbert's description of the goings-on at the Resurrection is perfectly traditional—unless you fail (or refuse) to notice that the descriptive conceits are conceits.

3. *Holy Sonnets* 7.3–7.
4. Ibid., 7.5.
5. My text for "The Retreate" and for other poems by Vaughan is *The Works of Henry Vaughan*, ed. L. C. Martin (Oxford: Clarendon Press, 1957).
6. Merritt Hughes oddly thought that Vaughan's infant starts out "pure." See "The Theme of Preexistence and Infancy in 'The Retreate,'" *Philological Quarterly* 20 (1941): 484–500, p. 494.
7. "The plaine of the valley of Jericho, the citie of palme trees" (Deut. 34:3). But in name (from Hebrew *jareah* = moon), Jericho is also the City of the Moon (see Jerome, *Liber de nominibus hebraicis*, Migne *PL* 23, cols. 899, 886, 900; Isidore of Seville, *Commentarius in librum Josue*, Migne 108, col. 1021; Rabanus Maurus, *De universo*, Migne 111, col. 379); and for Vaughan the moon is "the veil or partition drawn betwixt us and Immortality" (*Mount of Olives*, Martin ed., p. 176). According to Patristic tradition, the palm is an apt metaphor for unlimited endurance (Ambrose, *Hexaemeron* 58.17). Cf. Vaughan, "The Palm-tree," l. 16: "A Tree, whose fruit is immortality."
8. Fish, *Self-Consuming Artifacts*, p. 157.
9. No confession of faith implied here, of course; there are perfectly respectable truths about nonexistent things—e.g., that Santa Claus is fat, and Sherlock Holmes is lean.
10. The locus classicus of this commonplace is Hilarius, *De trinitate* 7. Cf. Paul's claim that "Christ is all *and in all things*" (Col. 3:11; italics mine). Cf. Col. 15:28. Protestant commentary interprets Col. 3:11 individualistically; see, e.g., John Diodati, *Pious Annotations upon the Holy Bible* (London: T.B., 1643), ad Col. 3:11; also Immanuel Tremellius, Franciscus Junius, *Biblia Sacra* (London: G.B., R.N., R.B., 1593), ad Gen. 1:26–27 ("all in all" glossed as "God's kingship"); also ibid., ad Col. 3:11 ("all in all" glossed as "holy concord" among the saints).

Almaricus Benensis (ca. 1210) was the best-known spokesman for the doctrine that God is all there is. Since this doctrine entails that Christian ideas of sin and redemption are absurd, it isn't surprising that the Almarican heresy *is* a heresy. Jan Ruysbroeck sounds as if he's reviving it in *Adornment of Christian Marriage*, but as his severe critic Gerson admits, Ruysbroeck explains that he's only talking *similitudinarie* (metaphorically). (See Gerson, *De theologia mystica*, p. 286.)

This goes double for Protestantism. Calvin is as committed as any Catholic mystic to the notion that "*in a sense* [i.e, in a figurative sense], the Lord will coalesce with his chosen" (italics mine). But he's quick to add language that implies the survival of human individuality after "coalescence": "Not only does the Bible promise everlasting life to the faithful, but a specific reward to each one of them" (*Institutio* 3.25.10). Cf. Richard Hooker, *Laws* 5.56.5.

At least one critic (A. L. Clements, "Theme, Tone, and Tradition in George Herbert's Poetry," *ELR* 3 [1973]: 264–83, p. 276) thinks the last couplet of

"Clasping of hands" is "plainly" anti-individualistic:

> O be mine still! still make me thine!
> Or rather make no Thine and Mine!

But abolishing private *ownership* of thee and me doesn't abolish the difference between us. In the previous stanza, to be owned by Christ gives the speaker *back* his individuality: "to be thine doth me *restore*."

11. Col. 3:11. See n. 10 above.

12. Fish takes the speaker literally (*Self-Consuming Artifacts*, p. 161). Richard Strier thinks that "Herbert's point is . . . that specification of places is . . . irrelevant" (*Love Known*, p. 232). But Herbert isn't (literally) talking about places *at all*—not even to dismiss them as irrelevant.

13. Aristotle, *Physics* 209a30–209b1. For the idea of all-inclusive place, or *koinos topos*, see ibid., 212b18–20.

14. According to Calvin and Protestant theology in general, faith implies assurance and rules out episodes of despair: "What kind of assurance will it be that will continually yield to despair? . . . Yet I do not deny . . . that certain interruptions of faith sometimes occur, according as the feebleness of faith is bent hither and thither between vehement impulses" (*Institutio* 3.2.25). This peters out ingloriously. Calvin is worried and can't quite own up to the fact. Herbert is braver and franker.

15. See n. 8 to this chapter.

16. Richard Hooker, *Laws* 5.56.1.

17. "Clasping of hands," ll. 19–20.

18. "The Improvment," ll. 19–24. My text here and hereafter is *Centuries, Poems, and Thanksgivings*, ed. H. M. Margoliouth (Oxford: Clarendon Press, 1958).

19. *Centuries* 4.18, 15.

20. "The Vision," l. 25; "Mankind is sick," ll. 44–45.

21. *Centuries* 2.93; "Hosanna," ll. 67–70.

22. *Centuries* 2.70.

23. Ibid., 4.55, 49. Despite Ellrodt (*Poètes métaphysiques*, 2:291), Traherne doesn't make self-love our *exclusive* or even *main* reason for loving God, only *one* (developmentally first) reason. Eventually we come to love him *more* than ourselves, and not just as a means to our gratification: God "hath made us upon the very Account of Self lov to lov him more then our selvs (*Centuries* 4.49). It's hard to see how God's love for us would make sense as a (biblically endorsed) *reason* for loving him back (1 John 4:10) if we didn't *care* whether we were loved or not— that is, if we didn't love ourselves.

24. *Centuries* 2.79.

25. Ibid., 2.70. Ellrodt reads the mirror passage as implying that Traherne

"makes of his fellows the instrument of his own happiness" (*Poètes métaphysiques*, 2:286).

26. "The Vision" ll. 25–30.

27. Matt. 22:37–40. Barbara Lewalski takes "lov me" quite literally (*Protestant Poetics*, p. 368). But the Gospel neglects to mention Traherne, who is innocent of ad-libbing dotty "laws of God" unless proved guilty. Cf. Augustine's comments on the same Gospel text: "At the same time [as love of neighbor was enjoined], self-love was not passed over" (*De doctrina Christiana* 1.26, col. 29).

28. *Centuries* 4.56.

29. Ibid., 4.55. It's not true that mutual love gets reduced to self-love here, overcoming the poet's alleged separation anxiety by "blurring boundaries between selves" (Joan Webber, *The Eloquent I: Style and Self in Seventeenth-Century Prose* [Madison: University of Wisconsin Press, 1968] p. 222). The speaker says explicitly that to love oneself *well* is to love others *better* (*Centuries* 4.55); this makes no sense if "self" equals "other." The neurosis reading is a figment of fudging the literal sense (Webber, p. 222); what overflows in Traherne's pool metaphor is love, not self.

30. *Centuries* 4.65.

31. "My Spirit," ll. 37–39.

32. *Centuries* 2.84.

33. "Misapprehension," ll. 62–65.

34. "Silence," l. 81.

35. Ellrodt attributes Berkeley-style "idealism" to Traherne (*Poètes métaphysiques*, 2:298). Later, the idealism reading is softened to lifelong "doubts" about "external and material reality" (2:309). Still later, "Berkeleyan idealism" is reinstated (2:316). But the accompanying quotes ("Silence," l. 80; "My Spirit," ll. 45–51) express no such doubts. In "My Spirit" the mind perceives by *conforming* to (external) reality. Ellrodt is closer to the truth when he says that for Traherne the external world is "sterile, as long as man's thought . . . does not reveal it at all" (2:311). "What fascinates him . . . is that things sensed appear in the mind as immaterially as realities that are purely mental" (2:316). "The natural phenomenon of perception throws him into ecstasies" (2:316). Compare the emphatically nonmystical Hobbes's wonder at the fact "that among natural bodies some contain models of nearly all things" (*De corpore* 25.1; *Opera latina* 1:316).

36. Quoted in Carol L. Marks, "Thomas Traherne and Cambridge Platonism," *PMLA* 81 (1966):521–34, p. 530. Instead, the mind contains by representing; cf. Hermes: "Contain all these things at once—places, times, masses, qualities, quantities. In that way you will come to understand God" (*Poimandres* 11; see Ficino's version, *Mercurii Trismegisti Pimander* [Lyons: Joannes Tornaesius, 1570], pp. 442–43). Cf. also Aquinas's metaphors of the thing known "in" the knower and the thing wished "in" the wisher (*Summa theologica* 1.8.3), where "thing

known" is later explained as a "mental concept . . . a thing called a [mental] word" (*Summa theologica* 1.37.1; cf. 1.27.1 and 1 ad 2).

37. *Centuries* 5.4.

38. The classical influence here isn't Plato but Aristotle (*De anima* 431b21–432a2).

39. "The thing known is in the knower and the thing willed is in the willer, so that . . . things are more in God than God is in things" (Aquinas, *Summa theologica* 1.8.3 ad 3).

Despite Stanley Stewart, "The Preparative" does not equate "the I" with God (*The Expanded Voice: The Art of Traherne* [San Marino: The Huntington Library, 1970], p. 179). Instead, "the I" is a clean slate for "Divine impressions" to be inscribed on—by God. Unlike God, the I's essence is mere capacity (ll. 51, 55; cf. "My Spirit," l. 8; *Centuries* 4.84; "The Circulation," ll. 11–14).

40. "My Spirit," ll. 110–17. Traherne's Latin jargon sends a precise double signal. The bread in the Lord's Prayer is "daily" in the Geneva and the King James Bible, but "supersubstancial" in Jerome's version. Not only the bread of the Sacrament but Christ himself is *supersubstantial;* he isn't here or there, now or then; he just *is*. What this comes down to is that for Traherne, things as registered in the mind are sacramental. They enjoy the Host's double life of dailiness and "rarity." They're "above themselves." See Jerome, *Commentarium in Matthaeum (6:11)*, Migne *PL* 11, col. 565; *Rustici Diaconi Ecclesiae Romanae contra Acephalos Disputatio, PL* 67, col. 1184 (*supersubstantiva res [Christus] est*); Ambrose, *De sacramentis* 5.4.24, *PL* 16, col. 452a (Ambrose avoids Jerome's confusion of *ep-iousios*, "[bread] for the coming [day]," with *epi-ousios* "[bread] above substance [*ousia*]").

41. See Calvin, *Institutio* 4.17.5.

42. "Dreams," ll. 52–56.

43. *Centuries* 2.79.

44. Ibid., 1.100.

45. "Poverty," ll. 25–27, 54–55.

46. In *Writing and Revolution in Seventeenth-Century England* (Amherst: University of Massachusetts Press, 1985), Christopher Hill argues that if only Traherne (like the social radicals called "Ranters") had come to grips with the requirements for communism in the literal sense, he would have abandoned his "communism of the imagination" (p. 234). But loving metaphorical communism is compatible with loathing the literal kind—and with being perfectly at home as the chaplain of Sir Orlando Bridgeman. Still, Traherne might just possibly be coopting Ranter talk. There may be a special shock value in his choice of diversionary *littera*.

47. *Centuries* 1.3.

48. Ellrodt, *Poètes métaphysiques*, 2:349.

49. "The Review," ll. 5–6.

50. For lack of appreciating the strategy, readers who manage to recognize

the ordinariness are in danger of backsliding into bizarre metaphysics. Michael J. Ponsford thinks that Traherne "often veers into solipsism"—even though in fact, "Traherne is merely asserting that every spiritual being has its center within itself" ("Traherne's Apostasy," *The Durham University Journal* 76 [1984]: 177–85, p. 177). But if this near tautology is all Traherne means by his "solipsism," then there's no (literal) solipsism for Traherne to "veer" into.

In the same vein, Ponsford assumes that in lines like "[I was] a little Adam in a Sphere / Of Joys!" Traherne jettisons Original Sin by literally claiming to have been born innocent—even though by the critic's admission Traherne acknowledges more than once that our "corruption" is "derived" from Adam, in the form of a "Poyson shed / On Men" (see references in ibid., pp. 181–82). Taken out of context, Paul himself would come out a Pelagian: "I had not known sin, but by the law: for I had not known lust, except the law had said, Thou shalt not covet" (Rom. 7:7)—where the point about sin and lust is their latency, not their absence.

Franz H. Woehrer softens the solipsism reading by writing of a "nature-mystical union," but this too is a figment of literalism (*Thomas Traherne: The Growth of a Mystic's Mind* [Salzburg: Institut für Anglistik, 1982], p. 149).

51. *Centuries* 1.41.
52. Ibid., 1.41–42.
53. Ibid., 1.45, 5.8.
54. Aquinas, *Summa theologica* 1.20.2 ad 2. Cf. ibid., 1.15.1: "The ideas of all things must necessarily preexist in God's mind, notionally [*objective*]." Cf. Marsilio Ficino, *Commentarium in Convivium Platonis* 6.18: "The real person and God's idea of that person are the same. That is why, severed from God, no one of us on earth is a real person, since we have been cut off from the idea and form of ourselves."
55. Ps. 139:16.
56. In *The Shadow of Eternity* (Lexington: University of Kentucky Press, 1981), p. 134, Sharon Seelig takes this dependency claim literally; it's "almost blasphemous." But all "The Demonstration," ll. 43–46 (her proof text), says is that without a creature to enjoy it creation can't be "prized" by God as "the best of all possible works" (*Centuries* 2.25). Similarly, in Traherne's "bold claim to be the 'End' of the Deity ["Love," l. 40]" (Seelig, p. 137) "end" means *purpose*, not *ultimate* purpose. In fact, Traherne thinks the series of God's ends comes full circle in God, not man ("The Demonstration," ll. 79–80). (Cf. Aquinas, *Summa theologica* 2–2.123.7.) The "end" claim just *sounds* bold—as it was meant to; that's the whole point of a diversionary *littera*.
57. "Eden," ll. 8–11.
58. *Centuries* 3.5.
59. *De rerum natura* 2.1028–39.

Chapter 5. Metaphor Dramatized: Deceit and Irony

1. Hermogenes, *De formis* 2.10, 374 Walz (405 Spengel); Quintilian, *Institutio oratoria* 9.2.26.

2. Quintilian, *Institutio oratoria* 9.2.29–30. "Making up characters" (*fictio personarum*) is Quintilian's translation of the Greek *prosopopoiia*. The translation substitutes the notion of shaping or fabricating (*fictio*) for the original's notion of making (*poiesis*). (This is a step closer to a full-fledged notion of fiction.) For "*dialog*ismos" Quintilian supplies "*sermo*cinatio." (In this context, *sermo* = *dialogos* = *conversation*. Compare the discussion in chapter 2 of the Protestant use of *Sermo* as a proper name of the Second Person of the Trinity.)

3. Cicero, *De oratore* 2.268–69 (on urbane dissembling); Quintilian, *Institutio oratoria* 8.6.54–55 ("[irony] is recognized by delivery [*pronunciatione*] or speaker or subject matter"); Dudley Fenner, *The Artes of Logike and Rethorike* (?1584), sig. C3r (on the "mocking Trope," "perceyued" by the "manner of vtterance"); Pseudo-Dionysius of Halicarnassus, *Ars rhetorica* 8.10–11 (on dramatic irony as a perfect overlap between an author's tacit act of mentioning speech *S* and his character's act of using *S*).

4. Unfortunately, the popular formula won't work; irony doesn't reverse or otherwise change sense, but tacitly *comments* on it while quoting or reciting a piece of language that *carries* it. See Jerrold M. Sadock, "Figurative Speech and Linguistics," in *Metaphor and Thought*, ed. Andrew Ortony (Cambridge: Cambridge University Press, 1979), p. 54. Sadock thinks that this phenomenon is evidence for the possibility that "immunity from contradiction" is "one of the purposes of figuration," but he misunderstands the phenomenon he's building this theory on. Irony is a figurative avowal of contempt for a statement the speaker pretends to express but is really only citing. "It's a likely story" is contradicted by "You're wrong to think it unlikely."

5. For Joseph Summers, in *George Herbert: His Religion and His Art* (London: Chatto and Windus, 1954), p. 104, a Herbert lyric is typically the written equivalent of a prayer "delivered in the presence of the congregation," but "addressed to God rather than the congregation." This analogy fails by oversimplifying both genres.

A public prayer is addressed to two audiences at once. For the benefit of his parishioners *only*—God doesn't need it—the preacher makes his style as understandable, forceful, and attractive as he can, and implicitly points out by tricks of emphasis the thoughts he hopes they'll emulate. He silently *comments* on his prayer text. The text occurs inside his silent framework of implyings and pointings as something *mentioned* (re-cited). And so as not to scandalize his congregation, he avoids or cuts out the embarrassments that spontaneity would have let by. In addressing the same prayer text to God at the same time, the preacher doesn't *mention* the words of his prayer text. He simply *uses* them.

The devotional poet has only one audience: the parishioners. And his deceitful, wavering, forgetful, partly inarticulate speaker has only one: God. The poet emphasizes the deceit, and so on, subtly or boldly as his dramatic purposes require. The last thing the poet would do if he could help it is inflict these things on God in a prayer of his own—much less emphasize them. Even if the poem is a recycling of some spontaneous prayer of the poet's, the act of recycling is not an act of prayer, and the speaker is the poet as he was (or will be again if he isn't careful), not as he is. Unlike the preacher, the poet does not use the prayer. Like the preacher, he too mentions, recites, and comments on it.

According to Barbara Lewalski, religious lyric aims to "discover" the "conditions" that "the soul experiences in meditation, prayer, and praise" (*Protestant Poetics*, p. 4). I don't see why Lewalski thinks this shows that religious lyric is a "private mode" (e.g., meditation, prayer, or praise), rather than a mimetic *study* of such modes.

6. Cf. Heather Asals's trenchant remark about Herbert's use of an "uninstructed persona," *Equivocal Predication: George Herbert's Way to God* (Toronto: University of Toronto Press), p. 55. Speaker or persona talk has been used to say true things about poems (e.g., the Psalms) from at least the days of Augustine, Ambrose, or Jerome. But it works well only if we're clear about what "persona" means. And the key to this is simply that drama and dialogue are elliptical narratives. (This too is an ancient truism. See Eucleides' description of his dialogue-writing procedure in Plato's *Theaetetus* 143c.)

7. At worst, according to Calvin, the impurities are pardonable (*Institutio* 3.20.13); at best—e.g., effusiveness, rambling—they're even desirable, "by David's example" (3.20.13). Calvin's notion of the psalm as a (public) prayer-*demonstration* is reflected in this formula (*exemplo suo praescribit {docet}*, 3.20.8, 3.3.18; also 3.20.12 [on Augustine's candidate for a paradigm case, Psalm 51]). For the Book of Psalms as a "manual" for "disciples," see Luther, *A Manual of the Book of Psalms*, trans. Henry Cole (London, 1837), p. 5. For prayer itself (what the Psalms demonstrate and obliquely comment on) as an intimate talk of the devout with God [*familiare piorum cum Deo colloquium*], see *Institutio* 3.20.16; cf. 3.20.2.

8. For the tradition of "free speech" (*parrhesia*) in prayer, see chapter 3, n. 68, and the accompanying discussion. The counterpart of *parrhesia* in Calvin is *intrepidus precandi spiritus* (*Institutio* 3.20.14).

9. Augustine, *Enarrationes in Psalmos*, Migne *PL* 36, col. 589.

10. See Augustine on David as representing "the multiplicity of the Church," *Enarrationes in Psalmos*, col. 713. On incongruity as a clue to prophetic role-playing, see ibid., col. 714; also *De civitate Dei* 17.12b. Cf. Luther on Isaiah and the Holy Spirit as impersonators (*Rationis Latomianae confutatio*, pp. 66, 61).

11. Calvin, *Institutio* 2.3.9.

12. *Enarrationes in Psalmos*, col. 598. Augustine tends to talk as if David were playing all, and not merely each member of the Church—as if the group were

itself a (corporate) person. "Here [Psalm 51] he speaks as if the speaker were an individual: but it is not an individual speaking, it is Unity speaking *as* an individual [*tamquam unus, Unitas loquitur*]. In Christ we are all a single person" (*Enarrationes*, cols. 723–24; cf. ibid., col. 1336). Is this a trope or a submerged piece of weird metaphysics? Cf. Aristotle: "It is possible . . . that people coming together become collectively a single person, as it were—a person with many feet, hands, and feelings, and so too with respect to character and thought" (*Politics* 2.611, par. 4; but notice "as it were"). Cf. Aquinas: "In political discourse all members of a single community are treated as a single body, and the whole community as a single person. Thus Porphyry says that 'by sharing a species many people are a single person' " (*Summa theologica* 1–2.81.1; notice "treated as").

I think it's a trope, overlaid on the figure of induction (see discussion in this chapter), but I'll spare the reader an argument. We won't find it in the seventeenth-century metaphorists—not in any crucial context, at least.

13. *De doctrina Christiana* 4.7. In the same passage Augustine comments: "I don't know whether this trope . . . is handed down by that art [of rhetoric] which I have learned and taught. But how beautiful it is, and how it moves readers who understand it, one need not trouble to tell anyone who has no personal experience of it."

14. "Obedience," ll. 36–38.

15. Summers argues convincingly that puzzles about the order of Herbert's poems disappear "if we conceive of The Temple as the symbolic record, written by a poet, of a 'typical' Christian life within the Church" (*George Herbert*, p. 86).

16. *Enarrationes in Psalmos*, col. 167. In "The Voices of George Herbert's 'The Church,' " reprinted in *Essential Articles for the Study of George Herbert's Poetry*, ed. John R. Roberts (Columbia: University of Missouri Press, 1979), pp. 393–407, Heather Asals claims that Christ is supposed to be speaking in the voice "of his mortality" (p. 396). When the speaker complains that God has abandoned him, his ignorance belongs to "the humanity of Christ" (p. 402). But this won't work. On Augustine's theory of the Incarnation, the human aspect of Christ *can't* be speaking for itself here. It was neither sinful nor ignorant (see Augustine, *Enarrationes in Psalmos*, cols. 167, 949; *Super Genesin ad litteram* 10.19–20).

In Augustine's terminology a "voice" is a role—in twentieth-century jargon, "the speaker" of a given passage. Herbert's fallible, troubled, labile speaker isn't Christ in either aspect. By the figure of induction, he's the Church, taken member by member. (The case of David is irrelevant here; his privilege of playing Christ is unique. See Calvin, *Institutio* 3.20.26.)

On *persona* in Herbert see also the contributions of John R. Mulder and Anne C. Fowler in *"Too Rich to Clothe the Sunne": Essays on George Herbert*, ed. Fowler and Pebworth (Pittsburgh: University of Pittsburgh Press, 1980).

17. George Herbert, *The Countrey Parson*, chap. 6.

18. *Soliloquia* 2.7, Migne *PL* 32, col. 869.

19. *Letters to Severall Persons of Honour*, ed. Charles Edmund Merrill, Jr. (New York: Sturgis & Walton, 1910), p. 223.

20. Cf. Terry G. Sherwood, *Fulfilling the Circle: A Study of John Donne's Thought* (Toronto: University of Toronto Press, 1984), p. 78: "Bodily action stamps the soul's imprint on other souls." This fudges the first term in the analogy. The object of stellar imprinting is air, not man, and what gets transmitted by air is destiny, not likeness to the relevant constellation. The point of the comparison is explicit: a grudgingly figurative "in-flowing."

21. Helen Gardner managed to convince herself that the great Prince is the "rationality" of "man's sense organs" ("The Argument about 'The Extasie,' " in *Elizabethan and Jacobean Studies* [Oxford: Clarendon Press, 1959], p. 302). With puzzling hesitancy, A. J. Smith gets it right ("The Metaphysics of Love," *Review of English Studies*, n.s., 9 [1958]: 374).

22. In "The Dismissal of Love," in *John Donne: Essays in Celebration*, ed. A. J. Smith (London: Methuen, 1972), A. J. Smith claims that the lovers refute Neoplatonism by invoking ecstasy to justify sex. But this justification is itself a kind of Neoplatonism (see Leone Ebreo, *Dialoghi d'amore*, ed. Santino Caramella [Bari: Laterza, 1929], p. 50, where sex complements [by "*correspondenzia*"] a "union" the souls already enjoy). Neoplatonist or not, the lovers Smith reads into the poem are his own invention; the bubble (or diversionary *littera*) that gets punctured in "The Extasie" is precisely ecstasy. Before sex or after, soul union (or communion) turns out to be absurd.

23. We seem to owe this old commonplace to Ovid, *Amores* 1.9. But *vagina* and *gladius* metaphors are prehistoric.

24. This notion dies hard. For one recent example among many, cf. Frank J. Warnke, *John Donne*, p. 60, where "The Extasie" is summed up as a "heartily holistic seduction poem."

25. Robert Ellrodt (*Poètes métaphysiques*) notices the highly erotic scene-setting that prepares us for the souls' lecture on ecstasy (2:179). He also shrewdly points out the ironic "libertine smile" in the speaker's "small change" remark, and in the parting invitation to qualified voyeurs to watch the lovers "when we'are to bodies gone" (2:180, p. 179, n. 34). At the same time, Ellrodt wants the poem to salvage the ecstasy, and the sincerity of the souls' testimony about it. Unhappily, the poem doesn't oblige. The lovers don't say they just *aspire* to ecstasy (2:180), they say they're *in* it. The soul-"contact" and "supersensible joys" (p. 180) are bogus— a diversionary *littera* that the opening undermines and the ending mocks. Finally, the speaker or his mouthpieces don't keep sex "clearly" and "distinctly" in mind during their "supersensible"—i.e., erotic—"joys," when, in fact, they clearly have nothing in mind. As Ellrodt himself admits, the souls start thinking about their experience by pretending that the ecstasy is purely spiritual (2:179).

26. A. B. Chambers thinks that the "teare-floods" and "sigh-tempests" that the speaker bans from this peaceful "melting" away of the lovers are the beaker mishaps referred to as floods and tempests in some alchemical texts ("Glorified Bodies and the 'Valediction: forbidding mourning,'" *John Donne Journal* 1 [1982]: 1–20, p. 3). But what makes "flood" refer figuratively to something alchemical when you're talking about beakers, and so on, is CONTEXT. By the same token, what *keeps* "flood" from referring figuratively to something alchemical when you're talking about lovers—and (a bit further on) what keeps the "refinement" of those lovers from referring *literally* to something alchemical—is CONTEXT again.

27. As in the Horatian tag: "I loathe the profane mob and keep them at arm's length" (*Carmina* 3.1.1).

28. There *is* a "tension" in this imagery, as Wilbur Sanders shrewdly points out (*John Donne's Poetry* [Cambridge: Cambridge University Press, 1971], p. 85)— but between figurative sense and literal, not "logic" and "hypothesis."

29. A. B. Chambers thinks the earthquake referred to here is the one that will herald Judgment Day—and that metaphorically heralds the resurrection and glorification of the lovers' bodies ("Glorified Bodies," p. 3). But the speaker's point is that what heralds the lovers' parting is precisely *not* an earthquake; it's a "trepidation of the sphere." Chambers's central thesis won't march; the refinement celebrated in the poem is of the lovers' *minds*—in contrast to the bodies that "element" lesser loves, but not theirs. And the refinement has *already* happened; it doesn't have to wait for a figurative death and resurrection.

30. John Freccero, "Donne's 'Valediction: forbidding mourning,'" *ELH* 30 (1963): 335–76. I'm focusing on the central issue of glossing. If Freccero's gloss won't stand up, neither will the structure of curious lore he builds on it.

Chambers, another champion of esoteric reading, thinks Freccero's "evidence" is "irrefutable"; but even he admits that the "poem's last two lines do appear to stress not the more or less roundness of a gyre but the perfect roundness of a just circle." To salvage the rest of the Freccero reading, Chambers is reduced to explaining that Donne is giving us a "self-contradictory juxtaposition" ("Glorified Bodies," pp. 14, 15). It's a handy move in exegetical dealings with one's author: when resisted, blame the victim.

31. For the classic recipe for the construction of a spiral, see *Archimedis Opera omnia*, ed. J. L. Heiberg (Leipzig: Teubner, 1881), 2:10.

32. *Platonis Timaeus interprete Chalcidio, cum eiusdem commentario*, ed. Johann Wröbel (Leipzig: Teubner, 1876), pp. 181–82. Chalcidius is imagining circles that spiral off by "accident" or by the "will" of the draftsman; not by the firmness of the fixed foot but by a "deflection from suitable rigidity" (ibid.). But then what is it for the unfixed foot to run "obliquely"? If the compass is drawing a just circle rather than a continuously skewed one, then "obliquely" will have to mean simply *curving*, not *curving in a spiral*. Both metaphors work the same way: slanting implies deviation, and the arc of a circle "slants" away from any given

radius (or homeward path). Read figuratively, coming "home" by coming full circle is cold comfort. It's just another kind of "roaming" away from the center.

33. Aquinas, *Summa theologica* 2–2.15.1 (on "voluntary intellectual blindness"; quotations from Vulgate Ps. 35:4 and 57:9). Compare Donald Davidson's theory that "the [self-deceiver's unpleasant] thought that *p*" causes a "directing of attention away from the evidence in favor of *p*" (*Actions and Events*, ed. Ernest LePore and Brian P. McLaughlin [Oxford: Basil Blackwell, 1985], p. 145). For a useful summary of recent analyses of self-deception, see chapter 2 of Mike W. Martin, *Self-Deception and Morality*.

34. This ploy may well result in a comforting belief-about-one's-beliefs—for example, that one believes cigarettes don't cause cancer ("Would I be smoking so happily if I really believed it would kill me?"). Maybe the second-order belief is what tempts Davidson and others to think that the self-deceiver has contradictory beliefs. Davidson's explanatory metaphor of "keeping apart" contradictory beliefs (*Actions and Events*, p. 147) is self-defeating. It conjures up a decision requiring the keeper-apart to keep tabs on both halves of the contradiction, lest they get together. But keeping tabs on both is precisely *not* keeping them (mentally) apart.

I think the contradictory belief analysis is more trouble than it's worth. A fuller unpacking of Aquinas's notion of self-distraction is more promising—and besides has more to tell us about a culture like Donne's, still very much under the shadow of Scholastic ideas.

35. *Othello* 4.1.46.

36. Indeterminacy is the iron pyrites of twentieth-century literary criticism. (a) I don't see how predicting the lady's unfaithfulness can be a way of "getting rid of her, and *appearing self-righteous at the same time*" (Carey, *John Donne*, p. 195; italics mine). How can the speaker be planning to "appear self-righteous" when he tells her *he* may yet feel just the way *she* does? (b) Carey's insecurity scenario is just as unconvincing (ibid.). If the speaker is afraid she'll lose interest, how does he prevent this by telling her he doesn't trust her? If the speaker is angling for reassurance, why doesn't he wait for a nibble instead of cutting the lady off with an insult? (c) Revenge in advance works no better; why pull his punch by saying he just *may* think so too?

But suppose Carey were right (p. 195), and the poem didn't decide among a–c. Would we then have a poem in which "insecurity and inconstancy insecurely and inconstantly mingle" (p. 195)? Hardly; this is just a fourth choice, d, combining a, b, and c. And Carey rightly says (ibid.) that if the poem doesn't tell us enough, we can't choose. If all we have are meanings the poem *might* have had if it had told us more about the lovers, then the poem has no *actual* meaning at all. It's literally pointless, and—again for lack of information—figuratively pointless, too; its pointlessness makes no point.

Terry Sherwood thinks the speaker is trying to "nullify [the Lady's] strategy by predicting it" (*Fulfilling the Circle*, p. 24). Why nullify a strategy he can "conquer" anyway? Why forearm the enemy by forewarning her—unless he doesn't much care if she *is* forearmed?

Is the speaker taking out earlier rejections on an innocent victim (Patricia Garland Pinka, *This Dialogue of One* [University: University of Alabama Press, 1982], p. 83)? But his parting shot isn't that the expected Dear John arguments will be unwelcome, much less vicious—only that they would be child's play for somebody with his IQ. This is nonchalance, not bitterness.

37. *Twelfth Night* 2.4.76–79.

38. This isn't one of Donne's poems of flashy sophistry (Frank Kermode, *Shakespeare, Spenser, Donne* [London: Routledge and Kegan Paul, 1970], p. 132). The speaker makes no attempt to justify his wildly self-defeating claim. Nor is "Donne the poet . . . claiming what Donne the theologian calls impossible"— namely, to "desire annihilation" (ibid.; ditto Carey, *John Donne*, p. 172). The speaker doesn't claim to *desire* annihilation, he claims to have *been* annihilated, along with his ability to desire anything at all (ll. 31–33).

Carey (p. 173) thinks the possibility of desiring annihilation, though denied by Augustine (*De libero arbitrio* 3.7–8), is affirmed by Aquinas (*Summa theologica* 3.98.3 ad 2). But Aquinas agrees that no one desires annihilation *as such;* a desire to end hell's pain by annihilation (he argues) is no exception to this rule. Bogus or not, the Thomistic pedigree is beside the point. The annihilation in "A Nocturnall" is only figurative; desiring it wouldn't discredit Augustine's thesis.

39. *Lateinische Gedichte Deutscher Humanisten*, ed. Harry C. Schnur (Stuttgart: Reclam, 1967), p. 232.

40. *Sermons*, 8:177.

41. Some critics have noticed the affirmativeness of the close while at the same time being distracted by the diversionary *littera* from the lusty affirmativeness of the whole poem. Cf. Wilbur Sanders, *John Donne's Poetry*, pp. 119–20; Arnold Stein, *John Donne's Lyrics* (Minneapolis: University of Minnesota Press, 1962), p. 179.

A step in the right direction is Frank Warnke's intuition (*John Donne*, p. 53) that the "Nocturnall" is both a love poem and a religious poem.

42. The speaker's fear of hell isn't the benign "godly sorrow" endorsed, e.g., in William Perkins's summation of Protestant teaching (Lewalski, *Protestant Poetics*, p. 21). "If there were no judge, no hel, nor death, yet we must be grieved because we have offended so mercifull a God and loving father" (*The Whole Treatise of Cases of Conscience*, ed. Thomas F. Merrill [Nieuwkoop: B. de Graaf, 1966], p. 106). By Perkins's standard, the speaker isn't redeemingly sorry, just corruptly terrified.

43. Unlike Donne, the speaker is no Calvinist. Calvin doesn't reduce justice to supremacy. John Stachniewski's claim to the contrary ("John Donne: The Despair of the Holy Sonnets," *ELH* 48 (1981): 607–705) is disproved by the Calvin

passage he cites for corroboration: "How could he who is the judge of the world commit any inequity? If rendering judgment belongs to God's nature, it follows that he loves justice and shuns injustice by nature" (*Institutio Christianae religionis* 3.23.4). Calvin's whole aim here is precisely to deny that Rom. 9:20 is an appeal to naked power. God is the supreme judge because he's supremely just, not because he's supremely strong. Stachniewski relies on the modern canard that Calvin thinks God is an (arbitrary) law unto himself. Actually Calvin damns this theory as "profane" and "loathsome." For God's will to be a "law unto itself" in the Platonic sense Calvin endorses instead is for it to be a model—a supreme example—of justice (*Institutio* 3.32.2). In his panicky groveling before the throne, Donne's speaker acts as if he had mistaken Calvin's use of the phrase for the classic definition of a tyrant.

44. If the speaker's heart is supposed to be seeking God the way iron seeks adamant, then "iron" doesn't mean *stubbornness toward God* here, *pace* Roston, *The Soul of Wit*, p. 156.

45. Donne's view that after receiving grace the sinner spontaneously "cooperates" with God is just Calvinism, not "soft Calvinism" (Lewalski, *Protestant Poetics*, p. 20); see *Institutio* 2.3.11. The catch is that grace does all the work. By the standard of the talk-postulates of Donne's Protestant audience, the speaker of the Holy Sonnets is right about his abject dependence on God. The sinner can cooperate, yes—when and if he's lucky enough to be made to.

46. *Enarrationes in Psalmos*, col. 959.

47. The speaker has a more compliant audience in Lewalski: "[The octave of Holy Sonnet 9] is a specious argument, as he [viz., the speaker] recognizes in his outcry: 'But who am I, that dare dispute with thee?' " (*Protestant Poetics*, p. 269).

48. "[The last tercet of 14 expresses] the Calvinist sense of man's utter *helplessness* in his *corruption* and total dependence on God's grace" (Lewalski, ibid., p. 272; italics mine). This is too general to capture the portrait the last three lines are clinching. The soul claims to love her besieger, but her excuse—betrothal to the devil—unmasks her hypocrisy. The poem is about somebody helpless. But it's not about his helplessness. It's about his corruption.

49. Sophisms like the ones in Sonnet 10 occur systematically in all the Holy Sonnets. They're usually transparent ploys, of the sort that turn up in the fallacy section of Renaissance logic textbooks. To follow Ellrodt (*Poètes métaphysiques*, 2: 190) and Carey (*John Donne*, p. 253) in making Donne the self-deceiver, we have to believe that the author of *Paradoxes and Problems* and "The Flea" could have written a logic howler without knowing it, and without noticing it once he'd looked at it. Anyhow, the poem has to be read in the language it was written in, including the pragmatic rules that go with the language—e.g., the rule of charity: the author is held innocent of gross ineptitude if the prima facie evidence of gross ineptitude can be otherwise explained.

50. In *John Donne*, p. 105, Frank Warnke agrees with most twentieth-century

critics that "there is little hope in Donne's Holy Sonnets, and not very much trust. What one encounters, rather, is naked fear." But in the Protestant view hope is precisely a capacity to live with a well-grounded fear; her facial expression in *The Faerie Queene* allows only two readings of the state of "her hart": "dread" and "anguish" (1.10.14). Even for a Protestant saint, to face one's naked self is to feel a naked fear. The portrait of the fear in the Holy Sonnets is unsparingly realistic. But realism has other uses than the counsel of despair, and inoculating oneself against despair is one of them.

51. I share Joseph Summers's view that the final prayer shows in its mended rhyme the beginnings of a happiness the speaker isn't yet aware of. Cf. Richard Todd, *The Opacity of Signs* (Columbia: University of Missouri Press, 1986), p. 51; Todd points out "the ironic interplay between poet and speaker"—though I can't agree that the "resolution" of "Denial" is merely "conditional." Cf. also Anne C. Fowler, "With Care and Courage: Herbert's Affliction Poems," in *Too Rich to Clothe the Sunne*, ed. Fowler and Pebworth, pp. 129–30.

This is not, as Strier objects (*Love Known*, pp. 190–91), to make the prayer (absurdly) "imply" that the speaker has "already received what [he] is requesting." A symptom isn't an implication. Far from implying that it's been granted, the prayer implies that it hasn't; while its delivery, unnoticed by the speaker, shows us that it has. "Before they call I will answer, and whiles they speake, I will heare" (Isa. 65:24; see Tudor Homilies 2:117; Calvin, *Institutio* 3.20.14).

Strier has a second objection to a redemptive reading: "The poet cannot mend his spiritual state by mending his representation of it." But the speaker's prayer for the ability to mend his rhyme implies that he thinks he can't mend it—much less mend it for some further end. Of course, the implication could be a trick. But by the principle of charity, he's held innocent until proved guilty.

52. Strier thinks that the final stanza shows a speaker who may not have suppressed his thought but isn't vulnerable to it any more (*Love Known*, pp. 112–13). But having it is being vulnerable to it.

53. Cf. "Lectori," in Justus Lipsius, *De recta pronunciatione latinae linguae* (Leyden, 1586): "Reader, accept this grammatical work from me—thin, fine-spun, nay cheap. . . . Evidently I have returned to my elements while my body too, little by little, returns to its own." Cf. also Horace, *Epistularum liber* 1.26.

54. *Certaine Sermons or Homilies* (London: John Bill, 1623), p. 59.

55. Cf. Daniel Dyke, *The Mystery of Selfe-Deceiving, or, A discovrse and discovery of the deceitfulness of mans heart* (London, ?1626)—in a discussion of "the deceit of the heart in translating the sinne from our selues vpon some other cause" (p. 138): "How vsuall is that translation vpon the flesh. O say the prophane, as of old in *Austens* time, so still when charged with their wickednesse, *not we, but the flesh*. We of our selues haue good wills to doe otherwise, we like and approue of the best things, but the *flesh* ouer masters vs, that, as a violent streame, carries vs away" (p. 139). Note that "translation" is, among other things, a familiar

seventeenth-century synonym for "metaphor." Taken literally, and absurdly, what the "prophane" have to say is a disavowal. Taken figuratively, it's a confession.

56. Gen. 3:19; Eccles. 10:9.

57. Ellrodt writes about the speaker's "pitiful dodge" with his usual brilliance; see *Poètes Métaphysiques*, 2:293. Some critics have been misled by modern speech patterns into reading sudden self-discovery into "My God, I mean myself"—on the analogy of "My God, the barn's on fire!" (See Fish, *Self-Consuming Artifacts*, p. 181; Vendler, *The Poetry of George Herbert*, p. 26; Gene Edward Veith, *Reformation Spirituality* [Bucknell University Press, 1985], p. 62.) Exclamatory "My God" is a profanity. For this devout speaker, it's out of the question. "My God" is a vocative, as it is elsewhere in Herbert.

The speaker has finally brought himself to make the point of "man" explicit. If nothing in the context or talk-postulates defeats it, the prima facie meaning is the meaning.

58. Isa. 66:11, 13. Maternity is an ancient metaphor for the nurturing aspect of a god, for example, in the iconography of the Jupiter with breasts. See Augustine's discussion of Juppiter Ruminus in *Civ. Dei* 7.11. Clement of Alexandria describes the Word as a mother in *Deus dominus et paedagogus* 1.6. See W. Deonna, "Les thèmes symboliques de la légende de Pero et de Micon," *Latomus* 15 (1956): 502–3, 509–11. There are many examples in the mystical writings of Saint Francis de Sales and other contemplative authors Herbert might have run across.

59. Calvin, *Institutio* 4.17.15. See Exod. 17:6; 1 Cor. 10:4.

60. Many critics have noticed the pun. See, e.g., Mary Ellen Rickey, *Utmost Art: Complexity in the Verse of George Herbert* (Lexington: University of Kentucky Press, 1966), p. 268.

61. See the discussion in chapter 3, sec. 1.

62. 1 Cor. 2:28, 38f.

63. 2 Cor. 12:7.

64. *Hamlet* 1.5.86.

65. For another opinion see Ira Clark, "'Love Unknown,' and Reading Herbert," *ELH* 39 (1972): 560–84; Anne C. Fowler, "With Care and Courage," p. 72.

66. In spite of all the speaker's broad hints, Strier (*Love Known*, p. 159) thinks he really is "naïve." Coming from one of the two or three best Herbert critics of the many I've read, this gaffe is puzzling.

67. See Pliny, *Naturalis historia* 11.8. According to Pliny, the spider web is the product of a "corrupted" stomach.

68. Ellrodt (*Poètes métaphysiques*, 2:250) thinks the speaker's "objectivity" is somehow untainted by the "transubstantiation" of his feelings.

69. Cf. Ps. 56:8; also Tibullus 1.5.38: "But grief had transformed all my wine into tears."

70. *Twelfth Night* 1.5.95.

71. Calvin, *Institutio* 4.19.28; in the same passage, Christ is "a priest in the order of Melchisedec, without end, without successor." Cf. Ps. 110:4; Heb. 5:6, 7:3. *Shalem* and *shalom* have a number of fairly obvious etymological cousins. By folk etymology, at least, the last element in "Jerusalem" is supposed to mean *peace*. Cf. Augustine, *De civitate Dei* 19.11b. "Solomon" means (roughly) *man of peace;* could the speaker's wise old informant possibly be Solomonic? Cf. 1 Chron. 22:9–10.

72. For the bees' homing instinct, see Virgil, *Georgics* 4.155, 180; also Virgil's pantheism (ibid.).

73. For weaving as a metaphor for the formation of skin and bones, see Porphyry, *De antro nympharum* 14.

74. Stanley Fish argues that " 'their' and 'they' refer indiscriminately to 'heavenly joyes' and 'my lines.' The displacement in his poetry . . . is here recreated in the verse, which moves away from . . . 'heavenly joyes' . . . to the self-absorbing problems of composition" (*Self-Consuming Artifacts*, p. 197). But in fact, on Fish's assumption, there *is* no egocentric "displacement" from "joyes" to "lines"; the pronouns refer "indiscriminately" to both—if you stop for guesswork after line 2. If you don't, the "lines" reference disappears; the speaker wouldn't be wondering how to write them if he had already. According to Fish, readers' mid-sentence or mid-phrase guesses are part of what a sentence or phrase means. But reading makes guesswork superfluous, and meaning guesses aren't meanings. (An illusory exception to this is *para prosdokian;* see chapter 6.)

75. Calvin, *Institutio* 3.25.10.

76. Augustine, *De doctrina Christiana* 1.26, col. 29. Richard Strier (*Love Known*, pp. 39–40) takes the speaker as Herbert's representative: "The witty conceits [of "Jordan (II)"] . . . dramatize and exemplify sinister processes. Herbert is not exempting his own ingenuity from that he is attacking." This pins some pretty glaring logical ineptitudes on Herbert—ineptitudes strategically placed to be obvious to anybody who shared Herbert's rhetorical culture. He should, as usual, be held innocent of them until proved guilty.

Herbert uses the "Jordan (I)" ploy of artfully bad-mouthing artfulness for frankly humorous effect in his own college oratory (see *The Works of George Herbert*, ed. F. E. Hutchinson [Oxford: Clarendon Press, 1954], p. 445). It's hard to believe that he had never seen Quintilian's shrewd advice on the forensic *technique* of speaking from the heart (*Institutio oratoria* 6.2.25–36). Herbert himself plays Quintilian to fledgling parsons, who need to keep their flocks' attention with "all possiblie art" (*The Countrey Parson*, chap. 6). A plain countryman should get a plain style; somebody better educated will be "sensible of fineness" (ibid., chap. 14)—where clearly Herbert sees nothing sinister in "fineness." After all, a benign gift of holy persuasion is sometimes given to the "wicked" (see Herbert's note on Valdesso's sixty-ninth consideration). "Herbert sometimes consciously mars poems in order to assert his sincerity" (Strier, pp. 195–96). But both of Strier's examples involve a standard rhetorical artifice (anacoluthon in the jargon).

77. "Heavenly" is literal here (*pace* Summers, *George Herbert: His Religion & His Art*, p. 111). Joys that "excell" without qualification and "trample" on the sun will excel what's available *under* the sun, even for a mystic.

Chapter 6. Figuration and Retort

1. Or "the answerer's keenness" (*acumen respondentis*). See the whole passage, *De oratore* 2.236.

2. See ibid., 2.273, 275.

3. Ibid., 2.278. See also n. 2 to this chapter.

4. Tesauro, *Cannocchiale*, p. 442.

5. Jacobus Bidermann, *Epigrammatum libri 3*, 4th ed. (Dillingen: Johann Bencard, 1692), p. 13; *Bernardi Bavhusii et Baldvini Cabillavi Epigrammata* (Antwerp: Plantin, 1634), p. 21.

6. The Christ child is allusively comparing himself with the wrestler Milo, who built up the strength to lift a bull by regularly lifting a calf until it grew up.

7. Metaphorical, that is, in contradistinction to the *literal* notion supplied by the Gospels, which represent Jesus' banter—especially his way of coming back at malicious questions with embarrassing ones—as rabbinical dialectic (*pilppul*); cf., e.g., Matt. 21:23–27.

8. *Francisci Remondi Epigrammata* (Pont-à-Mousson: François du Bois and Jacques Garnich, 1605), sig. B5r–v.

9. Paul A. Parrish stops just short of appreciating the complexity and audacity of what Crashaw is about here: in the *Epigrams* "the tone and pose are those of a superior observer commenting sarcastically on what he sees" (*Richard Crashaw* [Boston: Twayne, 1980], p. 53). But the sarcastic comments are events in the *story* Crashaw is implicitly telling, not just a matter of tone or pose. The speaker's comments are retorts. And the whole work is intelligible only if it implicitly contains the Gospel as a proper part, like a commentary in harlequin dialogue with the text it serves.

10. "In vincula Petro sponte delapsa, et apertas fores," *The Poems*, ed. Martin, p. 29.

11. "Verbum inter spinas," ibid., p. 25. "Crashaw, choosing to take the seed [of Jesus' parable, Luke 8:7] figuratively and the thorns literally, derives the 'Verbum inter spinas'—the Logos crowned with thorns" (Warren, *Richard Crashaw: A Study in Baroque Sensibility*, p. 87). This rejection of a meaning is the whole point of repartee (retort; antanaclasis).

J. B. Leishman, *The Art of Marvell's Poetry* (London: Hutchinson, 1966), p. 46: "[In the *Epigrammata sacra*, Crashaw] is magnifying and expanding [the

Gospels], . . . sometimes by, as it were, the inreading, or extraction, of unapparent paradoxes." The paradoxes are "unapparent" because they're barefaced importations, and bogus to boot. If "extract" means *take the meaning out*, then "inreading" is the opposite of extraction. The holy Jester is putting words in the mouths of the Evangelists, in the crazy confidence that repartee and devotion mix.

12. John 8:44, 48, 49.
13. *The Poems*, ed. Martin, p. 27.
14. Luke 11:27. The Geneva gloss sees repartee in this exchange. Christ was giving the woman a "privie taunt," with an equivocation on "worde."
15. *Poems*, ed. Martin, p. 94.
16. Acts 2:13, 15.
17. "In Spiritus sancti descensum," *Poems*, ed. Martin, pp. 17–18.
18. "Indignatur Caiphas Christo se confitenti," ibid., p. 21.
19. "Arbor Christi jussu arescens," ibid., p. 30.
20. "Christus ad Thomam," ibid., p. 16.
21. "Christus accusatus nihil respondit," ibid., p. 25.
22. John 10:22; "Christus ambulabat in porticu Solomonis, et hiems erat," *Poems*, ed. Martin, p. 56.
23. "Song" [signed "Earl of Pembroke" in Lansdowne MS 777], *The Poems of John Donne*, ed. Grierson, app. B.VIII.
24. In short, Herbert's parody goes far deeper than adapting Pembroke's "formal pattern," *pace* Rosemond Tuve in "Sacred 'Parody' of Love Poetry" (reprinted in *Essential Articles for the Study of George Herbert's Poetry*).

By the way, taking off a "formal pattern" is parody in seventeenth-century literary as well as musical theory, again *pace* Tuve, ibid. Quintilian records "parody" as a musical term (*para-* [prefix] = "askew" + *aoidia* = "singing") *already* extended to (legal) writing (see *Institutio oratoria* 9.2.35). Compare ibid., 6.3.96–97, where Quintilian speaks of "verses made up [by the public speaker] to resemble familiar verses." In a section on "the use of verses in prose," Hermogenes speaks of working familiar tags in "by way of parody—when the speaker follows a verse fragment with his own prose interpretation, and again when he finishes off the fragment with something he improvises, so that the result is a unitary form" (Spengel 451). There's nothing about burlesquing or other nose thumbing here—just appropriating formal pattern.

25. See Ps. 38:12–15 in the BCP version. The LXX, Vulgate, Geneva, and King James texts all read Hebrew *tishm'a* as "thou wilt hear." The Book of Common Prayer follows the Masoretic, reading *ta'aneh* as "thou wilt answer." On the other hand, for *thochahoth* = "chastisements," BCP has "reproofs" and LXX and Vulgate have *elegmous* and *redargutiones*, respectively, both of which can mean "refutations," which fits Herbert's scenario better.
26. Joseph H. Summers, ed., *The Selected Poetry of George Herbert* (New York: New American Library, 1967), p. 163.

27. Vendler (*Poetry of George Herbert*, p. 28) discovers a "reinvention" of doomsday iconography in the last stanza, by dint of taking the "tormentors" literally.

28. Rosemond Tuve (*A Reading of George Herbert*, p. 70) thinks that "Jesus's life is among our sins" means *Jesus is the vicarious bearer of our sins*. But then "among" would make no sense. The persecutors would have to say that Jesus' life "*is*" their sins. To name one of their sins—to refer to the result of an act of theirs—Jesus' "life" has to mean Jesus' *survival* (i.e., his survival as tolerated by *them*).

29. "With his love God the Father anticipated and got the start of our reconciliation in Christ" (Calvin, *Institutio* 2.16.3, quoting Augustine, *De praedestinatione sancta* 15). Cf. Donne, Holy Sonnet 16.5–6: "This Lambe . . . was from the world's beginning slaine." (The metaphorical idiom of this sonnet is very close to "Redemption's," by the way.)

30. Virginia R. Mollenkott's analysis in "George Herbert's 'Redemption,'" *English Language Notes* 10 (1973): 262–37, is just right. If she overlooks anything, it's the point I'm driving at in the current discussion: the studied absurdity the fiction builds up to.

31. Strier, *Love Known*, p. 53: "Christ is the speaker's 'deare Saviour' [l. 48], but the note of self-satisfaction is clangorous." This mistakes self-mockery for self-satisfaction by ignoring the speaker's joy in openly spoiling his own case. Strier thinks that Herbert is following Luther here in exposing the hubris in the Catholic notion of imitating Christ. But the speaker nowhere implies that his *imitatio Christi* will be anything but the fruits of Christ's grief—and grace, which "prevents" [= anticipates and causes] all goodwill (l. 4). By the way, there's nothing hubristic in *trying* to imitate Christ, and no hostility to this notion in classic Protestant theology—on the contrary; see Calvin, *Institutio* 3.3.6, 3.3.16, 3.6.3, 3.18.7.

32. B obeys A only if A tells B to do something. But in the usual theology it seems to be false that God tells himself to do anything.

33. "As for Augustine's statement elsewhere that grace does not do away with will but changes it from bad to good and helps it when it *is* good, all this means is that a person is not 'drawn' [by God] in the sense of being carried along without a motion of the heart; but that he is so affected inwardly as to obey from the heart" (Calvin, *Institutio* 2.3.14).

34. According to Stanley Fish, the question underlying "The Holdfast" is what the speaker has to do to be saved. When each of his answers is rejected in turn, "he hears another voice supply the one answer the implicit question would seem to have excluded—'Nothing!' Of course, that was always the answer, and the fact of the poem is a testimony to the speaker's unwillingness to consider it. . . . To do so would be to give up his sense of personal worth" (*Self-Consuming Artifacts*, pp. 174–75). But the speaker is "much troubled, *till*" he hears the "answer," not *when* he hears it. It brings an unexpected solution to the riddle that's nonplussing him, not an expected solution the speaker is trying to avoid. It takes a powerful

"unwillingness to consider" the obvious to read "when" for "till."

Fish does nothing at all to establish that the speaker really *is* indirectly asking how to get himself saved. Yet the burden of proof for this claim has to rest on the critic. All the speaker *says* he's looking for is a way of responding to "my deare God." This sounds pretty disinterested: what can I do to express my (love, gratitude)? Above all, the answer the speaker finally gets isn't "Nothing!"—not after the discouraging voice has conceded that the speaker "might" trust and "must" confess. The answer is more like: "Something—but the something (trusting and confessing) will belong to Christ as agent more than to you, and for that very reason it will belong to you *more* than before he was in the picture." This is the answer, and it no more crushes the speaker once uttered than it frightened him beforehand.

"Few men have made literature of their humbly attained *successes* in the immolation of the individual will" (Tuve, *A Reading of George Herbert*, p. 195). This pseudo-Augustinian version of humility is the kernel of the Fish approach—maybe the source? Augustine and his Protestant disciples actually say something different enough to qualify this as a caricature. (See n. 36 to this chapter.) As usual, Summers is easily the best guide: "The self-centred pride which wished to take 'the way that takes the town' must be rejected; but equally firm must be the rejection of a sense of unworthiness so strong that it prevented all action. The latter stemmed from a continuing preoccupation with 'self' which, carried to its logical conclusion, implied a distrust of God's grace—that grace which could create of 'earth and clay' a sacred vessel" (*George Herbert: His Religion & His Art*, p. 45).

This notion of grace doesn't rule out activism. It implies it. In fact, Herbert *is* an activist: "Being desirous (thorow the Mercy of God) to please Him for whom I am and live, and who giveth mee my Desires and Performances, and considering with my self That the way to please him is to feed my flock diligently and faithfully, since our Saviour hath made that the argument [= proof] of a Pastours love, I have resolved to set the Form and Character of a true Pastour, that I may have a Mark to aim at; which also I will set as high as I can, since hee shoots higher that threatens [N.B.: compare "The Holdfast," l. 1] the Moon than hee that aims at a Tree" (*The Countrey Parson*, "The Authour to the Reader"). The person God gives "Desires and Performances" is a person who desires and performs. "This is that which the Apostle cals a reasonable service, *Rom.* 12[:1]. when we speak not as Parrats, without reason, or offer up such sacrifices as they did of old, which was of beasts devoyd of reason; but when we use our reason, and apply our powers to the service of him that gives them" (chap. 6).

Strier is another critic who follows Fish in seeing in "The Holdfast" a speaker "forced into a new passivity" (*Love Known*, p. 73). Glossing "more ours" as *secure* (p. 72) is arbitrary. The would-be consolation would be way off target. What is it to us if somebody else's goods are safe? The arbitrary critic is forever repairing unbroken clocks. The first step should be to see if "more ours" might just possibly mean *more ours*.

35. 1 Cor. 11:27–29. Note that what Paul says here does *not* entail that "if [the speaker of "Love (III)"] approaches in a state of sin he will eat and drink damnation" (Stanley Fish, *The Living Temple* [Berkeley: University of California Press], p. 132). Everybody invited to approach *is* in a state of sin. To generate the dilemma he needs in order to tell his story about Protestant angst, Fish has to equate Paul's "unworthiness" with sinfulness in general. Reformation theology tells a different story. See n. 36 to this chapter.

36. Stanley Fish thinks that Christian catechists "place their charges on the horns of a dilemma: if the medicine of the sacrament is to be efficacious, the soul must feel the need of it . . . ; but the soul that feels its sickness too strongly will be 'terrified, and discouraged from the partaking of this sacrament'" (*The Living Temple*, p. 117). A victim of this terror, according to Fish, "is damned if he does and damned if he does not" (ibid., p. 118). This is a caricature of what Reformation writers actually say, which is simply that the terrors are natural but unfounded, and that having them isn't a sin so long as they are overcome. (See Calvin, *Institutio* 4.17.42; Martin Chemnitz, *Secunda pars examinis decretorum concilii tridentini* [Frankfurt, 1590], pp. 181–82; William Perkins, *The Whole Treatise of Cases of Conscience*, p. 136).

Fish compounds his fanciful Protestant double bind by claiming that in the Protestant view somebody who "rests in a sure hope of God's mercies" might conceivably "rest there too complacently, and lose the benefit of his faith by being proud of it" (*The Living Temple*, p. 120). But hoping for mercy is admitting one has no claim on justice and so has nothing to be proud of. And being sure of God's mercy is an unearned gift (*fiducia*, or saving faith) and so, once again, nothing to brag about—except in a sense of bragging explicitly endorsed by Saint Paul himself (2 Cor. 11:30, 12:5).

37. William Perkins, *The Whole Treatise*, p. 123.

38. *Pace* Vendler, *Poetry of George Herbert*, p. 55, Love is not a Magdalene Herbert making rigorous demands on the speaker, and going by a fanciful "image" of him as a worthy guest (that is, a person more deserving than the speaker conceives himself to be). The speaker conceives himself to be a sinner, and the Supper is precisely for sinners. His "claims to imperfection" aren't "put aside" as false, just as irrelevant. Armchair psychoanalysis is no substitute for getting the text and the underlying theology right.

39. *Pace* Strier, *Love Known*, p. 80, "let my shame / Go," etc., isn't a "demand." Introduced by "Lord," it's a *prayer for permission*. Nor does Love dismiss the appeal to desert (i.e., penal justice) as "rationalism." On the contrary, Love replies that the requirement of justice has already been met: Christ "bore the

blame." In replying so as to satisfy the speaker's reason, Christ if anything *endorses* "rationalism."

40. Fish, *The Living Temple*, p. 132.
41. Ibid., p. 133.
42. Ibid.
43. Ibid.
44. Ibid., p. 134.
45. Ibid., pp. 134–35; italics mine.
46. Many writers on Herbert have disagreed with the anti-Love (radical libertarian) reading of "Love (III)." So why another trip around the mulberry bush? This kind of reading isn't just a *failure* to comply with the conversational contract that lets figuration work, it's a principled *refusal* to comply. The principle is that in shrewd hands reading out of context gets at textual reality; interesting possibilities can no more be eliminated by context than anatomy by a zipper.

Professional readers-in have a guild status and an air of smart knowingness that naïve readers-in can't match—along with a roadrunner velocity of thought: objections that can't be met can be (ingeniously) outrun. Given Gresham's Law, all this makes it better to reply to them than not—but only barely.

For what it's worth, Stein also argues that "Love (III)" addresses the problem of the "human desire for absolute independence"; here that desire figures as "the human reluctance to accept love as a gift entire." But to his credit, Stein doesn't claim that Jesus is being portrayed as a bully. See Arnold Stein, *George Herbert's Lyrics* (Baltimore: Johns Hopkins University Press, 1968), p. 194.

47. Stein, *George Herbert's Lyrics*, p. 193n, describes Love's replies as "repartees" but doesn't see repartee as an organizing principle of the whole poem.

Chapter 7. Thinking in Metaphor: Windfalls and Searches

1. Roston, *The Soul of Wit*, p. 116.
2. *De oratore* 2.255, 260.
3. *De methodo vafritiae* 34, Spengel 453–54.
4. Mercutio plays on the same distinction in his retort on Tybalt:

> TYB. You shall find me apt inough to that [a quarrel] sir, and you will giue me occasion.
> MERC. Could you not take some occasion without [my] giuing?
> (*Romeo and Juliet* 3.1.53)

5. Fish, *Self-Consuming Artifacts*, p. 405.
6. Ibid., p. 406. Fish tries in vain (p. 402) to argue from uniformity of understanding among speakers of a language to uniformity of *mis*understanding.
7. *The Prose of Sir Thomas Browne*, ed. Norman J. Endicott (Garden City: Doubleday, 1967), p. 30. Quoted by Fish, *Self-Consuming Artifacts*, p. 384.

8. Fish, *Self-Consuming Artifacts*, pp. 384–85.
9. *The Prose of Sir Thomas Browne*, pp. 35, 239, 195, 212, 211.
10. The most celebrated is Heraclitus Fragment 51, preserved in Hippolytus, *Refutatio omnium haereseon* 9.9.1, which speaks of "a fitting-together-of-parts [*harmonia*] by a stretching-against-each-other [*palintonia*]—as of a bow and a lyre." Cf. Heraclitus Fragment 80, in Origen, *Contra Celsum* 6.42: "War is universal, justice is conflict [*eris*], and all things come to pass by conflict and necessity."
11. Vulgate Job 7:1: "Militia est vita hominis super terram."
12. 2 Tim. 2:6.
13. *The Countrey Parson*, chap. 32.
14. Eph. 2:19; Gal. 6:10; Calvin, *Institutio* 3.25.1.
15. *The Countrey Parson*, chap. 10.
16. Ibid., chap. 34.
17. For the pervasive social tensions and dislocations associated with entering service, see Derek Hirst, *Authority and Conflict* (Cambridge, Mass.: Harvard University Press, 1986), pp. 22–23. *Pace* Vendler, *Poetry of George Herbert*, p. 42, there's only one metaphor for God and no inconsistency. The employer's rank and activities of "enticing," bribing with perquisites, and "indulging" (Vendler's word, not Herbert's) are part of a single literal sense. "Bewitching" (quoted as if it were in the text) is a figment of the critic.
18. "Joyes" (l. 3), "delights" (l. 5), "mirth" (l. 12), "pleasures" (l. 13), "milk and sweetnesses" (l. 19), "flow'rs and happinesse" (l. 21), "no moneth but May" (l. 22).
19. The service is "brave" (l. 2; = splendid). The livery is "glorious" (l. 9; with overtones of *gloriosum*—i.e. [by metonymy], worth bragging about). His master isn't just any lord, but a king—and not just any king, but a special king (l. 13).
20. See n. 19 to this chapter. It makes sense for the speaker to make his lord's "furniture" "fine" *to himself* (ll. 7–8) if "furniture" has its older meaning of *array:* he puts the finery on and shows off. In other words, he glories in the livery that "entwines" him—"stuff" marked as belonging to the "household" of a great lord (l. 9). The speaker doesn't imply that he's playing Jacob to God's Laban (see Gen. 31:34–42). There's no salient parallel between the speaker's accusations and Jacob's grievances against his father-in-law. Camel "furniture" (the alleged clue to a parallel, Gen. 31:34) isn't the kind of "furniture" that attracts the speaker. But see Chana Bloch, *Spelling the Word* (Berkeley: University of California Press, 1985), p. 93).
21. This is a speaker who thinks being "just" (= "justified" = "righteous") is doing things to qualify for the justness label (ll. 59–60), or (equivalently) a speaker who thinks God's mercy is "wages" for services rendered (l. 13). So on the usual Protestant talk-postulate that no amount of moral industry can establish a claim on God, the speaker has a special *talent* for presumption. Of course, he's trying to *pin* caprice on God. To miss the way the effort backfires is to miss the

comic irony of his self-serving performance. To miss the comic irony is to miss the poem. But see Vendler, *Poetry of George Herbert*, pp. 43–44.

22. *The Countrey Parson*, chap. 28.

23. Cf. Hill, *The World Upside Down*, p. 99.

24. Ps. 102:3, 5; Ps. 38:3; Job 19:20. Bloch, *Spelling the Word*, pp. 264–65, recognizes stanza 5's kinship with the Psalms, but not with Job.

25. Soon after the lines quoted from Job, the tortured patriarch manages to affirm that "I am sure, that my Redemer liueth" (19:25).

26. Marion White Singleton thinks that line 66 expresses Herbert's newborn ambition of "accepting God's cross-biasses without repining"—combined with his lack of "assurance that he will be able to fulfil this condition" (*God's Courtier* [Cambridge: Cambridge University Press, 1987], p. 125). But Herbert doesn't have to wait for bad news on this score; the clause "if I love thee not," given the way he's been behaving, can't express a future condition. In context it has to mean (roughly) *if my unloving speech shows me up for what I am*. The "if," in short, is painfully close to "since."

Diana Benet's remark that line 66 "reaffirms [the speaker's] commitment to God" (*Secretary of Praise* [Columbia: University of Missouri Press, 1984], p. 118) seems to result from the same out-of-context reading of "if." By contrast, it seems to me that she's right on the central point: at the last minute Herbert "drops the metaphor that has facilitated his rash and dangerous threat" (ibid.).

27. Matt. 13:45.

28. Prov. 3:13–17.

29. This is Herbert's version of the commonplace that a just body of (civil) law is a combination of (a) natural law as it applies to the circumstances of the society being legislated for, and (b) arrangements left optional by natural law and dictated by utility. Cf. Calvin, *Institutio* 4.20.15.

30. For the musical terms in lines 21–23, see Summers, *George Herbert: His Religion & His Art*, p. 159.

31. See Job 6:12.

32. Strier thinks that the speaker of "The Pearl" surprises us in the end by rejecting the bargain mentality and the Covenant theology that grows out of it. The proof of this is that (a) the speaker comes to God "through grace, not understanding," and (b) "the mutuality essential to the covenant-as-contract falls away" (*Love Known*, pp. 90–91). But this distorts both the poem and the theology it's supposed to be repudiating.

a. The speaker's understanding, in the form of faith, and no thanks to his own "groveling wit," is precisely what leads him to God. That's the ironic point of the falcon metaphor: God's way of training *his* falcons is precisely *not* to seel their eyes shut but to open them. Grace *brings* a kind of understanding: the falconer's lure or silk twist "conducts" by "teaching" ("The Pearl," ll. 31–40). The speaker is claiming to be wise to the treacheries of the maze and at the same time disclaiming credit for the wisdom. This is perfectly in line with Covenant theology. The knowledge that saves is "a gift of God, whereby a man may judge, how to carrie himselfe warily, and uprightly before men" (Perkins, *The Whole Treatise*, p. 117). (Compare Calvin: "The human understanding finally begins to taste the things that belong to God's kingdom at the point when the understanding has been pierced with the light of the Holy Spirit" [*Institutio* 3.2.34]. "[Scripture teaches in various places] that understanding is joined with faith" [3.2.5].")

b. In the view of those who preach it, the Covenant of Grace doesn't stop being mutual just because the human partner can't carry out his side of the bargain "by his own powers" (Strier, *Love Known*, p. 91). He's *given* a power to carry it out, "to climbe to thee" (in the "Pearl" speaker's phrase), and thereby earn "Title in the Covenant of grace" (Perkins, *The Whole Treatise*, p. 121). "Repentance with the fruites thereof are on our part required; yet no otherwise, but as they are necessarie consequents [of faith] and the signes and the documents thereof" (Perkins, p. 60). For Covenant theology and for Herbert, this is mutuality enough—at least enough to justify the metaphor of the pearl merchant's financial killing. Wherever the power to do it came from, Herbert's speaker, and nobody else, is the falcon who does the flying and the climber who does the climbing—in short, the bargainer who keeps the bargain.

The theory that Herbert's poem is designed to undermine this metaphor and the covenant idea that goes with it is untenable. The original metaphorist in this case was Christ himself. The pearl bargain is simply a variant of the biblical metaphor of divine reward as wages earned. There's nothing Protestant about rejecting this metaphor; on the contrary. "God isn't thwarting or fooling us when he says that he 'repays' our works with that which he had given us free before we did them. Because he wants us to be exercised in good works . . . and to run through those good works in our race toward the blessed hope offered us in heaven, it is fitting for those works to be assigned credit for our enjoyment of the promises" (Calvin, *Institutio* 3.18.3). "Nothing is clearer than that God's promise of wages for good works is meant to relieve the feebleness of our flesh with some consolation—and not to puff up spirits with pride" (ibid., 3.18.4). "According to one Gospel passage [Heb. 6:10], it befits the justice of God not to forget his servants' acts of obedience. This is so put as to suggest that it would be almost unjust should he forget. The point here is that to spur on our laziness God has assured us that the toil we undergo to glorify his name will not be in vain. Let us always remember that this promise like all the others would bring us no fruit if the covenant of mercy freely given [i.e., the Covenant of Grace] did not go before it" (3.18.7).

Strier thinks that Herbert is too much of a Calvinist to find the covenant or bargain metaphor acceptable—but in fact it's Herbert's Calvinism that *makes* it acceptable (see the last quote, above). Scholarly myths die hard. Strier owes this one to John S. Coolidge: "[Luther and Calvin] do not notice, . . . or else do not care to exploit, the possibility of elucidating Paul's argument by a simple adjustment of terminology. . . . The Covenant with Abraham can be termed the 'Covenant of Grace' " (*The Pauline Renaissance in England* [Oxford: Clarendon Press, 1970], pp. 101–2). In Calvin's case, anyhow, the truth is exactly the opposite. He uses this metaphorical notion—sometimes in so many words—whenever it's relevant, which is pretty often. In the *Institutes* Calvin speaks of "the covenant that God has struck with us when Christ was made manifest" (2.10.1). "It is necessary to insist that the covenant by which the Jews were reconciled to the Lord was supported by no merits of theirs, but only by the mercy of God who called them" (2.10.2). "Until the coming of Christ, the Lord had singled out one nation [the Jews], in which to confine the covenant of his grace [*foedus gratiae suae*]" (2.11.11). "As in all the covenants of his mercy [*in omnibus misericordiae suae pactis*] God demands of his servants uprightness and holiness of life in return, so that his goodness may not be mocked, . . . so by this means he wishes to hold those people to their duty who have been admitted to the sharing of his covenant. Nevertheless the covenant itself is originally struck as a covenant of grace [*foedus gratuitum;* "covenant freely given"] and remains such forever after" (3.17.5). "And in the meantime we do not deny that for the faithful their uprightness, though halved and incomplete, is a step toward immortality. But what is the reason for this if not that the Lord does not reject as they deserve the deeds of those whom he has taken up into the covenant of grace [*foedus gratiae*], but instead kisses those deeds with the kindness of a father?" (3.17.15). See also Everett H. Emerson, "Calvin and Covenant Theology," *Church History* 25 (1956): 142.

33. It isn't true that the speaker must or does give up his giving up of the world; what the speaker must and does give up is *credit* for giving it up. So the speaker hasn't trapped himself in an infinite regress of givings-up, *pace* Fish, *Self-Consuming Artifacts*, p. 179.

34. *Sermons*, 3:152.

35. Vendler, *Poetry of George Herbert*, p. 38.

36. Ps. 144:2.

37. The Milky Way passage in Ovid's *Metamorphoses* 1.169–73 isn't an example of pagan afterlife doctrine and isn't relevant here, *pace* Mary Ellen Rickey, who is unaware of the standard ancient meaning of the Milky Way in late antiquity, viz., the heavenly destination of the just; see Cicero, *Somnium Scipionis* 16; Porphyry, *Antrum nympharum*. Cf. also Crashaw, "The Weeper," ll. 20–22.

38. *De doctrina Christiana* 3.25, Migne *PL* 34, col. 103.

39. *Ostia Oceani* and *pylai Gadeirides*, respectively. See Pliny, *Naturalis historia* 32.134; Pindar, Fragment 256.

40. See, e.g., Aquinas, *Summa theologiae* 2–2.184.2 and *passim*.

41. Matt. 7:14.

42. In Sermon 6.272–73 Donne explains a relevant figurative use of "now": the Resurrection happens "now" (at the moment of death)—but only in the sense that "*there is no more to be done with* the Body, *till* the Resurrection" (italics mine). To serve his deflationary reading of the "Hymne," Carey (*John Donne*, p. 223) arbitrarily interprets "done with" as "happen to": neurotically in love with his own body, Donne is whistling in the dark. But saying the body is exempt from further effort on its owner's behalf isn't saying that it's exempt from disintegration, or that the soul is exempt from parting with it until doomsday. And "till" obviously implies that death and resurrection *aren't* simultaneous—*literally* simultaneous, anyhow. The point of "now" is that they're *figuratively* simultaneous: the interval between them is a mere nothing—brief and undemanding. The soul can rest easy, like an archer who says his speeding arrow is "beyond the mark, though it be not come to the mark yet, because there is no more to be done till it be" (Donne, ibid.).

This particular critic is forever on the lookout for a chance, even at the cost of literalism, to catch Donne out in a spot of clinically narcissistic wish fulfillment. But to give credit where credit is due, the narcissism reading of this particular theme in Donne was pioneered by Ellrodt, who in turn (*Poètes métaphysiques*, 2: 222) cites Helen Gardner's remark that in sending the elect soul straight to heaven immediately after death, Donne showed an uncharacteristic "dogmatism" on a point Reformation theologians declare indifferent (*The Divine Poems* [Oxford: Clarendon Press, 1978], xliv).

But in fact, all Calvin (e.g.) does is warn against curiosity about "the interim condition of souls"; he takes it as a biblical truth that, "divided from the body, the soul has God present to it." What the soul receives right away, according to Calvin, is "happy rejoicing" in God's presence. What it has to wait for till resurrection is "glory." Since Calvin thinks all of this is implied in the Bible, he accepts it without reservation (*Institutio* 3.25.6). Donne is no more and no less "dogmatic" in arriving at the same conclusion (*Sermons* 7:70–71). So, for that matter, is the Tudor Homilist (*Certaine Sermons or Homilies {1623}*, p. 62). Clinical narcissists all.

43. John 10:9.

44. Annotations to Gen. 32:24 and 28, respectively.

45. See *Institutio* 1.13.10 (cf. 1.14.5).

46. See n. 10 to this chapter.

47. Fish (*Self-Consuming Artifacts*, p. 220) invites us to "step back" from the context of line 30. The speaker hasn't been advising mystics on holy dying but poets on decorum: secular love poetry should wear cheap "canvas," not costly "arras"—i.e., not "beauteous words." Such words "go together with" (befit) their source, the divine beauty they express in sacred poetry. What they "light" toward

heaven is *thoughts*, not (as in Fish) departing souls they somehow accompany ("go" with).

48. What the "paleness" of the chalk is to the royal festivities inside, white hair is to a faith that's "livelier than before": an outward sign that gives no inkling of the inner grace. This use of "pale" rules out death as the expected king, in spite of the "pale" horse he rides in Rev. 6:8 (another arbitrary sparkler courtesy of Fish, *Self-Consuming Artifacts*, p. 222).

Chapter 8. The Fellowship of the Mystery: Emergent Metaphor in Vaughan

1. Or as an internal accusative.
2. *The Works of George Herbert*, ed., Hutchinson (Oxford: Clarendon Press, 1954), pp. 85–86.
3. Eph. 4:17.
4. Migne *PL* 26, col. 537. Jerome goes on to say that the *physicus perscrutator* "dives beyond the earth's depth and the void, as it were, of the abyss." Herbert gives us a mercenary diver. With Jerome, compare Augustine's discussion of *experiendi noscendique libido, Conf.* 10.35.
5. Eccles. 3:22–23; cf. 1 John 2:16.
6. Col. 2:18; 2 Thess. 3:11.
7. Matt. 7:7.
8. *The Works of Henry Vaughan*, ed. L. C. Martin (Oxford: Clarendon Press, 1957), pp. 418–19.
9. *Anima Magica Abscondita*, by Eugenius Philalethes (London, 1650), p. 13.
10. Jer. 31:33.
11. For disappareling in the same sense, see Plotinus 5.3.17. The notion of the mind's clothing is an ancient commonplace, but the Hermetics dignify it with an essential role in their theory of embodiment. See, for example, *Poimandres* 10.16.–8, and *Reallexikon für Antike und Christentum* (Stuttgart: Hiersemann, 1972), 10 *s.v. Gewand (der Seele)*, esp. cols. 955–58.
12. Matt. 1:21.
13. Isa. 45:15. Vulgate *absconditus* ("hidden") softens the terror of the Hebrew reflexive *mistatter* = *se abscondens* ("hiding *himself*"). King James and Geneva are more faithful—and unsparing.
14. L. C. Martin, *Works of Henry Vaughan*, pp. 478–79. James Simmonds, in *Masques of God* (Pittsburgh: University of Pittsburgh Press, 1972), pp. 185–89, also finds a "symbolic exhumation" in the poem and identifies the root as an emblem, and hence as one of Vaughan's divine "prolusions and strong proofs." But Simmonds misses the crucial point that the "exhumation" is a ritual-histrionic act. He doesn't supply a clear account of the alleged distinction between emblem

and symbol. There is no recognition of the conflicting cues the poem supplies in a gradual and uneven process of self-clarification. And above all, merely saying that the exhumation is symbolic simply finesses the prior question of how the exhumation *language* applies to whatever it is describing. My answer, in brief: (a) figuratively, to the root digging; (b) literally, to a fictitious exhumation the root digging is used to act out; (c) figuratively, again, to an effort of the actor's speculative imagination. These meanings aren't a motionless array; the poem only gradually lets us see how they fit together. That process of semantic forthcoming is a crucial part of what the poem as a whole has to say.

15. L. C. Martin, *Works of Henry Vaughan*, p. 177.

16. Cf. *Poimandres* 12.16: "The dissolution [of bodies] is not death but the dissolution of a mixture. Bodies decay, not to be destroyed, but to become young." Ficino's version embroiders this a bit: "soluitur autem vnio [mistionis], non vt ea, quae sunt, intereant, sed vt vetera iuuenescant" (*Iamblichi de mysteriis liber {et alia opuscula}* [Lyons, 1570], p. 453; hereafter *Pimander*). The Greek edition from which I am translating is A. D. Nock's in *Corpus Hermeticum* 1 (Paris: "Les Belles Lettres," 1945), with A.-J. Festugière's French version. With Vaughan's thought compare also his own version of Nollius's *Chymists Key*: "Nothing can be animated and borne, unless it first suffer corruption, putrefaction, and mortification, saith Raymond Lullie in his testament" (L. C. Martin, *Works of Henry Vaughan*, p. 604). Cf. also *Anima Magica*, pp. 13–14: ". . . everything in the world is directed for [man's] Preservation by a *spice* or *touch* of the *first Intellect*." "Everything" will include the remains of the dead.

17. Ficino says that a particular Hermetic dialogue "hunts God from the center, the pole, place, and the forms of things" (*Pimander*, p. 388).

18. This last detail will depend on whether the tense of "is" in "those faint beams in which this hill is drest" (l. 7) is the present or the habitual, with "every evening" understood.

19. See Vaughan's life of Paulinus of Nola (L. C. Martin, *Works of Henry Vaughan*, p. 366; Paulinus, Epist. 40.8).

20. E. C. Pettet, *Of Paradise and Light* (Cambridge: Cambridge University Press, 1960), p. 165, suggests that "in the middle of the seventeenth century ['peep'] was entirely, or relatively, free of furtive, prurient, and comic associations." But in fact it seems to have this complex of associations at least by the time of Shakespeare and Spenser. "Why pry'st thou through my window? Leave thy peeping" (*Lucrece*, l. 1089). As the speaker of the *Epithalamion* enjoys his wedding night he asks playfully "who is the same, which at my window peepes" (l. 372). In a similar vein of whimsy the speaker of Shakespeare's Sonnet 24 mentions "windows to my breast, where through the sun / Delights to peep." Whimsy or not, the common thread here is a stealthy invasion of privacy, including sexual privacy.

21. For "true liberty," see Rom. 8:21 and Vaughan, "Waterfall," l. 37.

22. The notion that the soul is astral in substance is ancient and ubiquitous. See Franz Cumont, *Lux Perpetua* (Paris: Geuthner, 1949), *passim*. The adage that the body is a tomb (*Gorgias* 493a) is also familiar in various forms. It is a little more enterprising for the speaker to claim that on dying his inner star will irradiate the universe. He can claim Hermetic endorsement: man in his disembodied essence has power over everything (*Poimandres* 1.15). In the Neoplatonic scheme the human soul is at the same level of the cosmic hierarchy as the world soul, with which it potentially shares control of the universe. See Ficino's comment on Plotinus 4.4.16, reproduced in *Plotini Enneades*, ed. F. Creuzer and G. H. Moser (Paris, 1855).

23. *Invidia*, at its most primitive, is the evil eye. See Catullus 5.12, where the act of *invidere* is associated with spying on lovers. Cf. Isidore of Seville, *Etymologiae* 10.34: "Inuidus dictus ab intuendo felicitatem alterius." Spenser, *FQ* 1.4.31, seems to be playing with this traditional etymology when he makes envy a perverse response to seeing "good," and includes among Enuie's personifying attributes a kirtle "ypainted full of eyes."

24. Eph. 3:9. The glass one sees God through darkly is canonically a mirror, of course (*esoptron*, 1 Cor. 13:12). There is also a familiar Latin pun submerged in the notion of a "hill [*specula*, vantage point], / Where I shall need no glass [*speculum*]." "Speculation" is a kind of intellectual spying that the chosen soul is destined to rise above. (For the punning philosophical contrast between hill and mirror, see Ficino: "In a world that comes later [in the order of emanations from the One], you will, stepwise, reflect [*speculabere*] as if in a mirror [*speculo*] on the world that comes just before, and from the higher one in turn contemplate the lower one as if from a lookout hill [*specula*]" [*Plotini Enneades* 5.3.9].) The speaker is engaging in some serious play—to use Vaughan's term, in a "prolusion."

25. John 3:2, 4, 9.

26. John 7:50–53.

27. John 19:38–42.

28. Heb. 9:11; Exod. 25:8. Cf. John 1:14: "And the Worde was made flesh, and dwelt [*eskenosen*: literally, 'pitched its tent'] among us." In biblical idiom, the human body in general is a "tent." Cf. Immanuel Tremellius, Franciscus Iunius trans. *Biblia sacra* (London: G.B., R.N., R.B., 1593), Beza's annotation at 2 Cor. 5:1: "As that body is sorely afflicted in this life, Paul compares it to a tent both frail and apt to fall." See n. 35 to this chapter.

29. Exod. 26:33; Heb. 10:19–20. Cf. Iacobus Cappellus on Heb. 10:20, in John Pearson et al., eds., *Critici sacri* (London: James Flesher, 1660), vol. 7, col. 4298: "The veil may be regarded as offering or as withholding access to the Holy of Holies. Regarded as offering, it was the prefiguration of Christ: as no way opened into that sanctuary except through the veil, so to no one is there a way open to heaven except through Christ." Cf. also Tremellius-Iunius, *Biblia*

sacra, Beza's annotation ad loc.: "In this way the flesh of Christ shows us his godhead as it were under a veil. Otherwise the brightness of that godhead would be unendurable to us."

Alan Rudrum's case for a Hermetic and Boehmian reading in "'The Night': Some Hermetic Notes," *MLR* 64 (1969): 11–19, depends on a rigorous program of taking things out of context. To accept it, we have to abandon the notion that in verbal communication meaning is constrained by ongoing argument. This is a high price to pay. But if we don't pay it, then we gain nothing by bloating the glossary with esoteric usages that the logic of the text won't let us apply. The "virginity" of Christ's flesh, for example ("The Night," l. 1), can hardly express a mystical bisexuality unless there is some defect in the standard alternative meanings *sexually untried* and *inviolate* (supported by "pure" immediately preceding). There is something obvious that Christ's flesh *literally* has in common with virgins; so we've been given no reason to rummage for something (femaleness) that it only *figuratively* has in common with them. Having to invoke a notion of unsignaled or unmotivated figurativeness is another example of too high a price to pay for an esoteric reading.

30. Exod. 33:20.
31. Mal. 4:28.
32. Col. 2:9.
33. Vaughan is playing, of course, on the familiar virtuoso *topos* of spinning out alternative definitions of something. The sub-*topos* involving Sleep (as in *Macbeth* 1.2.33–7) is especially relevant. Praise sleep highly enough (to outdo the competition) and you will end up suggesting a contemplative state. Thus, in Drummond's sonnet, Sleep is "silence' child," and "Prince whose approach peace to all mortals brings." This hardly takes much revision to become a real rather than a mock prayer. In Vaughan's retort on the *topos*, the "care-charmer sleep" of secular poetry meets its pointed antithesis, the sacred vigil that is (without flattery this time) "cares check and curb."
34. Song of Sol. 5:2, 6.
35. Song of Sol. 5:2; cf. Rev. 3:30. The body is also a tent, 2 Cor. 5:1, 4— *corporis nostri tabernaculum*, Calvin, *Institutio* 3.9.5. See n. 28 to this chapter.
36. Song of Sol. 5:6.
37. Matt. 7:7.
38. I'm translating from Charles Butler, *Rhetoricae libri duo* (London, 1649), pp. 7–8. Cf. Gerard Vossius, *Rhetorices contractae libri quinque* (Leyden, 1640), p. 353.
39. "Euen-song," ll. 14–16 (Hutchinson, *Works of George Herbert*, p. 203). In Dionysian terms, God is without essence (*an-ousion*) and hence beyond predication or rational understanding. Union with God yields "a knowledge, beyond mind, of Nothing." See Pseudo-Dionysius Areopagita, *De divinis nominibus*, in Migne *PG* 3, col. 1001.

40. It may seem odd to speak of a conjunction as having a meaning. The meaning is a rule (R for short) that takes any pair of sentence meanings $M\,1$ and $M\,2$ and gives us back a third $M\,3$ ($M\,1RM\,2$) that is related to the pair in a specific way. Thus (roughly) a sentence of the form: sentence 1 + "because" + sentence 2 is true if and only if $M\,1$ and $M\,2$ single out actual states of affairs, and the $M\,1$ state of affairs is due to the $M\,2$ state of affairs. If "because" lacked a (literal) meaning, the theologians couldn't use it figuratively; there would be nothing for a trope to work on.

41. Cf. Vulgate Isa. 58:10: "And thy darkness will be as noon."
42. "Regeneration," ll. 68–71, 80; John 3:8; Acts 2:2.
43. "The Retreate," l. 25.
44. "The Water-fall," ll. 37–38.
45. L. C. Martin, *Works of Henry Vaughan*, p. 392. In his defense of a topical reading of "The Night" in *Henry Vaughan: The Unfolding Vision* (Princeton: Princeton University Press, 1982), pp. 203–4, Jonathan F. S. Post ignores both Vaughan's warning and the text of the poem. "That land of darkness and blinde eyes" is supposed to draw an "explicit" parallel between Nicodemus's and Vaughan's reasons for seeking Christ at night: both "blest believers" are avoiding persecution, whether from Nicodemus's fellow council members or from the Puritan enemies of Welsh Anglicanism. But stanza 2 doesn't even say this implicitly, much less explicitly. And security from persecution doesn't fit in with the advantages of night prayer actually listed in stanzas 5–6; the common denominator here is simply freedom from the distractions of the workaday world.

In fact, Vaughan would have *needed* to be fairly "explicit" to carry off any such implication. There is no single authoritative reading of Nicodemus's motive that Vaughan could count on his audience to take for granted. Luther thinks the night visit was dictated by fear of persecution, but Calvin opts for personal vanity: Nicodemus was too vain about his prowess as a teacher to risk being caught playing pupil to anybody. (See *Luther's Works*, 54 vols., ed. Jaroslav Pelikan [St. Louis: Concordia, 1957], 22:276; *Commentary on the Gospel According to John by John Calvin*, 2 vols., trans. William Pringle [Grand Rapids: Eerdmans, 1956], 1:105.)

In Vaughan's last stanza Post finds still another reference to church troubles in Wales, as well as a millenarian hint that world history is growing "late" and is about to end (*Henry Vaughan*, p. 209). But "lateness" comes into the speaker's actual line of thought only as a subjective *appearance*, not as a fact. See my analysis above.

Afterword

1. Ad-lib in the sense that the items on the selection list aren't checked to see if they are in fact talk-postulates of the poets' literary community. (On talk-postulates, see chapter 1.)

2. Some people will want to object that there are facts of the matter about recipes and contexts (see previous note). But readers of this persuasion who are up-to-date won't let themselves be sidetracked into arguments with naïve realists.

3. For the theory of conversation as a pervasive topic in seventeenth-century French literature, see Christoph Strosetzki, *Rhetorique de la conversation*, trans. Sabine Seubert (Paris: Biblio 17, 1984).

Appendix A

1. "A Nice Derangement of Epitaphs," reprinted in *Truth and Interpretation*, ed. Ernest LePore (Oxford: Basil Blackwell, 1986), p. 446.
2. Ibid., pp. 434–35.
3. Ibid., p. 443.
4. Ibid.
5. Ibid., p. 474.

Appendix B

1. R. Harris, "Comprehension of Metaphors," *Bulletin of the Psychonomics Society* 8 (1976): 312–14; A. Ortony, D. Schallert, R. Reynolds, and S. Antos, "Interpreting Metaphors and Idioms," *Journal of Verbal Learning and Verbal Behavior* 17 (1978): 465–77; D. Rumelhart, "Some Problems with the Notion of Literal Meanings," in *Metaphor and Thought*, ed. A. Ortony (Cambridge: Cambridge University Press, 1979), pp. 78–90; R. Gerrig and A. Healy, "Dual Processes in Metaphor Understanding," *Journal of Experimental Psychology: Learning, Memory, and Cognition* 9 (1983): 667–75; R. Gibbs, "Literal Meaning and Psychological Theory," *Cognitive Science* 8 (1984): 275–304.

2. Sam Glucksberg, "Metaphors in Conversation," *Metaphor and Symbolic Activity* 4 (1989): 129.

3. M. Dyer, "Comprehension and Acquisition of Figurative Expressions," *Metaphor and Symbolic Activity* 4 (1989): 180, 181.

4. Notice that literalization—status as a separate lexicon entry—also blocks the passive transformation; either "The bucket was kicked by X" is about X's kicking of a bucket or it's verbal slapstick. Compare "The gun was jumped by X."

5. R. W. Gibbs and R. J. Gerrig, "Context Makes Comprehension Special," *Metaphor and Symbolic Activity* 4 (1989): 148.

6. Ibid., p. 155.

7. Ibid., p. 152.

8. Dyer, "Comprehension and Acquisition of Figurative Expressions," pp. 180–82.

Index

Abelard, Pierre, 235 (n. 1)
"Affliction (I)" (Herbert), 177–82, 275 (n. 17), 276 (n. 26)
Agrippinus, 251 (n. 72)
Allusion, 200
Almarican heresy, 253–54 (n. 10)
Almaricus Benensis, 253–54 (n. 10)
Ambrose, Saint, 42–43
Antimetaphorism, 43–44, 46–47
Apology (Plato), 25
"Apparition, The" (Donne), 107–8
Apuleius, Lucius, 134
Aristophanes, 169
Aristotle, 4, 7, 223, 259–60 (n. 12); on metaphor, 11, 12, 22, 240 (n. 49), 240–41 (n. 57), 244 (n. 40); theory of speech acts, 14, 28–29, 237 (nn. 7, 8), 238 (n. 16); on simile, 23; and metaphorical deception, 43, 44–45; "ideas," 239–40 (n. 46)
Asals, Heather, 248–49 (n. 26), 260 (n. 16)
"Assurance" (Herbert), 120–22
Augustine, Saint, 7, 223, 246 (n. 75), 248 (n. 21); and biblical metaphor, 34, 35–36, 37, 38–39, 41–42, 46, 47; on Psalms, 36, 37, 97–98, 259–60 (n. 12), 260 (nn. 13, 16); on reading, 42–43, 242 (nn. 13, 17), 245 (n. 53); devotional cheering, 57–58, 59; and annihilation, 60, 264 (n. 38); on soliloquy, 99, 118, 121; on sin and confession, 114, 115; and individualism, 139; and Cyprian, 187; on Gospels, 255 (n. 27); on will, 271 (n. 33), 271–73 (n. 34)
"Autumnall, The" (Donne), 72–74, 251–52 (n. 78)

Baauwhuys, Bernaard, 142
Barigazzi, Adelmo, 251 (n. 72)
Benet, Diana, 276 (n. 26)
Bernard of Clairvaux, Saint, 248 (n. 21)
Bible, 191, 193, 253–54 (n. 10), 270 (n. 25), 279 (n. 42), 280 (n. 13); Gospel of John, 33, 215, 216, 218; Genesis, 33–34; divine conversation, 33–34, 39, 40–41, 42, 43, 244–45 (n. 49); Psalms, 35–36, 37, 96–97, 259 (n. 7); Ephesians, 60; Gospels, 63–64, 77, 139, 182–83, 255 (n. 27), 269 (n. 7), 276–78 (n. 32); pseudometaphor, 66–67, 152, 153; Isaiah, 126; Acts, 142; Crashaw's Gospel retort, 142, 143–44, 145, 146, 151, 269–70 (n. 11); and *para prosdokian*, 171, 172, 182–83; Song of Solomon, 215, 217–18; Lord's Prayer, 256 (n. 40)
Biedermann, Jakob, 142
Black, Max, 8
Book of Common Prayer, 161, 270 (n. 25)
Boswell, D. A., 236–37 (n. 3)
Bridgeman, Sir Orlando, 256 (n. 46)
Browne, Sir Thomas, 171–72

Butler, Charles, 26, 239 (n. 33)

Calvin, John: and biblical metaphor, 34, 40–41, 193, 244 (n. 40), 245 (n. 63), 279 (n. 42); and reading, 42–43; and metaphors of Christ, 83, 284 (n. 45); and Communion, 89, 128, 161; and Psalms, 97, 259 (n. 7); on faith, 253–54 (n. 10), 254 (n. 14), 276–78 (n. 32); and justice, 264–65 (n. 43)
Campanella, Tommaso, 58, 59
"Canonization, The" (Donne), 21
Carey, John, 251–52 (n. 78), 263–64 (n. 36), 264 (n. 38), 265 (n. 49), 279 (n. 42)
Castiglione, Baldassare, 223
Celsus, 55, 72
Centuries, Poems, and Thanksgivings (Traherne), 84–85, 91, 254 (n. 23), 254–55 (n. 25), 255 (nn. 27, 29)
Chalcidius, 106, 262–63 (n. 32)
Chambers, A. B., 262 (nn. 26, 29, 30)
Christianity, 77, 118, 165, 182, 191, 198; divine figuration, 36, 41, 42; devotional cheering, 57–58; mystic union, 59, 83–84; prayer and, 60, 96, 153; sin and redemption, 63, 253–54 (n. 10); and conscience, 129
"Church-monuments" (Herbert), 122–24
Cicero, Marcus Tullius, 223, 238 (n. 16), 244–45 (n. 49), 251 (n. 72); on metaphor, 23, 239 (n. 33), 240–41 (n. 57); on retort, 140–41; on comedy, 169, 170
Civil Conversation (Guazzo), 223
Civil law, 276 (n. 29)
"Clasping of hands" (Herbert), 83–84, 253–54 (n. 10)
Cognitive science, 231–32
Colloquies (Erasmus), 223
Comic irony, 275–76 (n. 21)
Comic non sequitur, 169
Comic zeugma, 170
Communication, 11, 140
Communion, 89, 128–29, 133, 161, 166

Confessions (Augustine), 38, 43, 57
Context, 10, 35–36, 223
Conversation, 76, 229; in reading, 31–32, 222, 223–24; of God, 33, 34; retort in, 140; emblem, 158
Coolidge, John S., 276–78 (n. 32)
Cooper, Robert M., 249 (n. 32)
Courtier (Castiglione), 223
Covenant theology, 276–78 (n. 32)
Crashaw, Richard: pseudometaphor, 49–54, 59–61, 63, 65, 67, 74, 248–49 (n. 26), 249 (n. 32), 249–50 (n. 48), 250 (n. 68); puns, 55–56, 57, 247–48 (n. 13), 248 (n. 14); retort, 151
—Works: *Musicks Duell*, 50–51; "The Weeper," 51–52, 247 (nn. 4–6); "The Flaming Heart," 59–60; *Sacred Epigrams*, 64, 142–46, 269 (nn. 9, 11)
Cumont, Franz, 282 (n. 22)
Cyprian, Saint, 187

Davenant, Sir William, 14
Davidson, Donald, 8, 227–30, 233, 263 (nn. 33, 34)
Dead metaphor, 232
Death, 191
"Death be not proud" (Donne), 124
Demetrius, 223, 241 (n. 59)
"Demonstration, The" (Traherne), 257 (n. 56)
"Deniall" (Herbert), 119–20
Derrida, Jacques, 8
Descartes, René, 239–40 (n. 46)
Devotional cheering, 56–61
Dialogism, 94
Dialogue, 200
Dionysius of Halicarnassus, 25, 223
Dio of Prusa, 251 (n. 72)
Diversionary *littera*, 24–25, 94, 99; of Herbert, 77, 79, 80–81, 82, 83, 84, 87, 119, 120, 124, 125–26, 127, 130; of Vaughan, 79–80, 212; of Traherne, 84, 85, 88, 90, 92, 93; of Donne, 103, 104, 107, 112, 114, 115, 116, 117, 118

Donne, John, 11, 47, 200, 263 (n. 34); diversionary *littera*, 24–25, 112–19; irony, 26, 79, 130, 132–33; pseudometaphor, 67–75, 252 (n. 86); diversionary *littera* dramatized, 100–112; exploratory metaphor, 189–92
—Works: "A Valediction: of weeping," 5–6, 75; "The Sunne Rising," 13, 16, 21, 22; *Sermons*, 19–20, 187, 279 (n. 42); "The Canonization," 21; Holy Sonnets, 41, 64, 112–19, 264–65 (n. 43), 265 (nn. 45, 49), 265–66 (n. 50); "Twicknam garden," 56, 132–33; "Loves growth," 67–70, 168, 170; "A Feaver," 70–72; "The Autumnall," 72–74, 251–52 (n. 78); "The Expiration," 74–75; "The Extasie," 100–103, 261 (n. 22); "A Valediction: forbidding mourning," 103–7, 146, 147, 262 (nn. 26, 30); "The Apparition," 107–8; "Womans constancy," 108–9; "Nocturnall upon S. *Lucies* Day," 109–12, 264 (nn. 38, 41); "Death be not proud," 124; "Hymne to God my God, in my sicknesse," 189–92, 279 (n. 42)
"Dooms-day" (Herbert), 77–79, 252 (n. 2)
Dramatic irony, 130–31

Ellrodt, Robert, 18, 19; on Crashaw, 247 (n. 5), 247–48 (n. 13); on Traherne, 254–55 (n. 25), 255 (n. 35); on Donne, 261 (n. 25), 265 (n. 49), 279 (n. 42)
Emergent metaphor, 173, 199–20, 203, 210, 213, 222
Empedocles, 43
"Employment (II)" (Herbert), 173–77
English, 32
Erasmus, Desiderius, 26, 97, 223
Euphemism, 126
Euphues, 29, 30, 34, 42, 43
Eutrapelia, 4
Existential psychoanalysis, 18–20
"Expiration, The" (Donne), 74–75

Exploratory metaphor, 173, 188–89, 192, 198
"Extasie, The" (Donne), 100–103, 261 (n. 22)

Faerie Queene, The (Spenser), 265–66 (n. 50)
Favorinus, 70, 251 (n. 72)
"Feaver, A" (Donne), 70–72
Ficino, Marsilio, 257 (n. 54), 281 (nn. 16, 17), 282 (n. 24)
Fiction, 74, 75, 96, 209
Figuration, 1, 10, 11, 14, 36, 70, 135, 223, 224
Figurational charity, 47; pseudometaphor and, 48, 56, 67–68, 72, 76, 168; diversionary *littera* and, 110, 117–18, 128; irony and, 135; retort and, 140; *para prosdokian* and, 170, 188
Figurative meaning, 2, 34; and literal meaning, 3, 4–5, 6, 7, 30, 35–36, 76, 165, 227, 228–29, 231–32
Figure of induction, 98
Fish, Stanley, 165, 166, 246 (nn. 74, 75), 254 (n. 12), 268 (n. 74), 271–73 (n. 34), 273 (nn. 35, 36)
"Flaming Heart, The" (Crashaw), 59–60
"Flower, The" (Herbert), 81–82, 83
"Forerunners, The" (Herbert), 80, 195–98
Freccero, John, 262 (n. 30)
Freer, Coburn, 248–49 (n. 26)
Free-Will, Of, 160
Fronto, 251 (n. 72)

Galen, Claudius, 55
Gardner, Helen, 279 (n. 42)
Gellius, Aulus, 251 (n. 72)
Gerson, Jean, 59, 253–54 (n. 10)
Golden Rule, 33
Góngora y Argote, Luis de, 52, 54, 247 (n. 6)
Goodman, Nelson, 8
Grammar, 199
Greek rhetoricians, 9, 223–24

Gresham's Law, 274 (n. 46)
Guazzo, 223

Hamlet (Shakespeare), 191
Hebrew, 134, 153, 270 (n. 25), 280 (n. 13)
Henry IV (Shakespeare), 2–4
Heraclitus, 83, 275 (n. 10)
Herbert, George, 6, 11, 96, 221; diversionary *littera*, 24–25, 77–79, 81–83, 84, 87; irony, 26, 133–39; and prayer, 97, 98, 99, 186–87, 188, 258–59 (n. 5), 260 (n. 16); diversionary *littera* dramatized, 119–30; retort, 142, 146, 147–67; *para prosdokian*, 173–88; exploratory metaphor, 192–98; emergent metaphor, 200–203, 204, 220; and sermons, 246 (n. 77)
—Works: "Praise (III)," 4–5; "Love (III)," 41, 161–67, 273 (nn. 35, 38), 274 (n. 46); "Dooms-day," 77–79, 252 (n. 2); "The Forerunners," 80, 195–98; "The Flower," 81–82, 83; "The Temper (I)," 82–83, 192–95, 254 (nn. 12, 14); "Clasping of hands," 83–84, 253–54 (n. 10); "Deniall," 119–20; "Assurance," 120–22; "Church-monuments," 122–24; "Miserie," 124–26, 267 (n. 57); "Longing," 126–28; "Love unknown," 128–30; "Peace," 133–35; "Jordan (II)," 136–37, 138–39, 268–69 (n. 76); "Jordan (I)," 137–39, 268–69 (n. 76); "Parodie," 146, 147–48, 270 (n. 24); "The Quip," 148–51, 152; "The Sacrifice," 151–52, 154; "Redemption," 152–54; "The Thanksgiving," 154–56, 271 (n. 31); "The Reprisall," 156; *The Temple*, 156, 260 (n. 15); "The Pulley," 156–57; "Hope," 157–58; "The Holdfast," 159–61, 271–73 (n. 34); "Employment (II)," 173–77; "Affliction (I)," 177–82, 275 (n. 17), 276 (n. 26); "The Pearl," 182–85, 276 (n. 29), 276–78 (n. 32); "Prayer (I)," 185–87;

"Vanitie (I)," 200–203, 205, 280 (n. 4); "Jesu," 204
Hermetic philosophy, 17, 18, 280 (n. 11), 281 (n. 17), 282 (n. 22), 282–83 (n. 29)
Hermogenes, 26, 169, 223, 249 (n. 32), 270 (n. 24)
Hilary of Poitiers, 242 (n. 17)
Hill, Christopher, 256 (n. 46)
Hilyard, Joseph P., 250 (n. 68)
Hindsight figuration, 173, 175, 188, 199
Hippolytus, 275 (n. 10)
History, 38–39, 43, 215
Hobbes, Thomas, 13–14, 43, 44, 45, 239–40 (n. 46), 255 (n. 35)
"Holdfast, The" (Herbert), 159–61, 271–73 (n. 34)
Holy Sonnets (Donne), 41, 64, 112–19, 264–65 (n. 43), 265 (nn. 45, 49), 265–66 (n. 50)
Homer, 23, 25, 94
"Hope" (Herbert), 157–58
Horace, 12, 95, 262 (n. 27)
Hoskins, John, 26, 239 (n. 33)
Hotspurism, 2–4, 5, 6–7, 13, 16, 54, 60, 158, 165, 247 (n. 4)
Hughes, Merritt, 253 (n. 6)
Hutten, Ulrich von, 110–11
"Hymne to God my God, in my sicknesse" (Donne), 189–92, 279 (n. 42)
Hyperbole, 21
Hypocrisis, 28–29

Iconoclasm, 245 (n. 63)
Idealism, 255 (n. 35)
Iliad (Homer), 243 (n. 29)
Importance of Being Ernest, The (Wilde), 169
Individualism, 139
Institutes (Calvin), 276–78 (n. 32)
Invention, 73
Irenaeus, Saint, 34, 223, 242 (n. 17), 245 (n. 50)

Irony, 21, 26, 94, 130–31, 258 (n. 4), 275–76 (n. 21)
Isocrates, 251 (n. 72)
"I walkt the other day" (Vaughan), 205–10, 213, 214, 280 (n. 14), 281 (n. 16)

Jerome, Saint, 202, 223, 242 (n. 13), 249–50 (n. 48), 256 (n. 40), 280 (n. 4)
"Jesu" (Herbert), 204
Johnson, Mark, 8
Jonson, Ben, 95
"Jordan (I)" (Herbert), 137–39, 268–69 (n. 76)
"Jordan (II)" (Herbert), 136–37, 138–39, 268–69 (n. 76)
Julius Caesar (Shakespeare), 55

Korshin, Paul J., 243 (n. 31)

Lakoff, George, 8
Landino, 223
Language, 32; literal and figurative meaning and, 8, 227–30; metaphor in, 11, 12, 13–14, 18, 19, 135, 224–25
Latin, 153, 282 (n. 24)
Lechner, Sister Joan Marie, 241 (n. 58)
León, Luis de, 61
Lewalski, Barbara, 255 (n. 27), 258–59 (n. 5)
Lewis, David, 235 (n. 1)
Literal meaning, 2, 34–35, 236–37 (n. 3); and figurative meaning, 3, 4–5, 6, 7, 30, 35–36, 76, 165, 227, 228–29, 231–32
Literary criticism, 4, 6, 263–64 (n. 36)
Literature, 94
Locke, John, 43, 45, 47
"Longing" (Herbert), 126–28
"Love (III)" (Herbert), 41, 161–67, 273 (nn. 35, 38), 274 (n. 46)
"Loves growth" (Donne), 67–70, 168, 170
"Love unknown" (Herbert), 128–30

Lucretius, 92
Lullie, Raymond, 281 (n. 16)
Luther, Martin, 12, 34, 161, 242 (n. 13), 245 (n. 63), 271 (n. 31), 284 (n. 45)
Lycidas (Milton), 95–96

Macbeth (Shakespeare), 9–10, 114
Mackay, Alfred, 230
MacKenzie, J. D., 252 (n. 89)
Madsen, William G., 243 (n. 31)
Malapropism, 136, 230
"Man" (Vaughan), 135–36
"Mankind is sick" (Traherne), 86
Manning, Stephen, 247 (n. 4)
Masque, 209, 214
Maternity, 267 (n. 58)
Measure for Measure (Shakespeare), 143
Meiosis, 191
Menapius, 70
Metalepsis, 26–27, 78, 109, 112, 114
Metamorphoses (Ovid), 278 (n. 37)
Metaphor, 1, 2, 4, 6–8, 27, 29, 31, 34, 77, 138; classic sense, 8, 231–33; and language, 11, 12, 13–14, 18, 19, 135, 224–25; Aristotle and, 11, 22, 23, 44–45, 240–41 (n. 57); tropes, 21–22, 23, 230; simile as, 22; Augustine and, 39, 45–47; antimetaphorism, 43–44, 46–47; mixed, 49, 65, 69; mock, 60, 61, 63, 69–70, 75; exploratory, 173, 188–89, 192, 198; emergent, 173, 199–20, 203, 210, 213, 222
Metonymy, 24, 38, 40, 191, 244 (n. 43)
Milton, John, 34, 241 (n. 5)
"Miserie" (Herbert), 124–26, 267 (n. 57)
Mixed metaphor, 49, 65, 69
Mock metaphor, 60, 61, 63, 69–70, 75
More, Henry, 88
"Münze und Wort" (Weinrich), 241 (n. 58)
Musicks Duell (Crashaw), 50–51
"My Spirit" (Traherne), 255 (n. 35), 256 (nn. 40, 46)

Neoplatonism, 261 (n. 22), 282 (n. 22)

Nietzsche, Friedrich Wilhelm, 8
"Night, The" (Vaughan), 215–22, 282–83 (n. 29), 283 (n. 33), 284 (n. 45)
Nijinsky, Vaslav, 8
"Nobody" (Hutten), 110–11
"Nocturnall upon S. *Lucies* Day" (Donne), 109–12, 264 (nn. 38, 41)
Nollius, 281 (n. 16)
Non sequitur, 169
Novels, 18, 19, 20–21

Our Lady's Tumbler, 65–67
Ovid, 52, 155, 278 (n. 37)

Paradise Lost (Milton), 33
Para prosdokian, 169–70, 171, 173, 182, 185, 188
"Parodie" (Herbert), 146, 147–48, 270 (n. 24)
Parody, 146, 270 (n. 24)
Parrish, Paul A., 269 (n. 9)
Paul, Saint, 60, 64, 214; on Psalms, 35, 36, 39; Augustine on, 38, 39; Herbert and, 82, 137, 161, 177, 202–3; tent metaphor, 215, 282 (n. 28); and sin, 256–57 (n. 50), 273 (nn. 35, 36)
"Peace" (Herbert), 133–35
"Pearl, The" (Herbert), 182–85, 276 (n. 29), 276–78 (n. 32)
Pelagianism, 256–57 (n. 50)
Pembroke, Earl of, 146–47, 148, 270 (n. 24)
Pericles, 25
Perkins, William, 264 (n. 42)
Persius, 12
Peter, Saint, 64, 144
Pettet, E. C., 281 (n. 20)
Pindar, 249 (n. 32)
Plato, 16, 25, 29, 223
Plautus, Titus Maccius, 26–27
Poetry, 1, 2, 18, 199, 223–24
Polytropia, 4
Ponsford, Michael J., 256–57 (n. 50)
Pope, Alexander, 170

Porphyry, 259–60 (n. 12)
Post, Jonathan F. S., 284 (n. 45)
"Praise (III)" (Herbert), 4–5
Prayer, 65, 97, 127, 153, 186–87, 188, 258–59 (n. 5), 259 (n. 7)
"Prayer (I)" (Herbert), 185–87
Prefiguration, 38–39, 243 (n. 31)
Presocratic philosophers, 174
Protestant theology: divine conversation, 33–34; Herbert and, 83, 160, 177, 221; Christ in, 83, 271 (n. 31); and sin, 116, 265 (n. 45), 273 (n. 35); dependence on God, 160, 161, 265 (n. 45); notion of God, 165, 244–45 (n. 49), 253–54 (n. 10), 264 (n. 42); Vaughan and, 221; faith in, 254 (n. 14), 265–66 (n. 50), 273 (n. 36); good works in, 275–76 (n. 21), 276–78 (n. 32)
Pseudometaphor, 44, 48–61, 63; consecrated wit, 61–67; and profane wit, 67–76
"Pulley, The" (Herbert), 156–57
Puns, 54–55, 129
Puritanism, 139
Puttenham, George, 45

Quantum physics, 230
Quilligan, Maureen, 235–36 (n. 16)
Quintilian, 10–11, 27–28, 44, 45, 258 (n. 1), 268–69 (n. 76), 270 (n. 24)
"Quip, The" (Herbert), 148–51, 152

Ranters, 256 (n. 46)
Rationalism, 116, 273–74 (n. 39)
Reading, 6, 42–43, 105, 171, 172, 199, 222, 223, 242 (n. 17)
Redemption, 191
"Redemption" (Herbert), 152–54
Reference, 18, 81
Reformation theology, 33, 279 (n. 42); and figurative reading, 34, 35–36, 42, 242 (n. 13), 245 (n. 63); and sin, 273 (nn. 35, 36)
Remond, François, 142

Renaissance, 7, 45, 52, 70, 97, 118, 190, 265 (n. 49)
"Reprisall, The" (Herbert), 156
Resurrection, 191
Retort, 140–41, 142, 145, 146, 154, 160, 161, 163
Retort-by-silence, 157
"Retreate, The" (Vaughan), 79–81, 253 (nn. 6, 7)
Ricoeur, Paul, 8
Roman Catholic church, 65, 78, 271 (n. 31)
Romeo and Juliet (Shakespeare), 48–49, 274 (n. 4)
Roston, Murray, 250–51 (n. 69)
Royal Society for the Arts, 44
Rudrum, Alan, 282–83 (n. 29)
Ruysbroeck, Jan, 253–54 (n. 10)

Sacred Epigrams (Crashaw), 64, 142–46, 269 (nn. 9, 11)
"Sacrifice, The" (Herbert), 151–52, 154
Sadock, Jerrold M., 258 (n. 4)
"Salutation, The" (Traherne), 90–91
Sarcasm, 232–33
Schema, 9
Scholasticism, 88–89, 91, 263 (n. 34)
Seelig, Sharon, 257 (n. 56)
Self-abasement, 125, 127
Semantic bad faith, 107, 109, 119
Sense, 81, 199, 231
Sermons (Donne), 19–20, 187, 279 (n. 42)
Shakespeare, William, 281 (n. 20)
Sherwood, Terry, 263–64 (n. 36)
Sidney, Sir Philip, 20–21, 138
Siemon, James, 245 (n. 63)
Silex (Vaughan), 222
Simile, 22–23
Simmonds, James, 280 (n. 14)
Sin, 114–15, 116, 191, 256–57 (n. 50), 271 (n. 28)
Singleton, Marion White, 276 (n. 26)
Smith, A. J., 261 (n. 22)
Socrates, 25
Soliloquies (Augustine), 99

Soliloquy, 118
Solipsism, 88, 256–57 (n. 50)
Sophistry, 74
Sophists, 174–75, 251 (n. 72)
Spenser, Edmund, 15–16
Sprat, Thomas, 28, 43, 44, 45
Stachniewski, John, 264–65 (n. 43)
Stein, Arnold, 274 (n. 46)
Strier, Richard, 244–45 (n. 49), 254 (n. 12), 266 (nn. 51, 52), 268–69 (n. 76), 271 (n. 31), 271–73 (n. 34), 276–78 (n. 32)
Sturm, Johann, 240–41 (n. 57)
Summers, Joseph, 149, 260 (n. 15), 271–73 (n. 34)
"Sunne Rising, The" (Donne), 13, 16, 21, 22
Synesius, 251 (n. 72)
Syntax, 199

Talk-postulates, 10, 14–18, 20, 21, 31, 36, 169–70
"Temper, The (I)" (Herbert), 82–83, 192–95, 254 (nn. 12, 14)
Temple, The (Herbert), 156, 260 (n. 15)
Teresa, Saint, 59, 61
Tertullian, 34
Tesauro, Emmanuele, 26–27, 29, 44–45, 240 (n. 49)
"Thanksgiving, The" (Herbert), 154–56, 271 (n. 31)
Theology, 152, 153, 220, 221
"They are all gone into the world of light" (Vaughan), 210–14
Thomas Aquinas, Saint, 34, 43, 244 (nn. 43, 46), 248 (n. 21), 259–60 (n. 12), 263 (n. 34), 264 (n. 38)
Tragedy, 133
Traherne, Thomas: antimetaphorism, 46–47; diversionary *littera*, 84–88, 89–90, 92, 93, 256–57 (n. 50)
—Works: *Centuries, Poems, and Thanksgivings*, 84–85, 91, 254 (n. 23), 254–55 (n. 25), 255 (nn. 27, 29); "The Vision," 86; "Mankind is sick," 86;

Traherne, Thomas: Works *(cont'd)*
"The Salutation," 90–91; "My Spirit," 255 (n. 35), 256 (nn. 40, 46); "The Demonstration," 257 (n. 56)
Tropes, 9, 10–11, 21–22, 23–27, 35, 111, 230, 237 (n. 6)
Tuve, Rosemond, 271 (n. 28)
"Twicknam garden" (Donne), 56, 132–33
Tychonius, 242 (n. 13)

"Valediction: forbidding mourning" (Donne), 103–7, 146, 147, 262 (nn. 26, 30)
"Valediction: of weeping" (Donne), 5–6, 75
"Vanitie (I)" (Herbert), 200–203, 205, 280 (n. 4)
"Vanity of Spirit" (Vaughan), 203–5, 207, 210, 213
Vaughan, Henry, 17–18, 46, 96, 282 (n. 24); diversionary *littera*, 79–81, 212; emergent metaphor, 199–200, 203, 213, 221–22; retort, 200
—Works: "The Retreate," 79–81, 253 (nn. 6, 7); "Man," 135–36; "Vanity of Spirit," 203–5, 207, 210, 213; "I walkt the other day," 205–10, 213, 214, 280 (n. 14), 281 (n. 16); "They are all gone into the world of light," 210–14; "The Night," 215–22, 282–83 (n. 29), 283 (n. 33), 284 (n. 45); *Silex*, 222
Vaughan, Thomas, 203–4
Vendler, Helen, 252 (n. 2), 275 (n. 17)
Vernacular, 8, 9, 10, 13, 29, 35, 70, 131, 236–37 (n. 3)
"Vision, The" (Traherne), 86

Waiting for Godot (Beckett), 127
Wallerstein, Ruth, 248 (n. 14)
Warning, Rainer, 236 (n. 19)
Warnke, Frank, 251 (n. 71), 264 (n. 41), 265–66 (n. 50)
"Weeper, The" (Crashaw), 51–52, 247 (nn. 4–6)
Wilde, Oscar, 169
Wit, 29, 44–45, 76; in Crashaw, 63, 64, 65, 143; in Donne, 67, 72, 75; in Herbert, 152, 163
Woehrer, Franz H., 256–57 (n. 50)
"Womans constancy" (Donne), 108–9
Women, 107, 109, 133

Young, R. V., 247 (n. 6), 249 (n. 46)

Zeugma, 170
Zwingli, Ulrich, 89

www.ingramcontent.com/pod-product-compliance
Lightning Source LLC
Chambersburg PA
CBHW011720220426
43664CB00023B/2896